The Cooperstown Symposium on Baseball and American Culture 2003–2004

The Cooperstown Symposium on Baseball and American Culture

2003–2004

Edited by
William M. Simons

<small>SERIES EDITOR: ALVIN L. HALL</small>

McFarland & Company, Inc., Publishers
Jefferson, North Carolina, and London

The Cooperstown symposium on baseball and American
    culture, 2003–2004
        edited by William M. Simons ; series editor Alvin L. Hall.

ISSN 1536-1195

ISBN 0-7864-2196-7 (softcover : 50# alkaline paper) ∞

Cover art © 2005 Wood River Gallery

Manufactured in the United States of America

McFarland & Company, Inc., Publishers
    Box 611, Jefferson, North Carolina 28640
    www.mcfarlandpub.com

Acknowledgments

William M. Simons

Alvin L. Hall created and continues to coordinate the Cooperstown Symposium on Baseball and American Culture.

National Baseball Hall of Fame president Dale Petrosky was again a gracious host. Hall of Fame librarian Jim Gates rendered invaluable help at every step of the way, including service on the Abstract Committee and the Editorial Board. The contributions of Tim Wiles, director of research at the Hall of Fame Library, and the library's superlative staff greatly facilitated the research underpinning this volume. Bill Frances, Gabriel Schechter, and Russell Wolinsky of the Hall of Fame's A. Bartlett Giamatti Research Center provided much appreciated copyediting and other editorial assistance. Becky Ashe, secretary at the Hall of Fame Library, deftly expedited the exchange of materials.

Catherine Kempf, affiliated with Cornell University publications, also lent her professional expertise to copyediting. SUNY-Oneonta reference librarian Nancy Cannon and Mark Boshnack, reporter for *The Daily Star* (Oneonta), read manuscripts and offered insightful criticisms. Stephen Walsh, stalwart of the Division of Economics and Business at SUNY-Oneonta, checked statistics and shared the expertise of his discipline. In addition to Jim Gates, academicians Dennis Shea, Daniel Payne, and Thomas Beal served on the Editorial Advisory Board.

SUNY-Oneonta president Alan B. Donovan, provost and vice president F. Daniel Larkin, and interim dean of graduate studies/continuing education Alfred Lubell contributed strong institutional support. College secretary Fawn Holland once again spent many hours producing the index, proofreading, and generously helping in diverse ways. Sharon Corna gave much appreciated secretarial assistance. Jay Wood provided valuable computer expertise.

A lady known as the *electric librarian* has a baseball field on her farm: For this and other reasons, the book is dedicated to Nancy Cannon.

Table of Contents

Preface

Alvin L. Hall

When I organized the first Cooperstown Symposium on Baseball and American Culture in 1989 to observe the fiftieth anniversary of the National Baseball Hall of Fame, I had no idea that the conference would have such legs. We all thought we would do it once and then move on to other things. As it turned out, one of the other things was the Second Cooperstown Symposium in 1990; and the rest, as they say, is history. I have relocated three times, and the Symposium seems to follow me wherever I go—though it seems to have a life of its own. Each year, we receive between 70 and 80 abstracts for papers from institutions all over the country and, occasionally, from foreign scholars. I have yet to determine the depth of interest in baseball in the Republic of Mongolia, but we did at least receive an inquiry from that quarter this year.

One good thing about the Sixteenth Symposium (2004) was that the jury decided to increase the number of papers we accepted. In previous years we had limited our selection to between 25 and 30 papers, and we always felt we were leaving some really good stuff on the cutting room floor. In order to have the greater number presented in the same time period, we planned several sessions in which two, or even three, papers on related topics were offered. This seemed to work well and will be continued in the future.

At the same time we increased the number of papers, we decided to reduce the number published. Instead of publishing all papers given in a single year, this volume includes only eight papers from the Symposium of 2003 and nine from the 2004 conference. Since this involved a second jury, the reader is assured of getting the best of the best.

In 2004, after fifteen years of simply playing the role of coordinator of the conference, I finally decided to take a chance and submit an abstract myself. Over the entire history of the Cooperstown Symposium, I have been very honest with the participants about the fact that my research interests have been in other areas. However, when I moved to East Stroudsburg University of Pennsylvania in 2001, I discovered that Zane Grey had lived only 30 miles from the campus during the first two decades of the twentieth century. I also learned that he was a first-rate baseball player and had written a couple of very autobiographical novels about baseball in the late nineteenth century. I decided to submit an abstract on a topic related to this discovery. To my complete surprise, it was accepted for presentation. Since the selection process is blind and the jury did not know I was the author until I told them after being selected, I was even more pleased. I did not submit my final paper for consideration for this publication; if you must know, the title was *Zane Grey, Cy Young, and Images of the American West*. If you want to know the connection between Zane Grey and Cy Young, let me quote Casey Stengel: "You can look it up!"

As coordinator of the Symposium, I have always had dinner with the keynote speaker the night before the opening sessions. These dinners are always enjoyable, but this year was special. Marvin Miller was the keynote speaker, but we also invited a special guest, the first Hall of Famer to participate in the Symposium: Bob Feller. Both are in their mid-eighties, and both are giants of the game, although for quite different reasons. As I sat at the dinner table, bracketed by Miller and Feller, joined by their wives, Dale Petrosky (president of the Hall of Fame), and Jim Gates (librarian at the Hall), I just listened. Toward the end of the meal, Mrs. Miller looked at me and said, "Dr. Hall, you haven't said much." I resisted the urge to use my usual comment when engaged in conversations about baseball: "It's better to remain silent and appear a fool than to open your mouth and remove all doubt." Instead, I said, "Mrs. Miller, I'm a historian, and I know primary material when I hear it." Actually, Bob Feller gave the most memorable line during his session on Thursday morning. During the period of questions following his remarks, someone asked Feller to name the most dangerous hitters he had faced. He rambled off a half dozen names. In a follow-up, the questioner persisted, "But what about Ted Williams? Did you face him?" Feller responded that he had pitched to Williams many times but did not regard him as particularly dangerous because he knew what *not* to pitch him. Then, Bob Feller — "Rapid Robert," known for his blazing fastball, and ever the country boy from Iowa — said, "Trying to sneak a fastball past Ted Williams was like trying to sneak a sunbeam past a rooster in the morning."

Finally, the Sixteenth Cooperstown Symposium was especially sweet for me. After planning and attending the first fourteen from 1989 to 2002, I had to miss the fifteenth in 2003 because of open heart surgery. When I consider the alternative, being able to attend and participate in the sixteenth took on special meaning.

In closing, I want to thank Dale Petrosky, Jim Gates, and all the other staff members at the Hall of Fame for their support and assistance over the years. Without this help, I simply could not have continued to put the whole thing together, especially from a distance. I would also like to thank the State University of New York at Oneonta, its president, Alan Donovan, and its staff for their continuing sponsorship. The co-sponsorship of the National Baseball Hall of Fame and SUNY-Oneonta has assured that the Cooperstown Symposium has become and continues to be the premier scholarly conference on baseball in the world.

I have reserved special thanks for William Simons, professor and past chair of history at SUNY-Oneonta and volume editor of the last four volumes of the proceedings. Bill is one of the best baseball scholars I know. I especially appreciate his Herculean efforts to corral the scholarly and creative energies of some 40 to 50 college faculty members, as most of the presenters and authors are. I'm sure he now really understands every university administrator's lament: "Leading faculty is like herding cats!"

East Stroudsburg University of Pennsylvania
November 2004

Introduction

William M. Simons

The *Cooperstown Symposium on Baseball and American Culture, 2003–2004* anthology consists of seventeen of the very best papers presented at the last two meetings of the annual conference with which it shares a name. These baseball essays are notable for their original scholarship, significance, and engaging readability. The June 11–13, 2003, and June 2–4, 2004, gatherings were, respectively, the fifteenth and sixteenth sessions of the Cooperstown Symposium on Baseball and American Culture. As it has since its inception in 1989, the Symposium, co-sponsored by the National Baseball Hall of Fame and Museum and the State University of New York at Oneonta, continues to attract top baseball scholars from various disciplines. As the game's symbolic, yet fictive, birthplace, Cooperstown, home to the Hall of Fame and Doubleday Field, provides a splendid setting for the Symposium.

Through the years, the Symposium has played a crucial role in legitimizing baseball scholarship in academia. At the time of the first conference, liberal arts deans largely scoffed at the idea that baseball research constituted serious scholarship. Eschewing baseball as baseball, the Symposium has consistently featured presentations illustrating how the game provides an important vantage point for understanding culture, society, economics, politics, and other components of American civilization. By bringing together talented practitioners of the craft and facilitating publication of their work, the Symposium has contributed significantly to the notable expansion, in recent years, of university and college courses, in diverse disciplines, on baseball. The annual conference continues as a vital forum, providing a setting for leading scholars and young doctoral candidates to share, across the generations, serious baseball research. While the African American presence in Major League Baseball is, sadly, in precipitous decline, at the Symposium it is vital and growing. Women continue to figure ever more prominently in the Symposium, and the papers of four of them are published in this anthology.

Intellectual endeavors at the Symposium are leavened by an infectious, enthusiastic, even joyful, celebration of the game. Rigorous formal panels find second life over food and drink at convivial, impromptu gatherings that linger far into the night. The Symposium often includes an evening devoted to an "open mike," featuring brief, informal, off-the record presentations, including baseball short stories, poetry, drama, music, humor, and miscellany. During the second night of the conference, a bountiful communal meal is preceded by (unless rain intervenes) a rousing game of townball, a mid–nineteenth century antecedent to baseball. By tradition, before festivities conclude, the mighty Casey, dressed in full regalia, always appears, courtesy of the Hall of Fame's Tim Wiles, to recite the most famous of baseball poems.

Over the years, the Symposium has elicited extensive commentary in books, magazines, newspapers, radio, and television, including mention by *The New York Times*, CBS News, and National Public Radio. The Symposium has become a phenomenon, and cultural commentators look to it for clues to both the soul of baseball and the American national character. Nor does this attention show any sign of abating. Writing for the July 18, 2003, edition of *The Chronicle of Higher Education*, Jeffrey Selingo observed that the presenters at the three-day Symposium are "serious scholars," and that, over the years, "some 40 books have come out of the papers presented at this conference." Recognizing however, that "not all the conference business was serious academic work," Selingo captured the Symposium's other side: "Participants played a nearly two-hour game of pickup ball one evening under a light rain and then feasted on barbecued chicken, pork and beans, apple pie, and ice cream." Players in the annual ballgame vary in skill, ranging from former Yankees third baseman Clete Boyer to those who knew primarily sunbaked sandlot diamonds. The Symposium is a wonderful, unique, yeasty, ever evolving epiphany of scholarship and camaraderie. It is the best scholarly conference on baseball, and it possesses a unique fellowship that envelops attendees.

Keynote Speakers

Make no mistake, however: The Symposium features important contributions to the literary canon of baseball and American culture. The roster of keynote speakers from past years includes many of baseball's great muses, writers, celebrants, and historians. Through the years, Symposium keynoters—among them baseball's first academic historian, Harold Seymour; Harvard paleontologist and Renaissance man Stephen Jay Gould, novelist W.P. Kinsella; documentary filmmaker Ken Burns; chronicler of *The Boys of Summer* Roger Kahn; and Walter Mitty sportsman and writer George Plimpton —

have invariably spoken with memorable eloquence about baseball and its place in the American culture. The two most recent keynotes continued this tradition of excellence.

The 2003 keynote address was presented by Josh Prager, the young, talented, and protean *Wall Street Journal* investigative reporter. It highlighted the formidable talents of a new generation of baseball chroniclers. Prager examined one of the most celebrated moments in baseball history, "the shot heard 'round the world"— New York Giants outfielder Bobby Thomson's home run on October 3, 1951, in the bottom of the ninth inning of the third and decisive game of a playoff series at the Polo Grounds. Thomson hit an inside fastball thrown by Brooklyn Dodgers pitcher Ralph Branca into the left-field stands, granting the euphoric Giants faithful the National League pennant. Memorably rendered in contemporary radio and newspaper coverage, and subsequently burnished in novel and memory, the Thomson home run, culminating the Giants' dramatic comeback from a 13½ game deficit in August against their archrival, the Dodgers, is one of the game's most celebrated episodes. A half-century after the Thomson home run, however, Prager, through tireless and meticulous research, revealed that the Giants, via use of a telescope and a bell-and-buzzer system installed at the Polo Grounds, had been stealing signs from opposing teams since mid-season. Prager acknowledges that his research does not necessarily refute Thomson's retort to the recent revelations that the Giants star, an honorable man, refused information based on the stolen signs. Prager also points out that sign stealing in baseball is not illegal, and prior to 1961, the use of doing so by mechanical means, albeit morally dubious, was not prohibited. Nonetheless, the Symposium audience was enthralled by Prager's findings, which made headlines across the nation. Based on sources once hidden, including discovery of an electrician's receipt and the secrets of aged men, Prager's presentation at the Symposium provides a model for historical research and methodology that transcends baseball.

Marvin Miller, the iconic director of the Major League Baseball Players Association (MLBPA) from 1966 to 1982, was the keynote speaker at the 2004 Symposium. Miller spoke with a vigor, passion, and conviction that belied his 87 years. His presentation, relating the life and times of an individual named by ESPN Sports Century the fourth most influential person in twentieth-century American sports, constituted an important contribution to the oral history of the game. Miller noted that it was only after serving a long labor apprenticeship as chief economist, associate director of research, and assistant to the president of the United Steelworkers that the MLBPA — until that time a moribund organization that accommodated management — selected him as its executive director on March 15, 1966. Reconfiguring labor relations in the national pastime, Miller converted the MLBPA into an assertive union. By 1982, when Miller stepped down as executive director of the MLBPA, he had fundamentally transformed the business of baseball.

In his presentation, Miller — employing by turns logic, polemic, humor, law, politics, and ethics— discussed the epic battles and triumphs that occurred during his tenure as MLBPA executive director: abrogation of the reserve clause, the birth of free agency, arbitration, strikes in 1972 and 1981, dramatic increases in player salaries, and augmented pensions. Commenting on current events, Miller, an unabashed liberal, opposed mandatory drug testing of players and likened tabloid speculation concerning abuses by certain players as journalistic McCarthyism. Whether they agreed or disagreed, the Symposium audience witnessed firsthand the qualities that gave Marvin Miller a reputation for never being afraid to take an unpopular stand. They were also treated to a very human moment when Miller hesitated briefly after a question about baseball's continued vitality in the face of doomsayers; Miller's wife of over 60 years, Terry, punctuated the silence with a deft response: "Good game."

Only two years younger than Miller but, like the former labor leader, unbowed by age, 85-year-old Bob Feller regaled 2004 Symposium attendees with a special presentation. The presence of "Rapid Robert"— Hall of Famer, the greatest of all Cleveland Indians, one of the most dominant pitchers in the history of baseball, possessor of a legendary fastball and a wicked curve, winner of 266 major league games, author of three no-hitters and twelve one-hitters, purveyor of 18 strikeouts in a 1938 game and 348 "K's" in 1946 (both then records), and World War II hero— demonstrated that baseball scholars are also fans of the game. Bob Feller, still bigger than life (at least when holding court at the Hall of Fame), graciously posed for photographs and signed autographs. Although Feller, a native of rural Iowa, is as conservative as Marvin Miller is liberal, these two outspoken octogenarians got along famously, bound by a belief in player rights and a love of the game. A curmudgeon, but a charming one, Feller buttressed his lecture with a phenomenal memory, wry humor, and excellent timing as he recalled, with vignettes, anecdotes, and memorable stories, a storied major league career that spanned the years from 1936 to 1956. An audience member noted that Feller led the American League in victories (25) in 1941 and, because of naval service, did not play another complete season until 1946 — when he again paced the circuit in wins (26). The enthusiast then asked the old Indians ace to comment on what the baseball record book might have looked like had he not missed nearly four seasons at the peak of his prowess. Feller, ever the patriot, retorted, "Many of you are historians. A more important question is: What would the history books look like if we had lost World War II?"

Feller brings to mind another age, before steroid use and other misdeeds, when the diamond was the home of true heroes. Indeed, Feller, oblivious to fatigue, 68 years after his major league debut, drove with his wife to Cooperstown from Washington, D.C., immediately after playing a prominent role in the dedication of a monument to honor World War II veterans. Save for hotel accommodations, he neither asked for nor received remuneration for participating in the Symposium.

Subsequent to his own session, Feller attended, as an appreciative audience member, a presentation by his friend and greatest fan, Dr. Edwin L. Plowman, chair of the sociology department at Florida Southern College. Plowman's paper, *From the Cornfields of Iowa to the National Baseball Hall of Fame: A Profile of Bob Feller,* displayed an encyclopedic knowledge of the pitcher's life and times. It was priceless to watch the pride and enjoyment in Bob Feller's face as he listened to his friend's tribute, a deft amalgam of baseball erudition, storytelling, and humor.

Following Plowman's presentation, a Hall of Fame staff member approached Feller to inform him that a limousine was waiting to drive him to the Hotel Otesaga; Feller thanked the woman but said he would prefer to walk. That was a great sight — Bob Feller walking vigorously, sans entourage and unnoticed, down Cooperstown's Main Street, heading to his hotel several blocks away. Then, Feller and his wife, departing the Symposium, drove by themselves to Iowa for a board meeting of the Bob Feller Museum at his boyhood home near the Raccoon River, where long ago, between milking cows and pitching hay, a father and son played catch on their own field of dreams.

Structure of the Anthology

An abstract committee subjected paper proposals for the 2003 and 2004 symposia to a rigorous and blind selection process. Such was the quality of these abstracts that many good proposals were not chosen for inclusion in either the 2003 or 2004 programs. Following both the 2003 and 2004 symposia, presenters were invited to submit their papers for possible publication. This anthology contains seventeen outstanding essays on baseball and American culture, chosen by an editorial advisory board from the approximately sixty papers delivered, cumulatively, at the 2003 and 2004 symposia. Thus, articles tapped for the anthology truly represent an all-star lineup, subject to two demanding and distinct selection processes. Subsequent to initial presentation, papers were revised and edited for publication.

The anthology is divided into five parts. *Gender: Perceptions of Masculinity and Femininity on and off the Diamond* explores the intersection of sport and sexual identity. *African Americans and the Game* chronicles the black experience in the national pastime. *Other Minorities: Beyond Baseball's Melting Pot* ruminates on baseball as a microcosm of multiculturalism in the larger society. *Baseball Media: Literature, Journalism, and Audiovisual Reproduction* analyzes depictions of the game in the popular arts. *The Business of Baseball* examines sport from a commercial perspective. Each part contains multiple essays related by theme and topic, as described below.

GENDER: FEMINISM AND MASCULINITY ON AND OFF THE DIAMOND

A Cup of Coffee in the Show: My Seven Games in the Majors by Dan Ardell is a poignant and witty autobiographical account of the coming of age of a young man through his odyssey in baseball. A former major leaguer, Ardell was subsequently a commercial real estate developer as well as a volunteer in micro-credit projects in the inner city and developing world.

Cuba Libre Versus Women's Lib: A Comparison of the Feminine Side of Baseball in Cuba and in the United States by Jean Hastings Ardell constitutes a cross-cultural analysis of gender. Her article perceptively contrasts the history of women's baseball in the United States and Cuba. Hastings Ardell, a freelance writer, is the author of a monograph on women in baseball, scheduled for publication in 2005 by Southern Illinois University Press.

Defending Masculinity: Brawling and the Unwritten Rules of Major League Baseball by Paul J. Olson offers telling perspective on the distinctive rituals governing fighting during games, a practice prompted by symbolic assertions of hegemonic manhood. A Ph.D. candidate in sociology at the University of Nebraska–Lincoln, Olson includes sport and social justice among his research interests.

AFRICAN AMERICANS AND THE GAME

Bases Loaded: Race, Reconstruction, and Baseball in Washington, D.C., 1865–1876 by Ryan Swanson constitutes a brilliant exploration of racial fluidity in baseball and society during Reconstruction, offering a case study of the nation's capital that links the microcosm of sport to the central issues of the age. Swanson, a Ph.D. candidate in United States history at Georgetown University, is a staff assistant at the Federal Research Division of the Library of Congress.

"Between Memory and History": Black Sportswriters and the (Re)construction of Negro League Baseball by Robert Cvornyek and Lawrence Hogan provides a telling interpretation of the African American press's interpretation of baseball history from the vantage point of race. Cvornyek is director of the labor studies program and professor of history at Rhode Island College, and Hogan is senior professor of history at Union County College.

Down in the Dugout: Why Baseball Is No Longer the National Pastime for Blacks by Jessica A. Johnson offers perceptive and bold analysis on the dramatic decline of the game's appeal in the African American community. Johnson teaches composition and literature courses at Columbia State Community College, serves as special correspondent for the *Columbus Dispatch*, and writes a monthly column, "From the Desk of Dr. J," that appears on Black Sports Network.

OTHER MINORITIES: BEYOND BASEBALL'S MELTING POT

Who Is a Jewish Baseball Player? by Rebecca Alpert provocatively investigates ethnic identity within the national pastime, raising important questions about Judaism that transcend sport. Chair of the department of religion and associate professor of religion and women's studies at Temple University, Alpert, ordained as a rabbi at the Reconstructionist Rabbinical College, is the author of *Like Bread on the Seder Plate: Jewish Lesbians and the Transformation of Tradition* (Columbia University Press, 1997).

Constructing the Cuban Pipeline: Papa Joe Cambria Brings the Cubans to Williamsport, Pennsylvania, 1944 to 1945 by James P. Quigel, Jr., employs original sources to relate an important and little known passage in baseball's multicultural past: the resourceful response of the Washington Senators' legendary owner Clark Griffith to the game's personnel shortage during World War II. A prolific author of works on labor history and minor league baseball, Quigel is the director of the Historical Collections and Labor Archives at the Eberly Family Special Collections Library, the Pennsylvania State University Libraries.

The Chinese Wall and Murakami, Too: The Baseball Establishment and Post–World War II Perceptions of the Asian Other by Ron Briley insightful analyzes representations of Asians in baseball and American culture, giving special emphasis to Japan's Masanori Murakami, Major League Baseball's first Asian player. Assistant headmaster at Sandia Preparatory School and adjunct professor of history at the University of New Mexico, Briley received the 1999 SABR/Macmillan Award for his article "As American as Cherry Pie: Baseball and Reflections of Violence in the 1960s and 1970s."

BASEBALL MEDIA: LITERATURE, JOURNALISM, AND AUDIOVISUAL REPRODUCTION

Imagining the Action: Audiovisual Baseball Game Reproductions in Richmond, Virginia, 1895–1935 by Eric Dewberry provides an engaging portrait of the mechanical and electronic display boards that once offered play-by-play recreations of baseball. This case study links the history of these displays to the main currents of society and culture in a bygone era. Recipient of a master of arts in history from Virginia Commonwealth, Dewberry plans to pursue a Ph.D. in his discipline and to continue his baseball research.

Joe McCarthy and the Fourth Estate: A Window onto Baseball and Media Relations in the Mid-Twentieth Century by Alan H. Levy investigates, with flair and verve, the role of the press in molding public perceptions of the game, utilizing as a vantage point the complex figure who managed, with notable success, the Chicago Cubs, New York Yankees, and Boston Red Sox. Professor of history at Slippery Rock University, Levy is the author of *Rube Waddell* (McFarland, 2000), *Tackling Jim Crow* (McFarland, 2003), and *Joe McCarthy* (McFarland, 2005).

Playing Catch Inverted: August Wilson's Fences *and Other Departures from Baseball's Cultural Stereotypes* by Edward J. Rielly provides spirited content analysis of iconoclastic, even disturbing, images of baseball in plays, novels, films, and biographies, offering a counterbalance to celebrants of sacred myth. Professor and chair of the English department at Saint Joseph's College of Maine, Rielly has edited several volumes of poetry and baseball literature.

THE BUSINESS OF BASEBALL

Yankees Profits and Promise: The Purchase of Babe Ruth and the Building of Yankee Stadium by Kenneth Winter and Michael J. Haupert employs original franchise accounting records in a compelling chronicle of the player acquisition and ballpark construction that provided the foundations for baseball's most famous and successful dynasty. Haupert is chair and professor of the economics department at the University of Wisconsin–La Crosse, and Winter is chair and assistant professor of the accountancy department at the University of Wisconsin–La Crosse.

Evolution of the Sunday Doubleheader and Its Role in Elevating the Popularity of Baseball by Charlie Bevis provides an illuminating history of the practice of admitting fans to two games for the price of one, a promotional strategy that burgeoned during the 1930s and helped the game rebound from the hard times of the Great Depression. Bevis, editor-in-chief of research studies at Financial Research Corporation in Boston, Massachusetts, is the author of *Mickey Cochrane* (McFarland, 1998) and *Sunday Baseball* (McFarland, 2003) and a prolific baseball writer.

The Kansas City Royals' Baseball Academy: Expanding the Science and Pedagogy of Baseball by Richard J. Puerzer relates, in a presentation attuned to nuance, team owner Ewing Kauffmann's attempt to transform athletes into ballplayers via a "school," a bold entrepreneurial enterprise to manufacture future major leaguers that defied the game's conventional wisdom. An assistant professor of industrial engineering, Puerzer has published previous writings on baseball in *Fan, Spitball, Nine,* and past editions of *The Cooperstown Symposium on Baseball and American Culture.*

The Cost of Competitiveness in Major League Baseball by Herbert F. Lewis,

Thomas R. Sexton, and Kathleen A. Lock provides clear and rigorous analysis of the relationship between franchise success and market size in the age of free agency. Lewis, Sexton, and Lock are affiliated with the W. Averell Harriman School for Management and Policy at Stony Brook University as, respectively, visiting assistant professor, professor and director, and graduate student.

The Elements of Major League Contraction by Paul D. Staudohar and Franklin Lowenthal clarifies, through lucid exposition of seminal research, the legal, economic, and political ramifications of eliminating baseball franchises. Staudohar, professor of business administration at California State University, Hayward, is the author of *Diamond Mines: Baseball and Labor* (Syracuse University Press, 2000). Lowenthal is professor of accounting and computer information systems at California State University, Hayward.

Part I

GENDER: FEMINISM AND MASCULINITY ON AND OFF THE DIAMOND

A Cup of Coffee in the Show: My Seven Games in the Majors

Dan Ardell

It has been forty-four years since I played Major League Baseball. And this is the first time I have given a formal account of my cup of coffee in *the show*. The story begins with Coach. Rod Dedeaux, my coach at the University of Southern California (USC), made possible my journey to the majors; he was the best baseball teacher I ever encountered.

Dedeaux emphasized the mental aspects of the game. In 1961, USC had a number of players who were all-city, all-county, or all-state in high school. Consequently, their basic baseball skills were good. Augmenting those skills, Dedeaux imposed upon us a thought process that related to every pitch and every play of the game. Preparing for a game against the University of California, Berkeley, Coach gathered all of us around a chalkboard, and proceeded to ask us the following: "It's the sixth inning, you're on second, and the score is 3–2, with Cal leading. What are you thinking and why?" This does not appear to be a particularly difficult question, but he expected you to ask yourself the following before answering:

- How many outs are there?
- How does each of their outfielders throw?
- Are their relief pitchers stronger or weaker than ours?
- Who's batting for us?
- Who's pitching for them?
- What place are we in the standings, and how important is this game?
- Is the third base coach likely to be aggressive on a close play in trying to score me; and how aggressive should I be in rounding third base?

Dedeaux was really asking, "Do you understand that you're not just a runner on second base, but that you are an integral part of the game and your thought process could easily affect its outcome?"

Another example from 1961: After USC won the College World Series, we went to Hawaii to play the Japanese college champions. I was on deck in one of the games. With one out, the batter hit a fly ball to short-medium left-centerfield, and the runner on third tagged up and was out by a mile at home plate to end the inning. The following inning, I led off and struck out. Dedeaux called me over, and said, "Tiger" (he calls everybody *Tiger*), "that's got to cost you twenty-five cents." (Twenty-five cents was the maximum fine for a mental error, with the minimum being a dime.) I indicated that my strikeout might constitute a mental error, but that he had never before imposed a fine for striking out. Coach indicated that he was not fining me for the strikeout, but for the runner making the third out at home in the previous inning. Dedeaux asked if I really wanted the runner to score. I told him *yes*. Coach asked if I *really* wanted the runner to score. Dedeaux then asked if I knew which side the runner slid best on. I indicated no. Coach stated he would not fine me for that, although that after 60 games, I should certainly have known. I then said, "It didn't make any difference which side he slid on; he was going to be out by a mile." Coach stated, "That is the problem": Dedeaux asserted that if I had been *really* thinking I would have recognized immediately the futility of the runner racing toward home. Instead of having the runner slide, I should have held my hands up to get him to stop and be in a rundown, which, Dedeaux indicated, would have given the runner a far better chance of scoring than simply sliding into the third out. "Tiger, got to fine you twenty-five cents," concluded Coach.

Coach Dedeaux is still the man. About a year ago, the USC baseball team accepted an invitation to play three exhibition games in Cuba. Dedeaux, at age 89, along with a number of USC alumni and supporters, made that trip. I was sitting next to Dedeaux during the third game. In the seventh inning, a Cuban player hit a one-hop, short-hop ball to the USC shortstop, who gloved the ball nicely, took three steps, and got the runner by half a step. Turning to my old coach, I said, "Just the way you used to teach it." Looking me square in the eye, Dedeaux retorted, "Not quite, Tiger." He asked me how many steps the shortstop took. I was not particularly cognizant of the answer, but guessed it was three. Dedeaux agreed, but said that the shortstop should have taken only two steps. Once again, Coach could have fined me twenty-five cents. In baseball and life, Dedeaux taught us to anticipate what might take place next based on understanding the past and present. That perspective made possible my journey to the majors and beyond.

In July of 1961, following my sophomore year at USC, I signed a contract with the then Los Angeles Angels, an American League expansion team in its inaugural year. Angels owner Gene Autry, the old cowboy star, had acquired the team the previous December for $4 million. Interestingly, he had originally anticipated paying $3 million for the broadcast rights, but realized that for the extra million he could buy the ball club. I received a signing bonus of $37,500, which was paid out, at my request, over five years. As my Dad had never made more than $10,000 in one year, the bonus seemed immense to me. When I signed and decided to defer some of the bonus, my Dad asked Roland Hemond, who was the Director of the Farm System (and subsequently one of the best baseball administrators in history), what rate of interest the Angels would pay on the amount I did not take the first year. I told Dad and Roland that since I was the one who was asking for the money to be deferred, no interest should be paid. To his credit, Dad did not correct me because he sought to make me responsible for my own decisions, and that was more important than compounding interest.

After signing the contract, Hemond indicated that if I did well, I would be called up at the end of the year. The Angels had only two farm teams, a Triple-A affiliate in Dallas-Fort Worth, and a Class D team in Statesville, North Carolina. The Statesville team did not have an opening for another player, and, for about a week, I was not sure where the Angels would send me; then, I received a call, instructing me to report to a Dodger farm team in Artesia, New Mexico. I had no idea where Artesia was. It turned out to be about 30 miles from Carlsbad Caverns and was in the appropriately named Sophomore League (Class D). The other teams included Carlsbad, Hobbs (NM), Alpine (TX), El Paso, and Albuquerque. The Sophomore League was so bad that it folded at season's end.

The Angels were able to send me to a Dodger farm team because the Dodgers needed additional players in their large farm system, and because this was possibly the worst professional team ever assembled. When I arrived in Artesia, some of the players told me that when they left spring training they flew on the Dodger plane into the Artesia airport. The only problem was they had no way to exit the plane because it would have taken a fairly high ladder to reach the door of the plane. Consequently, the town's one hook-and-ladder fire engine came to help them out. This was only the beginning of Artesia stories. We were paid three dollars a day meal money, and each ball player was responsible for finding his own housing. I ended up rooming with one of the team's catchers in a two-bedroom apartment for $40 a month, including utilities and furnishings. This was about $39 too high.

The team was so bad that a writer from *Sports Illustrated* had been sent out to interview a number of townspeople and players about the team. Our manager was a former ballplayer named Spider Jorgensen, and I seem to remember we were some fifty games out of first place. One of our better pitchers was known as "Iggy," which was often shortened to "Ig." As ballplayers are prone to do, they look for weaknesses, not only in opponents, but also among teammates. I was informed that Iggy was short for "ignorant." One night we were leading 2–1, with Iggy pitching an excellent game. In the sixth inning, however, he proceeded to walk the first three batters. Spider came out of the dugout and, as I was the first baseman, I went to the mound along with the other infielders to hear what the manager had to say. The manager told Iggy that he had pitched a good game, but given the three walks, he was getting the hook. Iggy was displeased. He responded by stating that he had knocked in our two runs and that if Spider was really going to take him out, he would take those runs with him. Spider had a look on his face that I had never seen before. He told Iggy that he was done and to go in and take his shower. Iggy did not head directly for the dugout, however; instead, he trotted out to the centerfield scoreboard and literally removed his two runs from the scoreboard before proceeding to the dugout.

Summer in New Mexico brings giant mosquitoes and bugs, and the lights of the ballpark seem to attract every insect in the neighborhood. Luckily for us, we only had 56 lights that actually worked. The good news was that we had less bugs; the bad news was that it was a little tough to see the ball coming from some of the flame-throwers. Still, it was my first adventure in professional baseball. The team consisted of eighteen players, and we traveled in station wagons. With all the equipment and fairly good-sized players, this was not a picnic.

I particularly remember our first trip to El Paso, one of the two good-sized cities in the circuit. I had grown up in Los Angeles and had seen segregation, and had read about a different kind of segregation in the South. I did not think of El Paso as being the South, but quickly learned that it was. We had a day game there, and that night four of us walked to the local movie theater to see *The Guns of Navarone*. Another white guy and I were walking in front of two black teammates and entered the theater before they did. In the theater lobby, I noticed that there were two drinking fountains, one of which read "Colored Only." I remember my shock and amazement that this really existed. My white teammate and I proceeded into the lower level of the theater and saved two seats for our teammates, but they did not show up. After the movie, we saw them in the lobby, and said something smart like, "Where the hell did you guys go?" They looked at us like we were complete idiots, and said, "Obviously, we were in the balcony." I naively asked, "Why did we save the seats for you?" The response went, "We don't get to sit in that part of the theater." That was my first direct experience with that kind of segregation.

The season in Artesia ended thirty days after my arrival, and the Angels felt that I had done well enough to be called up. Just sixty days before, I was at USC being fined twenty-five cents for a mental error and often sitting on the bench while an All-American played first base ahead of me; now I was in the big leagues. Minimum pay was $7,500 a year for a major leaguer, and I received $1,250 for my thirty-day cup of coffee. Players in those days generally did not make enough money to live on and consequently virtually all had off-season jobs ranging from sales and marketing to gas station attendant. Most players simply took it for granted that they would work in the off season. My situation was different. Since I had spread my bonus over five years, I had enough money in the off-season to not work, and my intent was to complete four more semesters and get my college degree, which, in fact, I did.

Coming to the ballpark that first day at Wrigley Field in Los Angeles was exciting. The Angels were a team of colorful characters—Ted Kluszewski, Eddie Yost, Rocky Bridges, Leon "Daddy Wags" Wagner, Eli Grba, Tom Morgan, Steve Bilko, Lee Thomas, George Thomas, Art Fowler, and Albie Pearson. I was known as *Big Dan*, but Kluszewski, with his enormous biceps, had a vaccination mark bigger than my head.

I had read about so many of these guys who were now my teammates; some had been in the Pacific Coast League (PCL), which, when I was growing up, included my beloved Hollywood Stars and the "hated" Los Angeles Angels. Hollywood played at Gilmore Field, the present site of CBS Television Studios. The PCL Angels had played at Wrigley Field, just as the brand-new major league Angels now did. As a twenty-year-old baseball player, I was thoroughly convinced I belonged in the major leagues. My fielding was suspect, and I did not hit left-handers well, but I was sure I could work through these problems. My optimism outran my talent.

For several weeks, I did not get an opportunity to play. Then, on September 20th in the ninth inning at Detroit, Angels manager Bill Rigney yelled, "Hey, rook. Get a bat and hit for Dean Chance." (This is a far cry from pinch hitters today who know their role and are fully warmed up prior to stepping into the batter's box.) At first, I was not sure Rigney meant me because there were other "rooks" there, too, but he kept pointing in my direction. So I picked up my bat and headed for the on-deck circle. Ron Kline was on the mound for the Tigers. We were down 6–3, with a runner on first, actually a pinch-runner who was one of our pitchers. We were playing in Detroit's old Briggs Stadium, which had a short right-field porch. I saw myself as a power hitter, and did not think Kline looked overpowering. It was clear to me that I could hit a home run and make it a 6–5 ball game. It was probably also clear to Kline that I was a big, young rookie thinking about hitting a home run. He threw me pitches that were around the plate, ones that were not overpowering. Finally, he threw one that looked very hittable. I swung and almost broke my knuckles, but the ball had enough on it to get over the second baseman's head for a single. The pinch runner on first rounded second too aggressively. The right fielder gunned the ball to second and the runner was tagged out. The game was over. And I was standing on first base, batting 1.000. I was unhappy that we had lost, but ecstatic about getting on base in my first at-bat. I was confident that many more at-bats and hits lay ahead.

The following day in Chicago, Rigney asked me to pinch-run. I do not remember much about that, but, after the game, I joined a group of the ballplayers signing autographs. Some of our players were very recognizable, while others, like me, were unknown. But we all signed autographs like we were veterans. One boy of about eight held out his baseball for me to sign, which I did, and handed it back to him, at which point, he read the autograph and said, "Dan Ardell. Who are you?" I assured him I was one of the players.

About a week later, we were in the last week of the season. Again, Rigney asked me to pinch-run, and I found myself on third base. Watching the pitcher wind up, I knew I could steal home on him. The third base coach simply looked at me and said, "No." Some years later, I found out that if I had been successful, I would have been the first Angel to have stolen home. To this day, I am convinced I could have done it.

Finally, on September 27th, I got my first and only start in the major leagues. It was USC Trojan Night, and Tom Satriano and I were honored as the first Trojans to play for the Angels. I did not hit lefthanders well, and lefty Claude Osteen was on the mound for the Washington Senators. My 1.000 batting average was at risk. Osteen, like Kline, probably knew that I would overswing and proceeded to strike me out my first time up. *Oh, well: I was still hitting .500.* The second time up, he jammed me, and I grounded right back to him. *Oh, well, still hitting .333.* In my last at-bat in the majors, he once again jammed me, and I once again grounded out to him. Unbeknownst to me, I had just finished my major league career as a .250 hitter. The season ended a few days later, and Rosie Gilhausen, the longtime scout who recommended me to the Angels, assured me I was just getting started, and there was no doubt in my mind he was right.

During the off-season, I took classes at UCLA, confident that I would be with the major league club for spring training. At that time, the Vic Tanny gyms (much like today's 24-Hour Fitness) offered any major leaguer a free membership. I was told by executives of the Angels to refuse that offer because the team did not want muscle-bound players. Unlike today, ballplayers of my time did not generally follow a year-round regimen. Nonetheless, I stayed in pretty good shape during the off-season, particularly compared to my contemporaries.

In February 1962, I reported to spring training along with four other players who had also been brought up the previous September. This was just the beginning for Jim Fregosi, Buck Rodgers, and Dean Chance. It was also the start of Bo Belinsky's career with the Angels. I still remember the first day of spring training; we rode bicycles through downtown Palm Springs, with

Gene Autry and Bill Rigney, also on bikes, leading us to the ballpark. In those days, spring training was quite different. In addition to not reporting in good shape, players also partied hearty.

The first week of spring training reminded me of my time in Army boot camp; it was not fun. But then we started inter-squad games. I remember facing future Cy Young award winner Dean Chance. Although I was a power hitter, prior to facing Chance, I had only one home run that really stuck out in my mind — and that was in high school, where I hit a ball over the Hollywood High School gym. I did well against Chance — hitting the only other home run I remember, but did not do well enough against other pitchers. When spring training ended, I was sent to San Jose of the Class-C California League. I was disappointed but was young and knew I could work my way back.

In San Jose, I started the season slowly, and then, in June, facing another of those dreaded left-handed pitchers, I took a fastball in the forehead. It happened at twilight, when it was difficult to see the ball. I had a no-ball, 2-strike count, and was going to "hang in" at all costs, not realizing that the cost would be a dented forehead. I literally did not see the pitch, and have never talked with anyone who has seen anything comparable. The ball bounced off my forehead and went past third base. I was unconscious but not paralyzed as they took me from the field. I came to only once that night, remembering that my mouth was full of liquid, most of which was deposited on the doctor, at which point, the doctor asked, "Why didn't somebody tell me this man was bleeding internally?" The next morning I woke up with my right eye swollen shut and the seams of the baseball outlined on my forehead. The pitch had broken the orbit in the back of my right eye and given me a concussion, but other than that I was OK. Gene Autry offered to have any doctor in the country flown in to assist, but the doctors there were more than competent, and outside help was unnecessary. The main decision that had to be made was whether or not to operate. There were two issues relating to the orbit in my right eye and the forehead area of my skull. After some days, the doctors determined that it was more dangerous to operate than to simply allow the injury to heal on its own. I was lucky; vision returned, and pain subsided. The only thing that seems to affect me today is watching pitchers come inside; I occasionally find myself flinching.

About six weeks later, I was playing again. Although I finished the season as poorly as I had begun it, I did have the winning RBI in the final game to win the league championship. During the off-season, I transferred to San Jose State, continuing to chip away at a degree. I also invested some of my bonus, purchased my first piece of real estate in Santa Cruz, and worked part-time for the realtor from whom I bought the property. The major leagues now seemed far off but still reachable.

In 1963, I went to spring training with the minor league clubs. Although I had not done well in 1962, I was still a prospect and started the season in Double-A Nashville. Unlike the previous season, I started well in 1963, and for the first two weeks was hitting over .400, and leading the league. The next two weeks saw my average drop to about .320, and management called me in to tell me I was going to be reassigned. Still believing that I was going to be a major leaguer again, I hoped the assignment was to Triple-A Hawaii. Instead, it was back to San Jose.

Disappointed, I had a so-so season during my second San Jose stint. I returned to San Jose State in the off-season, and belatedly started to show finesse as student.

In 1964, I again reported to the minor league training camp, now not knowing what was in front of me. Despite enjoying playing baseball, I was coming to realize that I did not enjoy the life of a minor league player. Traveling long distances by bus or station wagon, sleeping in cramped beds in second rate hotels, and eating mediocre food at odd hours, my life in the bushes was consumed by a day-to-day fight for survival. Additionally, the male tendency to descend to the lowest common denominator meant that if you did not like to screw around (particularly on the road), then you were probably going to be by yourself figuring out what to do in Hobbs, New Mexico, or Bakersfield, California, or Wenatchee, Washington. I was beginning to realize that I had better finish school and make a real living.

Still, there were some distinctive moments along the way. In Salinas, of the California League, a new ballpark had been constructed on what appeared to be a very limited budget. It also appeared that some of the people involved did not know baseball. Upon entering the locker room for the first time, I saw nine nails, one for each of our players to hang up their clothing. Since we were the first team to use that locker room, the overseer of construction was there to proudly display his new facility. Our manager asked why there were only nine nails. He looked at our manager with disbelief: "Do you think I'm stupid? I know baseball has nine players on each team."

One of the California League clubs was located in Bakersfield, necessitating travel through the summer heat belt of California's Central Valley. In an old bus bereft of air conditioning, we drove by many fruit stands. Finally, we stopped at a stand featuring cherries. On a team populated by men defined more by youth than wisdom, we each bought and consumed two pint containers of fresh cherries, and, sadly to say, not much other food. The game started some four hours later, and by the third inning, player after player needed to leave the field to finish off the cherry experience. Ah, to be twenty-two again!

Later that season, we were again driving toward the Central Valley through a range of hills when the brakes on the bus went out. Luckily our driver (who in the minor leagues was often also the trainer) skillfully banked the bus against the side of the hill, and no one was hurt. Overall the year was very disappointing, but it did not mean I was not going to return to *the show*. Still, the odds were starting to lengthen against me.

The following year I again went to spring training with the minor league teams and was assigned to the Tri-City Angels. This was Kennewick, Pasco, and Richland, Washington, located in the extreme southeasterly plains of the state, only a few miles from the Oregon and Idaho borders. As was the case in Artesia, housing alternatives were unattractive. In one large apartment complex, which had been in foreclosure, some of the players found the amenities lacking.

My most vivid memory of that apartment related to a late-night party after a Sunday game. But Washington was a dry state on Sunday, and the closest beer outlet was 80 miles away, in Umitilla, Oregon. On such occasions, a single player was typically designated to drive the 160 mile round-trip, beer-run. A number of players drank too many beers, and at around 1:30 AM, one of the players decided that the apartment unit domiciling the party was far too dirty. He felt the best way to remedy this situation was to bring in a garden hose and simply hose down the apartment: Not a good decision. The police soon joined us, and some weeks later approximately $3,000 was transferred from a ballplayer account to that of the apartment owner.

I finished the 1964 campaign with 17 home runs, 65 RBIs, and a .265 batting average. It was now clear to me that I needed to finish school and leave baseball. I talked with Roland Hemond and asked him if my contract allowed this since I had one more payment due me in 1965. He indicated this was OK, because I was the one who chose to spread the bonus over five years. After talking with Hemond, I felt relieved and ready for life after baseball. It was time to move on. I graduated from college in June 1965. No remorse with my decision to leave the game: I had a short but good run in the game.

In 1966, I attended a ball game and was going to meet one of the players whom I knew after the game. I was still only 25 years old, and looked like a ballplayer. As I stood and waited, a boy of about eight came up and asked for my signature, pointing to his friend and telling him that I was Rick Reichardt. I told the boy that I was not Reichardt, and his comment was, "Sure, Rick!" My friend and a number of other ballplayers came out and the other kids went to them for autographs, but the one boy stayed by me. I did not know what to do, but it was clear that he believed I was Reichardt. I looked around and the boy was the only one left near me, so I decided I would sign Reichardt's name. I only had two problems: Reichardt is right-handed; I am left-handed; and I didn't know how to spell his name. Therefore, I wrote quickly and illegibly, but not quickly enough. My friend saw me signing the autograph, and told all the kids to get my autograph. With that, a horde descended upon me. Since I had signed for the first boy, I felt obligated to sign more and proceeded to autograph approximately a hundred balls or pieces of paper. Therefore, if you are a collector and find Reichardt's signature from 1966, be forewarned.

Fast-forward several decades. I am a fan, and the Angels are still my team. The Angels have had only one magical year in their entire history: 2002. The 2003 year was a tremendous disappointment, but in that year Arte Moreno made the decision to buy the Angels. Much has been said about Moreno, almost all of it good. My experience, although it is limited, affirms this evaluation. In 2004, he gathered former Angels players for a dinner and update on the team. I am a former Angel, and this had never taken place before. About fifty of the former Angels, including Fred Lynn, Dave Winfield, Don Sutton, Jim Abbott, Bob Boone, Buck Rodgers, and Albie Pearson, gathered simply to hear the new owner and see for themselves if all the good comments really meant anything. Moreno is wealthy, but he is a humble person without pretense. During the NBA playoffs in June of 2004, Moreno was invited to Staples Center for one of the Lakers' games. It is customary for the executive chefs for each of the teams to contact one another for the appropriate menu when one owner is visiting another's venue. The executive chef at Staples Center e-mailed the gourmet menu to Anaheim Stadium and asked if the menu was good enough for Mr. Moreno. The executive chef at Anaheim Stadium e-mailed back that Mr. Moreno preferred hot dogs, taquitos, and chicken wings. Of course, the Staples Center chef knew this was a joke, and again asked if the gourmet menu was satisfactory. The Anaheim Stadium executive chef reiterated Mr. Moreno's preferences. This time, the Staples Center executive chef was running short of patience and asked for a real answer. Finally, someone in the front office called the executive chef and told him this was not a joke.

Remembrance of seasons past and on-going rooting for the Angels continue to connect me to baseball. My sense of humor still carries the resonance of the game as does my facility for anticipating situations, an attribute derived from the teachings of Coach Dedeaux. So many people want to hear about ballplayers' experiences. Although I played only briefly, I find that talking baseball with fans brings a special smile and a camaraderie. I have got a lot of mileage out of my cup of coffee in *the show*.

Cuba Libre Versus Women's Lib: A Comparison of the Feminine Side of Baseball in Cuba and in the United States

Jean Hastings Ardell

In January 2004, the University of Southern California baseball team opened its season in Cuba. Alumni were invited along. USC had worked hard to win a governmental sanction for this "cultural" exchange, but a few days before our departure the Bush Administration apparently decided that too many American citizens were enjoying far too much culture in this communist country. Suddenly the only way U.S. citizens could legally visit the island was under the umbrella of religion. The university was obliged to send a letter, which read, in part, "We would like to reiterate that the purpose of your visit to Cuba is for religious purposes and you will participate in a full-time religious program developed by the University Church of Our Savior."[1] If anyone wanted to cancel, the university would grant a refund. I did not want my money back. As a lifelong member of the Church of Baseball, I was eager to make a missionary outreach to the Cuban branch of the church. Besides, I had been tracing the history of women's baseball in the United States and was intrigued by the opportunity to compare how Cuban women had fared in the Church of Baseball. For the purposes of this paper, three periods in history will be discussed: the late 1800s, the 1940s and 1950s, and the 1990s to the present.[2]

I started out in search of contrasts between the two countries' historic attitudes toward baseball, but instead found similarities. For example, national identity figures in both countries' early responses to the game. Although historians have repeatedly demonstrated that baseball as we know it arose from town ball, earlier English games, such as rounders and stool ball, which were played by girls and boys, and, going way back in time, ancient fertility rites, some of professional baseball's promoters of the late nineteenth century wanted America's new pastime clearly distinguished from anything English. When the star pitcher and shortstop John Montgomery Ward published his treatise of 1888 on the game's origins and history, he attempted to plant baseball firmly in American soil. "[I]f base-ball is neither sprung from rounders nor taken bodily from another English game, what is its origin? I believe it to be a fruit of the inventive genius of the American boy.... In the field of out-door sports the American boy is easily capable of devising his own amusements, and until some proof is adduced that base-ball is not his invention, I protest against this systematic effort to rob him of his dues."[3] Out of such reasoning, it was a short jump two decades later to the creation of the Abner Doubleday-Cooperstown creation myth.

Cubans also connected baseball with their national identity. During the 1860s, Cuban college men often returned from their studies in the U.S. full of talk about the game just as visiting U.S. sailors were bringing the game ashore in Havana. The people of Cuba were engaged by baseball's resemblance to their old game of *batos*, which was played by the indigenous inhabitants, the Tainos. The bat was made of wrapped tree branches and the ball composed of resins and leaves. Today, Cubans like to claim that the English term for "bat" comes from their own "batos." And Batos is now the trademark of all Cuban-made sporting equipment.

The Cubans also appreciated baseball because it put cultural distance between them and Spain. By the mid-1800s, Cuba was straining against Spanish domination. Adopting baseball as its game of preference fostered Cuba's ties with its closest Western Hemisphere neighbor, the United States, rather than anything connected with imperialistic Europe. The Spanish understood this and in 1868, the Spanish General Captain of Cuba banned baseball because it was an "anti-Spanish game, and of insurrectional tendencies against the Spanish language."[4] Statements like this surely moved the Cubans to only love the game more. To this day, Cuba favors baseball, unlike other Latin American countries that consider soccer their national sport.

If its promoters of the nineteenth century wanted baseball to be a game of the Western Hemisphere, they also wanted it to be a masculine game. For example, John Montgomery Ward attempted to separate the game not only from England but also from any taint of the feminine. In his discussion of the game's origins, Ward wrote:

> The fact that in the three instances in which we find the name [baseball] mentioned it is always a game for girls or women, would justify the suspicion that it was not always the same game, and that it in any way resembled our game is not to be imagined. Base-ball in its mildest form is essentially a robust game, and it would require an elastic imagination to conceive of little girls possessed of physical powers such as its play demands.[5]

This was news to the tomboys of the late 1800s. As the game grew in popularity throughout the United States, girls and women were falling for the game. Many of them, discontent with sitting on the sidelines as spectators, took up the game despite resistance from medical authorities, who feared injury to a young woman's health, purveyors of social mores, who feared injury to her femininity, and the sports media, which resented her invasion of the manly domain of baseball. When Vassar College opened to students in 1866, its young women quickly organized baseball clubs. Despite administrators' concerns for the students' safety and parental disapproval, such clubs persisted for decades. Stronger reactions attended the professional women's teams that by the 1880s were barnstorming the country. While individual women of talent were indeed found, the recruitment of a fully competent team often proved difficult, given the cultural resistance toward women playing baseball. When two players of one traveling club quit in New Orleans, a local girl filled in at centerfield, and the local press reported with sarcastic diplomacy, "It was evidently the first time she had ever seen a baseball outside of a shop window, and she has not exactly acquired the art of handling it yet."[6] Also under scrutiny was the moral fiber of both the promoters of women's baseball and the players themselves. When Harry H. Freeman attempted to organize such a team, rumors circulated that he was recruiting the players for prostitution. In 1886, *The Sporting Life* ran this series of notes: May 12th: "Freeman's Female Base Ball Club is in New Orleans. During an alleged game recently, a young man ran out of the crowd, caught one of the girls by the neck and began dragging her out of the grounds. He was arrested, but on proving that the girl was his sister he was released. He took her home." July 7th: "The Freeman's Female Base Ball Club turned up in Nashville, Tenn. The Nashville Club wisely refused to let their ground to the disreputable party." September 8th: "The female base ball club seems to have extinguished itself. The only decent connection women can have with the game is as spectators."

This attitude surfaced in Cuba, too. In a dispatch dated March 6, 1893, *The Sporting News* reported that the American Female Base Ball Club "has been going about playing against Cuban clubs and otherwise exhibiting themselves with more or less success."[7] It all went bad, however, in Almendares during a game the women played against a local club. While the report describes the spectators as generally "respectable and well behaved," the crowd also included "a share of the lowest degrees of society." These latter quickly found fault with the women's quality of play, and raised the cry that "the women — were, in fact, not players at all, and that the money of the spectators had been received under false pretenses." Refunds were demanded, and when that did not happen, the mob tore apart the seats and set fire to the fence surrounding the field. Several of the women ballplayers reportedly "nearly swooned with fright." Things got worse. The crowd turned on the female ball club, which was "gallantly defended" by the opposing players and others in the stands as "[h]orrible confusion ensued and the shrieks of the frightened women would be heard." Pursued by the mob, both teams then fled to a nearby residence. But the mob broke in and began to tear the house apart. The Cuban players tried to protect the women but by the time the police arrived to restore order, some of the women had been injured.

Baseball developed in popularity amid the Victorian Age (1837–1901), and far into the twentieth century, strongly held tenets of Victorian thinking attached to the idea of women playing baseball in both Cuba and the U.S. It was unseemly and unfeminine. Tomboys who persisted in playing the game as adults were suspected of being lesbian. Indeed, some of them were and some were not. While World War II gave women a chance to play hardball in grander arenas for good pay, the players' sexual orientation was a perennial issue. The organizers of the All-American Girls Baseball League (1943–1954) mandated that its players play ball like men but look traditionally feminine. Number One on the League's list of rules was the command: "ALWAYS appear in feminine attire when not actively engaged in practice or playing ball."[8] The front office continued the drive to maintain this image throughout its existence. At the start of the 1950 season, Don H. Black, the owner of the Racine Belles, urged the team to remember that they were selling both baseball and femininity. Black's newsletter of March 1950 reveals his preoccupation with the issue: "You'd be surprised at the importance [femininity] holds with the average fan. Nobody is especially surprised or impressed if a rough, tough mannish looking babe shows some ability at sports. But to realize that a truly feminine creature can reach the top ... is refreshing and pleasing."[9] Warming to his role as fashion advisor, Black told the Belles in his next newsletter to "avoid the mannish touches in jackets and shirts. Keep the little feminine frills and fancies where you can.... I've got a special personal feeling about shoes. I know it isn't so comfy to wear high heels after bouncing around in spikes for a few hours but there is nothing like a neat, feminine shoe ... to set off womanly charms."[10] Such standards sent the lesbians of the AAGBL deep into the closet, literally and figuratively.

During the 1940s, Cuba also had a women's league. Organized along the lines of the AAGBL by Rafael de Leon, a Cuban distillery owner, the *Estrellas Cubanas* gave the most talented of the island's female athletes, who had grown up playing on the streets and with boys' and men's teams, a chance to continue playing baseball into adulthood. Isabel Alvarez and Eulalia "Viyaya" Gonzalez were two such women, born at the beginning of the Depression, who demonstrated sufficient talent for the game that the crowds that saw them play were not moved to launch an attack a la 1893. Alvarez and Gonzalez reveal further similarities between the two countries' attitudes towards women's baseball. Eulalia Gonzalez grew up in the Havana neighborhood of Plaza del Vapor. Tightly circumscribed by apartments was a baseball diamond, the home of the Deportivo Tacon Club. Four gates led to the field, one from each of the access streets. Hard-hit balls had a tendency to enter the lower floors of the apartments, so special rules were in effect. According to the Cuban newspaper *Juventud Rebelde,* spectators following Tacon's games from the windows of the upper floors; those who disagreed with a call or a play were known to drop bags of urine upon the field of play. Gonzalez was good enough and tough enough to play first base for this men's team and made quite a name for herself, traveling throughout the country with Tacon. "She was so good that many were calling her the 'Regino Otero' (after a famous Cuban first baseman) of the amateur baseball."[11] Gonzalez typified the elite female ballplayer able to play alongside men — much like her near contemporary in the U.S., Babe Didrikson, who toured with the House of David before moving on to sports more hospitable to women.

In April 1947, Max Carey brought players from the AAGBL to Havana for spring training. The U.S. played three exhibition games against local women's teams. Rafael de Leon acted as agent for the Cuban women deemed talented enough to be considered for the AAGBL. *Juventud Rebelde* reported that after seeing Gonzalez play, Max Carey quickly offered her $300 (another source said $350) a month to come north to play. On May 4th, she traveled to the U.S. She probably would have done well because she had always played men's baseball, unlike the players from the U.S. and Canada, who had grown up mostly playing softball. However, Gonzalez missed the island and she missed her family, and she quickly returned to Cuba. She continued to play men's baseball for years, becoming widely known throughout the island. Baseball researcher David Skinner reported that the Municipio de Centro Habana Museo del Historia del Deporte (Central Havana Sports History Museum) features an extensive display of Gonzalez's career. Skinner concluded, "[She] was apparently the most famous baseball player from the Central Havana municipality. At least there was more material on her than the several pros from Centro, who included Edmundo (Sandy) Amoros."[12] Gonzalez reportedly passed away recently on Cuba's Isla de la Juventud.

Isabel Alvarez was only fourteen when AAGBL scouts returned to Cuba in 1948 to sign four older players; her time would come the following year when, at fifteen, she was deemed old enough for such an adventure. Any concerns about the idea of a girl playing baseball held no sway with Alvarez's mother, a strong-willed woman who was passionate about the game. Growing up, Isabel remembers her mother habitually seated close by a tiny radio, following the games of the Almendares ball club. Although she did not attend the Roman Catholic Church of her faith, Isabel's mother was a prayerful woman who maintained a household shrine, where she often lit a candle when a favorite player needed a hit. Alvarez reminisced in a telephone interview:

> I grew up in what we say is a dysfunctional family, with everyone fighting all the time. I think for my mother, baseball was my ticket out of there.... I don't think I loved baseball as much as my mother did.... I was very shy when young — my mother was very strict about boys— but not about baseball. She always dressed me in long pants and let me climb trees. We'd play *pelota* in the street with balls covered with strips of cardboard from cigarette cartons wrapped around crumbled up newspaper. Of course, they came apart quickly, and we spent a lot of time repairing them. [13]

Isabel and her mother were very close. It was her mother who managed her baseball career, keeping a detailed scrapbook, calling the press with news of her daughter and promoting interviews, and persuading Gollito, their dark-skinned neighbor and former ballplayer, to coach Isabel. During the 1930s, sufficient food was hard to come by in their neighborhood of Cerros, but her mother always made sure her daughter was taken care of. These special attentions caused jealousy in Isabel's brother.

If neighbors wondered at Isabel's tomboy ways, her mother kept the criticism from her. That innocence ended during a family argument. According to Alvarez,

> I was just a child. My brother got mad and called my mother and me lesbians. I never forgot that. Then, when I started playing professional baseball, it all came back on me.... I didn't want people talking about me that way, so I've never had a roommate even though it would have let me live cheaper.

Over the years, Isabel made several attempts to reconcile with her family, traveling to Cuba in 1979 and 1986, before inviting her brother and his son for a visit to her home in Indiana in 2000. By the second week, the old recriminations had again begun; and finally, in the midst of one bad moment, she recalls her nephew saying, "Look at you — you're a lesbian." Isabel recoiled in pain: "I felt crucified by that — all just because I once played baseball. What kind of mentality would say something like that? I was raised a Christian, I read the Bible, I go by it." Alvarez called the assumption that women who play baseball must be gay to be "a curse — one you carry all your life. After the League ended, I seldom told anyone I played baseball." The release, however, in 1992, of Penny Marshall's film *A League of Their Own* transformed Alvarez's feelings on the subject. The hit movie made celebrities of the players; suddenly it was all right, even cool, to be a woman who played baseball. Ever since, Alvarez said she has felt more acceptable, more comfortable about her career in baseball.

Alvarez's mother pushed her daughter to play baseball and she pushed her to leave Cuba. For years, Alvarez felt somewhat abandoned by her mother's determination in these matters. Like Viyaya Gonzalez, she, too, was homesick when she joined the AAGBL, but she felt obliged to stay. In 1949 and 1950, she pitched for the AAGBL's touring team, the Chicago Colleens. Her statistics are somewhat sketchy; these are taken from the *AAGPBL Record Book*: 1950: 6–6; 39 ABs, 10 hits, .256 B.A.; 1951, with Fort Wayne and Battle Creek, 209, 3.71 ERA; 21 ABs, 2 hits, .095 ERA; 11 assists, 1 error, .917 fielding average. Without her mother around to push her, Isabel, in retrospect, thinks she could have tried harder. After the Revolution of 1959, Isabel's visits to the country left her appalled by the conditions there. During one stay, she went to see Viyaya Gonzalez. "It was awful — oh, how she lived in a tiny room, hardly even a bed; and so very thin. She was living like a cat. She had been a fine athlete; the government should have taken care of her."

For women, access to the game of baseball is closely tied to gender politics. In the U.S., as the Women's Movement of the 1960s grew more powerful more women were able to enter the manly game of baseball, a few as umpires at the amateur and minor-league levels, and many more as beat sportswriters and front office executives. But after the AAGBL folded in 1954, we heard little about women playing baseball until the 1990s, when *A League of Their Own* educated the public. The film was the impetus that enabled Bob Hope, a former front office executive with the Atlanta Braves, to persuade the Coors Brewing Company to sponsor the Colorado Silver Bullets, the first professional women's baseball team since the AAGBL, for three seasons. Meanwhile a young lefthander named Ila Borders was living out her dream of playing professional baseball, becoming in 1993 the first woman to earn a college baseball scholarship, playing four years of varsity college baseball, and playing for three seasons in the independent Northern League before her retirement in 2000. At the amateur level, women's leagues sprang up around the country, notably in the Midwest, along the Eastern seaboard, and in California, thanks in great part to the efforts of Jim Glennie, a Michigan assistant attorney general, who organized the American Women's Baseball League in 1992, and Justine Siegal, of Toronto, whose Women's Baseball League has fostered amateur play from youth to adult leagues as well as the international Women's World Cup tournament. At a women's tournament in Bethesda, Maryland, during the Labor Day weekend of 1999, I was struck by the diversity of the players. With names like Amundson, Deutsch, Ng, Provenzano, and Strozynski, the women were housewives, mothers, attorneys, office workers, firefighters, and students. They play on such teams for no money and little glory, just the love of the game. Through the power of the Internet, particularly Siegal's website, www.baseballglory.com, such women are able to connect with one another as never before. However, during the games in Bethesda, I noticed men and young boys stopped by to gawk at women playing baseball, rather than softball. And I watched as an elderly black man engaged in ongoing banter about the subject with first-base coach Mamie "Peanut" Johnson, who had played for the Indianapolis Clowns in the waning years of the Negro Leagues. Johnson just shook her head over the fact that, even in 1999, this stranger felt surprise at women playing baseball.

As for Cuba, Castro's Revolution of 1959 preceded by a decade our social revolution of the late 1960s and 1970s. Cuban women were deeply involved in the events leading to the Revolution. During my visit in January, we were taken to a Santeria church and adjacent museum in Regla, where we learned that men deemed sympathetic to the rebels were kept under close surveillance by the Battista dictatorship, while women, presumed to be occupied with the cares of home and hearth, were often able to escape such scrutiny. Consequently many women served as key agents in passing essential messages and arms to Fidel Castro's rebels in the mountains. After Castro took power, women, who had risked their lives for Revolutionary ideals, quickly gained new freedoms in education and the workforce. I queried Kit Krieger, who has traveled to Cuba nine times since 1998, regarding his impressions of gender equity there, and he replied:

> I suspect that Cuba follows the pattern in other socialist nations. The "triumph of the revolution" made a priority of ending discrimination on the basis of gender. It meant that women could become doctors, professors and engineers. But "machismo" is deeply rooted in Cuban society. Cuban women gained equality in the workplace but probably continue to carry the load at home as care-givers and managers of the household.... Among the biggest improvements for women were universal day care (from 6 weeks on) and both pre-natal and post-natal care. In summary, Cuban women are doing okay by Latin standards, but their lives remain difficult, and I doubt that many Cuban women would suggest that they are treated equally by men. Watch the news on Cuban TV and you don't see a lot of women in key government positions.[14]

Luz de Alba, a retired schoolteacher who showed me around in Havana, remembered well the thrills and hopes of the late 1950s. She still keeps a framed photograph of Che Guevara on the living room wall in her Havana home. Luz had arranged to meet me at Ciudad Deportiva (Sports City), and when we found one another amid the complex of playing fields, I asked whether Cuba's gender equity extended to baseball. (Here we can only speak of amateur baseball, since, by Castro's decree of 1961, Cuba has no professional sports.) Luz responded by saying that she and many other workers, men and women, had spent their evenings, after their day jobs were done, to help build Estadio Latinoamericano, the Cuban equivalent of Yankee Stadium. Yet while Cuban women are encouraged to compete in other sports, only recently, with international amateur competition now available to female baseball players, was a league formed. Luz was here to introduce me to one of these new teams as they practiced. The Femenino Ciudad Habana de Besibol team has 18 players. Its director is Constantino Herrera Toyo, a congenial man who formerly played baseball; the entrenadora (trainer) is Maria Menendez Gonzalez. Constantino directed the brisk workouts. The women, clad in brand new turquoise T-shirts and black hats emblazoned with "Cerros," looked fast and fit as they ran drills, but only three or four stood out as well-developed baseball talents. Their last names ranged from Sanchez, Pedroso, and Montenegro to Mesa. Among them were teachers, students, a physical therapist, security guard, factory worker and two housewives—much like their U.S. counterparts. Their equipment, however, was sorely worn, the gloves thin and battered, the balls held together with tape. Only one woman wore cleats; the others wore tennis shoes. The offering of a box of 24 new baseballs was greeted with great excitement by all involved with the team. As happened in the U.S., a small crowd of boys and men gathered to watch but did not seem at all surprised to see the women playing baseball. Luz translated their comments. "In Cuba, everybody is fond of baseball.... We have women in administrative positions, as secretaries, as janitors and groundkeepers, announcers and in ticket sales, so why not baseball players?" Two of the twelve umpires of the new women's league are women. (Umpires, I was told, have day jobs, and call games because they love the work.) Some spectators spoke of their mothers' interest in baseball. But when asked whether the star male players attract groupies, I was met with quizzical looks: "Women come to the stadium for the game, not as groupies. From the Revolucion and our parents, is planted our love for the country—that's where the intensity for baseball comes from. Since childhood, we are stimulated to what do we *like* to do, not for greed."

Here, then, was a distinction between the women of Cuba and at least some of the women of the U.S. major leaguers exude an aura of power and glamour that has always attracted some women. As early as 1890, columnist Ella Black complained from Pittsburgh in *The Sporting Life* that women were throwing themselves at such heartthrobs as John Tener and Tony Mullane. We have continued to see such behavior (and its unhappy results) in the scandals attending Wade Boggs, Steve Garvey, and others. Cuba, as the freewheeling playground of the United States, would have seen similar behavior in its pre-Revolution days when women were disadvantaged and U.S. teams, led by Babe Ruth, came to play in every sense of the word. When I asked Kit Krieger whether he agreed that Baseball Annies were not a part of the Cuban baseball scene, he replied:

> I suspect that the absence of groupies may reflect the fact that sexuality in Cuba is somewhat less repressed than in Canada or the United States. It is my understanding that a young woman, upon reaching the

age of fifteen, is expected to behave as an adult when it comes to sexuality.... Some of the things that may account for groupies in major league baseball are the celebrity and economic status of athletes. In Cuba, neither of these apply. Ballplayers are very accessible to Cubans. They live in the community, earn no more money than their neighbors, live in the same kind of housing and struggle with the same daily challenges that face other Cubans. Even the great athletes are treated with respect rather than with the idolatry we see in our culture. I have met with a number of elite Cuban athletes and have observed how unimpressed most Cubans seem to be in their presence. I would describe Cuban athletes as physical culture workers rather than superstars. The Cuban media coverage of athletics may also explain why women don't hang around the ballpark looking for a ballplayer. Cuban sports are team — rather than individual star-focused. The emphasis is on winning for the sake of national achievement rather than personal glory or gain. When athletes retire, they become coaches. All the great players in Cuba are members of the ... National Teachers' Union.[15]

I saw this for myself after a Cuban all-star game when one of the players came out of the stadium and joined his wife and child. There was no aura of celebrity to him, no crowd of idolatrous females elbowing their way to get close to him, as happens here. He was just another man, done with his job for the day — to use Krieger's term, a "physical culture worker." On another occasion, I witnessed one of the country's star players come over to greet one of the coaches of the women's team. As director of sports for the municipality of Cerros, Julian Herrera had coached him as a youth, and the player wanted to pay his respects. While this could also happen in the U.S., the two men clearly related to one another as equals. In the same fashion, I witnessed mutuality between the men and women I met in Cuban baseball.

To conclude, the women of the U.S. and Cuba have both long contended with the prejudice that baseball is a man's game. This has required perseverance in the face of social constraints and the withstanding of moralizers' scrutiny as to their sexual orientation. Women such as Eulalia "Viyaya" Gonzalez and Isabel Alvarez remind us of the cost to a woman who pursues the life of baseball player. The women of both countries who play amateur baseball today remind us that the game belongs also to everyday women who struggle to carve out time to play from their day jobs without hope of the recognition and glory that attends men's professional baseball. Playing for love of the game, these women can be seen as throwbacks to 150 years ago, when town ball and early baseball were enjoyed as social recreation rather than cut-throat competition. Of course, many female amateur players also want to test themselves against the best of their opponents. They will get the opportunity in August 2004, when the best of the Cuban women players plan to travel to Edmonton, Canada, for the Women's World Championship, where they will play Justine Siegal's Team Canada as well as teams from the U.S.,

Japan, and Australia. Wherever they come from, the players will find they have much in common.

Some day the political constraints that bind official relations between the United States and Cuba will unravel, and the two countries will be free to rediscover the commonalities that unite them. In this, the game of baseball should prove a serviceable missionary outreach. Something of this spirit was expressed by a young Cuban fan in 1999, when the Baltimore Orioles came to Havana to play the Cuban national team. According the *Los Angeles Times*, "Tania Mancebo painted a Cuban flag on the left side of her face, an American flag on the right, and a peace symbol in the center of her forehead. 'It's a game of friendship' she said, explaining her facial adornment. 'It's not important who wins. It's important to be friends.'"[16]

Notes

1. Letter to the author, 21 January 2004.
2. I thank those who lent assistance with this paper: Kit Krieger of Cubaball Tours, who introduced me to the world of Cuban baseball; Luz de Alba of Havana, who introduced me to contemporary female Cuban players and served as translator; Mike Sharpe, who helped me understand the ancient game of *batos*; Cuban émigré Bill Torres, who helped with translations of Spanish-language articles; and Tim Wiles and the staff of the National Baseball Library and Museum, who always seem to come through with just the right article or two.
3. John Montgomery Ward, *Base-Ball: How to Become a Player* (Philadelphia: The Athletic Publishing Company, 1888) 21, 23. (Republished 1993 by the Society for American Baseball Research).
4. Francisco Forteza, "Cuba-USA: Baseball, A Shared Passion," *CubaNow* (no date) http://www.cubanow.net.
5. Ward, 20.
6. "The League Clubs Keep out of the Rain But the Females Play," *New Orleans Daily Picayune,* 5 January 1885, 8.
7. "The Female Twirlers," *The Sporting News,* 11 March 1893.
8. Marjorie L. Pieper, "Chapter," undated, 3.
9. Don H. Black, *Racine Belle*, Racine, WI, 22 March 1950, 1.
10. Black, 18 April 1950, 4.
11. Elio Menendez, "Viyaya' Was Sharp in Baseball," *Juventud Rebelde,* (no date).
12. David Skinner, e-mail to the author, 15 January 2004.
13. Isabel Alvarez, telephone interview, 25 May 2004.
14. Kit Krieger, e-mail to the author, 20 May 2004. Krieger qualified his response by saying, "I am pleased to offer my impressions, qualified only by the fact that I know little about this subject. I have made nine trips to Cuba over the past six years and confess that my probings have been more in the political and economic realms rather than sociological."
15. Kit Krieger, e-mail to the author, 20 May 2004.
16. Mark Fineman, "Baseball, Music Bridge U.S.-Cuba Gap," *Los Angeles Times,* 29 March 1999, sec A, 8.

Defending Masculinity:
Brawling and the Unwritten Rules
of Major League Baseball

Paul J. Olson

"Baseball is about remaining a boy and becoming a man."
— Michael S. Kimmel[1]

Rituals pervade major league baseball (MLB). Players have idiosyncratic rituals that they perform before each game, at bat, or pitch. Batting virtuoso Wade Boggs invariably ate chicken before games, and relief pitcher Turk Wendell chews black licorice and brushes his teeth between innings. Teams perform rituals during spring training, the regular season, and the playoffs. Beyond the singular rites of individual players and teams, the game itself is replete with generic rituals, including infield chatter and the seventh inning stretch.

Rituals are performed for a variety of reasons. Personal rituals help individuals prepare for the day's game. Practical jokes, forcing rookies to perform demeaning tasks, and other group rituals bring a team closer together, establish a social order, and initiate novitiates to the majors. Other rituals, transcending individual players and teams, solidify the importance of baseball in American culture. For example, the singing of the national anthem and the ceremonial first pitch, separate the baseball game from ordinary time and space. Other rituals reinforce an American culture that the national pastime embodies. In addition, baseball teaches boys the meaning of manhood in America.[2]

This study examines one particular MLB ritual, brawling. Two distinct types of brawls occur during games. The first is the "symbolic brawl" in which players from one team threaten the other team, but no punches are actually thrown. The other is the "real brawl," marked by actual fighting. Brawls do not occur spontaneously, but instead follow a violation of one of baseball's "unwritten rules": these informal guidelines of baseball etiquette will receive attention. Baseball's unwritten rules have been constructed, at least in part, to allow players to defend their claim to hegemonic masculinity.

Masculinities and Hegemonic Masculinity

Social scientists who study gender, sexuality, and sports recognize that various "masculinities" exist in different cultures.[3] For example, homosexual behavior is considered a normative component of masculinity in some parts of the world while other cultures consider homosexual acts to be the antithesis of masculinity.[4] Masculinities are cultural constructions that are created, maintained, and altered by social institutions over time. Moreover, competing masculinities exist within the same culture and impact differently on men of divergent social classes, ethnic backgrounds, and sexual orientations.

Multiple masculinities, however, are not equal in status within a society, but exist in a hierarchy. Sociologist R. W. Connell defines hegemonic masculinity as the dominant form of masculinity in a particular culture.[5] According to Connell, hegemonic masculinity, exalted through the mass media, religion, sports, and other institutions, is the "culturally idealized form of masculine character."[6] The ascendancy of this form of masculinity is so complete that most members of the society acknowledge it as "what it means to be a man."[7] The men who best exemplify the hegemonic form of masculinity in a particular culture, however, need not actually exist, or may be so rare that the vast majority of men could never attain their status. These ideal men may be "fantasy figures"[8] like the movie characters Rambo and Rocky or celebrities like Muhammad Ali, Michael Jordan, or Roger Clemens.

Although the unlikelihood of becoming an iconic hero is generally recognized by most men in the Western world, Connell argues that many males still benefit from the social structure that promotes these figures. In Western nations, hegemonic masculinity is sexist, promoting the cultural ascendancy of men over women. Because men benefit from the subordination of women, the social institutions that historically have been controlled by men, professional sports included, are organized to sustain this domination. Hegemonic masculinity in its Western form is also exclusively heterosexual. Homosexual and bisexual men are the victims of ideological warfare and direct discrimination not only by individual men, but by a system that benefits from their subordination.[9]

In his description of the life of a champion Australian "iron man" (a sport that includes swimming, running, and surf-craft racing), Connell identifies additional traits that are associated with hegemonic masculinity in a Western context. Physical strength and athletic success are vital to the iron man's life. This leads iron-man competitors to focus obsessively on their bodies. The particular iron man interviewed by Connell placed great emphasis on his ability to make money through sponsorships. Cognizant that time and physical decline are enemies, Connell's iron man recognized that he had but a few years to earn big money. Connell's case study emphasizes the centrality of capitalism, ageism, and physical prowess to hegemonic masculinity.[10]

The connection between sports and hegemonic masculinity in the Western world is well established in the academic literature. Sociologist Michael A. Messner employs the concept in his discussion of violence in sports,[11] and in their edited volume *Sport, Men, and the Gender Order* Messner and collaborator Donald Sabo link sports to hegemonic masculinity.[12] Social scientist Michael Kimmel contends that baseball resolved the late nineteenth-century crisis of middle-class, white American masculinity,[13] and scholar Nick Trujillo posits that the media used Nolan Ryan, as it has others, as a paragon of hegemonic masculinity.[14]

Hegemonic Masculinity and the Major League Baseball Player

Professional baseball players possess many of the traits that have come to be associated with hegemonic masculinity in the United States. They live in a hyper-masculine subculture that, with the exception of ball girls, a handful of auxiliaries, and groupies, generally excludes women. Heterosexuality is certainly assumed. When New York Met catcher Mike Piazza found his sexual orientation questioned, the perennial All-Star felt compelled to hold a press conference to announce that he is, in fact, straight. The pursuit of occupational and financial success has always been present in MLB, and the recent contracts given to players like Alex Rodriguez and Kevin Brown illustrate the ubiquitous role of capitalism in baseball. Like Connell's iron man, major leaguers understand that their sport is a business and their bodies a vehicle toward wealth.

Emphasis on youth and physical prowess are endemic to the national pastime. The media highlights Bo Jackson breaking a bat over his knee, Albert Belle flexing his biceps, Mark McGwire's mammoth home runs, and similar images of physical strength. Trujillo notes Nolan Ryan's venerable age when he recorded his seventh no-hitter, perhaps astonished at such mastery from a pitcher of more than two score years.[15] And, in 2004, pundits expressed wonderment at Roger Clemens' ability to win games at the age of forty-one. Despite the achievements of Ryan, Clemens, and other older stars, baseball remains a game that values young arms and legs.

Defending Masculinity in the Context of Professional Sports

Laying claim to hegemonic masculinity is difficult, and the claim must constantly be defended. Baseball players' claim to hegemonic masculinity is more vulnerable than the claims of athletes in North America's three other major professional sports. Violent behavior is ubiquitous and sanctioned on the gridiron, and football players are expected by teammates, coaches, and spectators to endure and dispense pain. The masculinity of football players is heightened by juxtaposition to the frenetic sexuality of female cheerleaders.[16]

Basketball players, wearing uniforms that showcase masculinity, demonstrate physical prowess through powerful dunks, followed by primal screams. As on the gridiron, the masculinity of basketball players is juxtaposed to the subordinate femininity of scantily-clad members of gyrating dance teams. While there are no cheerleaders or dance teams at hockey games, the sport allows players to show their masculine prowess in ways that are consistent with the rules of the sport. By violently checking opponents, hockey players can legally retaliate when their manhood is challenged. And fighting with opponents is embedded within professional hockey, usually resulting in a minor penalty.

None of these hyper-masculine epiphanies are part of baseball. Head-to-toe uniforms cover the physical features of ballplayers. Despite the proliferation of muscles, honed by weights and pharmaceuticals, the bodies of baseball players remain the subject of humor. Pitcher David Wells appears to suffer the same addiction to complex carbohydrates that bedeviled his personal hero (and the game's greatest figure), Babe Ruth. Many ballplayers deviate from the physical ideal. Furthermore, no women undulate before male potency at MLB games. And the official rules of baseball offer virtually no means for retaliation when a player feels his masculinity has been challenged. The only option baseball players have is to break the formal rules of the game.[17]

In an effort to defend their claim to hegemonic masculinity, baseball players have developed a three-tiered system for preventing emasculation. The first tier involves unwritten rules, prohibitions against derisive behavior. Symbolic brawls, the second tier, inform the other team, through threats of violence, that the offended contingent will not tolerate behavior that compromises the masculinity of one or more of their number. Finally, real brawls are violent reactions to the breaking of baseball's unwritten rules in which players from one team actually fight with players from another team within a somewhat controlled context.

The Unwritten Rules of Major League Baseball

The sport of baseball has an extremely complex set of formal, bureau-cratically-mandated rules that govern the game. In addition to this formal structure, however, there exists an informal set of unwritten rules. The unwritten rules are rather vague, uncodified, and are prone to change over time. Practices that were not acceptable a generation ago, like a batter wearing "body armor," are now part of the game. Similarly, behavior that was once part of the game, such as pitchers throwing inside to back hitters off the plate, is now seen by some as violating the unwritten rules.[18] The changing of the unwritten rules over time creates problems because MLB is played by men who range in age from their late teens through their early forties. The gap that exists between the oldest and youngest players concerning proper baseball etiquette often appears to be at the heart of bench-clearing brawls.

The unwritten rules that, if violated, will often lead to retaliation include, but are not limited to the following:

1. Pitchers are not to intentionally throw at or behind a batter's head. When pitchers retaliate with a beanball, they need to keep it below "the letters."[19]
2. After surrendering a home run, pitchers are not supposed to hit the next batter [20]
3. Pitchers are not to celebrate excessively after striking out a batter.
4. Runners are not to steal bases if their team has a large lead.
5. If a batter hits a home run, he should not watch it from home plate.
6. If a batter hits a home run, he should not take too much time circling the bases.
7. Batters should not attempt to peek at the catcher to steal signs.
8. Superstars are not to be targeted for retaliation and must be protected by their teammates during brawls.[21]

These rules provide a framework. However, not all players agree on their meaning, and some simply refuse to adhere to the protocols. When these unwritten rules are violated, the offended party often retaliates. This frequently leads to a cycle of retaliation in which the breaking of the rules becomes more overt, culminating in a brawl.

Symbolic Brawls

Both symbolic brawls and real brawls possess ritualistic elements. They employ specific scripts, assigning players temporary roles that deviate from normative conduct. Nonetheless, like many other rituals, brawls often bond a team more closely. Symbolic brawls are more numerous than real brawls, and the latter is almost always preceded by the former. In Goffmanian terms, symbolic brawls are "keyings" of real brawls.[22] Symbolic brawls are not started with the intent to injure players from the other team, but are instead an effort to show the opposing team that the aggrieved are not going to be bullied. Symbolic brawls are governed by a complex set of norms that render them potentially unstable. Each player must act in a precise manner in order for the symbolic brawl to be carried out properly with all parties involved saving face. The players involved in a symbolic brawl must recognize the preceding. If even one player fails to act accordingly, a real brawl will almost inevitably break out.

The primary responsibility for deciding if a brawl is going to be real or if it is going to be merely symbolic falls on the batter. His reaction to being hit by a pitch will determine the roles of the other players. In a symbolic brawl, the batter, after being hit by a pitch, will not run at the pitcher at full speed. Instead, he may take a few slow steps toward the mound, giving the catcher enough time to come between him and the pitcher. Allowing the catcher to restrain him, the batter will then point, glare, or yell at the pitcher. The pitcher, in return, will walk slowly toward the batter or may simply yell and point back at him.

In the case of a symbolic brawl, the catcher may appear to be a bodyguard for his pitcher, but his role is more like that of a negotiator. The catcher physically places himself between his pitcher and the batter, attempting to convince the hitter that attacking the pitcher is unnecessary. The infielders form a buffer zone between any base runners and the pitcher, giving the impression that they are prepared to defend their pitcher if anyone actually goes after him. As with real brawls, the benches and bullpens clear, but the players only jog or walk slowly toward the field, each team being careful not to go any further onto the field than is absolutely necessary. Both benches give the impression that they are ready to fight to defend their teammates. Finally, the coaches for both teams make their way onto the field in an effort to keep their players from getting into a real brawl or getting ejected from the game. Overall, the symbolic brawl is much more about posturing and giving the impression of team solidarity than it actually is about fighting members of the other team.

Real Brawls

The ultimate manifestation of hegemonic masculinity is the real brawl. Real brawls are violent in nature with at least some of the players attempting to inflict physical damage on their opponents. Real brawls are usually the result of a number of factors that gestate over time. As noted by Arizona Diamondbacks manager Bob Brenly, players from one team may hold a grudge against players from the other team, dating back to the minor leagues or even to college baseball.[23] A player may have made derogatory comments about his opponents prior to the game, or, more commonly, following a previous game played by the two teams. Typically, real brawls begin after both teams have violated baseball's unwritten rules, most frequently in a "beanball war" during which opposing pitchers threw at batters in a cycle of retaliation.[24]

Although serious injuries are rare, real brawls are potentially dangerous. During real brawls, players are punched, kicked by shoes with metal cleats, find themselves under piles of other players, and, on occasion, even bitten. A potentially lethal attack occurred on August 22, 1965, when the Giant Juan Marichal hit Dodger catcher John Roseboro on the head with a bat.[25] In 1987, Chicago Cub Andre Dawson was struck in the face by a 90 mile-an-hour fastball that opened up a cut requiring twenty-four stitches. Dawson charged the mound, trying to get to Padre pitcher Eric Snow, who had yielded a home run ball to Dawson in the first inning.[26] And in 1993, Mariner pitcher Chris Bosio reinjured his broken collarbone during a brawl with the Baltimore Orioles.[27]

Despite the chaos that appears to reign over real brawls, they are governed by established norms. In a real brawl, a batter, after being hit by a pitch, charges the mound in an attempt to assault the pitcher. Interestingly, the batter almost always drops his most dangerous weapon, the bat, before charging the mound. Oftentimes, the pitcher will motion for the batter to advance, occasionally moving toward the batter. In a 1998 incident, Oriole pitcher Armando Benitez, after hitting Yankee first baseman Tino Martinez, turned toward the Yankee dugout, raised both hands in the air, challenging the entire team to confront him, which the Yankees promptly did.[28]

While the pitcher and batter are usually the two primary combatants, other players have specific duties during real brawls. The catcher's job, a "bodyguard" role, is to run after the batter and attempt to tackle him before he reaches the pitcher. The infielders attempt to keep any base runners from getting to the pitcher. From the dugouts and bullpens, players pour onto the field; it is expected that every member of the team will participate. Prior to a legendary 1984 melee between the Padres and Braves, Milwaukee third baseman Bob Horner, then on the disabled list, was sitting in the press box, wearing street clothes. When the tension rose in the early innings, Horner rushed down to the clubhouse, put on his uniform, and went to the dugout. When the actual brawl began, Horner was in the middle of it.[29] Coaches also participate, and, on occasion, have gotten into fights with members of the opposing team. During the 2003 American League Championship Series, venerable

Yankee coach Don Zimmer charged Red Sox pitcher Pedro Martinez. Nonetheless, during real brawls, the coach's primary responsibility is to keep his players from getting hurt, separating them from the other team. But, as in the Zimmer incident, this "negotiator" role is broken from time to time if the violation of the unwritten rules is severe enough.

Discussion

Baseball reflects perceptions of American masculinity. The game instills in boys the masculine traits that society has historically valued, including hard work, perseverance, competitiveness, and a willingness to stand up for self and team when challenged. In the major leagues, players are expected by teammates, media, and fans to conform to the dominant masculine image. Compliance may create or worsen physical injury.[30] Brawling, the need to do what "real men" are supposed to do, may make some players uncomfortable, but baseball's unwritten rules have been constructed to allow players to pose as exemplars of hegemonic masculinity while minimizing physical risk.

Many of baseball's unwritten rules mandate against players "showing up" opponents. Rules prohibiting the excessive celebration of a home run are in place to deter batters from embarrassing pitchers. And pitching protocols eschew embarrassing a batter after a strikeout. Likewise, stealing a base while holding an insurmountable lead violates the unwritten rules. As Trujillo notes, a successful career is a component of hegemonic masculinity,[31] and baseball's unwritten rules caution players not to deride their opponents. The unwritten rules constitute a prophylactic against emasculating behavior.

The masculine ideal emphasizes physical strength, including the ability to defend self and friends when challenged. Not all players like to fight, but they are expected to support their teammates by rushing onto the field during brawls. This marginalizes players who do not want to fight; baseball brawls are essentially bonding ritual for teams, reminding participants and observers of the dictates of the dominant masculinity. In 1987, Cleveland Indian second baseman Brett Butler charged the mound after Kansas City Royal pitcher Danny Jackson threw one pitch behind Butler and the next pitch at him. Butler commented, "You've got to do something. I don't like to fight. I just want to play ball."[32] Butler may not have wanted to fight, but he believed that Jackson violated the rules of the game, rendering an aggressive response necessary.

A player failing to participate in a brawl would endure negative sanctions from teammates. The player's commitment to his team would be questioned by his teammates and coaches, as well as by the media; everyday interactions between the player and his teammates would sour. Since the devaluation of women and homosexual men is common in the bonding process of male athletes,[33] players participating in brawls would likely term a non-participating teammate as feminine or gay. Such activity would reinforce the claim to hegemonic masculinity by members of the team who participated in the brawl while marginalizing a non-participant.

Perceptions of masculinity play an important role in baseball brawls. Following a 1993 brawl between Nolan Ryan and Robin Ventura, White Sox pitcher Jack McDowell praised Ventura for attacking Ryan. He then criticized other players who had been thrown at by Ryan, but refused to retaliate: "He's been throwing at batters forever, and people are gutless to do anything about it."[34] Being considered "gutless" is certainly not beneficial to a player's reputation.

After the Yankees and Orioles brawled in 1998, the Yankees were treated like heroes by their fans and owner. When reliever Graeme Lloyd, the first Yankee to land a solid punch on an offending pitcher during the brawl, took the field the next day, fans chanted his name repeatedly. Lloyd had never before received such attention from the Yankee faithful.[35] New York owner George Steinbrenner was clearly proud of the way his team responded: "If we can't win the game, we win the fight."[36] For defending their masculinity, the Yankees were rewarded with the adulation of the crowd and the praise of their autocratic owner.

The media encourages brawling in baseball, equating it with masculinity. Some commentators overtly advocate retaliation. The White Sox's television broadcast team of Tom Paciorek and Ken Harrelson urged Chicago pitchers to retaliate against the Milwaukee Brewers after White Sox hitters were brush backed.[37] Likewise, after the previously mentioned fight between Nolan Ryan and Robin Ventura, sportswriter Neil Hohlfeld praised the picher: "Ryan's six-punch KO of Ventura was a thing of beauty. A middle-aged legend met a 26-year-old upstart head-on and provided all middle-aged men with yet another reason to love Nolan."[38]

Beyond the need of a player to defend himself and his teammates as evidence of his physical prowess and loyalty, other aspects of hegemonic masculinity are also evident. American men are expected to be the financial providers for their families, and to that end, baseball's unwritten rules help players protect themselves against potentially career-threatening injuries. Pitchers are not to throw at or behind batters' heads, because this could lead to a career — ending injury. Knowing that the batter and his teammates are willing to fight provides even greater discouragement from throwing high and inside.

Emphasis on competition and winning, hallmarks of hegemonic masculinity, pervade baseball's unwritten rules and brawls. For the most part, superstars are off-limits during brawls and in the cycle of retaliation that typically precedes them.[39] Having a superstar injured by a beanball or during a brawl severely damages a team's chance at winning. To prevent this from happening, the best players are well protected by their teammates.

Conclusion

During baseball brawls, chaos sometimes appears imminent. Brawling, however, is not completely chaotic. The unwritten rules of the game are a preemptive form of defense, constructed to prevent players from emasculation. Symbolic brawls operate as a warning of resolve against opponents. Real brawls occur when the game's unwritten rules are violated.

Major league players are held up as role models of what a "real man" is like, yet their claim to the hegemonic form of masculinity is fragile, as is that of any man. Baseball players can be emasculated in front of tens of thousands of fans at the game and millions more watching on television. To prevent this from happening, baseball's unwritten rules, particularly the protocols governing symbolic and real brawls, have been established by the players themselves. Theses rules create the appearance that baseball players embody the ideal of American masculinity.

Notes

1. Michael S. Kimmel, "Baseball and the Reconstitution of American Masculinity, 1880–1920," in *Sport, Men, and the Gender Order*, ed. M. A. Messner and D. F. Sabo (Champaign, IL: Human Kinetics Books, 1990), 55–66, and 56.

2. Walter E. Schafer, "Sport and Male Sex-Role Socialization," unpublished paper presented at the World Congress of Sociology (1998), Montreal, Canada; and D. Whitson, "Sport in the Social Construction of Masculinity," in *Sport, Men, and the Gender Order*, 19–30.

3. See Harry Brod, ed., *The Making of Masculinities: The New Men's Studies* (Boston: Allen & Unwin, 1987); R. W. Connell, *Gender and Power: Society, the Person and Sexual Politics* (Cambridge: Polity Press, 1987); R. W. Connell, *The Men and the Boys* (Berkeley, CA: University of California Press, 2000); and Jim McKay, Michael A. Messner, and Don Sabo, eds., *Masculinities, Gender Relations, and Sport* (Thousand Oaks, CA: Sage Publications, Inc., 2000).

4. Connell, *The Men and the Boys*, 10.

5. Connell, *Gender and Power*, 183–188.

6. R. W. Connell, "An Iron Man: The Body and Some Contradictions of Hegemonic Masculinity," in Messner and Sabo, *Sport, Men, and the Gender Order*, 83–96.

7. Robert Hanke, "Hegemonic Masculinity in *thirtysomething*," *Critical Studies in Communication* 7 (1990): 231–248, and 232.

8. Connell, *Gender and Power*, 184.

9. Ibid.

10. Connell, "An Iron Man," 83–96.

11. Michael A. Messner, "When Bodies Are Weapons: Masculinity and Violence in Sport," *International Review for the Sociology of Sport* 25, no. 3 (1990): 201–219.

12. Messner and Sabo, *Sport, Men, and the Gender Order*.

13. Kimmel, "Baseball and the Reconstitution of American Masculinity," 58.

14. Nick Trujillo, "Hegemonic Masculinity on the Mound: Media Representations of Nolan Ryan and American Sports Culture," *Critical Studies in Mass Communication* 8 (1991): 290–308.

15. Ibid.

16. Mary Jo Deegan and Michael Stein, "The Big Red Dream Machine: Nebraska Football," in *American Ritual Dramas*, ed. Mary Jo Deegan (Westport, CT: Greenwood Press, 1989).

17. John Schneider and D. Stanley Eitzen, "The Structure of Sport and Participant Violence," *Arena Review* 7, no. 3 (1983): 1–16.

18. Steve Wulf, "Basebrawl," *Sports Illustrated*, 16 August 1993, 12–17; and Larry Stone, "Take Me Out to the Brawlgame: Fights on the Field," *Baseball Digest*, 1 August 1999, retrieved 26 February 2002 from www.britannica.com.>

19. Stone, "Take Me Out to the Brawlgame," and Tom Verducci, "Fevered Pitch," *Sports Illustrated*, 1 June 1998, 60–65.

20. Tim Kurkjian, "Stop the Fighting." *Sports Illustrated*, 6 July 1992, 73.

21. Stone, "Take Me Out to the Brawlgame."

22. Erving Goffman, *Frame Analysis: An Essay on the Organization of Experience* (New York: Harper and Row, 1974), 40.

23. Stone, "Take Me Out to the Brawlgame."

24. Ibid; and Buster Olney, "Five Players Barred After a Nasty Brawl in a Yankee Game," *The New York Times*, 21 May 1998, A1 and C3.

25. John T. Talamini, "Social Problems in Major League Baseball," *Free Inquiry in Creative Sociology* 12, no. 1 (1984): 65–70; and Stone, "Take Me Out to the Brawlgame."

26. Hank Hersch, "It's War Out There!" *Sports Illustrated*, 20 July 1987, 14–17.

27. Stone, "Take Me Out to the Brawlgame."

28. Verducci, 62; and Buster Olney, "Dramatic Rally Leads to Rumble in the Bronx," *The New York Times*, 20 May 1998, C1.

29. Stone, "Take Me Out to the Brawlgame."

30. Michael A. Messner, *Power at Play: Sports and the Problem of Masculinity* (Boston: Beacon Press, 1992), 71–76.

31. Trujillo, 295–297.

32. Hersch, 14.

33. Michael A. Messner and Donald F. Sabo, *Sex, Violence, and Power in Sports: Rethinking Masculinity* (Freedom, CA: The Crossing Press, 1994).

34. Wulf, 16.

35. Jack Curry, "Day After Brawl, Retaliation Is Still in the Air," *The New York Times*, 21 May 1998, C3.

36. William C. Rhoden, "Brawling Extinguishes An Afterglow," *The New York Times*, 20 May 1998, C1.

37. Wulf, "Basebrawl," 17.

38. Ibid., 16.

39. Stone, "Take Me Out to the Brawlgame."

Part II

AFRICAN AMERICANS AND THE GAME

Bases Loaded: Race, Reconstruction, and Baseball in Washington, D.C., 1865–1876

Ryan Swanson

"This game has become a perfect mania," exclaimed one Washington, D.C., reporter in 1866.[1] The Civil War had ended, and as soldiers returned to civilian life they happily traded the battlefield for the ball field. Baseball's popularity exploded. In the District of Columbia, teams formed by the dozens. Government offices picked teams to represent them in local tournaments. Social clubs, such as the Cicero Debating Society, decided that baseball, among all sports, was meant for gentlemen, and thus quickly began to learn the game. And then there were the truly serious ballplayers. The Nationals and Olympics became "all-star" teams, composed of the District's best players and chosen to compete against the elite teams from New York City, Philadelphia, and Boston.

Of course, in the 1860s and 1870s, much was happening in Washington, D.C., and the rest of the country besides baseball. Reconstruction policies, first directed by Andrew Johnson and later by Congressional leaders, were being used to create a new legal structure for post–Civil War America. The strained relationship between the conquered South and the victorious North was on the mend. However, it was the societal position of the former slaves that remained the most perplexing and divisive issue of the day. Just how equal would the freedmen be? This question persisted on various levels—including the legal, economic and cultural realms—with few simple answers to be found.

By examining baseball in D.C. during the Reconstruction Era, a historian can not only study what happened between the races, but also gain some understanding of what *could* have happened. In this instance, a look at baseball suggests that racial integration was possible sooner rather than later, and that the end result of segregation was far from predetermined. Baseball was unique because it held both an esteemed position in D.C. society, and it had a proclivity for racial tolerance. And it was this rare combination that made the game both a potential agent of change and an institution meriting historical attention.

In looking at the Reconstruction Era, some historians have asserted that the United States following the Civil War was on a one-way street to a racist, segregated society — even if some Reconstruction policies resisted this fate temporarily. But a look at the "broader baseball experience" in Washington, D.C., suggests otherwise. This study grapples with, and in the end comes to support, C. Vann Woodward's aging but still highly influential thesis that strict segregation developed gradually and only after a lengthy period of racial fluidity. Woodward argued in *The Strange Career of Jim Crow* that the path leading to legalized segregation was not forged until long after Reconstruction ended.[2] As he worded it, "stiff conformity and fanatical rigidity that was to come had not yet closed in and shut off all contact between the races ... there were still real choices to be made."[3] Despite the fact that Woodward concentrated much of his scholarship on the post-Reconstruction era, his overarching idea that there was a window of opportunity for racial progress still resonates when considering the case of Washington, D.C., baseball. And conversely, D.C. baseball provides some evidence that Woodward indeed got it right.

As should be expected, many historians have challenged Woodward's conclusions. Joel Williamson, Leon Litwack, and Howard Rabinowitz, in particular, led the assault on Woodward's delayed-segregation thesis. Williamson's argument focuses on the dichotomy that existed between Reconstruction's legal and cultural standards, and suggests Woodward's thesis missed the point by focusing primarily on legal statutes. "The real color line," Williamson argued in *After Slavery*, "lived in the minds of individuals of each race, and it had achieved full growth even before freedom for the Negro was born."[4] He further concluded that "whites ... tended to withdraw from public places where the color line could not be firmly fixed and the Negro could easily assert his equality."[5] Thus in Williamson's estimation, the cultural boundaries defining race had been entrenched from before emancipation and they remained fixed even in the midst of Reconstruction reform efforts.

Leon Litwack also concentrates on the cultural aspect of racism. In largely dismissing racially progressive legal decisions, Litwack contends, "the racial distinctions that characterized the immediate post-emancipation years were almost always understood rather than stated." Blacks understood that a series of unwritten rules still dominated society and that these rules frequently overrode "official" laws. "To the blacks themselves, the differences might have seemed minimal and the risks incurred in flaunting deeply rooted social customs were no less pronounced than those which would later inhabit Jim Crow."[6]

Finally, Howard Rabinowitz not only dismisses the idea that there was a window of opportunity, but argues even further that blacks faced complete exclusion from most aspects of society. He contends that because a period of exclusion preceded segregation, segregation actually represented an improvement for blacks.[7] Unlike Williamson, Litwack, or even Woodward, Rabinowitz comments specifically on baseball in the South, stating, "with the exception of New Orleans, athletic events were rigidly segregated ... and, since there were no games between the organized teams of blacks and whites, there were city championship games for each race."[8] While one can argue over whether Washington D.C. was part of the "South," ample evidence exists to show that black baseball players were never completely excluded or segregated from D.C. ballgames during the 1860s and 1870s. On the contrary, the racial tolerance exhibited by Washington D.C. baseball teams supports Woodward's theory of delayed segregation.

This case study in many ways engages Woodward's detractors on their own turf — in the cultural realm of society. By first establishing that baseball was indeed a significant institution in Washington, D.C., and subsequently demonstrating that it exhibited unusual racial tolerance, we can gain some further insight into everyday race relations and also ponder what Reconstruction might have accomplished. After all, if Litwack's theory extended to baseball, Jackie Robinson would have actually been the first black to ever play professional baseball, rather than the player who broke baseball's fifty plus years of segregated play.

Following the Civil War, Reconstruction efforts and baseball stood at parallel points of development. Both had their most foundational issues decided. For Reconstruction, the death of slavery and the cohesion of the Union were beyond question. For baseball, a codified set of rules and solid fan base had emerged.[9] But practical details and complex issues for both remained undetermined. Reconstruction leaders pondered the social status of the freedmen, the options for state reentry to the union, and the proper punishment for rebel leaders. Baseball leaders faced questions of how scheduling, leagues, and the commitment to amateurism would play out. Most significantly, however, the often unspoken debate over blacks' place in baseball mirrored society's overarching racial confusion.

The choice of Washington, D.C., as the geographical focus of this study allows the parallels between Reconstruction and baseball to be explored on a relatively clean canvas. The historiography dealing with both the impact of Reconstruction and baseball on the District of Columbia remains rather sparse. This paucity stems not only from the fact that most Reconstruction historians have logically chosen to concentrate on the former Confederate states, but also because Washington, D.C., defies most historical paradigms. During the 19th century, a time defined by sectionalism, D.C. existed in a proverbial no-man's land and could not be strictly classified as either North or South. Geographically, D.C. sat between two slave states— and just across the Potomac River from Confederate General Robert E. Lee's home. It came within a hard day's march of being overrun by Confederate rebels during the fighting and in many ways was merely a Northern bastion among Southern sympathizers.

In terms of its economy and citizenry, Washington resembled a Southern city more than a Northern one. In the years following the Civil War, Washington experienced little of the industrial growth or the influx of foreign migrants that cities such as New York and Boston enjoyed.[10] Southerners dominated the white population. According to census data, before the war, residents originating from one of the soon-to-be Confederate states composed 56% of D.C.'s entire population, and 76% of those D.C. residents not originally born in the District.[11] The end of the war did little to alter North-South balance. In 1870, the census found that 72% of D.C. residents were of Southern origin.[12]

During Reconstruction, Washington, D.C., experienced a population surge that dramatically altered the racial composition of the city. In a special census taken in 1867, D.C.'s population was recorded as 126,990, with 88,327 white and 38,663 black residents. Population in 1860, as a comparison, had been 75,080 with 60,764 white and a total of 14,316 black residents (11,131 free blacks and 3,185 slaves). Thus in a period of 7 years, the white population had increased by a robust 17%. But the black population, due to an influx of blacks migrating from the South, increased by nearly 170%.[13]

The District of Columbia contained slaves before the Civil War, but never in great quantities and always in the midst of a large free black population. This large presence of free blacks distinguished D.C. from much of the South. Within slave states, only the cities of St. Louis and Baltimore had a higher percentage of free blacks than slaves at the beginning of the Civil War, as Washington, D.C., did.[14] But D.C. should hardly be viewed as a safe haven for blacks, before or after the Civil War. District leaders enacted a series of black codes (before they were called that) in the early 19th century, which limited the social freedom of free blacks. Regarding political rights, a referendum for black suffrage in the fall of 1865 resulted in a tally (from white voters) of 7,303 votes against, and only 36 in favor.[15] Similarly, the city council fought against the black suffrage bill of Congress in 1865 by arguing that the white man, as the superior race, had the responsibility to govern society.[16]

In short, Washington, D.C., makes an acceptable case study for Woodward's thesis and the impact of Reconstruction policy because of its demographics, but also because the region often foreshadowed the events that took place during the southern Reconstruction process. Washington, D.C., fell under the jurisdiction of the United States Congress and thus on at least two significant occasions served as a testing ground for Reconstruction policies. First, Congress emancipated District slaves in April 1862, six months before Lincoln's Emancipation Proclamation and years before slavery was completely abolished following the war's conclusion. Second, District blacks gained suffrage in January of 1867, three years before the passage of the 15th amendment and many months before the reconstructed Southern states individually granted their black citizens the right to vote.

From the perspective of baseball fans, Washington had a long, newly ended, hiatus from the game. From the Senators' relocation in 1971 until the 2005 return of Major League Baseball to the District of Columbia, Washingtonians had been forced to traverse the I-95 to Baltimore in order to enjoy the "national pastime." What made this lack of a baseball presence particularly surprising from a historical standpoint was that the District of Columbia was at the forefront of baseball's development in the 19th century. Through local participation and leadership in national baseball organizations, Washington surpassed nearly all cities but New York in its involvement in the game. As one New York newspaper declared, "Washington did more for baseball when it was needed than any city in the United States."[17]

While on-the-field baseball during the Reconstruction Era would have been recognizable to today's fan, most other aspects of 19th century baseball would seem quite foreign. Until 1869, almost all baseball teams remained publicly committed to the virtues of amateurism. Gentlemen's social clubs pursued the game in dignified fashion, often inviting the visiting team for dinner following a prearranged match. There were no binding schedules or leagues. Nor were there any prohibitions on which teams could play each other. It was perfectly acceptable for an elite (and later professional) team, such as the Washington Nationals, to play against an unorganized group of high-school students. To find an opponent one club simply issued a challenge to another. This flexibility undoubtedly eased the entry of blacks into the baseball realm.

Eventually baseball's organizational structure evolved and professionalism became acceptable. But even in the midst of such changes the game held a consistently prominent and respected place in society because of its association with government employees, its vast number of players and fans, and its positive relationship with the local press. The game was "mainstream" and this separated it from other entertainment such as boxing and cockfights, which also had integrated crowds and participants. As Eric Foner has reminded historians, integration must be looked at in context. During Reconstruction, for example, brothels operated with black and white prostitutes, and often served integrated clienteles.[18] But just as miscegenation between white slave owners and their slaves did not represent progress in creating an integrated society before the Civil War, neither did integrated, but illegal prostitution, boxing or cock-fights promote equality during Reconstruction.

Baseball attracted influential people from the most important sectors of D.C. society — the government and political parties. Federal government employees filled the rosters of many early teams. William Ryczek has noted that it was not coincidence that most of Washington's baseball fields were located near federal office buildings.[19] "As soon as the hour for closing business in the departments arrived, there was a general march for the ballgrounds," one D.C. journalist explained.[20] In looking at the roster of the Nationals in 1866, one sees that seven of the nine players worked for the treasury department.[21] When the *New York Times* in 1870 provided a list of how National Association teams would compensate their players in the new professional league, the two organizations from Washington — the Nationals and the Olympics— stood out. Instead of listing "salary" or "a share of the gate" as methods of compensation as the other teams did, the D.C. clubs simply listed "appointed to office."[22]

Most government departments fielded their own teams. The local papers were filled with games between teams such as the Redemptive Division of the Treasury Department and the Third Auditor's Club.[23] While these teams generally approached baseball more casually than elite clubs, as evidenced by whimsical names such as the "Typos, " who represented the Government Printing Office, they often played extensive schedules before large and appreciative crowds.[24] A look at D.C. newspapers shows that in a period of only a few weeks in 1870, games involving the Quartermaster General's Office, Internal Revenue Office, Census Office, Post Office, and Surgeon General's Office took place. There were also intradepartmental games such as those between the "Don't Bodder Me" and "Shoo Fly" nines of the Census Office.[25]

While today baseball's connection with politics, seen in acts such as the President throwing out the season's first pitch, is largely taken for granted, such associations provided baseball with a unique and unexpected stamp of approval during the Reconstruction Era. The fact that teams hosted games near the White House and that notables such as President Andrew Johnson were known to attend games granted the game legitimacy.[26] The Washington Nationals went so far as to arrange for visiting clubs to meet the President, a show of prestige that did not go unnoticed by the press. President Johnson, reported one newspaper, "held the National Club in high esteem and reporters similarly noted President U.S. Grant's attendance in subsequent years"[27]

The exact number of baseball teams in existence in the District of Columbia during Reconstruction remains an elusive figure. Teams frequently formed, disbanded, and reorganized under new names. It is certain, however, that dozens of teams existed for various durations. Among the longest lasting clubs were the Nationals, Olympics, Jeffersons, Union, Empire, Mutuals and Alert — the latter two being black clubs. Other teams such as the Enterprise, Americas, Artic, Mohawk, and Gymnastic surfaced only briefly, and failed to remain intact.[28] There were also a significant number of teams organized directly through government offices and the area's universities.

Washingtonians took to baseball not only because of the sheer number of area teams, but also because D.C. claimed one of the country's most prominent clubs of the 19th century — the Washington Nationals. Formed in 1859, the club's constitution limited membership to forty, set the initiation fee at fifty cents, and determined that voting members would elect leadership.[29] In 1867, the Nationals were considered the "champions of baseball" and their president, Arthur Gorman, who would later be elected to the U.S. Senate from Maryland, determined that the club should embark on a national tour. What transpired was the most ambitious trip that had ever been embarked upon by a ball club, and an endeavor that received lavish coverage from newspapers across the country. The Nats (as they were affectionately called in D.C.) traveled to five states and over three thousand miles, at a cost exceeding $5,000.[30] The tour marked the first time that an eastern team traveled as far west as Missouri and Illinois or as far south as Louisville. Major Ellerbeck, President of the District Association of Baseball Clubs, voiced the widespread admiration felt for the Nats when he toasted their successful tour at a banquet held in the team's honor: "I cannot see why it is not an event in your lives that will stand inscribed on the records of time in such glowing letters as to well afford you the greatest pride and satisfaction."[31]

Exact attendance figures for the baseball games in the District during this time are difficult to calculate. Most teams, at least during the 1860s, charged no admission, and thus rarely counted the exact number of fans in attendance. As a benchmark figure, Harold Seymour has estimated that in the United States 200,000 paying customers attended baseball games in 1868, a total drawn almost exclusively from professional games.[32] In D.C., where approximately seventy-five percent of baseball games played were between amateur teams, such a number provides only a crude indication of what fan support might have been. When estimates were offered, they confirmed the popularity of the game. *The Ball Players' Chronicle,* for example, reported that even an intra-club game in Washington, D.C., between two nines from the Cicero Debating Society drew nearly two thousand spectators.[33] Newspapers almost always offered "ballpark" figures (perhaps coining the term) of how many fans attended. Descriptions such as "a large number of our citizens assembled to watch the sport," or that the game transpired "in the presence of a large number of spectators" were most commonplace.[34]

While attendance numbers do not necessarily equate to respectability in the realm of entertainment, D.C. baseball during the Reconstruction Era counted among its participants and supporters some of society's most distinguished citizens. Arthur Gorman, U.S. Senator from Maryland, played outfield and served as president of the Washington Nationals, and was later elected President of the Association of Baseball Players. Influential men serving as president of the Washington Olympic Club included Colonels A.G. Mills and C.M. Alexander. Nicholas Young, a former aid to Abraham Lincoln, not only served as President of the Nationals, but later of the entire National League. Additionally, Charles Douglass, the son of activist Frederick Douglass, was a member of the Washington Alert.

The press played no small part in cementing baseball's popularity and respected place in D.C. society. Frequent articles not only increased general knowledge of the game, but also fostered its image as a moral recreation. The nation's most famous baseball writer, Henry Chadwick, claimed that baseball deserved the "endorsement of every clergyman in the country ... [as] a remedy for the many evils resulting from the immoral associations boys and young men of our cities are apt to become connected with."[35]

In that vein, journalists frequently showed as much interest in the activity in the stands as that on the field. Since there were no sports sections in the newspapers at this time, the reports of games were intermixed with daily news of politics and foreign affairs. Making clear their focus, *The Daily Morning Chronicle* stated of one contest, "We do not give a detail of the game, as it would be uninteresting, for toward the close it was simply a bat and run on one side and chase ball on the other." The reporter concentrated instead on the social scene, saying that "a large number of ladies were in attendance, which speaks well for the gallantry of the gentlemen. Among those present we noticed the Secretary of the Interior, Commissioner Parker, and many others of our best citizens."[36] *The Evening Star,* which provided extensive baseball coverage, often took a similar tone. "The 'Stay-at-Home Club' numbering about fifteen hundred strong, visited the grounds of the Olympic Base Ball Club yesterday afternoon," the paper reported in July of 1870, "and witnessed one of the most beautiful games of the season."[37]

As journalists promoted baseball as a "moral recreation," they also took gender roles into consideration. Recalling the return of the Nationals from their national tour, Chadwick reminisced that "youths with vicious tendencies were transformed into beings with manly characters."[38] Newspaper accounts paid special attention to the attendance of women at ball games, as it was widely presumed that their presence would preserve proper decorum. In 1866, for example, the Washington Nationals hosted the New York Excelsiors, in an event brought together arguably the two finest teams in the country. But *The Daily National Intelligencer,* among others, found discussing the gentlemanly characteristics of the sport more important than the action on the field:

Old players say they have never before seen so many ladies present at a game and the number of persons of note in attendance was unusually large. The President [Johnson] was on the ground in his carriage, an honor deeply appreciated by the base ball fraternity. As is usually the case on such occasions, the best of order prevailed, the character of the spectators, as well as of the members of the clubs, contributing in no small degree to the just appreciation of the necessity of decorum. When we see gentlemen escorting their wives, mothers, and sisters to the ground, we take it as a pretty good evidence that nothing will occur contrary to the roles cultivated in American society.[39]

Journalists felt it their duty to encourage women to attend games. "Ladies are not only admitted free on all occasions, but seats are specially reserved for them," *The Richmond Whig* noted. "The Southern ladies of Washington make it 'a point' to attend all the first-class games ... it is the only out-door sport they can grace with their presence."[40] The *Sunday Herald* in advertising upcoming games simply stated, "Ladies are particularly requested to grace the occasion with their presence."[41]

Clearly "respectable society" embraced and participated in baseball. Yet baseball teams and players generally exhibited a level of racial tolerance that was out of step with societal norms. This demands some explanation. It should first be noted that there were no integrated teams in Washington D.C. All rosters, as far as conventional sources show, consisted either entirely of white or black players throughout the Reconstruction Era. This might seem to contradict the thesis of this article. If the teams were not integrated, how can it be argued that significant racial tolerance existed? But by looking at the relationships between white and black teams, the press coverage surrounding black teams and the occurrence of interracial games, one sees a significant pattern of racial tolerance and cooperation.

Charles Douglass, son of Frederick Douglass, was a leader among black baseball players in Washington, D.C. Charles and his father corresponded frequently during the 1860s, while Frederick lived in Rochester, New York, and Charles resided in Washington, D.C. In doing so, they often discussed D.C. baseball. Charles issued frequent updates on the status of his baseball club, the Washington Alerts and later the Washington Mutuals. On August 16, 1867, for example, Charles wrote, "It is the wish of everybody here that you will come to Washington on the occasion of the visit of the Pythians of Philadelphia."[42] When Charles wrote requesting money for his family and for his team, Frederick not only donated five dollars, but he also wrote an open letter to the club that did a "great deal of good" in fundraising efforts. Charles happily reported back to his father that some members of the club gave upwards of ten or fifteen dollars in order to support the visit of the Pythians.[43] These sizable donations, equivalent to giving over one hundred dollars in today's currency, suggest that black baseball players and club members likely came from middle-class society.

By all indications, Charles' teams consisted only of black players. Most likely, many were agents of the Freedmen's Bureau, as Charles Douglass was. *The Evening Star*, a paper that at times proved very critical of the freedmen, provided coverage of black teams that was equitable to its coverage of white teams.[44] While some announcements were brief ("A match game is to be played this afternoon on the National Grounds between the Mutual and Country Clubs, both colored"), few records exist of newspapers disparaging black teams.[45] Even on one occasion when the *Sunday Herald* did report that in a match between two black clubs— the Metropolitans and Mutuals— the first basemen of the Mets disagreed so adamantly with the umpire that the game had to be called to an early end, the reporter refrained from unduly harsh criticism. Instead he merely stated, "We regret that the M's should have met trouble in their first important match, and we think from all that we heard remarked by an officer of the club that a repetition is not likely."[46] *The Evening Star, The Herald* and other D.C. papers also often exhibited their respect for black teams, stating that the Alerts, for example, "play a very strong game."[47]

Baseball fit into a larger strata of social and professional clubs that played an important role in nineteenth century society. During Reconstruction, many new groups formed —for both blacks and whites. Eric Foner lists "burial societies, debating clubs, Masonic lodges, fire companies, drama societies, trade associations, temperance clubs, and equal rights leagues" among the organizations formed by blacks during Reconstruction.[48] Without exception in the District of Columbia, these clubs were either exclusively white or black. Blacks petitioned for admittance to both the Sons of Temperance society and the local YMCA, but were denied. Perhaps most detrimental was the failure of black doctors to gain admittance to the District of Columbia Medical Association. In 1869, three black physicians from Howard University, fully qualified to practice medicine, applied for membership, only to also face rejection.[49] In each of these cases, blacks created parallel organizations to the ones that rejected them (the Frederick Douglass Total Abstinence Society, the Negro YMCA, and National Medical Society).

Thus it should come as no surprise that baseball club membership remained segregated. But the interaction between white and black baseball clubs represented something unique. White baseball clubs allowed and even fostered interaction with their black counterparts. They met frequently for competition and regularly shared use of their facilities. Such commingling was not characteristic of other segregated social groups. The Masonic Lodge, for example, when disallowing black membership also explicitly forbid blacks to participate in their events.

The promising relationships between white and black clubs came at a time when the social status of blacks remained open to question. By 1869, blacks in Washington D.C. enjoyed optimism that their legal status in society would continue to improve. They were no longer slaves, had won the right to vote, and hoped that the D.C. Congressional committee might pass a local anti-discrimination bill.[50] But the question of how much contact the two races would have on a daily basis remained far from decided. Black leaders formed a Social Equality Republican Club to discuss such issues. Frederick Douglass, as he often did, pushed to clarify the positive social standing of former slaves. "What is social equality?" he asked. "Is it to walk the streets with others, to ride in the cars, to drink the same water? If these constitute social equality, then I am for it…. But if it be understood that we are endeavoring to force our white neighbors to invite us to their drawing rooms, to allow us to marry their sons and daughters … then I contend that it is wrong to confound the common school subject with this idea."[51] Perhaps it meant, in baseball terms, the right to play on the same field but not necessarily always together or on the same teams.

On the "official" level certainly, obstacles existed for black baseball players in the District. The National Association of Base Ball Players in 1867 voted to ban black players and teams. But even in the face of such resistance, D.C. baseball teams pursued their own courses. *The Evening Star*, on August 6, 1869, reported "the Olympics have received a challenge from the Alert Base Ball Club, (colored) of this city, for a series of home and home match games, which challenge will undoubtedly be accepted."[52] And although the newspaper remarked that it would be "undoubtedly" accepted, it marked a significant event. Not only would there be a gathering of white and black clubs, but it came at the invitation of the black club.

As the event neared, the Washington press piqued public interest and seemed to more adequately understand the event's significance.

> The Olympic Base Ball Club of this city, received a challenge from the Alert Base Ball Club (colored) for a series of home and home match games. As a white and colored club had never met in the District of Columbia in a match game, considerable attention was manifested in the fraternity to know what the action the directors of the Olympics would take. On Friday the directors, Motlee, Smith, Hoyt and Young directed the Secretary to return a communication accepting the challenge…. The next match will therefore, take place on the National grounds Monday, the 20th, instant, and as the Alerts play a very strong game it will be both a novel and interesting match.[53]

Undoubtedly race remained at the forefront of public discussion, but it did not derail the competition or even put it under a cloud of social unrest. Fans, both white and black, came in large numbers to witness the groundbreaking event. It marked the first time that a "major" white club met a black nine, anywhere in the United States.[54] That the Olympics belonged to the National

Association of Base Ball Players, which denied black clubs admittance, only made the event more significant. Playing the Olympics who would be crowned the "Champions of the South" in 1870 meant that indeed the Alert played against the best.

The score of this historic game suggests that the white team won the day on the field, by a score of 56–4. But clearly the Alert, and the black citizens of D.C., gained something too. *The Evening Star,* one of the local newspapers most attentive to baseball in D.C., failed to even mention the final score. While it did express some disapproval of the Alerts' baseball skills, ("it seems that as the game progressed their apparent proficiency diminished") overall the coverage remained positive:

> The game yesterday on the National Grounds being rather a novel sight here, that of a white and colored club playing together, attracted a large concourse of spectators, comprising the friends of both organizations.... Good feelings prevailed throughout, the game being equally enjoyed by the contestants and spectators.

The place of the game, the National Grounds, bucked demographic trends. The field was located at 16th, 17th, and South streets, in the Northwest quadrant of the city. In close proximity to the White House, this area also had the lowest percentage of black residents of any sector of the city.[55] Black players and fans came to the sight for this game and others. In fact, only a few weeks later the Washington Mutuals (the city's other prominent black team) visited the grounds for a game with the Olympics.[56] While they too fell to the Olympics, the Mutuals took pride in the closeness of the score. Charles Douglass wrote to his father: "The club to which I belong in a game of base ball with the Olympics (white) were beaten by a score of 24–15 so you see we played them as close as the Mutuals of New York did."[57]

Unlike barnstorming games of the 1920s and 1930s, which filled the time between "real" seasons; the interracial games in the 1860s and 1870s were on par with other games that took place. A fan in the 1860s could show up at the National Grounds one day to watch the Nationals versus the Olympics, and the next day, at the same field, see the Nationals take on a black team such as the Alert or Mutuals.

While integrated games were never an everyday occurrence, other connections existed between white and black clubs in D.C. George B. Kirsch in his work on the formation of team sports notes the collegial attitude between fellow baseball players, stating "the leading [black] clubs of Brooklyn, Newark, Philadelphia, and Washington D.C. were on good terms with the white organizations and frequently obtained permission to use their grounds for feature contests."[58] Record exists of D.C. black teams playing casual intra-city games as well as entertaining clubs visiting from Philadelphia and New York on the grounds of both the Nationals and Olympics. On one occasion in the summer of 1870, the Olympics lent their field to the Mutuals for a fund-raising game. The *Evening Star* reported the occurrence:

> The Olympic Base Ball Club have donated the use of their grounds for a match game to the Mutual Base Ball Club, a well known colored organization in this city.... The Mutuals who have maintained an organization for over five years, are preparing a tour through western New York for next month, and this game is intended both as an exhibition and benefit game for the Mutuals.[59]

This goodwill broke down barriers within the city because it invited black teams and their fans to areas primarily inhabited by whites. The "White Lot," utilized most extensively from 1865–1870, was on the southwest grounds of the White House away from the poorer areas of the city — typically the marshy areas currently known as Foggy Bottom and Georgetown — where blacks tended to settle. Since both blacks and whites could be counted among baseball's most enthusiastic fans, even those games that did not mix races on the field were often experiments in integration in the stands. When the Nationals traveled to Richmond to play the Pastime Club, reporters took notice of the diverse crowd, even in the former capital of the Confederacy:

> a large assemblage, composed of ladies, gentlemen, soldiers, boys and Negroes, seated on benches, chairs, and on the ground; some perched on fences and housetops, while others filled numerous carriages in the outskirts of the field, greeted them [the Nationals] all eager for the opening of the game. About seven thousand persons are estimated to have witnessed the progress of the game.[60]

While sources are unclear about the details, it appears that the only segregation at ballparks themselves came by providing an area of seats reserved specifically for ladies.

Segregated rosters were less detrimental to blacks than they became in the 20th century. Blacks formed their own teams, elected their own officers, traveled as schedule dictated, hosted teams from other cities, and initiated contests with their white counterparts. It seems unlikely that positions of leadership that blacks found by forming their own clubs would have been available had they been allowed on white rosters. In addition, while this "defense" of segregation might sound similar to the argument that Howard Rabinowitz used to rebut C. Vann Woodward's thesis, it must be recognized that complete exclusion did not exist. Rather the combination of black autonomy and the fact that black teams could still compete and interact with white organizations provided significant integrating opportunities.

For D.C. and baseball nationwide, the season of 1871 was the beginning of a significant shift away from integrated play. The formation of the National

Association of Professional Baseball Clubs, with ten charter members including the Washington Nationals and Olympics, began to institute more official and structured league play.[61] The years from 1865 to 1870 had been enthusiastic and exciting times for baseball teams—both black and white. Paralleling Reconstruction in general, they were years of optimism for blacks that a "raceless" baseball society might emerge. Certainly such hopes persisted beyond 1871, and blacks continued to find encouraging instances of the game's racial tolerance. But a sense of dread began to emerge regarding the increasingly exclusive nature of the game.

The National Association ultimately ruled against allowing the participation of black players and teams. This disappointment only piled on the many other obstacles that black Washingtonians would face in the 1870s. In 1871, the U.S. Congress essentially rescinded the vote from residents of the District. Citizens of D.C., black and white, lost the local autonomy that they had enjoyed in the years following the Civil War. In 1873, the D.C. Supreme Court nullified the D.C. non-discrimination law enacted under Mayor Bowen in 1870 that had protected blacks' rights to access public places such as theaters and restaurants. Additionally in 1874, the *New National Era*, D.C.'s black newspaper, published by Frederick Douglass, quit circulation for lack of funds. And in the same year, the Freedmen's Bank failed, costing hundreds of blacks their life savings. After the initial post–Civil War years of hope, a new reality threatened to dash aspirations.

Black baseball, however, continued to serve as a beacon of hope for black Washingtonians. In August of 1870, the Washington Metropolitan Baseball Club was formed, and the team made their presence felt in the District in the 1870s by frequently playing both white and black teams. The Mutuals took extensive tours in both 1870 and 1871, winning all their games in the former year.[62] Interracial games continued as well, even in the face of the previously discussed setbacks. In 1871, the Mutuals (black) competed against the Creightons (white). In 1872, the two teams met for a rematch, and something truly unusual happened. The black team won. The *Herald* reported the occurrence rather matter-of-factly: "On Friday a match game of base ball was played on the White Lot between the Mutual and Creighton Clubs. The former won by a score of 19 to 14."[63] It marked one of the first times that the press reported on a game in which a black team defeated a white one. In 1873, again D.C. residents read in the newspaper about a black baseball team defeating a white one, this time the Monumental over the Capital.[64] Near the end of the season, the Washingtons, a white professional club who had emerged as one of D.C.'s most respected, agreed enthusiastically to play two games each against the District's premier black teams—the Mutuals and Alert.[65]

Mirroring society in general, baseball's window of racial opportunity closed gradually. Fewer integrated games took place and more negative press coverage of black clubs appeared in 1874 and 1875. Perhaps most significant among these reactionary moves was the restriction of play at the White House grounds. "The White Lot has been closed to all ball players except the Creightons," reported the *Herald*. "The gangs of lazy negroes and other vagrants infesting the grounds made this action necessary."[66] Thus play in the shadow of the Executive Mansion, which had fostered geographical integration, abruptly came to a halt.

Even with the setbacks that became increasingly common in the 1870s, baseball, on balance, during the Reconstruction era in Washington D.C. brought measures of respect and opportunity for blacks that few other institutions could match. In what other realm, could blacks engage in a contest of skill with white opponents, being watched by a large audience of racially mixed spectators, and enjoy an equal opportunity for victory? Howard Rabinowitz, among others, argued that such occurrences rarely, if ever, took place. And yet on the baseball fields of Washington, D.C., they did. It was on the baseball field that black social clubs gained overwhelming respect and positive coverage from the white press. Thus it must be concluded that this snapshot of history provides support for C. Vann Woodward's theory of late-developing segregation. There was a window of opportunity. Ultimately, however, Washington, D.C., along with the rest of the United States, moved away from baseball's example of inclusion and instead chose a path that led to the blighted days of Jim Crow segregation and ongoing racial repression. The results of choosing this path continue to plague America, calling into question its ideals of equality and freedom for all. So it is with a sense of regret that we look back at baseball during this time to see that the course of the United States might have proceeded differently, more positively, and ask ourselves the question of what might have been.

Notes

1. *The Daily National Intelligencer* (Washington D.C.), September 11, 1866.

2. C. Vann Woodward, *The Strange Career of Jim Crow, Third Edition* (New York: Oxford University Press, 2002).

3. Ibid, 44.

4. Joel Williamson, *After Slavery: The Negro in South Carolina During Reconstruction, 1861–1877* (New York: W.W. Norton & Company, Inc., 1965), 80–81.

5. Ibid, 291.

6. Leon F. Litwack, *Been in the Storm So Long: The Aftermath of Slavery* (New York: Vintage Books, 1980), 262.

7. Howard N. Rabinowitz, *Race Relations in the Urban South, 1865–1890* (Urbana, IL: University of Illinois Press), 1980.

8. Rabinowitz, 189.

9. William J. Ryczek, *When Johnny Came Sliding Home: The Post-Civil War Boom, 1865–1870* (Jefferson, NC: McFarland & Co., Inc., Publishers, 1998).

10. Constance McLaughlin Green, *The Secret City: A History of Race Relations in the Nation's Capital* (Princeton, NJ: Princeton University Press, 1967), 120.

11. *Eighth Census, Vol. 1: Population of the United States in 1860*, 589. Cited in Thomas R. Johnson, "The City on a Hill: Race Relations in Washington D.C., 1865–1885" (Ph.D. Dissertation, University of Maryland, 1975), 24.

12. U.S. Census Office, *Ninth Census, Vol. L: The Statistics of the Population of the United States*, 380–385.

13. Green, 33.

14. Letitia Woods Brown, *Free Negroes in the District of Columbia, 1790–1846* (New York: Oxford University Press, 1972), 14.

15. James H. Whyte, *The Uncivil War: Washington During the Reconstruction* (New York: Twayne Publishers, 1958), 49.

16. Green, 76.

17. John B. Foster, "Washington Challenged the West," in *The New York Sun*, October 8, 1924.

18. Eric Foner, *Reconstruction: America's Unfinished Revolution, 1863–1877* (New York: Harper and Row Publishers, 1988), 371.

19. Ryczek, 24.

20. Edward F. French Papers, newspaper clipping, April 25, 1866, 83.

21. A.G. Spalding, "Speech of AG Spalding at the Convention of the National League in 1901," In the Mills Commission Papers, A. Bartlett Giamatti Research Center.

22. *New York Times*, April 7, 1870.

23. *The Daily National Intelligencer*, September 29, 1866.

24. *The Evening Star*, October 22, 1869.

25. *The Sunday Herald and Weekly Intelligencer*, August and September issues.

26. Michael Benson, *Ballparks of North America: A Comprehensive Historical Reference to Baseball Grounds, Yards, Stadiums, 1845-Present* (Jefferson, NC: McFarland and Co., Inc., Publishers, 1989).

27. Edward F. French Papers, newspaper clipping, 154; *The Sunday Herald and Weekly Intelligencer*, June 20, 1873.

28. A look at *The Ball Players' Chronicle* and the *New York Clipper* provides the most comprehensive evidence of D.C.'s many teams.

29. Edward F. French Papers, The Washington D.C. Historical Society, *The Constitution and By-Laws of the National Base-Ball Club of Washington D.C.*, Organized November 27, 1859, 7–19.

30. A.G. Spalding, *America's National Game*, Originally published in 1911, (San Francisco: Halo Books, 1991), 73.

31. Edward F. French Papers, newspaper clipping, 202.

32. Harold Seymour, *Baseball: The Early Years* (New York: Oxford University Press, 1960), 7.

33. *The Ball Players' Chronicle*, October 31, 1867.

34. *The Daily National Intelligencer*, August 29, 1866; *The Evening Star* (Washington D.C.), October 5, 1869.

35. Henry Chadwick, *Hanley's Baseball Book of Reference* (1866), vii; cited in Tygiel, 18–19.

36. *The Daily Morning Chronicle* (Washington D.C.), May 24, 1870.

37. *The Evening Star*, July 5, 1870.

38. Ryczek, 126.

39. *The Daily National Intelligencer*, September 19, 1866.

40. Edward F. French Papers, newspaper clipping, *The Richmond Whig*, October 24 (no year listed), 154.

41. *The Sunday Herald and Weekly National Intelligencer*, July 27, 1873.

42. Charles Douglass to Frederick Douglass on August 16, 1867. Frederick Douglass Papers, Library of Congress.

43. Ibid, August 10, 1867.

44. Rayford W. Logan in *Howard University, The First Hundred Years, 1867–1967* (New York: New York University Press, 1969) states that "One reason why most whites thought that Negroes would never make good citizens was the unflattering portrayal of colored Washingtonians by *The Evening Star*." (pg. 70) He cites a MA Thesis by Virginia Scott of Howard

University, which chronicles the *Star's* incendiary descriptions of blacks such as "chicken-stealin, razor-totin negros."

45. *The Evening Star,* September 18, 1869.

46. *The Sunday Herald and Weekly National Intelligencer,* September 18, 1870.

47. *The Evening Star,* September 18, 1869.

48. Foner, 95.

49. Johnson, 129–136.

50. Green, 96.

51. *Washington Chronicle,* May 10, 1872.

52. *The Evening Star,* August 16, 1869.

53. Ibid, September 18, 1869.

54. The Olympics of Philadelphia met the Pythians of the same city on September 3, 1869 in the first mixed race game on record. Thus by a few days, Philadelphia beat Washington D.C. to interracial baseball. However, the Olympics of Philadelphia held little of the prestige of their counter-parts in D.C., nor were they members of the National Association. See Ryczek's *When Johnny Came Sliding Home,* as well as the late August, 1869 editions of *New York Times* and *New York Clipper.*

55. Johnson, 7; U.S. Census Office, *Eighth Census of the United States,* Vol. 1, Population, 279.

56. *The Evening Star,* October 13, 1869.

57. Charles Douglass to Frederick Douglass, *The Frederick Douglass Papers,* The Library of Congress.

58. George B. Kirsch, *The Creation of American Team Sports: Baseball and Cricket, 1838–72* (Urbana: University of Illinois Press, 1989), 166.

59. *The Evening Star,* July 7, 1870.

60. Edward F. French Papers, newspaper clipping, 151.

61. James C. Roberts, *Hardball on the Hill: Baseball Stories from Our Nation's Capital* (Chicago: Triumph Books, 2001), 18; Leonard Koppett, *Koppett's Concise History of Major League Baseball* (Philadelphia: Temple University Press, 1998), 16–20.

62. *The Sunday Herald and Weekly National Intelligencer,* August 13, 1871.

63. *The Sunday Herald and Weekly National Intelligencer,* June 30, 1872.

64. Ibid, September 14, 1873.

65. Ibid, September 21, 28, 1873.

66. Ibid, September 6, 1874.

"Between Memory and History": Black Sportswriters and the (Re)construction of Negro League Baseball

Robert Cvornyek and Lawrence Hogan

Perhaps we are the greatest.
'Cause we give you all the latest
In the world of sport:
Oh, we give them plenty matter
All the news and also chatter.
We never have to sort.
If we lead, with sixteen pages
Make history for the coming ages
You're left forever more
With more space o'er which to wander
And more news with which to ponder.

Romeo Dougherty
"The Sportive Spotlight"
New York Amsterdam News, June 23, 1926

In 1948, Effa Manley, co-owner of the Negro National League's Newark Eagles, challenged Brooklyn Dodger Jackie Robinson to a public debate on the past importance and credibility of black baseball. She criticized Robinson for his remarks in a widely publicized *Ebony* magazine article where he disparaged Negro League baseball as an unprofessional business and accused franchise owners of disrespect toward their players. Robinson's recollection of black baseball was ill-timed given Manley's efforts to keep the sport alive in the post-integration era, and it clearly clashed with her own experience as a long-time owner and backer of the game. Manley possessed an intimate knowledge of "shadowball" that allowed for her genuine appreciation of baseball's historical importance and vital role within the African-American community. Robinson's criticism angered and hurt Manley. After all, she claimed, the Negro Leagues helped place Robinson "where he is today." More importantly, it confirmed her suspicion that black sportswriters failed to construct a usable baseball past because of their overwhelming desire to advance the interest of integration. "Negro baseball has always been treated as a stepchild of American sport," Manley stated. Black fans knew only Satchel Paige and Josh Gibson because the black press never "built up" or "conscientiously" covered the game.[1]

Although Manley correctly asserted the role of the black press in promoting integration, she underestimated the capacity of sportswriters to create the common language and memories needed for African Americans to remember their baseball past and comprehend how these memories shaped black America's cultural outlook. In the years between the publication of Sol White's monumental *History of Colored Baseball* in 1907 and the outpouring of scholarship on the black game after 1970, the history and cultural relevance of Negro League baseball fell mainly to local black writers and sports reporters who kept the public memory of the game intact.[2] For most of the twentieth century, these chroniclers approached their subject in numerous forms, but one outcome remained constant: namely, their private efforts to (re)construct the game became part of a public transcript that fashioned the black community's collective memory of baseball and the game's cultural importance. Sportswriters who recalled and interpreted the "long and honored history" of black ball occupied the ambiguous and oftentimes conflicted position of writing, indeed existing, "between memory and history."[3]

While scholars have recently focused their attention on the relationship between the black press and the integration of professional baseball during, and immediately after, World War II, few have examined the sportswriter's role in explicating the proud heritage of black baseball, identifying past heroes to be emulated, developing a critique of the present in the context of the past, and celebrating the game's contributions to black culture. An examination of the role of the black press, with its potential to reach broad segments of the African-American population, in preserving this history provides one method of assessing how blacks exercised their right to interpret and make use of their baseball past.[4]

Black sportswriters enjoyed their widest readership in city newspapers, but they also published more interpretative pieces in journals and magazines. As early as 1920, the *Competitor* (1920–1921), a national monthly magazine under the editorship of *Pittsburgh Courier* publisher Robert L. Vann, provided extensive coverage of black baseball and its history. The magazine hosted Ira F. Lewis of the *Courier* as its sports editor and included articles by reporter David Wyatt of the *Chicago Defender* and insider C. I. Taylor, owner of the

Indianapolis A.B.C.'s baseball club and vice-president of the Negro National League from its start in 1920 until his death in 1922.

In an article entitled "The Future of Colored Baseball," Taylor recounted that after "a quarter of a century as a player, promoter, and baseball manager" he learned how the game had fully cast itself into the community "on the corner lot; in every school yard; in the great pleasure parks and playgrounds for children." Black neighborhood culture had become intricately linked to America's national game. He observed that the future success of the sport depended on organization, and to that end he concluded his article by reprinting a letter he sent to fellow player, promoter and manager Andrew "Rube" Foster in 1916. The letter summarized his correspondence with Foster, since 1912, on the need to construct a formal professional league. History, according to Taylor, had witnessed the undoing of the game's "old order" and the "beginning of a new era is upon us."[5] Taylor suggested that both men set aside their differences and join together to "keep alive the great sport among us." But it was the pen of Ira Lewis that inked the most thoughtful connections between baseball's past and present. Lewis regarded baseball as the "fourth meal of the day," and his articles grounded the legitimacy of blackball in its history. He noted that "players of other days," including Sol White and Nathan Harris, had been on hand to assist Foster and Taylor in their historic meeting in Kansas City on February 13 and 14, 1920, to create a black national baseball league. The erudite Lewis rarely missed an opportunity to educate his readers on the game's historic past and players' heroic achievements. In a commentary on the hiring of William "Dizzy" Dismukes as manager of the Pittsburgh Athletics in 1921, Lewis painstakingly contextualized the early game by examining the players, teams and notable events associated with Dismukes's distinguished career that began in 1908. Lewis even included a few words on Dismukes's managerial efforts with a black service team during World War I, noting that he piloted one of the only black teams in the American Expeditionary Force (A.E.F.) League while stationed in Heddesdorf, Germany.[6]

Throughout the first half of the twentieth century, baseball articles also appeared in the journals of major civil rights organizations, such as *The Crisis* (1910-present), sponsored by the National Association for the Advancement of Colored People, and *Opportunity* (1911-present), published by the National Urban League, as well as independent publications like the *Messenger* (1917–1928). The more popular black magazines, including *Negro Digest* (1942–1975) and *Our World* (1946–1955), carried stories that placed the sport in the broader context of the community's cultural life. Since all of these monthly and quarterly publications served a national audience, writers were not as concerned about updating their readers on the current status of their local teams and players as they were on recounting timeless events that significantly impacted the game and its fans. Consequently, sports reporters writing in magazines, more so than in newspapers, became the exemplars of two important functions relating to the history and memory of black baseball. By definition, the events they favored to remember and retell helped construct a usable baseball past, and stories they devoted their attention to in the present were certain to become history.[7]

It was the black weekly newspapers, however, that provided the images and words that fans consulted on a regular basis. City papers served as a lifeline to the baseball community, often creating the shared language and memories associated with black cultural identity. In particular, sportswriters crafted a vernacular that was contemporary to the period and familiar to the fans. The *Pittsburgh Courier* (1907-present) enjoyed the widest circulation of any black paper and offered the most comprehensive coverage of Negro League baseball. In 1932, the paper announced that it gathered "one of the greatest arrays of baseball writers ever assembled, who will cover the country like a roof." The array included veteran sportswriters like Ira Lewis, William G. Nunn, and Chester L. Washington, who cooperated with correspondents scattered nationwide to report the "grand old game." The *Courier* also invited Negro League notables such as the legendary C.W. "Cum" Posey, founder of the East-West League and owner/manager of the Homestead Grays, and Dizzy Dismukes, manager of the Detroit Wolves, to share their perspectives in guest editorials.[8] The *Courier*, in company with two other leading papers, the *Chicago Defender* (1905–1997) and *New York Amsterdam News* (1909-present), will serve as the basis for an examination of how sportswriters remembered and conveyed the history of the game, memorialized its finest players, and celebrated the Negro League's impact on the cultural lives of African Americans.

The press generated interest in the game's past by simply writing articles that recalled either the "greatest game" played in Negro League history or the "greatest plays" ever performed on the ball field. Both types of stories carried little or no historical context or interpretation; writers merely committed to paper the exploits of players and teams that had previously existed only in oral tradition. Exemplars of this practice included Ira Lewis, Cum Posey, Chester Washington, and Randy Dixon, all of whom wrote for the *Pittsburgh Courier*. By reminding readers of yesteryear's classic contests and player heroics, the press helped construct a mythology around the game that influenced black culture and identity. Strong articles, like Cum Posey's "Reviewing Great Plays, Players, and Games at Forbes Field," Ira Lewis's "The Greatest Play I Have Ever Seen," and Chester Washington's "Josh, Ruth, or Doby: Who Hit the Longest Ball," helped identify an authentic black baseball heritage. Columnist Randy Dixon periodically turned his attention to the "sepia diamondeers" of the past and assembled "all-time teams" from the

Golden Age of blackball that began around 1915 and lasted until the early 1920s. Writing in 1942, Dixon concluded that today's players and fans owed a collective "salaam" to the old-timers.[9]

Sportswriters also entwined the game's history with feature stories on former players' careers. According to *New York Amsterdam News* columnist St. Clair Drake, "characters, in the newspaper sense, are persons in whose lives or exploits diligent members of the Fourth Estate often find good copy." In the process of finding "good copy," reporters frequently shaped the game's public memory through "characters" who influenced blackball's history. These players were not remembered as much for their "prodigious wallops, sensational base running, stellar fielding, and brilliant all-around playing" as they were for advancing the interests and progress of the game. The press covered special occasions like retirements, managerial and front office appointments, and neighborhood commemorations of local heroes to familiarize their readers with individuals whose memory proved worthy of consideration. It was common for communities to hold celebrations in honor of favorite sons who left their mark on the game. Blacks in New Orleans, for example, staged a tribute night for Winfield "Lucky" Welch to honor his legacy as an architect of championship teams. He received recognition as a "past master of strategy in sports" who led local teams like the Black Pelicans, and later the Negro League's Birmingham Black Barons, to championship seasons. The community, however, elected to highlight his impact on the game by honoring his selflessness in developing unknown local talent "from the sandlot grades to stardom."[10]

In addition, feature stories allowed former players to comment on the present in the context of the past. Chappie Gardner, whose career as a player, manager and owner lasted from 1908 to 1925, observed in 1940 that current players performed just as well, if not better, than those in the past. Yet, he concluded, they allowed themselves to be more easily exploited by owners and promoters. He contrasted past owners like John Connors of the Brooklyn Royal Giants, Colonel Charles Strothers of the Harrisburg Giants, and Mose Corbin of the New York Colored Giants—men who knew the game and how to treat their ballplayers—with contemporary moguls, who failed to promote the financial interests of their players. Today's athletes, Gardner believed, needed to demand more accountability from those they entrusted with the sport and its future.[11]

The intersection of race and gender, evident in reporters' recollections of past players, led to a popular construction of black masculinity. Sportswriters related the way in which African-American men created a gendered self, particularly in opposition to the dominant cultural representations offered by white society. Black ballplayers owned their own bodies and freely sold their services in a black-controlled labor market. They traveled within the country and exercised a considerable degree of geographic mobility by relocating to Mexico, Puerto Rico, the Dominican Republic, and Latin America in the off-season to participate in winter ball. Once outside the United States, players commented that the color veil lifted and they experienced a genuine sense of manhood. Most importantly, players displayed a measurable degree of financial independence. In 1933, sports reporter William Nunn reflected on the sensational career of William Monroe, one of the earliest black stars, whose playing days began in 1896 and lasted until his untimely death in 1915. Nunn penned a column that added another dimension to the customary depiction of black players, offering his readers an example of how gender identity formation operated within one of several modalities, in this case, the sports world. The Pittsburgh scribe recalled that:

> Mayhap you people don't remember about Bill "Money" Monroe. Money played in the days when ball players sold their services to the "highest bidder." Idol of the fans and a great "box office" attraction, Money played his racket to the limit. He would never arrive on the playing field until the game was to start. Then, through the crowd would come "Money." Cheers would greet his arrival. He would walk to the center of the field, throw up his hand, and in a stentorian voice would announce: "Cease — Monroe is now here." "What are you going to do today, Money," the fans would yell. "Knock a homer the first time up" would be the reply...and he would do it.[12]

Monroe's boastfulness and swagger challenged the etiquette and expected behavior of black men set by polite white society and perhaps that of the black middle-class. Historians engaged in the study of black masculinity have generally ignored baseball and its impact on identity formation. Scholars prefer to examine literary sources in the construction of black masculinity. Their focus has marginalized the impact of the stadium as a site of gender construction and the complex role sports has played in shaping gender identity formation among blacks in the early twentieth century.[13]

Newspaper coverage of the death of black ballplayers evoked an outpouring of stories and memories that turned otherwise private mourning ceremonies into public expressions of the history and meaning of black baseball. Sportswriters assessed the legacy of recently deceased players and provided readers with an early glimpse of how history would later record their importance in relation to the game. This type of news story placed their remarks squarely between "memory and history." To this day, memorials remain an underutilized source of information on the black past. Reporters commented on how memorial services illustrated the vital connection between black baseball and the community. Journalists described the large number of people "from all walks of life" who attended funeral services and sat alongside political leaders and civic organizations representing the community at large. The passing of dominant figures like Rube Foster received considerable attention, but so did the funerals of lesser figures whom the community embraced for their commitment to the sport.[14]

In particular, the death of controversial figures encouraged writers to be more interpretive in their columns. The circumstances surrounding the death of legendary catcher Josh Gibson made explicit the link between the commemoration of a dominant ball player and the ideological purpose that commemoration served. Given the multiplicity of voices in the black press, the meaning of Gibson's death proved a hotly contested item. According to Gibson's biographer Mark Ribowsky, Wendell Smith, of the *Pittsburgh Courier,* portrayed Gibson as a martyr in the struggle to end segregation. Smith wrote that the thirty-five-year-old Gibson died from a broken heart because he was barred admission into the white major leagues. According to Smith, segregation rendered Gibson "downhearted and resentful" and eventually "sent the 'king' to his grave." Smith's polemics helped insure that Gibson's memory would forever be tied to the crusade to integrate baseball, a crusade that Smith championed above all else.[15]

Other writers contested Smith's viewpoint and challenged his one-dimensional interpretation. They placed Gibson's memory and legacy fully in the context of the black game. *New York Amsterdam News* reporter Joe Bostic found "the sincerest tribute to Gibson's matchless prowess was the respected awesome deference with which fellow ball players, friends and foe alike, looked upon him." Bostic honored Gibson for his performance as the greatest hitter to thrill black fans and for his role as a box office attraction in keeping the Negro Leagues a viable business. Dan Burley, Bostic's colleague at the *Amsterdam News*, echoed similar sentiments and claimed that Gibson "was playing the game for the fun he got from it." Burley concluded that Gibson's death resulted from a number of idiosyncrasies and destructive behaviors that "kept his name in the fore of dugout chatter" for years, certainly not a broken heart over a missed opportunity. In their mission to memorialize sports figures, writers found themselves edged between "memory and history" and could not always do justice to the complex, and oftentimes conflicting assumptions regarding how history is remembered and how it is conceived.[16]

The sports press moved beyond the construction of a usable black baseball past and examined traditions-in-progress to further influence the community's collective identity. These traditions-in-progress included opening day ceremonies, Old-Timers' days, and the annual East-West All-Star Game. Newspaper accounts of these festivities established their contemporary social and cultural importance and helped guarantee their later historical significance. Many African Americans marked their calendars with baseball's summer rituals and celebrated their arrival with city-wide revelry. Such occasions reinforced a sense of race pride among African Americans and instilled a sense of themselves as a people.[17]

In 1923, the *Kansas City Call* described opening day for the city's Monarchs as "the day that the local fans have been looking forward to for some time." Monarch fans, after all, enjoyed opening games as social and cultural gatherings as well as sporting events. Mostly, it was a day organized by blacks for the sole benefit of their community. The *Call* carefully outlined the itinerary for the day's events. Fans assembled at a predestined spot and formed a parade that included a police escort leading the way for marching bands and color guards representing the city's black high schools. Historian Janet Bruce observed that during the 1920's, the Monarchs Booster Club, a group she described as a "loose amalgam of neighborhood fans, including the 12th Street Rooters, the Vine Street Rooters, the 18th Street Rooters, the Kansas City (Kansas) Rooters, and the North End Fans Association," organized the parade year after year well into the 1950s. The procession toured the city's black neighborhood before making its way to the ballpark where the parade continued on the field. Once inside the stadium, local politicians and black celebrities from the world of sports, music and theatre greeted the procession and played a part in raising the American flag and throwing out the first pitch to symbolically begin the game. This tradition, more so than any other celebration associated with black baseball, assumed ritualistic status within black communities nationwide. Sports historian James Overmyer's description of opening day ceremonies in Newark, New Jersey, for example, recalls similar images and echoes the sentiments of Eagles fans on the importance of their day. Overmyer concluded that the "relationship between the Eagles and their audience was best demonstrated by opening day, each season's rite of renewal."[18]

On occasion, an exhibition game signaled such political or social importance that fans displayed the festivities usually reserved for opening day. At the onset of the Great Depression, New York City promoters staged a charity game at the Polo Grounds between the Black Giants, comprised of former Negro League players, and the city's Police Department. The proceeds of the game benefited the "unemployed and furloughed Pullman Porters and Maids," many of whom lost their jobs in a labor dispute with the Pullman Railroad Car Company. The event opened with a "monster" parade through Harlem that included displaced workers, their supporters, and the Henry Lincoln Johnson band. At game time, A. Philip Randolph, president of the Brotherhood of Sleeping Car Porters, and local dignitaries, including the mayor, assemblymen, judges and local councilmen, assisted in the flag-raising ceremonies. The fundraiser linked black baseball with the community and its efforts to help the Pullman workers in their struggle for union acceptance. It also connected the game with its historic past as the Black Giants featured the legendary pitcher "Cyclone" Joe Williams as an attraction for Harlem "fans of yesteryear" who remembered him as "the speed ball king [who] used to put over some of the most sensational shutout games in these parts."[19]

It was Old-Timers' days, however, that demonstrated the strongest relationship that existed between the game's historic past and racial identity, set within the broader context of the community's social life. These celebrations encouraged sports writers to reflect on the game's history and the accomplishments of former players worthy of emulation. In anticipation of an Old-Timers' contest to be held on New York's Randall's Island in August 1938, columnist St. Clair Bourne wrote that "one of my esteemed contemporaries recently opined that one of the many ills now afflicting Negro baseball is unfamiliarity of the public with any of its stars or their records." Bourne confessed that he became intrigued by the comment and "motivated by the announcement of the old-timers game" began researching the lives of the teams' opposing pitchers, "Cannonball Dick" Redding and "Smokey Joe" (also known as Cyclone) Williams. Bourne considered both men legitimate black folk heroes and found much praise in their dedicated service and accomplishments to relate to his readers. In featuring the "veteran diamond stars of yesteryear," the game evoked a sense of racial pride, but it also evidenced an in-group cohesion and solidarity in the form of self-help. Part of the proceeds of the Old-Timers' games went to help the retired players now in need of financial assistance. Williams, who became a regular feature during Old-Timers' contests around the country, came to embody the game's history and stable presence in the black community.[20]

The single most important event in black baseball and its affiliation to the African-American community was clearly the East-West All-Star Game. According to Wendell Smith, "the history of the East-West game is a fascinating story — one that has no equal, and might have been written by a Hollywood script writer. It packs all the drama, color, pathos, and interest of a 50 reel best-seller from movieland." He added that the excitement surrounding the game proved baseball "is the number 1 sports attraction insofar as Negroes are concerned." African Americans made the annual pilgrimage to Comiskey Park in Chicago, some traveling great distances by plane or rail, to participate in the weekend's social events and to take in the "Dream Game" of the baseball season.[21]

The East-West game originated in 1933 at the request of Gus Greenlee, owner of the Pittsburgh Crawfords, and Roy Sparrow, a reporter with the *Pittsburgh Sun-Telegraph,* to showcase the talent of black players. During its twenty-year run, the event attracted more people and generated more revenue that any other sports event sponsored by the black community. The *Pittsburgh Courier's* William Nunn described the game as "our connecting link with organized baseball" since it mirrored the white major leagues' mid-summer classic. Nunn also identified the contest as black baseball's "big opportunity to show…under perfect conditions…just what we are capable of producing through the years." Others, like Wendell Smith, chose to highlight another aspect of the game's importance. The birth and subsequent development of the all-star game was a story "that should make every Negro swell with pride whether he is a baseball fan or not. For the story proves convincingly that we can…if we will."[22]

The all-star game raised expectations that blacks, as a people, could accomplish much in the future, but it also recognized the contributions of past players who struggled to advance the game and the race. Promoters of the East-West contest consciously inserted veterans and old-timers into the event because their presence "unveils in fitting fashion the saga of the men who contributed so much to the game down through the years, and exposes in bold relief the great possibilities the future holds." Nowhere was the all-star game's connection between past and present more evident than in the selection of both teams' coaches. Beginning in 1933, Greenlee authorized the practice whereby fans could vote for any retired player to serve as a coach. The top six choices were selected, with three men going to each team. The *Courier* noted that the presence of former players legitimized the black game's history by turning "back the pages of ten, twenty, thirty, and possibly forty years [to] reveal those pioneers who did diamond service with bare hands." The press emphasized the role of history in authenticating the present by recalling a past tradition of professional organization and athletic excellence that sanctioned the present. Sportswriter W. Rollo Wilson devoted an entire column to all-star players of "other years" who would have graced Comiskey Park had that possibility existed during their careers. The event's magnitude and the vitality led William Nunn to conclude that the all-star game served as the black community's single greatest festival. Nunn argued that African Americans needed to embrace the game for its social and cultural value and work tirelessly to insure that the competition never lost its glamour. He believed that the game had overtaken the Howard-Lincoln college football rivalry as the sports world's premier contribution to racial identity and black cultural expression.[23]

The black press recognized and created numerous opportunities to examine the history of the Negro Leagues and their players. In their efforts, sportswriters provided the earliest attempts to interpret the meaning of the game from a black perspective. As such, they spoke directly to African Americans and assisted them in appreciating the past within the context of their own experiences. Baseball established a new cycle of public celebrations, in some ways replacing the older nineteenth-century freedom and emancipation festivals, by reflecting the urbanization and modernization associated with black America following the Great Migration and the artistic rise of the

"New Negro." Sportswriters celebrated significant aspects of black culture in the events and personages connected to the black game and the rituals they established. Operating as middlemen, somewhere between memory and history, they fashioned a usable past that was selective and incomplete. Yet, they did succeed in promoting an authenticity of the game that only history can provide. The press corps remains an important, but neglected, source of information for today's scholars interested in the relationship between baseball and the formation of racial and gender identity.

Notes

The authors wish to acknowledge their colleagues, Ron Dufour and Denise Cassel Ehrich, for their critical commentary and editorial assistance in writing this paper.

1. Effa Manley, "Negro Baseball Isn't Dead," *Our World* (August 1948), 27–28. For additional information: see James Overmyer, *Queen of the Negro Leagues: Effa Manley and the Newark Eagles* (Lanham: Scarecrow Press, 1998), 232–234; and Gai Ingham Berlage, *Women in Baseball: The Forgotten History* (Westport: Praeger, 1994), 125.

2. Jerry Malloy, ed., *Sol White's History of Colored Baseball with other Documents on the Early Black Game, 1886–1936* (Lincoln: University of Nebraska Press, 1995). Robert Peterson's *Only the Ball Was White: A History of Legendary Black Players and All-Black Professional Teams* (New York: Oxford University Press, 1970) initiated interest in the game and stimulated subsequent scholarship.

3. For an analysis of the public and private transcript in African American history, see: Robin D. G. Kelley, *Race Rebels: Culture, Politics, and the Black Working Class* (New York: Free Press, 1996); and on the historical construct of "between memory and history" see: Genevieve Fabre and Robert O'Meally, *History and Memory in African-American Culture* (New York: Oxford University Press, 1994); A.S. "Doc" Young, "A Batch of Reasons Why You Should Support Negro Baseball," *Cleveland Call and Post*, 8 May 1948, 6.

4. Examples include Bill L. Weaver, "The Black Press and the Assault on Professional Baseball's "Color Line," October 1945-April 1947," *Phylon* (Winter 1979): 303–317; David K. Wiggins, "Wendell Smith, the *Pittsburgh Courier-Journal* and the Campaign to Include Blacks in Organized Baseball," *Journal of Sport History* (Summer 1983): 5–28; Chris Lamb, "What's Wrong With Baseball: The Pittsburgh *Courier* and the Beginning of its Campaign to Integrate the National Pastime," *The Western Journal of Black Studies*, (Volume 26, Number 4, 2002): 189–192; Chris Lamb and Glen Bleske, "Democracy on the Field: The Black Press Takes on White Baseball," *Journalism History* (Summer 1998): 51–59; and Brian Carroll, "The Black Press and the Integration of Baseball: A Content Analysis of Changes in Coverage" paper presented at the 14th Annual Cooperstown Symposium on Baseball and American Culture. Jim Reisler's *Black Writers/Black Baseball: An Anthology of Articles from Black Sportswriters Who Covered the Negro Leagues* (Jefferson: McFarland Press, 1995) includes several excerpts on integration, and Leslie Heaphy's comprehensive history, entitled *The Negro Leagues, 1869–1960* (Jefferson: McFarland Press, 2003), places the efforts of black sportswriters within the broader context of integration, see pages 188–190 and *passim*.

5. C.I. Taylor, "The Future of Colored Baseball," *The Competitor* (February 1920): 76–79.

6. Ira F. Lewis, "National Baseball League Formed," *The Competitor* (March 1920): 66–67; "Baseball Men Hold Successful Meeting," *The Competitor* (January-February 1921): 51 and 54; and "Dismukes to Manage Pittsburgh Club," *The Competitor* (May 1921): 40.

7. There are too many articles to cite in one footnote, see, for example H.B. Webber and Oliver Brown, "Play Ball," *The Crisis* (May 1938): 136–137, 146.

8. *"Courier's* Brilliant Battery of Writers for '32 Season," *Pittsburgh Courier*, 19 March 1932, 5. The *Courier* maintained the practice initiated by its sister publication, *The Competitor* magazine, of inviting the game's "insiders" to contribute their perceptions.

9. *Chicago Defender*, 6 March 1919, 9; *Pittsburgh Courier*, 8 May 1926, 14; 2 May 1936, 4; 11 May 1940, 17; 7 September 1940, 17; 15 August 1942, 16; and 22 May 1948, 14.

10. *New York Amsterdam News*, 12 February 1938, 14 and 19 August 1925, 5; *Chicago Defender*, 22 June 1912; and *Pittsburgh Courier*, 24 April 1926, 14; 18 May 1940, 17; and 15 July 1944, 12.

11. *New York Amsterdam News*, 17 August 1940, 15.

12. *Pittsburgh Courier*, 25 February 1933, 4.

13. The major works on the construction of black masculinity are Hazel Carby, *Race Men* (Cambridge: Harvard University Press, 1998); and Martin Summers, *Manliness and Its Discontents: The Black Middle Class and the Transformation of Masculinity, 1900–1930* (Chapel Hill: University of North Carolina Press, 2004).

14. On Rube Foster's funeral see the *Pittsburgh Courier*, 20 December 1930, 6; and the *New York Amsterdam News*, 17 December 1930. See, for example, David W. Kellum, "John Connors, Veteran Sportsman, Laid to Rest," *Chicago Defender*, 17 July 1926, 11. On the memorializaton of Frank Warfield see, *Chicago Defender*, 30 July, 1932, 5; 6 August 1932, 4; and *Pittsburgh Courier*, 31 December, 1932, 4.

15. Mark Ribowsky, *The Power and the Darkness: The Life of Josh Gibson in the Shadows of the Game* (New York: Simon and Schuster, 1996), 297–307; and Wendell Smith, "Grays' Home-Run King Dies at 36," *Pittsburgh Courier*, 25 January 1947, 1.

16. *New York Amsterdam News*, 25 January 1947, 1 and 10.

17. *Memory and Meaning in African American Emancipation Celebrations, 1808–1915* (Amherst). This discussion draws on the theoretical work of Mitch Kachun, *Festivals of Freedom* (Amherst: University of Massachusetts Press, 2003).

18. *Kansas City Call*, 27 August 1923; Janet Bruce, *The Kansas City Monarchs: Champions of Black Baseball* (Lawrence: University Press of Kansas, 1985), 45–47; Overmyer, *Queen of the Negro Leagues*, 63–64; and *Newark Herald*, 20 May 1939, 8.

19. *New York Amsterdam News*, 26 July 1933, 8; August 2, 1933, 8; and 9 August 1933, 8.

20. *New York Amsterdam News*, 20 August 1938, 4. For additional information on Old-Timer's Day, see *Pittsburgh Courier*, 13 August 1938, 17; and *Chicago Defender*, 13 August, 1932, 4.

21. *Pittsburgh Courier*, 12 August, 1944, 12; and 19 August 1944, 12.

22. Larry Lester, *Black Baseball's National Showcase: The East-West All-Star Game, 1933–1953* (Lincoln: University of Nebraska Press, 2001), 9–19; William Nunn, "Don't Kill the Goose That Lays the Golden Egg, Nunn Warns Moguls; Lauds Game," *Pittsburgh Courier*, 14 August 1937, 16; and July 1943, 19.

23. *Pittsburgh Courier*, 19 August 1933, 4; 19 August 1933, 5; 14 August 1937, 16; 31 July 1943 19; 5 August 1944, 5 and 12; 12 August 1944, 12; and 19 August 1944, 12.

Down in the Dugout:
Why Baseball Is No Longer the
National Pastime for Blacks

Jessica A. Johnson

One of the most touching scenes in the movie *Hardball* is when Coach Conor O'Neill (Keanu Reeves) takes a player on his Kekamba baseball team home to the hellhole of a Chicago ghetto. Anxiously eyeing the volatile surroundings as they walk through the grungy hallway, O'Neill asks, "What do you do for fun around here?" "Play baseball with you," the kid succinctly responds.[1]

If you asked this same question to black youth who actually live in the inner city, they would more than likely say they play basketball or football. You won't find too many sandlots embellishing the landscape around today's housing projects, and unlike the Kekamba team portrayed in *Hardball*, most black youth do not have a passionate love for baseball. This results from a deep cultural disconnection because most of them view baseball as a white man's sport. They don't see many faces on the field like their own and few probably know who National League MVP Barry Bonds is. Although Bonds is presently baseball's most dominant offensive player, he is not an ambassador for the sport the way Michael Jordan was for the NBA in the 1990s. Just seven years ago, it appeared that Major League Baseball was getting its "Michael Jordan" when Ken Griffey, Jr.'s career was blossoming with the Seattle Mariners. At this time, Griffey had an annual salary of $8.5 million, was the American League MVP, and had endorsements totaling $5 million.[2] He regularly appeared in Nike and Nintendo commercials, and if his career had not been beset with injuries he would be on pace with Bonds in the chase for Hank Aaron's home run record. Griffey could have been that marketing magnet for the inner city that baseball so desperately needs now as the NBA and the NFL promote their leagues with elite athletes like LeBron James and Donovan McNabb.

James and McNabb were among the athletes selected as role models by black youth in the sample size of this study who play basketball in public high schools in Columbus, Ohio. One respondent did select a current black base-ball star, New York Yankee shortstop Derek Jeter; however, some youth listed legendary black athletes who began their careers in sports other than base-ball before they were born — Jerry Rice, Muhammad Ali, and Julius Erving to name a few. This shows that the intrinsic historical connection baseball once had in the black community has been deeply severed as no respondent mentioned Dave Winfield, Tony Gwynn, or Rickey Henderson.

Things have certainly changed since the heyday of the Negro Leagues when no black athletes in any other sport could rival the likes of Cool Papa Bell, Buck Leonard, Josh Gibson, and Satchel Paige. Negro League games were main events as African Americans avidly flocked to the stands in antic-ipation of dynamic nine-inning duels, especially the East-West All-Star Game. However, within the 57 years since Jackie Robinson became the first African-American ballplayer in the modern era, the number of black players has dras-tically waned.

According to the *2003 Racial and Gender Report Card* published by Richard E. Lapchick of the Institute for Diversity and Ethics in Sport at the University of Central Florida, African Americans comprised only 10 percent of the major leagues in 2002, compared to 17 percent in 1995.[3] On opening day 2004, the percentage was just under 10, mirroring the 1959 season when the Boston Red Sox became the last team to integrate their roster.[4] The num-bers get even worse in the college ranks. NCAA data from 2001 revealed that only 6.7 percent of African Americans playing Division I baseball — exclud-ing historically black colleges — were on scholarship.[5] Moreover, in a special report titled "Blackout" for *Sports Illustrated* last July, Tom Verducci pointed out that only 11 African Americans were on the eight teams competing in the College World Series and just 52 blacks were on baseball rosters in the six largest Division I conferences (ACC, Big East, Big Ten, Big 12, Pac-10, SEC).[6]

Some studies such as Don E. Albrecht's "An Inquiry into the Decline of Baseball in Black America" contend that equipment costs and space are the major reasons black youth in the inner city choose not to play baseball.[7] How-ever, critics of this study have pointed out that youngsters in the inner city still manage to get money for other sports that require equipment such as football. Cultural scholar Gerald Early maintains that if a poor kid can buy shoes for football would he not be able to incur the costs of a baseball glove? Early also argues that although pickup baseball games are seldom played in the inner city today, football games are still popular and football demands a reasonable amount of space.[8] The popularity of football and basketball show that black youth in the inner city play sports that appeal to them and that their parents can lend financial support to their athletic activities. Thus, the current lack of interest in baseball has a more complex social meaning that embodies a shift in cultural trends.

Baseball in the Black Community — The Preeminence of the Negro Leagues

"There is no way that black success in basketball compares in magnitude to what blacks accomplished in baseball."

Gerald Early

Although the NBA's Charlotte Bobcats can proudly claim the 21st century's first African-American majority owner of a professional sports franchise, this historical feat comes 84 years after Andrew "Rube" Foster laid the foundation that made Negro League Baseball a multi-million-dollar enterprise during its prime. When Foster formed the first Negro National League (NNL) in 1920, average attendance on a Sunday afternoon was around 5,000,[9] and crowds of 8,000 to 10,000 would show up for holiday and weekend games in budding black metropolitan hotspots Indianapolis and Kansas City.[10] Foster's vision, however, was much broader than just giving talented black ballplayers an opportunity to earn a paycheck and showcase their talents during baseball's period of segregation. His objective was to make the NNL an economic mainstay in the black community that would, as Steven A. Riess asserts, "not only encourage opportunities for black capitalists but would also generate jobs for blacks on and off the diamond, as scouts, umpires, clerks, and secretaries."[11] In working to establish a firm economic base and solid fan support for the NNL, Foster planned to get his teams in position to enter the majors in full rank.[12]

Guided by Foster's business and baseball savvy, NNL teams survived during the early 1920s despite scheduling and financial problems, and three years after the league's inaugural season, Foster promoted the founding of the Eastern Colored League. Comprised of teams from Philadelphia, New York and Baltimore, the formation of the Eastern Colored League gave the Negro Leagues an equivalent organizational structure of Major League Baseball.[13] The best teams in both leagues usually played a 60–80 game schedule, drawing large weekend crowds, and in 1924 Foster added extra games in the NNL by formulating a split-season schedule. This new format allowed each half's winner to play a flag series at the end of the season, which increased profits and thrilled fans as players such as Oscar Charleston, John Henry "Pop" Lloyd, and Willie Foster were becoming legends in black baseball lore.[14] The first Negro World Series was also played in 1924 between the Philadelphia Hilldales and the Kansas City Monarchs. The Monarchs won the nine-game series that featured future Hall of Famers Wilbur "Bullet" Joe Rogan and Julius "Judy" Johnson.[15]

Unfortunately, the success of the NNL was short-lived as the organization suffered a tremendous loss when Rube Foster passed away in 1930. Many teams returned to an independent status after Foster's death; however, a second Negro National League was formed in 1933 by Pittsburgh racketeer Gus Greenlee. Four years later the Negro American League was created, which consisted of teams from the deep South and former NNL clubs in the Midwest. As the Negro Leagues were reinvented in the 1930s, Greenlee and Abe Saperstein, owner of the Harlem Globetrotters, created what Negro League historian Kyle McNary calls the "crown jewel of black baseball": the East-West All-Star Game.[16] More popular than the Negro League World Series, the East-West Game was played at Comiskey Park from 1933 through 1960. Fans voted for the players to appear in this classic through the *Pittsburgh Courier* and the *Chicago Defender*, the leading black national weeklies of the 1930s and 1940s. In 1934, a quarter-million votes were cast and by the late 1940s over 50,000 fans were making their annual Chicago pilgrimage to see their favorite players do battle on the diamond. More than any other sporting event, the East-West All-Star Classic symbolized the cultural institution of baseball in the black community and became "the highlight in the affairs of the elite."[17]

As the Negro Leagues began to peak in the 1940s, this decade, ironically, was the beginning of their demise. Greenlee's Negro National League folded in 1948, and many of the teams were consolidated into the Negro American League, which endured until 1960. When Major League Baseball began to integrate with young stars like Jackie Robinson, Larry Doby, Monte Irvin and Don Newcombe, faithful Negro League fans followed. More than half of the 26,623 fans who showed up for Robinson's Brooklyn Dodger debut in 1947 were black.[18] Doby, Irvin and Newcombe's entrance into the majors contributed to the decrease in attendance of Newark Eagles' games as the club's fan base dropped from 120,000 to 35,000 between 1946 and 1948.[19] Although the Negro Leagues began to lose their best players to the majors in the late 1940s, Bob Kendrick, the Negro League Baseball Museum's director of marketing, points out that baseball remained enormously popular in the black community.

"We were still going to the ballpark after the Negro Leagues ended in the 1960s," said Kendrick. "Jackie Robinson was Michael Jordan historically and virtually every African American wanted to see Robinson play. Somewhere the black community disconnected itself from the game as we stopped attending and playing."[20]

That disconnection is blatantly obvious today as African Americans comprise only 3.5 percent of Major League Baseball's fan base.[21] Furthermore, black player percentages are at an all-time low since their peak in 1975 when they represented 27 percent of MLB rosters.[22] Basketball has replaced baseball as the dominant sport in the black community and is an integral component of, as Douglas Hartmann claims, the "critical social space for the development of an African American identity and aesthetic."[23] Thus, many youngsters dream of playing in the NBA — a league that is 78 percent African American[24] — because they can identify with influential stars like Allen Iverson and Jermaine O'Neal. Although Major League Baseball is sponsoring programs such as Reviving Baseball in the Inner Cities (RBI), Kendrick contends that the game must be better marketed to urban black youth to revitalize interest.

"Our RBI program in Kansas City has been very successful as we have over 700 kids participating annually," said Kendrick. "We are giving them the opportunity to play and we have filled a niche, but 700 is only a fraction of those who need to be reached."[25]

Indeed, in addition to providing playing opportunities, Major League Baseball will have to find a way to make the game "cool" for a generation incognizant of the history of the Negro Leagues. Only then will baseball be able to regain the cultural influence it once had in the black community.

Basketball in the Black Community — A Meritocracy and Cultural Identity Model

Historian Robin D.G. Kelley contends that for African-American males "basketball embodies dreams of success and possible escape from the ghetto."[26] With the recent influx of high school players into the NBA, many young black males envision themselves becoming the next Tracy McGrady or Kobe Bryant, elite hardwood stars who bypassed big-time collegiate athletics and now have multi-million dollar endorsements. Since 1995, the year Kevin Garnett became the patron saint of the present generation of players skipping college for the pros, roughly 80 percent of high schoolers who made it to the NBA became millionaires by age 21.[27] Bryant and McGrady followed Garnett as first round prep selections in 1996 and 1997 respectively. Adidas landed both players during their rookie seasons, signing Bryant for $5 million, and coming to terms with McGrady for $12 million.[28] Also in 1997, Garnett became the second youngest player to compete in the NBA All-Star Game, and he signed a six-year $125 million deal with the Minnesota Timberwolves, the richest professional sports contract at that time.[29]

Presently, the most prominent African-American sports figure is the NBA's sensational Rookie of the Year LeBron James. In *Sports Illustrated*'s 2004 report on the 101 most influential minorities in sports, James is listed at number 4, up 97 spots from last year's rankings.[30] Christened "The Cho-

sen One" by *Sports Illustrated* in 2002, James has definitely become the savior the NBA so desperately needed since Michael Jordan's retirement. When
Jordan ruled the court, NBA merchandise sales increased from $44 million
to $2 billion, and he was estimated to be an overall $10 billion dollar industry.[31] Hoping to continue the success of the NBA's appeal that Jordan fashioned, the league and advertisers have aimed to make James' image palatable
to the mainstream yet hip enough for Generation Next. Advertisers cleverly
marketed Jordan to black, white, young, and middle-aged audiences throughout his career. His Coke and McDonald's commercials had the all-American
family appeal, while the Mars Blackmon spots with Spike Lee drew the urban
crowd. Jordan has been considered "more popular than Jesus, except with
better endorsement deals," and has also been dubbed "basketball's high
priest," and the "new DiMaggio."[32] Thus, he became not just a superstar athlete but also a cultural icon. Jordan is the meritocracy model of sport because
he represents the heroic semblance of the American spirit. James, raised by
his mother in a government-subsidized apartment complex in Akron, Ohio,
also symbolizes the economic and social mobility that personifies the American dream, especially since sport has been a primary vehicle for blacks achiev-
ing material success.

James' impact in the NBA has been truly Jordanesque in court performance as well as marketing appeal. Television ratings soared for cable net-
works TNT and ESPN during James' professional debut, and this year's NBA
All-Star Game, which attracted 8.2 million viewers, was the second most
watched NBA game on cable.[33] As far as endorsements are concerned, the
Cleveland Cavaliers' rookie has deals worth approximately $135 million. In
addition to his $90 million deal with Nike, James landed a $5 million contract with Bubblicious bubble gum, and agreed to a $14 million pact with
Coca-Cola.[34] As the apparent heir to Jordan's throne, James is taking the NBA
to its next level and is now truly anointed as the league's leading man.

The commercial appeal of James and other rising black NBA stars such
as Carmelo Anthony, another Nike endorser, will continue to influence the
cultural trend of basketball as a racial emblem for young African-American
males. In their study "It's Gotta Be the Shoes," Brian Wilson and Robert
Sparks found that black youth wearing apparel endorsed by African-American NBA players felt "a sense of cultural power and belonging." Taken from
a series of Nike "Barber Shop" commercials in the mid-1990s, Wilson and
Sparks' research also shows that young black males look to African Americans in the NBA as "reference points" to express their masculinity.[35] One of
the black adolescents in their study alluded to the racial labeling of basketball, differentiating between the allure and playing styles of whites and African
Americans:

you have to remember, when you do a commercial, you want something that catches the eye ... and if there were basketball commercials with stuff like that, for example, that Chris Webber commercial, if it was like Rony Seikaly and John Paxson, and Larry Bird and Kevin McHale, I don't think that people would look at that commercial. You wouldn't see like Larry Bird crowning Chris Webber or anything like that, man. Like when you see dunks and stuff ... all you see is black people. I would rather see 12 black people play. The basketball looks different. When you see white people play it's so fundamental.[36]

David G. Ogden and Michael L. Hilt link this "cultural branding of basketball" evident in Wilson and Sparks' findings to what racial theorist K. Anthony Appiah deems collective identity. Using Appiah's theory, certain activities are culturally marked for particular ethnic groups and Ogden and Hilt contend that basketball has "become a pillar in the construction of modern black culture."[37] Thus, in cultural terms, the court has become what Hartmann calls a "contested racial terrain" where racial images and inequalities clash.[38] Whites who do succeed in basketball then begin to measure their effectiveness by the skills of black players. This ideology was recently expressed in Larry Bird's astounding claim on ESPN that nothing irritated him more than having a white guy guard him when he played in the NBA. Reminiscing on the days when he and Kevin McHale were part of the great Boston Celtic's teams of the 1980s, Bird further argued that the league needs more white players to hold the interest of white fans. Although LeBron James and Carmelo Anthony disagreed with Bird and insisted that race is not a significant factor, subtle racial overtones have always shaped how the league is viewed, especially when it comes to assessing black and white players. And as long as the NBA is predominately black, race will continue to be an underlying issue.[39]

Bird's assertion that basketball is a "black man's game" reinforces the belief that the court is now a place where few whites have the athletic ability to compete; however, whites are not vanishing from professional basketball in the manner that blacks are currently disappearing from Major League Baseball. Although whites only comprise 20 percent of the players in the NBA,[40] young white males do have stars they can identify with such as the Minnesota Timberwolves' Wally Szczerbiak and the Milwaukee Bucks' Keith Van Horn.

When assessing baseball, there are only a handful of black stars and Yankee shortstop Derek Jeter is one of the few with an apparel deal with a major sneaker company. Promoting Jordan's athletic gear through Nike and serving as a pitchman for Visa, Jeter is the most visible African American baseball star but his image is not inventively packaged with the cultural flare of Nike and Reebok commercials that feature NBA stars like James and Allen Iverson. Most urban black youth do not relate to Jeter's Visa commercials that show Yankees owner George Steinbrenner casually reprimanding him for being out all night "carousing with his friends." However, they can identify with Nike's "Book of Dimes" commercial featuring James in a black church with comedian Bernie Mac acting as the preacher. In the spirited oratory fashion symbolic of African-American ministers, Mac fervidly asks the congregation, "Can I get a lay-up?," which is akin to "Can I get an Amen?" Thus, there is no mistaking who Nike's target audience is, especially when James emerges in the sanctuary and anoints the basketball as soon as he touches it.[41] Nike's arch-rival, Reebok, is known to run ads using a "hip-hop urban basketball scene." This approach was evident in the company's RBK brand ads that featured Harlem's Ruckers Park street team, and it is illustrative in their spots showcasing Iverson, their main pitchman.[42]

The Nike and Reebok commercials featuring black NBA stars are indicative of what Todd Boyd describes as a "cultural space where an overall sense of Blackness can be communicated to both marginal and mass audiences."[43] The marketing of this cultural space, in addition to the social mobility associated with the success of African Americans in the NBA, will enable basketball to continue to perpetuate the collective identity that labels the sport a black man's domain.[44]

Survey Results and Discussion

In assessing the survey responses of the 101 African American males in this study who play public high school and college basketball in Columbus, Ohio, there were similar fundamental patterns of distinctive racial themes in their reactions to open-ended questions imploring why baseball is viewed as a white sport and why basketball is more popular in the inner city. The respondents' ages range from 14 to 23, and they were selected from the Hoop Basketball Training and Fitness Center, Eastmoor Academy, Northland, Brookhaven, Mifflin, and Marion-Franklin High Schools, Columbus State Community College, and Otterbein College. The typical response from the majority of the athletes surveyed regarding baseball as a white sport was simply that more whites play baseball and that the sport has deep roots in white American culture. Consider the following comments:

> Baseball is viewed as America's pastime. Since we are not naturally Americans, we don't feel this is our pastime.
>
> Because whites were basically the founders of baseball, the first Hall of Famers dealing with baseball were guys like Babe Ruth.
>
> Because all the pastime legends are white.
>
> Because it initially started out as only white and recently it has improved enough to let minorities in.
>
> Because it is played more in white communities.

As they acknowledged baseball's segregated past, some of the respondents' observations also mirrored the racial connotations of Bird's statements implying black athletic prowess in basketball. Five explicitly supported this stance in their remarks:

> Baseball requires the least amount of athleticism of all the major sports (baseball, football and basketball).
> Baseball comes natural through their (whites) generation.
> Because you do not have to be as athletic to play baseball.
> It takes no athletic ability.
> Because it's harder for blacks to adapt to baseball. Basketball comes natural for most.

Other athletes commented that "baseball is slow" and that "most white people are slow." Although there is no legitimate scientific evidence that proves that blacks have an innate athletic gene, the belief that blacks are better suited to play basketball by many of the respondents in this study show they have embraced this stereotype. This racial typecast also exemplifies what John Hoberman terms a "sports fixation," that is, an imposed "athleticized identity on blacks." This identity in turn has made sport a dominant factor in the black community and basketball, as Hoberman claims, has become the "black sport par excellence."[45]

Regarding basketball's popularity in the inner city, the respondents attributed the game's appeal mainly to the easy access of the courts. "There is a basketball court on every corner," one replied. "You can't play baseball anywhere."

"There are many basketball hoops, recs and opportunities to enjoy the game," another added. "Other sports aren't really out to grab the people in the inner city."

The accessibility of basketball was also linked to respondents' explanations of what needs to be done to bring baseball back to the inner city. Many stated that more Little League teams need to be established, more equipment needs to be provided, and more black players in the majors need to be exposed. The following comments demonstrate these viewpoints:

> I think you should get more urban figures in baseball that represent the struggle and lower class inner city. Such as the way Deion Sanders was.
> Start inner city leagues and help enable blacks to participate in select programs.
> Make baseball equipment more available to the inner city.
> More tryouts in the inner city instead of the suburbs.

Only 38 of the athletes surveyed played Little League baseball, and 45 never stepped on the diamond at all. Twenty-one respondents indicated that their fathers never played baseball and only 18 in the survey sample currently play. While these athletes see the need for more Little League teams in the inner city, it will be very difficult to establish clubs without the active participation of fathers or other influential men in the black community. John Young, an African American, former major league scout, and founder of RBI, refers to these role models as "pied pipers," and he believes baseball has lost most of them.[46]

Exposure of more blacks in the majors was a crucial point emphasized by many respondents. It is evident that the dearth of black ballplayers heavily accounts for their lack of interest in baseball. Several suggested using black baseball players in more advertisements, which shows from a cultural standpoint that the young black males in this study do not identify with baseball. One respondent effectively conveyed this position stating, "There's more basketball players who appeal to inner city kids. They wear our clothes, shoes and have our style. We sort of can relate to that."

In addition to clothing style, the respondents said they respected players like LeBron James, Tracy McGrady, Kevin Garnett, and Stephon Marbury because they are from backgrounds similar to their own. This year's NBA draft also had players such as New York high school phenom Sebastian Telfair who expressed the need to get out of the "projects" and support his family.[47] As the 13th selection by the Portland Trail Blazers in the first round, not only will Telfair's family be well taken care of, but he will also be very visible commercial wise as Adidas gets ready to cash in on its $15 million investment.

Major League Baseball does have promising young black players working their way up through the minor leagues, but none have received the hype of the prep athletes who make it to the NBA. Expectations are very high for the Milwaukee Brewers' Rickie Weeks, the 2003 Rotary Smith Award winner, and Prince Fielder and Anthony Gwynn, sons of former big league sluggers Cecil Fielder and Tony Gwynn. Weeks led the nation in batting, RBI, triples, and slugging percentage in 2002 while playing at Southern University, a historically black institution.[48] Along with Gwynn and Fielder, Weeks is having a solid season this year for the Brewers' Huntsville Stars (AA), but no major endorsement deals have come the way of these Brewers' hopefuls. Thus, they have yet to rival their peers in the NBA, the athletes whose social mobility is most visible to young black males in the inner city.

Like the professional basketball players they idolize, 66 percent of the respondents surveyed aspire to play in the NBA. These respondents' choice of basketball sadly reveal that many black youth have passed on the national pastime. Although RBI programs are thriving across the country in cities like Atlanta and Houston, the program has yet to reach the heart of the inner city in Columbus. "RBI is most popular in the suburbs," said Shawn Jeter, an assistant basketball coach at Brookhaven High School. "There are no RBI programs in the rec centers but there are a lot of basketball and football camps. These sports surround us."[49] Jeter, a former Chicago White Sox outfielder and cousin of Yankees shortstop Derek Jeter, has tried to establish Little League teams in the inner city in Columbus, but he has not been successful due to lack of parental support. Thus while still passionate about baseball, Shawn presently runs several basketball camps at the Hoop.

When putting baseball's lack of appeal to black youth in Columbus in perspective with the overall decline of blacks in the sport, the problem, as former commissioner Fay Vincent contends, is a "20-year fix."[50] Baseball has missed the present generation, but league officials are taking steps to attract black youngsters back to the diamond. Last summer a $3 million youth academy in Compton, California, opened that is modeled after the complexes of many teams in Latin America.[51] Baseball is also donating $250,000 to Little League each year to expand its urban programs.[52] While respondents in this study stated that more opportunities are needed for Little League teams in the inner city, their observations regarding the lack of advertising exposure of black baseball players clearly indicate that the national pastime must make some inroads to market its game to an urban audience. Meanwhile sneaker companies continue their ad campaigns with African American basketball players. And 1, whose leading endorser is New York Nick Stephon Marbury, recently launched a Mix Tape Tour featuring streetballer Rafer "Skip to My Lou" Alston. The company's target audience is inner-city 11–17 year-olds.[53] Until baseball delves into this cultural mode that highlights black NBA stars, basketball will remain the predominant sport in the African-American community.

Appendix A: Eastmoor Academy and Northland, Brookhaven, Mifflin, and Marion-Franklin High Schools, Columbus, OH

- Players surveyed: 69
- Ages: 14–18
- Median years playing basketball: 7.1
- Median years playing baseball: 1.5

- 12 athletes currently play baseball
- 32 athletes never played baseball
- 11 athletes' fathers played baseball
- 43 athletes want to play in the NBA

Appendix B: High School Athletes Surveyed from The Hoop, Columbus, OH

- Players surveyed: 13
- Ages: 14–17
- Median years playing basketball: 9.5
- Median years playing baseball: 2.9

- 1 athlete playing baseball
- 7 athletes never played baseball
- 2 athletes' fathers played baseball
- 9 athletes want to play in the NBA

Appendix C: Columbus State Community College & Otterbein College Men's Basketball Teams, Columbus, OH

- Players surveyed: 19
- Ages: 18–23
- Median years playing basketball: 10
- Median years playing baseball: 3.3

- 5 athletes playing baseball
- 6 athletes never played baseball
- 8 athletes' fathers played baseball
- 15 athletes want to play in the NBA

Notes

1. *Hardball*, dir. Tom Richmond, 1 hr. 46 min, Paramount, 2001, videocassette.
2. Rod Little, Doug Stern, and Josh Chetwynd, "Then ... And now," *U.S. News & World Report*, 24 March 1997, 59.
3. Richard E. Lapchick, *2003 Racial and Gender Report Card*, University of Central Florida, The Institute for Diversity and Ethics in Sport with the DeVos Sport Business Management Program, 14.
4. John Shea, "Big Leagues a black hole for African Americans," *The San Francisco Chronicle*, 18 April 2004, C7.
5. Lapchick, 15.
6. Tom Verducci, "Blackout," *Sports Illustrated*, 7 July 2003, 58.
7. Don E. Albrecht, "An Inquiry into the Decline of Baseball in Black America: Some Answers-More Questions," *Nine: A Journal of Baseball History and Social Policy Perspectives* 1, no. 1 (Fall 1992): 34.
8. Gerald Early, "Why baseball was the black national pastime," in *Basketball Jones*, eds. Todd Boyd and Kenneth Shropshire (New York: New York University Press, 2000), 36–37.
9. Donn Rogosin, *Invisible Men: Life in Baseball's Negro Leagues* (New York: Macmillan, 1983), 6.
10. Robert Peterson, *Only the Ball Was White*, (New York: McGraw-Hill, [1970] 1984), 84.
11. Steven A. Riess, *Touching Base: Professional Baseball and American Culture in the Progressive Era*, (Urbana and Chicago: University of Illinois Press, 1999), 200.
12. Kyle McNary, *Black Baseball: A History of African-Americans & the National Game*, (New York: Sterling Publishing Company, Inc., 2003), 20.
13. Rogosin, 11.
14. McNary, 20.
15. Rogosin, 11.
16. McNary, 29.
17. Rogosin, 25–26.
18. Early, 37–38.
19. James E. Overmyer, "Something to Cheer About: The Negro Leagues at the Dawn of Integration," in *The Cooperstown Symposium on Baseball and American Culture: 1997 (Jackie Robinson)*, ed. Peter Rutkoff (Jefferson, N.C.: McFarland, 2000), 72.
20. Bob Kendrick, interview by Jessica A. Johnson, 31 May 2004.
21. Early, 38.
22. Verducci, 56.
23. Douglas Hartmann, "Rethinking the Relationships Between Sport and Race in American Culture: Golden Ghettos and Contested Terrain," *Sociology of Sport Journal* 17 (2000): 240.
24. Lapchick, 14.
25. Kendrick, interview by Jessica A. Johnson, 31 May 2004.
26. Robin Kelley, "Playing For Keeps: Pleasure and Profit on the Postindustrial Play-

ground," in *The House That Race Built*, ed. Wahneema Lubiano (New York: Pantheon Books, 1997), 204.

27. David Shields, "Why Not Go Pro?," *New York Times*, 6 May 2004, sec. A.

28. "Great Moments in Athlete Endorsement History," *Sporting Goods Business*, 1 July 2003, in LexisNexis Academic [database online] [cited 29 May 2004]; available from Columbus State Community College Educational Resources Center.

29. "Garnett Signs With Timberwolves; Becomes Second Highest-Paid In NBA," *Jet*, 20 October 1997, 46.

30. Richard Deitsch, Gene Menez, Elizabeth Newman, Melissa Segura, and Andrea Woo, "The 101 Most Influential Minorities in Sports," *Sports Illustrated*, 28 June 2004, 80.

31. Kevin Chappell, "Can LeBron James Repeat the Jordan Miracle?," *Ebony*, January 2004, 124; Douglas Kellner, "The Sports Spectacle, Michael Jordan, and Nike: Unholy Alliance?," in *Michael Jordan, Inc.: Corporate Sport, Media Culture, and Late Modern America*, ed. David L. Andrews (Albany, New York: State University of New York Press, 2001), 44.

32. Michael Eric Dyson, "Be Like Mike?: Michael Jordan and the Pedagogy of Desire," in *Michael Jordan, Inc.: Corporate Sport, Media Culture, and Late Modern America*, ed. David L. Andrews (Albany, New York: State University of New York Press, 2001), 259.

33. R. Thomas Umstead, "ESPN, TNT Enjoying NBA's Ratings Revival," *Multichannel News*, 23 February 2004, 24.

34. "NBA: LeBron blowing bubbles," *The Gazette*, 24 February 2004, C6; Branson Wright, "NBA LeBron soar together," *Plain Dealer*, 15 February 2004, C1.

35. Brian Wilson and Robert Sparks, "It's Gotta Be the Shoes: Youth, Race and Sneaker Commercials," *Sociology of Sport Journal* 13 (1996): 414,421.

36. Ibid., 416.

37. David C. Ogden and Michael L. Hilt, "Collective Identity and Basketball: An Explanation for the Decreasing Number of African-Americans on America's Baseball Diamonds," *Journal of Leisure Research* 35, no. 2 (2003): 218.

38. Hartmann, 241.

39. Jessica A. Johnson, "Bird underscores racial overtones of sports," *Columbus Dispatch*, 19 June 2004, 8A.

40. Lapchick, 14.

41. Barry Janoff, "The World NOT According to Kobe," *Brandweek*, 12 January 2004, in LexisNexis Academic [database online] [cited 22 May 2004]; available from Columbus State Community College Educational Resources Center.

42. R. Linnett, "Reebok rebrands for hip-hop crowd," *Advertising Age*, 28 January 2002, 3, 27.

43. Todd Boyd, "The Day Niggaz Took Over: Basketball, Commodity Culture, and Black Masculinity," in *Out of Bounds: Sports, Media, and the Politics of Identity*," eds. Aaron Baker and Todd Boyd (Bloomington, Indianapolis: Indiana University Press, 1997), 134.

44. Ogden and Hilt, 218.

45. John Hoberman, *Darwin's Athletes* (New York: Houghton Mifflin, 1997), 5–6.

46. Verducci, 61.

47. Tom Allegra, "Telegenic Telfair," *New York Sportscene*, May 2004, 29.

48. Lee Feinswog, "Black college is home to big-league talent," *USA Today*, 20 May 2003, 3C.

49. Shawn Jeter, interview by Jessica A. Johnson, 24 May 2004.

50. Murray Chass, "On Baseball; Game Fights Trend of Fewer Blacks," *New York Times*, 19 April 2004, sec. D.

51. Richard Justice, "Baseball Tries to Win Back Black Players with Youth World Series," *The Houston Chronicle*, 10 August 2003, in LexisNexis Academic [database online] [cited 10 May 2004]; available from Columbus State Community College Educational Resources Center.

52. Chass, sec. D.

53. Janoff, "The World NOT According to Kobe."

Part III

OTHER MINORITIES:
BEYOND BASEBALL'S
MELTING POT

Who Is a Jewish
Baseball Player?

Rebecca Alpert

Most recent scholarship suggests that baseball once played an important role in American Jewish life, and that role was to make Jews into Americans. The argument goes on to suggest that now that Jews are no longer predominantly immigrants, have less to fear from anti-Semitism, and do not need to prove their American credentials, their connection to the world of baseball has been normalized and is no longer freighted with significance. Yet in the past five years, a major best-selling book on Sandy Koufax, an award-winning documentary film about Hank Greenberg, numerous articles about Shawn Green in the general circulation and Jewish press, an anecdotal history of Jewish baseball, a website produced by the leading American Jewish historical society, a set of baseball cards including all Jews who played in the major leagues, and many other manifestations of interest in Jews and baseball have appeared in print and on the Internet. This outpouring of interest about Jews in baseball suggests that baseball still has a particular hold on the American Jewish sensibility.

While Jews have been heavily involved as fans, owners, sportswriters, and novelists, only a small number have actually played in the major leagues. But the exact answer to the question "how many?" has puzzled scholars of baseball. In recent years, a proliferation of lists has appeared that claim to incorporate all the Jews who played Major League Baseball, from Lipman Pike, who is generally acknowledged as the first Jewish professional ball player, until the current day.[1] The lists vary in size, including between 124 and 150 Jewish ballplayers.[2] The variations relate primarily to the date of compilation, as more Jewish ballplayers have been discovered, and there has been a marked increase in the number of Jews playing in the major leagues in recent years. But another significant difference in these lists is that not all the list makers agree about whether certain players were, in fact, Jewish.

Deciding Whom to Include

Deciding whom to include should be a simple matter, but in reality deciding who is a Jew is complex, even for religious experts, who do not agree upon a simple definition. Being Jewish has both ethnic and religious connotations. Judaism is the religion practiced by Jews, but one can be Jewish without involvement in religious practice. Even the definition of a Jew in Jewish law suggests this complexity. Jewish law dictates that one can claim Jewish identity simply by being born of a Jewish mother. But one can also become Jewish through conversion which is a religiously defined process. Yet because Judaism is primarily defined through descent, if one is born a Jew, one is always a Jew. According to Jewish tradition, even conversion to another religion does not change one's status: the individual is still considered part of the Jewish people.

Prior to the modern era, not many people outside of the Jewish community were interested in conversion to Judaism. Jews generally married other Jews, and maintaining a consistent understanding of who was Jewish was a fairly simple matter despite the complexity of definition. In the modern era, however, Western European societies permitted greater Jewish contacts with the outside world, and Jews began to marry outside the faith. There were also changes among liberal groups regarding the requirements for conversion (that is, the Reform omission of the requirement for male adult circumcision) that were not accepted by traditionalists. This has created confusion about who, precisely, is a Jew.

The Nazis contributed further to this problem by providing their own definition of a Jew, declaring anyone with one Jewish grandparent to be Jewish, and creating degrees and categories of Jewishness based on that definition. This was unlike Jewish tradition where one can either be Jewish or not, but never part or half-Jewish. The creation of the State of Israel further complicated this definition by including anyone Hitler would have defined as Jewish in the Law of Return (automatic citizenship is granted in Israel to anyone who can prove he/she is Jewish) while maintaining a very strict adherence to the traditional Jewish definition for purposes of marriage and divorce (issues of personal status). And American Jewry's liberal denominations (Reform and Reconstructionist) further complicated this question in 1983 by breaking with the imperative of matrilineal descent and encompassing anyone with at least one Jewish parent (although in some cases requiring that person be raised as a Jew or study Judaism to qualify). Intermarriage is much more common in the Jewish community today. People who have married Jews often convert officially, but sometimes they do not. Children with non-Jewish mothers who are raised Jewish, or who have Jewish stepparents and siblings and are raised with a connection to Judaism, while not recognized by religious traditionalists as Jews, are growing in number and often desire inclusion. All these changes have created a need within the organized Jewish community about making clear boundaries of belonging, but not any agreement among religious authorities about who is a Jew.

Who Is a Jewish Ballplayer?

It is not surprising, then, that there is some confusion in the process of determining whom to include in a definitive list of Jewish Major League Baseball players, and which ones should be left out. But what is surprising is the variation of guidelines that list makers use, and the extent to which they differ from the rules made by religious authorities.

Chroniclers of Jewish athletes formerly employed impressionistic criteria as to who should be identified as a Jewish baseball player and demonstrated little interest in precise definitions. Bernard Postal, who, with his collaborators, compiled a pioneering compendium in the *Encyclopedia of Jews in Sport* (1965), remarked that "learning the ancestry of an athlete was not an easy job," but he did not define the criteria he used to make his judgments about whom to include. Postal noted that he discovered many Jewish athletes were now "closely tied to [Jewish] communal affairs" and that there were a half-dozen who preferred not to be listed because they "had left Judaism."[3] This amorphous treatment of the selection process followed in other books about Jewish athletes. As he had in his earlier, generic works about Jewish athletes, Harold Ribalow's *Jewish Baseball Stars* (1984), written with his son Meir, indicated that there was a "problem" figuring out who was Jewish and who was not, but did not suggest how he resolved the problem.[4] The same applies to Erwin Lynn's book the *Jewish Baseball Hall of Fame* (1986), which includes players "of Jewish heritage" and "several converts."[5] These works, with their casual comments about criteria for inclusion, would appear to employ less than rigorous adherence to the traditional manner of deciding Jewish identity.[6]

Journalistic assertions complicate the task of identifying Jewish baseball players. Old lists and anecdotal stories told in newspapers tended to include many players who were presumed to be Jewish because of the sound of their names but who were not Jewish by any criteria, including Ed Reulbach, Benny Kauff, Chief Roseman, and John Lowenstein. Historian Peter Levine assumes there was an interest in enlarging the list of Jewish players, which he attributes to "a host of Jewish writers in the 1930s and after who, for a variety of reasons yet to be explored, found it useful to herald the accomplishments of Jewish ballplayers, however questionable some of their credentials might have been."[7]

Enlarging the list of Jewish ball players increased ethnic pride. Moreover, these men may have appeared on lists of Jewish players simply because writers assumed they were Jewish based on the sound of their names. It also was not always easy to figure out who was a Jew because prior to World War II many Jews, fearing anti-Semitism, still hid their identities and some players without Jewish-sounding names turned out to be Jews who had changed their names. The story that best exemplifies this is an oft-repeated tale about St. Louis Browns catcher Ike Danning and songwriter Harry Ruby who, when playing in a celebrity game in the 1940s, gave signals to one another in Yiddish. Jimmie Reese, the New York Yankee best known as Babe Ruth's roommate, got several hits during the game. When it was over, Danning commented that he was surprised that Reese could hit that well. "What you didn't know," said Reese, "was that my real name is Hymie Solomon."[8] Given that Jewish identity was not always something Jews were proud of, it is no wonder then that writers wanted to enlarge the list of Jewish players as a way to encourage Jewish pride. Questioning ballplayers' Jewish credentials was of little interest to writers promoting Jewish pride.

Today Jewish identity is no longer so heavily stigmatized in the United States. Now those who make lists are less interested in padding them with people whose Jewish identity can not be verified. In fact, the opposite impulse seems to be at work. In keeping with the mores of the contemporary Jewish community, they want to make boundaries around Jewish identity. The list makers want to be very clear not only about who is a Jew, but who is not. They are very interested in proof. The *Jewhoo* website goes so far as to suggest that for them to accept a reader's suggestion that someone is Jewish, the reader would have to provide "a bar mitzvah invitation and/or photograph."[9] But definitive boundaries are not so easy to make. And those who exist in the margins raise some interesting questions that are not easily resolved by creating a definition.

In Martin Abramowitz's introduction to his newly published set of Jewish baseball cards, he argues that the matter has been settled for scholars of Jewish baseball, setting the number of Jewish players at 142 (through the 2003 season). He acknowledges the pioneering work of Postal and Ribalow, and credits baseball historian David Spaner's 1997 essay in *Total Baseball*[10] with setting a definitive standard. According to Abramowitz, *The Jewish Sports Review*, (*JSR*)[11] refined that standard, and so for his baseball cards, he followed the guidelines set by *JSR*. He describes how *JSR* made decisions for inclusion as follows: "The JSR standard is inclusive, welcoming converts and, where there has not been conversion to Judaism, asking only that at least one parent have been Jewish, and that the player was not raised in or did not practice a religion other than Judaism."[12]

I would argue, however, that these criteria, while more inclusive in certain respects, are less inclusive in other respects than definitions made by Jewish religious authorities and by other list makers. And they do not necessarily solve the problem of whom to include. I want to focus now on seven contested cases: five who would be left out and two who are included in the set of Jewish Major Leaguers and raise questions about whether the standard set by *JSR* and followed by Abramowitz truly settles the question of who is a Jewish baseball player.

Those Who Converted Out or Were Not Raised as Jews: Bo Belinksy and Lou Boudreau

To exclude those who were born of Jewish mothers but were either not raised as Jews or who converted out of Judaism is problematic from the perspective of Jewish law. While people who leave the faith are not considered part of the community, there is no doubt, according to traditionalists, that they are still Jews and that they have the right to return to the community. Like *JSR*, historian Steven Riess discounts those who convert to another religion. He argues that this is "a greater signal of unidentifying from one's birth group than parents' conversion or choice not to raise the child in their ancestral faith (and culture)."[13] This definition of course disregards traditional Jewish law, which does not exclude those who convert out of Judaism. Author Peter Horvitz, on the other hand, retains the traditional definition and does not eliminate converts to another faith, but makes an exception for anyone "with proverbial Jewish lineage who joins Jews for Jesus."[14]

Despite these concerns, most lists (though not *JSR*) include Bo Belinsky, a pitcher of the 1960s who developed a reputation as an "underachieving, oversexed, unobservant Jewish player."[15] Belinsky was indeed born of a Jewish mother, but never practiced Judaism. He described himself as a "Polish Russian from Trenton" who not only pitched on Yom Kippur, but "caroused on Kol Nidre."[16] At the end of his life, he became a born-again Christian. His obituary makes mention of his affiliation with the Trinity Life Church, but not of his Jewish ancestry.[17] Should Belinsky be included? He certainly was of interest to Jewish baseball fans and sportswriters in his era, often being contrasted to Sandy Koufax. Peter Bjarkman, who categorizes Belinsky as a Jewish "supernova," includes him with the comment that although he was a "carefree, ne'er do-well prodigal son" he did pitch the first Jewish no-hitter.[18] There is an argument to be made that Belinsky made an impact on Jewish-American consciousness, and that he should be considered a Jewish baseball player.

The same argument could be made about Lou Boudreau. He gets excluded by *JSR* (but not by Spaner and others) because he was not raised as a Jew, and was not known to have Jewish ancestry until after he retired. But his mother was Jewish, and his mother's parents were observant. Boudreau recollected that they had "special plates" they used on holidays. But Boudreau's parents were divorced when he was young, and he was raised by his French-Canadian father. Despite this slim connection, Boudreau is always included in lists that assume having a Jewish mother is a good enough criterion for traditional Judaism and would be for them. Nonetheless, Jonathan Tobin had some qualms about including Boudreau on his all-star team, considering the selection "cheating a little bit." Tobin, the editor of the *Philadelphia Jewish Exponent* and a passionate baseball fan, not only selected an all-star team but played the team in a fantasy league. The team did not do well, due to injuries and the fact that "Boudreau has been terrible, which, I suppose, serves me right."[19] Tobin's anecdote illustrates just how difficult these decisions are for those who care about Jews and baseball.

Conversion or Not: Johnny Kling and Rod Carew

Conversion to Judaism has become more common as Jews intermarry. Once conversion takes place, the Jewish identity of the convert is never questioned, although the conversions carried out by liberal rabbis are not always accepted by Orthodox authorities. Yet once someone converts, Jewish tradition emphasizes that the status of the convert is no different from that of people who are Jewish by virtue of parentage, and they are not to be reminded of their status as converts. Again, in conflict with Jewish law and practice, all these lists specify who the converts are. The list in *JSR*, for example, labels converts with the letter "C," including only those who converted while they were still active as players.[20] Other lists count any player who had at any time made a decision to convert to Judaism, but their conversions are always noted.

Some of the list makers do not include those players who, although they never officially converted, were married to Jews and raised their children as Jewish. Two ball players, Chicago Cubs catcher Johnny Kling and Minnesota Twins/ California Angels infielder Rod Carew, fall into that category. Neither ever stated explicitly that he was not a Jew. Although they played in different eras—Kling at the beginning of the twentieth century and Carew from 1967 to 1985—their stories are similar, and complicated by the fact that both were stellar players and would vastly improve the number of Jewish players of all-star caliber. One or both are frequently included in lists made of all-Jewish all-star teams.

The debates about Kling and Carew are extensive and inconclusive. Noted Jewish baseball writer Eric Solomon discusses his ongoing disagreement with Steven Riess over Kling's Jewish identity.[21] Solomon wants to include Kling because his daughters married Jews and he was buried in a Jewish cemetery. Peter Levine does not count him, based on evidence from a letter written by Kling's wife after his death to the National Baseball Hall of Fame Library in Cooperstown. In her letter, Mrs. Kling indicates that Kling was baptized in the Lutheran Church, and although she was Jewish and they were married by a rabbi, Johnny never converted officially. Yet, she says tellingly that Johnny never wanted to say anything publicly and was willing to be mistaken for a Jew: "he didn't care what was written about his religion."[22] In an era when Jews were changing their names and intermarriage was rare, Kling was known as a Jew, married a Jew, raised his children as Jews, and was buried in a Jewish cemetery. For some, that is enough evidence to include him.

Batting champion Rod Carew was also married to a Jew and raised his children as Jews. For a time, Carew studied Judaism, and claimed that he would convert when his career was over and he had time for more extensive study.[23] During his playing career, his marriage to Marilynn Levy was of great interest to the Jewish community, and there were many articles about Rod's interests and his desire to convert. For many years, he did not play on Yom Kippur. Carew wore a Star of David, a gift from his mother-in-law, around his neck during his playing days. His family observed Shabbat and the High Holidays, and considered travel to Israel. And, when his eighteen-year-old daughter died of leukemia in 1996, Carew sat *shiva* and reminisced about the *tallis* and *yarmulke* she kept as treasures from her bat mitzvah. In 1978, Carew was quoted as saying, "We are all searching for something ... and I know that Judaism will lead me to what I want."[24] But, after his divorce, Carew subsequently remarried a woman who was not Jewish, and never did go through an official conversion.

Despite the attention Carew's marriage and interest in Judaism received, his election to the Baseball Hall of Fame, and his inclusion in Adam Sandler's Hanukkah song, which celebrates famous Jews, many list makers are adamant in their efforts to exclude him:

> This great Panama born baseball player and Hall of Famer has often been erreonously [sic] reported to have converted to Judaism following his marriage to a Jewish woman. However, whenever Carew is actually asked he politely says that he did not convert. His wife is Jewish and his children have been raised Jewish. Adam Sandler simply got it wrong in his Hannukah [sic] song. *Sports Illustrated* got it wrong in a fairly recent issue that featured its 'all time' Jewish baseball team.[25]

Peter Bjarkman considers the debate about Carew to be "legitimate."[26] Harold Ribalow would not include him, but Erwin Lynn considered Carew's case to be a "special situation"[27] since he was understood to be in the process of studying for conversion at the time. One anonymous response to excluding

Carew from a Jewish all-star team was also passionate: "So he never converted. He's still a better Jew than those not raising children in the faith. I say we should count him."[28]

The desire to include Carew (and Kling) stems in part from their status as "great" players and welcome additions to a Jewish all-star team. But it also uncovers a sentiment in the Jewish community that has no interest in official definitions of who is a Jew and cares more about the quality of the player's relationship to Jewish life than the actual conversion. Other players, like Ron Cey, who raised their children as Jewish, are often listed "for informational purposes," and achieve inclusion in that way. These arguments about ballplayers reflect the confusion among American Jews about how to figure out who counts as a Jew and who does not, and raises questions about whether the old desire to be broadly inclusive is really a thing of the past.

Having One Jewish Parent: Buddy Myer and Mike Lieberthal

Almost all the lists include "half-Jews," players with one Jewish parent. In terms of traditional Jewish religious law, such a category does not exist. Players with a Jewish mother are Jews; players with a Jewish father and a gentile mother are not. David Spaner and most other list makers ignore this nuance. Spaner advocates a "broad ethnic definition" that accepts as Jewish anyone with one Jewish parent of either gender; he appears unaware that liberal movements in Judaism have for the most part adopted this standard of patrilineal as well as matrilineal descent.[29] Horvitz also includes patrilineal Jews, but his rationale rests on the standards of "liberal tradition and cues from the women's movement," presumably in its impulse to give men equal rights as parents.[30] He is aware that there are those traditionalists who might be offended by including players with Jewish fathers and gentile mothers, acknowledging that traditionalists "will want to mark up the margins of some of our entries." All the list makers seek to make some point of discussing this issue, even if they are not aware that they are entering into a controversial arena in Jewish life. Including those with a Jewish father but not a Jewish mother is deeply disturbing to traditional Jews, and some Orthodox rabbis will not perform weddings between Orthodox and liberal Jews because they cannot be sure that liberal Jews meet their definition of being of Jewish descent any longer. Pundit Jacob Traub compared patrilineal descent to playing baseball games with four outs, a shift so major it would constitute a fundamental violation.[31]

Yet few Jewish all-star teams exclude Charles "Buddy" Myer, a gifted second baseman of the Depression Era. Myer was the son of a Jewish father and Christian mother. In 1935, columnist Dan Daniel reported that the Yankees were interested in obtaining Myer's contract from the Washington Senators, because "the big army of Jewish fans ... would be lured by a Jewish star."[32] Myer was also involved in an altercation with the famously anti-Semitic (and racist) player Ben Chapman and so his status as a Jewish hero who fought anti-Semitism was thus established. But Myer made neither public affirmation nor private affiliation with Judaism, and he played many years before the Reform movement made its historic decision to affirm patrilineal descent. Nonetheless, popular perceptions about Myer illustrate that Jewish religious authorities and personal affirmation are not the only means of defining group inclusion.

Even more problematic is whether to include Philadelphia's current all-star catcher, Mike Lieberthal. His father is Jewish, but Lieberthal has told reporters that he does not want to be identified as a Jewish ballplayer. A reporter for a Philadelphia Jewish newspaper decided to exclude him after finding a photograph, in the Phillies yearbook, of the Lieberthal family posed in front of a Christmas tree.[33] *Jewhoo.com* suggests that individuals should "view him as you choose."[34] But Lieberthal is included in the *JSR* list, and most of the other lists (though not Spaner's) despite these facts. A woman named Molly summed up the dilemma of deciding who is a Jew, with reference to Lieberthal, on her website quite thoughtfully:

> Mike Lieberthal ... was apparently born to a Jewish father, but was not raised Jewish. That's what some people say, at least. Several years ago, he denied being Jewish, but some of the media decided to deny that, as well, and kept insisting that he was. Now I'm not positive anyone knows for sure what he is, and it makes me wonder why there is such confusion around the issue. Do people simply want him to be Jewish, and can't cope with the fact that he may not be? Are we not quite sure what makes someone officially Jewish, or at least a Jewish athlete? Are sports writers just desperate for interesting players or interesting stories? Or could it possibly be that Philadelphia is not a good place for sports figures of any Jewish background?[35]

Molly has reminded us that the old desire to claim Jewish heroes and expand the number of Jews who play ball has not completely disappeared. Since we lack a universally held definition of who is a Jew, the subject will remain open to debate. Ironically, lists of those who are not Jewish but are sometimes mistakenly identified as Jews are so ubiquitous that this negative inclusion allows them to be counted anyway.

The Strange Case of Jose Bautista

Consider the strange case of Jose Bautista, a pitcher for the Chicago Cubs and other teams during the early 1990s. Bautista, a native of the Dominican

Republic, is omitted from *JSR* and Abramowitz's collection of Jewish baseball cards, with the following explanation:

> married to a Jewish woman and their children are raised Jewish, but Jose's tale (of which there are several versions) of being the son of an Eastern European Jewish mother (named Arias?) who married a Dominican and raised eleven children, of whom only Jose is Jewish, in the town of Bari, D.R., stretches our credulity.[36]

Although traditional Jewish law gives no credence to self-definition, it gives pause when Bautista's story is questioned and the self-affirmation of other players is not. One must wonder whether Bautista's Dominican background is the reason for his exclusion.

Taken together, these cases illustrate why it is impossible to claim that there can be a definitive list of Jewish ballplayers. In the majority of situations, of course, the Jewish identity of the ball players is not debatable, and the recent scholarship that carefully documents Jewish identity is to be commended. But those players whose Jewish identities are complicated and who exist at the margins of the Jewish community raise important issues about the value of creating definitive lists. Neither religious authorities, nor baseball scholars, agree about criteria related to descent or conversion. The question of who has the authority to decide who is to be included and who is to be excluded (religious authorities, list makers, or the individuals themselves) is also open to question. At this stage of history, when these questions are in doubt, it is premature to deem any particular list or set of criteria as definitive. Ultimately, this question transcends baseball, and the debate over who is a Jew continues.

Notes

1. Lipman Pike, a Jew of Dutch ancestry, who also had several brothers who played the game, is generally considered be the first Jewish professional player although some sources cite Al Reach as the first Jewish professional player.

2. The complete lists I found were made by Peter C. Bjarkman, "Six-Pointed Diamonds and the Ultimate Shiksa: Baseball and the American-Jewish Immigrant Experience," in *The Cooperstown Symposium on Baseball and American Culture*, ed. Alvin Hall (Westport, CT: Meckler, 1990); Peter S. and Joachim Horvitz, *The Big Book of Jewish Baseball* (New York: S.P.I. Books, 2001); David Spaner, "From Greenberg to Green: Jewish Ballplayers," in *Total Baseball: The Official Encyclopedia of Major League Baseball*, ed. John Thorn et. al, 5th ed. (New York: Viking Press, 1997); The American Jewish Historical Society, *Jewsinsports.com*; and Shel Wallman and Ephraim Moxson, "Big League Jews," *Jewish Sports Review* 2, no. 16 (November/December 1999): 5–7. Other scholars and writers, including Steven Riess, "From Pike to Green with Greenberg in Between: Jewish Americans and the National Pastime," in *The American Game: Baseball Ethnicity*, eds. Lawrence Baldassaro and Dick Johnson (Carbondale: Southern Illinois University Press, 2002); Eric Solomon, "Jews, Baseball and the American Novel," *Arete* I, no. 2 (Spring 1984): 43–66; and Peter Levine, *Ellis Island to Ebbets Field: Sports and the American Jewish Experience* (New York: Oxford University Press, 1992),

have created their own definitions of who is a Jewish player. There are also innumerable all Jewish all-star teams. See Adam W. Green, *The Jewish All-Star Team*. 2002, Baseball. Library.Com, 03 June 2003 www.baseball.library.com; Ed Levitt, "How About a *Matza* Ball Nine?" *Baseball Digest* 31, no. 9 (September 1972): 20(2); Joel Oppenheimer, *The Wrong Season* (Indianapolis: Bobbs-Merrill, 1973); Dan Schlosberg, "Baseball's Jewish All-Stars," *World Over*, 6 October 1972, 12–13; and "All-Time Jewish Baseball Team," *Jewish Heartland*, June/July 1999, 22–23.

3. Bernard Postal, et al., *Encyclopedia of Jews in Sports* (New York: Bloch Publishing Co, 1965), 1.

4. Harold Ribalow and M.Z. Ribalow, *Jewish Baseball Stars* (New York, NY: Hippocrene Books, 1984). See also Harold Ribalow, *The Jew in American Sports* (New York: Bloch Publishing Co, 1966).

5. Erwin Lynn, *The Jewish Baseball Hall of Fame: A Who's Who of Baseball Stars* (New York: Shapolsky, 1986).

6. Postal, Ribalow, and Lynn wrote popularizations and thus did not employ the canons of academic scholarship.

7. Levine, *Ellis Island to Ebbets Field: Sports and the American Jewish Experience*, 102.

8. Horvitz and Horvitz, *The Big Book of Jewish Baseball*. A variation on the story comes from a letter to the editor after Reese's death from Philip R. Blustein, who reports having read that while the signals were being called when Reese came to bat he "said, in perfect Yiddish: 'S'vet dir nit helfen.' (It ain't gonna help.)." Philip Blustein, Letter to the Editor, 23 July 1994. Jimmie Reese clipping file, A. Bartlett Giamatti Research Center, National Baseball Hall of Fame. Cooperstown, New York,

9. "Rod Carew," *www.Jewhoo.Com*, 1999, June 2003.

10. Spaner, "From Greenberg to Green: Jewish Ballplayers."

11. Wallman, "Big League Jews," 5–7.

12. Martin Abramowitz, *America's Jews in America's Game: The Making of a Card Set* (New York: American Jewish Historical Society, 2003), in Jewish Major Leaguers: Baseball Cards Set.

13. Riess, "From Pike to Green," 136.

14. Horvitz, *The Big Book of Jewish Baseball*.

15. Jonathan Mahler, "New York Observer," 12 December 2001. Bo Belinksy clipping file, A. Bartlett Giamatti Research Center, National Baseball Hall of Fame Cooperstown, New York.

16. Myron Cope interview, *True Magazine*, n.d., Bo Belinksy clipping file, A. Bartlett Giamatti Research Center, National Baseball Hall of Fame, Cooperstown, New York.

17. Richard Goldstein, Bo Belinsky obituary, *The New York Times* 27 November 2001. Bo Belinsky clipping file, A. Bartlett Giamatti Research Center, National Baseball Hall of Fame Cooperstown, New York,

18. Peter C Bjarkman, "The Yiddish Connection: Jewish Ball Players and the National Pastime," *Dugout* 3, no. 2 (June 1995): 15- 20.

19. Jonathan Tobin, "Big League Jews: Scouting the All-Time Jewish Baseball All-Stars," "*Jewish World Review*, April 16 2001, June 2003 <*www.jewishworldreview.com*>.

20. Wallman, "Big League Jews," 5.

21. Solomon, "Jews, Baseball and the American Novel," 46.

22. Peter Levine quotes Kling's wife and her claim that Kling was a Lutheran from a letter she wrote. See Mrs. John G Kling, Kansas City, to Lee Allen, letter, 12 February, 1969. Johnny Kling clipping file, A. Bartlett Giamatti Research Center, National Baseball Hall of Fame, Cooperstown, New York. It should be noted, however, that Mrs. Kling had written to clarify this previously, and in the other letter in the file, dated, 2 December 1948, she stated that Kling was a Baptist. .

23. Gerald Eskenazi, "Carew Plans to Convert to Judaism," n.d. Rod Carew clipping file, A. Bartlett Giamatti Research Center, National Baseball Hall of Fame, Cooperstown, New York.

24. Michael Elkin, "Baseball's Most Valuable Player and Judaism," *Jewish Digest* 23 (February 1978): 19.

25. "Rod Carew," *www.Jewhoo.Com*, 1999, June 2003.

26. Bjarkman, "Six-Pointed Diamonds and the Ultimate Shiksa: Baseball and the American-Jewish Immigrant Experience," 318.

27. Lynn, *The Jewish Baseball Hall of Fame: A Who's Who of Baseball Stars*, intro.

28. Terry Mattingly, *Reading the Sporting Jews*. 25 April 2001, 03 June 2003 <*http://tmatt.gospelcom.net/column/2001/04/25/*>.

29. Spaner, "From Greenberg to Green: Jewish Ballplayers," 172.

30. Horvitz, *The Big Book of Jewish Baseball*, intro.

31. Jacob Traub, "Reform Movement Trying to Play Baseball with 4 Outs," *Jewish Bulletin*, 23 January 1998, 102.4, 25.

32. Dan Daniel, 24 October 1935. Charles Myer clipping file, A. Bartlett Giamatti Research Center, National Baseball Hall of Fame, Cooperstown, New York.

33. Tobin, "Big League Jews: Scouting the All-Time Jewish Baseball All-Stars."

34. *"Mike Lieberthal."* April 2003 <*www.jewhoo.com*>.

35. Molly, *All Things Jewish: Popular Destinations for Jewish Major-Leaguers*. 2002, 03 June 2003 <*http://www.shawngreen.net*>.

36. Wallman, "Big League Jews," 7.

Constructing the Cuban Pipeline: Papa Joe Cambria Brings the Cubans to Williamsport, Pennsylvania, 1944 to 1945

James P. Quigel, Jr.

Shortages and rationing shaped American life and culture during the World War II era, and no shortage was more acute than that of professional baseball players during the war years. Many baseball players, from stars to bush leaguers, enlisted or were drafted into the armed services. Some players, classified as 2-B by the United States Selective Service, toiled in vital war industries where overtime wages could exceed salaries paid by parsimonious owners of baseball clubs— especially at the minor league level. Those declared physically unfit for military service (4-F), but able to run, throw, and hit, were prized commodities as baseball team owners struggled to fill roster spots depleted by the war. Due to the players' shortage, major league teams fielded sub-par talent and suffered accordingly on the field and at the gate.[1]

Organized Baseball's economic crisis hit the minor leagues especially hard during the war years. Prohibitive transportation costs owing to gas rationing and restricted rail service, limitations (blackouts) on night baseball to conserve electric power, and the shrinking players' pool forced many minor league team owners to suspend operations. At the close of the 1943 season, the National Association of Professional Baseball Leagues (NAPBL) reported that fifteen affiliated leagues had suspended operations—leaving only nine surviving minor league circuits to operate for the 1944 season. Baseball journalists conjectured whether professional baseball could survive wartime economic sanctions, and the propriety of operating Organized Baseball as war raged on. Rather than suspend the national pastime, President

Franklin D. Roosevelt issued his famous "Green Light" letter to the Commissioner of Baseball, Judge Kennesaw Mountain Landis, and encouraged the playing of baseball to boost morale on the home front. FDR commended America's game as a vital part of the war-time effort.[2]

To address baseball's manpower shortage, major league club owners adopted novel solutions to leverage the player pool. None was more resourceful, or penurious, than the Washington Senators' legendary owner Clark Griffith. Once a proud franchise and heir to the legacy of Hall of Fame Pitcher Walter "The Big Train" Johnson, the Senators had fallen on hard times in the late 1930s and early 1940s. A celebrated stage wisecrack found its way into American popular culture: "Washington — First in War, First in Peace, Last in the American League."[3] To address his organization's player shortage at all levels, Griffith cast a covetous eye toward the Caribbean Basin — specifically to Cuba. He was no stranger to the importation of Cuban baseball talent. As the young manager of the Cincinnati Reds in 1911, Griffith signed the first Cuban players to play in the major leagues — third baseman Rafael Almeida and outfielder Armando Marsans.[4]

Much of this Cuban baseball talent, however, lay beyond the reach of major league clubs due to the great racial divide and organized baseball's adherence to Jim Crow. Though black Cuban baseball players remained off-limits, promising white Cuban amateur and professional prospects could be signed on the cheap. Griffith wanted to secure a firm scouting foothold on the island. By no means an integrationist, he was a shrewd baseball businessman who hedged whichever way the racial winds were blowing before Major League Baseball embarked on integration in 1947. In Griffith's mind, signing Cuban players of lighter and mixed-skin color was preferable to the employment of Negro League stars in Washington Senators uniforms. Washington was, after all, a Southern city.[5]

The crucial link between Washington and Cuba, and by extension Washington and Williamsport, was a minor league impresario and self-proclaimed "super scout," Joe Cambria.

An Italian immigrant, Cambria operated a lucrative commercial laundry business in Baltimore during the 1920s, earning the monikers "Laundryman Joe" and "Wet Wash Joe." He and his brother John also invested in the ownership of the National Negro League's Baltimore Black Sox in 1933. Presumably, his players had shared their experiences playing in Cuba against seasoned professional ball players — both black and white. Leaving his brother to manage their minor league interests, Joe Cambria ingratiated himself to Clark Griffith and moonlighted as a roving scout for the Senators. Cuba became Cambria's primary beat and he established a "bird dog" scouting network to tap into the rich baseball talent from the Cuban amateur and professional leagues. Beginning in the mid-1930s, Cambria constructed and operated the "Cuban Pipeline" that led to thirty-one native Cuban players appearing in a Washington Senators uniform between 1935 and 1960. Seventy more Cubans, signed by Cambria, toiled in the Senators minor league system without reaching the big leagues during that same twenty-five year period.[6]

The colorful and charismatic Cambria became a legend on the pro baseball scouting circuit, garnering a reputation for his unorthodox methods and ability to discover baseball talent in unusual locales. Some of his signings were highly controversial and bordered on the novelty — such as tendering a contract to one pitching prospect (Allen W. Benson) from the barnstorming House of David team, and signing a former Sing Sing Prison inmate, Edwin (Alabama) Pitts, to the Class AA Albany Senators, an Eastern League team owned by the Cambria brothers.[7]

Cambria's legacy is subject to scrutiny. Though largely responsible for the "Cuban Baseball Invasion," his wholesale approach in signing the youngest Cuban prospects gutted the Cuban amateur league. For every bona fide prospect signed, other less-talented players languished in the lower echelons of the minors. Younger and marginal Cuban baseball players faced overwhelming odds in their climb up the Washington Senators' farm chain.

Cuban baseball historian Roberto González Echevarría noted that Cambria's "profit lay in quantity, not quality." Columnist Robert Considine, writing for *Collier's Magazine,* accused Cambria of "going ivory hunting in Cuba" — a reference to "Wet Wash Joe's" search for white Cuban baseball talent.[8] Washington Senators' historian Morris A. Bealle observed that "Joey-the Laundryman hadn't done so badly, and would do even better if he could get over his predilections for signing *Cubanolas.*"[9] Lured by the promise of lucrative pay and big league glamour, the Cuban players confronted a different reality once in America. Considine described their unenviable lot in the minor leagues:

> They get bean balls thrown at their heads by closed-shop (and closed-brained) rivals. They face pitchers who willingly throw away their arms bearing down on them in an effort to escape the "ignominy" of yielding a hit to them. They get a measure of grass-singeing abuse from the "jockeys" on the enemy bench. From their own team they get rock-bottom pay, and from many of their own teammates they get a wintry ostracism. Those who want to befriend them are halted by the differences in languages.[10]

On the eve of the 1944 season, Cambria and Griffith stockpiled the Washington ball club with at least thirty-nine Latin American ball players — all Cuban with the exception of one Venezuelan player.[11] Two considerations then came into play that nearly thwarted their master plan. In early April, the United States Selective Service ordered the Cubans to register for the

Army draft by June 12, 1944, or face deportation. Many of the Senators' Cuban players, especially those with families to support, indicated they would not play ball and planned to return to Cuba before opening day. Third baseman Luis Suárez and outfielder Roberto Ortiz, potential starters for the Senators, were among this group. Although the Selective Service ruling cast a pall over the 1944 season, Griffith and Cambria convinced a sufficient number of Cubans to remain in the United States and cast their fate with the draft board — averting a disaster for the Senators.[12]

A second stumbling block involved the question of where to assign the new Cuban prospects. Washington ticketed the more advanced and polished Cuban professionals to Chattanooga of the Class AA Southern Association, but the Senators had no working agreement with a lower-level Class A franchise to which to assign the younger Cubans — many of whom were fresh from the Cuban amateur league. Where the younger prospects would be assigned was crucial not only for their development as professional ball players, but also for their acculturation and adjustment to American life. The Cambria brothers owned controlling interest in the Springfield, Massachusetts team of the Class A Eastern League (EL). A dismal financial season in 1943 forced them to relocate to another city.[13]

In early January 1944, the Cambrias approached EL president Tommy Richardson to discuss new sites.[14] Richardson, a celebrity baseball humorist and owner of a Williamsport, Pennsylvania Buick dealership, had been a prominent baseball booster in his hometown since the early 1930s. Before his election to the presidency of the EL in 1939, he served as a business manager and publicist for the Williamsport Grays. The Grays had enjoyed a long association with the Philadelphia Athletics, but suspended baseball operations in 1943 due to the financial crunch and shortage of players. Richardson wanted to return Class A baseball to his hometown. He also perceived a potential marketing opportunity in affiliating with Washington to promote the Cubans as the best road attraction on the EL circuit.[15] The Cambria brothers needed to find a home for Griffith's Cubans.[16]

After a month of negotiations involving the Cambrias, Griffith, Richardson, and the Williamsport Community Baseball Association, the Senators signed a working agreement with the Grays on April 7, 1944. Williamsport became the primary baseball haven for Griffith's unique player development program. Bealle summed it up best: "Clark Griffith had signed so many Cubans that he had to establish a special farm for them in Williamsport."[17]

In early April 1944, the Williamsport Grays assembled a squad of 23 players — sixteen of them were Cuban — for spring training in College Park, Maryland. With less then three weeks to prepare for opening day, the Grays' new manager, Ray Kolp, received a "crash course" in Spanish and went about the task of meshing the Cuban and American players. His patience would sorely be tested during his two-year tenure as manager of Williamsport's Cuban teams from 1944 to 1945.[18]

Arriving in Williamsport in early May, the young Cuban players had a short period of time to adjust to the colder spring climate of north-central Pennsylvania. This disadvantage was mitigated by the early-season advantage the Cubans enjoyed after playing winter league ball in their native Cuba. Over the course of two seasons the pattern became clear. The "Cuban Grays" jumped out to a quick start, but faded in the "dog days of summer" when the rest of the Eastern League caught up.[19] Louis Pickelner, sports editor for the *Williamsport Gazette and Bulletin,* believed that they simply wore down as the long season progressed. By his estimation, the Cubans played close to two hundred games a year—factoring in the Cuban winter league season, exhibition games and barnstorming, and Caribbean tournament play. Pickelner wrote: "Fast starters and slow finishers, Cuban ball players will wind up on baseball's ash pile in the United States if they insist on continuing to play Winter Ball on their home island ... that is the consensus of opinion of a number of baseball experts." He failed to mention that the Cubans needed to play year-round to earn enough money to support themselves and their families.[20]

The biggest challenges the Cubans faced were off the field — adjusting to a new language, a foreign culture, and the reaction of the fans, both at home and away. The Cuban prospects assigned to Williamsport were relatively isolated from the community. But they had the advantage of comprising a majority of the team's members, and were billeted as a group five miles outside the city at the Haleeka camp grounds.[21] It is not clear if management's decision to house the Cubans at Haleeka was designed to prevent the isolation of individual Cuban players, or to sequester the team as a whole from contact with the public. American members of the Grays were free to arrange their own living quarters within the city. The Grays hired an interpreter/trainer to assist the Cubans with the English language and ease their transition to life in Williamsport.[22]

By all accounts, written and oral, the Cuban players were generally well-received by the Williamsport community, and in turn, conducted themselves well in public. During their two seasons in Williamsport, the Cubans often convened at the Lycoming Hotel, or one of Williamsport's many Italian restaurants to celebrate victory with dinner, drinks, and camaraderie.[23] My father, as a young boy, related that the Cubans often hiked back from center city to the camp grounds following games and a night on the town. He fondly recalled their joyful singing and boisterous laughter as they walked along North Route 15 near his old family home by the Lycoming Creek. Such fellowship and song surely provided a buffer against the periodic homesickness and loneliness the Cubans must have felt.[24]

Dorothy Parsons, long an avid Grays fan and one of the few women to sit in on the Williamsport baseball management sessions, remembered the players as young and well-behaved. Their hustling and energetic spirit endeared them to local fans, especially the city's female fandom. Parsons recalled that the Cubans were "young and cute," and elicited both maternal instincts and mild flirtations from Williamsport's "bobbysoxers."[25] She was impressed with their curiosity about American culture and willingness to learn a few English phrases in order to communicate with Williamsport residents. Parsons also remembered that the Cubans were subject to prejudice outside the ballpark. She recalled one incident involving EL president Tommy Richardson and a Cuban player:

> Well, you know us girls used to like to get together ... socialize, and go downtown for a drink now and then. There was this one young Cuban ball player who used to walk downtown with an open English dictionary in his hand. And he would stop to talk to us girls and try to learn a few words of English, just to get by. We admired him for that because he didn't just want to live here [Williamsport] and not communicate with the people. Well, one day Tommy [Richardson] came up to us as we were talking to the Cuban player and he yelled at him "You stay away from these girls ... you are not supposed to associate with these girls ... leave these girls alone. You girls stay away from these players ... they are no good." Now that is what I learned to hate about Tommy Richardson. Oh my, of all the stupid things for him [Richardson] to say. These kids were so cute and tried so hard. Can you imagine that ... to be that prejudiced.[26]

On the field, Williamsport's fans had never seen anything like the Cubans before. League beat writers dubbed them "The Rumba Rascals," "The Laughing Latins," or simply "The Williamsport Canebrakes," indicative of the stereotyping of Latin Americans prevalent among sportswriters of the era and the public at large.[27] Al Decker, former sports editor of *The Grit,* noted that their "constant chatter, blazing speed, and defensive athleticism set them apart from the other EL teams." He recalled that the Williamsport Cuban teams of 1944–1945 lacked a legitimate power hitter. The Cubans played what baseball purists labeled the "inside game," winning by bunting, advancing runners one base at a time, stealing bases, and using hustle and speed to force defensive errors by the opposition. Their erratic play and daring on the base paths often exasperated Kolp to the point of "hitting the bottle." Following a defensive or base running blunder by the Cubans in one game, Decker witnessed Kolp retiring to the back of the clubhouse between innings and imbibing from a flask concealed in his warm-up jacket.[28]

Kolp's tirades against Cuban players were well worth the price of admission. Fans howled in delight when the veteran skipper "dressed down" a Cuban player in front of the home dugout, his eyes bulging and head and shoulders twisted in all manner of contortions. Invariably, the poor Cuban ball player would "blink and nod ... and utter *"Sí Señor Kolp,"* and return to the end of the home bench — only to break out in laughter with his compatriots.[29]

The 1944 Williamsport Grays broke out of the EL starting gate early, and played above .500 ball for the first half of the season. The team was anchored by its speedy and athletic centerfielder, José Antonio "Tony" Zardón, dubbed "Speed Zardón," "The Canebrake Comet," and "The Havana Fleet Fly Hawk." Zardón possessed modest power, but led the league in doubles and triples well into the season until injuries and bean balls forced him to miss many games. A gap ball hitter, he caused major problems for opposing outfielders by stretching singles into doubles, and doubles into triples.[30] In a double-header against the Hartford Laurels on May 21, 1944, Zardón stole four bases, including two steals of home plate. At mid-season, he had racked up twenty-six stolen bases, including six swipes of home.[31] But Zardón also possessed a volatile temper that not only impacted his performance as a ballplayer, but also incited Williamsport fans to shower umpires and opposing players with bottles and debris following his demonstrative antics on the diamond. In one incident, Zardón, after an unsuccessful attempt to steal home, attacked a Wilkes-Barre pitcher with a baseball bat. He might have been suspended for the remainder of the year but for the quick intervention of teammate Juan Hernández, who tackled him before he reached the pitcher. Though the local press did not condone Zardón's violent behavior, they rationalized his anger as pent-up frustration with the Cubans being convenient targets for escalating ethnic taunts and "purpose pitches."[32]

The Grays remained in playoff contention until Zardón sustained an ankle injury and concussion that forced him out of the lineup for much of August. He still finished with a respectable .294 batting average and stole 33 bases. Four consecutive double-header losses in late August dropped the Grays out of the first division and they eventually fell to a fifth-place finish with a record of 64–75.[33]

In addition to Zardón, the 1944 Grays were paced by other outstanding Cuban players. While few advanced to the major leagues, several had respectable careers in the Cuban professional leagues and played for Cuban teams in the Caribbean (Latin American) Series. Francisco "Sojito" Gallardo, the Grays' sure-handed second baseman, epitomized the dashing and entertaining play of the Cubans. One of the most popular players during the "Cuban Seasons," he impressed fans and his teammates with his quick and acrobatic turning of double plays. Louis Pickelner labeled Gallardo "the slickest Keystone guardian of the Eastern League."[34] In early August, however, Gallardo informed management that he needed to return to Cuba to tend to his wife and child. His departure left a gaping hole in the Gray's middle infield; even manager Kolp acknowledged the team's inability to turn double plays after Gallardo left.[35] Besides his stellar defense, Gallardo finished second on the team in batting with an average of .283 and even slugged a few homers despite his bantam size. In the late 1940s, Gallardo played professional baseball in Cuba as a reserve infielder for the legendary Almendares Blues and participated in his team's historic rivalry with the Habana Reds.[36]

Two other Cuban Grays made their mark in Williamsport in 1944. Daniel Parra, a slightly-build left-hander with a nasty curveball and deceptive change-up, led the team in pitching with a 14–9 record. He played a key role in Williamsport's tumultuous 1945 season, highlighted by brawls with the hated Utica Blue Sox. Before his two-year stint in Williamsport, Parra pitched for Club Fortuna, a premier team in the Cuban amateur league. He later returned to Cuba to play professionally for Almendares.[37] Catcher Rogelio Valdés, Parra's battery mate, played solid defense and provided power to complement the Grays' speed. But he also departed for Cuba in early August, ostensibly to avoid the U.S. Selective Service.[38]

In hardscrabble towns like Scranton, Wilkes-Barre, and Utica, the Cubans confronted bigots and ethnic taunts from the grandstands, engaged in brawls with opposing teams, and suffered from a steady diet of "dusters." This baseball "reign of terror" was not just a conspiracy theory concocted by the hometown press. Scranton's "Chick" Feldman, dean of the EL sportswriters, wrote:

> It grieves me to report that some Eastern League players and even some managers went out of their way to abuse the Cuban kids.... This blind hate may have been responsible for Williamsport's failure to crash the first division in 1944. It would be a hard allegation to prove, yet there was talk in reliable circles that the other clubs 'ganged up' on Williamsport. Yes, even saving their best pitchers to toss at the once-laughing Latins.[39]

Unfortunately, these allegations and rumors were later confirmed during the course of the 1945 EL season — dubbed the "Summer of Fisticuffs" by league sportswriters.

The Grays entered 1945 without the services of speedster Zardón who was initially assigned to Chattanooga, but later called-up by the Senators. Catcher Rogelio Valdés joined him in Washington for a brief period after splitting the bulk of the season between Williamsport and Chattanooga.[40] A big bonus for the team was the return of Gallardo and pitching ace Parra. Cambria also signed additional Cuban players who later became the nucleus of "Kolp's Kiddy Corps." They included pitcher Leonardo Goicochea, a fierce competitor with an intimidating fastball. Goicochea's penchant for pitching high and tight to hitters earned him his Spanish nickname *"Guillotina,"* or Guillotine. Other stellar players included a slick-fielding shortstop, Manuel *"Chino"* Hidalgo, whose Chinese ancestors had immigrated to Cuba to labor in the sugar cane fields.[41] Cambria also discovered and signed a seventeen year-old pitching sensation, Fernando *"Trompoloco"* Rodríguez, whose moniker derived from his spinning-top pitching delivery. [42]

Hidalgo and Gallardo were by-far the best double-play combination in the Eastern League in 1945, and arguably the best in Williamsport's baseball history. At the end of the EL season, Hidalgo returned to Cuba to play for the Habana Reds in the Cuban professional league. He was a member of Habana's 1948 championship ball club and also played on the Reds team that captured the 1952 Caribbean Series Championship for Cuba. Hidalgo was later inducted into the Cuban Hall of Fame in Miami, Florida in 1997.[43] A new first baseman, Héctor Aragó, and a catcher, Mario Díaz, provided additional offensive support to compensate for the loss of Zardón. Aragó played for Almendares in the Cuban professional league from 1944 to 1946, and later joined many of his ex-Williamsport teammates with the Havana Cubans (1946–1947) of the Class B Florida International League.[44]

Despite new talent, the 1945 Grays sank to the bottom of the standings by mid-season and never recovered. The frequency of double-headers, owing to rainouts and a compacted schedule to reduce travel, played havoc with the Grays threadbare pitching staff.[45] The team's lack of focus, evident in defensive and base-running errors, did not escape the notice of the press. Williamsport baseball writers chided the Grays for their poor performance on the ball diamond and specifically targeted the Cubans. One local sports scribe offered this assessment: "The way the Williamsport Grays are playing ball a lot of them will be cutting sugar cane next summer instead of going through the pretenses of being ball players."[46]

The Grays' precipitous slide coincided with the increased hostility and bigotry the team encountered in other EL cities. Beginning in July and extending well into August 1945, the Grays became mired in several baseball brawls with opposing teams and fans described as "near riots" by the press. [47] The most serious of these escalating incidents involved Williamsport's rivalry with the Utica Blue Sox, a farm club of the Philadelphia Phillies that produced several future members of the 1950 National League pennant-winning "Whiz Kids," including Richie Ashburn, Granny Hamner, and Putsee Caballero. The Blue Sox also had a tobacco-spewing bigot by the name of Cecil "Turkey" Tyson. Tyson's specialty was ethnic-baiting and provoking fights with opposing teams. Throughout the long season, the Utica first baseman directed his choicest barbs and epithets at the Williamsport Cubans.[48]

Things came to a head on July 8th at Williamsport's Bowman Field. Grays' pitcher Leonardo Goicochea sent Tyson sprawling to the ground with a deliberate brush-back pitch. Whipped into frenzy, Williamsport fans serenaded Tyson with the "Turkey Call," a derisive cacophony of gobbling that reverberated from the stands. This goaded Tyson to take menacing steps toward the mound with a bat in hand before the plate umpire intervened to

prevent the bludgeoning of Goicochea. Surprisingly, neither player was immediately ejected. Play resumed with Goicochea striking out Tyson to end the
inning. Tyson, however, went directly for the Cuban pitcher, setting off a
bench-clearing donnybrook that also involved Williamsport fans pouring out
of the stands before city police quelled the "riot." EL's president Tommy
Richardson levied fifty-dollar fines and three-day suspensions on Tyson and
Goicochea, and lesser punishment to their teammates. [49]

One disturbing footnote to the July 8th brawl was the fight between
Williamsport teammates, reserve infielder Héctor Aragó and first baseman
Bill Schaedler, in full view near the Grays' dugout. Although an under-card
to the main bout, the Aragó-Schaedler fight had a more deleterious impact
upon team morale. Described as a "private scrap," this fracas signified that
the Grays had come unglued, and that ethnic tension divided the Williamsport
clubhouse into two camps— the Cubans against their American teammates. [50]
On July 11th, Aragó and Schaedler renewed their pugilistic display prior to a
game with the Binghamton Triplets. Aragó precipitated the second fight by
criticizing Schaedler's poor work ethic and absence from practice owing to
an alleged injury. Schaedler responded by punching Aragó in the nose. Aragó
had to be restrained by his Cuban teammates when he attempted to grab a
bat to hit his assailant. The fight brought immediate reprisal as the Grays'
management released Schaedler outright. Sportswriter Louis Pickelner aptly
summed up the fight: "Aragó told Schaedler he was saffron-hued because he
disdained a practice session ... the net results ... one sore nose, one gone first
baseman, and a bunch of lost games."[51] He viewed the recent fistic outbreak
as a serious matter, and not the standard "showing off for the bobby soxers."
Schaedler's dismissal was a forgone conclusion because "... nothing can be
done by segregating the players into two groups," a direct reference to the
ethnic tension permeating the Grays' clubhouse.[52]

Fines and suspensions did not quell the desire for retribution as the
Utica-Williamsport rivalry played out to its ugly conclusion in the later stages
of the 1945 season. The Blue Sox were among the league leaders and enjoyed
the luxury of goading the Cubans to the point of breaking their concentration on the playing field. The final straw came on July 16, 1945, in a game in
Utica when Tyson went after another Grays' pitcher, Daniel Parra. By all
accounts, Parra stood his ground, verbally and physically, before the Utica
constabulary restored order. Following the customary round of fines and suspensions— this time Tyson received an unprecedented fifteen-day suspension
from Richardson — things finally settled down for the Grays.[53] The constant
fan abuse on the road and internal fighting, however, had finally worn the
Cubans down. Pickelner weighed in with his opinion: "The damage Tyson
inflicted on the Williamsport club is beyond estimation ... the Grays haven't
been the same since their contact with 'the Turkey' and their disastrous July

debacle can be traced directly to his Cuban-baiting."[54] They finished out the season with the dismal record of 52–85, a record fifty-two games behind the hated Utica Blue Sox. However there were a few bright spots for the 1945 Grays. Chino Hidalgo batted .307 and was named to the Eastern League All-Star team. Héctor Aragó—when he wasn't punching Bill Schaedler—hit .298, and Daniel Parra led the Grays' pitching staff with a respectable record of 16–14.[55]

The tumultuous Cuban seasons came to an end in 1945. Griffith and the Cambria brothers had grown weary with the level of hostility exhibited towards Williamsport's Cuban players throughout the EL circuit. More importantly, they harbored resentment towards league officials for their failure to discipline team owners and curb fan abuse. As a result, they decided not to renew the Senators' affiliation agreement with the Williamsport Grays. But the "Cuban Experiment" would continue in other minor league outposts the following year—chiefly Chattanooga, Tennessee and Havana's new entry, the Havana Cubans, in the Class B Florida International League.[56]

In early 1946, Williamsport signed a new working agreement with the Detroit Tigers and embarked on a new era. The colorful cast of Cuban Grays faded into distant memory. Within five years, the Senators' farm chain began churning out many new Cuban players— Pedro "Pistol Pete" Ramos, Conrado Marrero, Sandalio Consuegra, and Camilo Pascual — who later became recognizable names to many Washington Senators' fans. Williamsport could at least boast that four players associated with its own Cuban era—José Zardón, Rogelio Valdés, Fernando Rodríquez, and Héctor Aragó—made it to the big leagues, if only briefly. Other Cuban players returned home to establish successful careers in the Cuban professional league, or continue their minor league sojourn with the Havana Cubans in the Florida International League from 1946 to the early 1950s.

One Williamsport sports commentator provided a fitting capstone to the Grays' Cuban era:

> The coming of the Cubans to Williamsport was a war time measure, and there is no intention that it be a long-term policy. You may remember that Williamsport got out of the league, and then suddenly we wanted to get back in, we had no players, no uniforms, no nuthin! John Cambria filled in the void by promising to get us a team of Latins, and while the club has had its ups and downs, they have done pretty well ... the Canebrake Kids surely have 'upped' the gate receipts at every ballpark in the league.[57]

Though their time was brief in Williamsport, the Cuban baseball players left an indelible impression upon local fans. Their experiences and hardships in adjusting to a foreign culture, and encountering prejudice and attitudes approaching racism, reveal how formidable and entrenched intolerance was in American society. Moreover, the Williamsport community's interaction with the Cubans was a microcosm of America's complex ethnic struggles and racial attitudes on the eve of Organized Baseball's great integration initiative. Williamsport can rightfully claim that it played a part in providing a more receptive social environment for the acceptance of Cuban players during the pre-integration era of baseball, and contributed to multiculturalism and the eventual integration of Latin American players into the mainstream of American baseball culture.

Notes

1. Richard Goldstein, *Spartan Seasons: How Baseball Survived the Second World War* (New York: Macmillan Publishing Co., 1980), 3–28; David Quentin Voigt, *American Baseball*, vol. 2, *From the Commissioners to Continental Expansion* (Norman, Oklahoma: University of Oklahoma Press, 1970; University Park, Pennsylvania: The Pennsylvania State University Press, 1992), 255–59; David Finoli, *For the Good of the Country: World War II Baseball in the Major and Minor Leagues* (Jefferson, North Carolina: McFarland & Company, 2002), 142–43; Geoffrey C. Ward and Ken Burns, *Baseball: An Illustrated History* (New York: Alfred A. Knopf, 1994), 275–79.

2. National Association of Professional Baseball Leagues, *The Story of Minor League Baseball, 1901–1952: A History of the Game of Professional Baseball in the United States With Particular Reference to Its Growth and Development in the Smaller Cities and Towns of the Nation — The Minor Leagues* (Columbus, Ohio: The Stoneman Press, 1953), 44–46; Daniel M. Day, "Roosevelt Saved Baseball With His 1942 Letter to Judge Landis," *Baseball Magazine* 75 (June 1945): 227–29. The importance of the national pastime in boosting the morale of servicemen abroad was evident in the formation of highly competitive fleet and base teams by the service branches during World War II. These military leagues and barnstorming teams included many major league stars. For a comprehensive history of baseball within the armed services during World War II, see Steve R. Bullock, *Playing for Their Nation: Baseball and the American Military during World War II* (Lincoln, N.E.: University of Nebraska Press, 2004).

3. Morris A. Bealle, *The Washington Senators: An 87-year History of the World's Oldest Baseball Club and Most Incurable Fandom* (Washington, D.C.: Columbia Publishing Co., 1947), 3.

4. Collie Small, "Baseball's Improbable Imports," *Saturday Evening Post*, 2 August 1953, 29; Mark Rucker and Peter C. Bjarkman, *Smoke: The Romance and Lore of Cuban Baseball* (Kingston, New York: Total/Sports Illustrated, 1999), 41–45; Brad Snyder, *Beyond the Shadow of the Senators: The Untold Story of the Homestead Grays and the Integration of Baseball* (New York: McGraw-Hill, 2003), 66.

5. Snyder, 68–76; A comparative study of American and Cuban racial, ethnic, and cultural perspectives is crucial to understanding how social integration in baseball played out in both societies. The most authoritative study on the dynamics of race, ethnicity, and class and the history of Cuban baseball is Roberto González Echevarría, *The Pride of Havana: A History of Cuban Baseball* (New York: Oxford University Press, 1999). For a discussion of the thesis that darker-skinned Cuban ballplayers— Rafael Almeida, Armando Marsans, Jacinto "Jack" Calvo, José Acosto, Mérito Acosta,and Tomás de la Cruz — pioneered racial integration in baseball before the signing of Jackie Robinson, see Peter C. Bjarkman, *Baseball with a Latin Beat: A History of the Latin American Game* (Jefferson, North Carolina: McFarland & Company, 1994), 194–205.

6. The number of Cuban players signed by Joe Cambria for the Washington Senators varies by account. A large majority of Cambria's Cubans ended their respective careers in the lower-level minor leagues. Citing a 1945 article by a Cuban sports journalist, Jess Losada, which appeared in the magazine *Carteles*, Echevarría places the number at seventy-three —

though one player was the Venezuelan pitcher, Alejandro Carrasquel. As Cambria often employed dubious methods to induce young Cubans to sign away their amateur status—using blank contracts—it is very hard to get an accurate and reliable figure for the number of players he is credited with signing. See González Echevarría, 268–70; Bjarkman, 200; Rucker and Bjarkman, 152–56; Collie Small, writing for the *Saturday Evening Post* in 1952, reported that the Senators had forty-nine Cuban players under contract, dispersed throughout Washington's minor league farm system. See Small, 29.

7. Snyder, 73–74. Cambria was at the center of the Pitts Case. Commissioner Landis moved to ban Pitts from organized baseball, perceiving his signing by Cambria as a publicity stunt to bolster attendance at Albany. Clark Griffith interceded on Cambria's behalf and convinced Landis to rescind the ban on Pitts. The matter was moot, however, as Pitts failed as a player in the International League. See Bealle, 152–53.

8. Robert Considine, "Ivory from Cuba," *Collier's*, 3 August 1940, 19; Echevarría, 269.

9. Bealle, 162.

10. Considine, 19; For an account of ethnic and race-baiting within the Washington Senators' clubhouse, see "Cuban Ball Players On Washington Senators Snubbed By Own Team Mates," *Pittsburgh Courier*, 8 June 1940, 16; This article was excerpted from a piece written by Rob Ruark for the *Washington Daily News*, 6 June 1940. Ruark reported that Washington manager Bucky Harris had a visible disdain for the Cubans and referred to them as "trash," even going further to state, "If I have to put up with incompetents, they must at least speak English."

11 "A Little Something Extra," *Williamsport Gazette and Bulletin*, 11 April 1944, 2 (hereafter cited as *WG&B*); Bealle, 170–71; Snyder, 71–72;

12 The status of the Cubans as draft fodder for the United States Selective Service during World War II remains a topic ripe for scholarly research by baseball and social historians. In May 1944, the United States Selective Service declared the Cubans "non-resident aliens" and issued them six-month visas—in effect, granting immunity from the draft. However, in July 1944, the Department re-defined the Cubans' status as "resident aliens," subject to the draft if they chose to play the entire baseball season. The specter of the draft forced several Cuban players on the Senators and Williamsport Grays to leave before the end of the season, though many cited other reasons for returning to Cuba. See Goldstein, 189–90; "Cubans Ordered To Register for Draft or Return," *WG&B*, 10 April 1944, 4; "Selective Service Rules Cubans Eligible for Draft—Most of Cubans on Washington Roster to Leave," *WG&B*, 11 April 1944, 2; "Griffith Not Alarmed by Selective Service Ruling—Boss of Senators Says Grays Will Not be Affected," *WG&B*, 12 April 1944, 2; "Cuban Ball Players May Have to Register," *WG&B*, 17 July 1944, 9; William B. Mead, *Even the Browns: The Zany True Story of Baseball in the Early Forties* (Chicago: Contemporary Books Inc., 1978), 229.

13. "A Little Something Extra," *WG&B*, 11 April, 1944, 2; Synder, 73. In his history of the Washington Senators, Bealle noted, "All the Cubans excepting ...Guerra, Torres, and Ulrich, were sent to Williamsport in the New York-Pennsylvania League [Eastern League], more to get rid of them than for development." Throughout the 1944 season, a constant stream of players moved back and forth between the Chattanooga Lookouts and Williamsport Grays, particularly between April and early May when rosters were being pared for the beginning of the season. See Bealle, 171.

14. "Cambria Willing to Bring Franchise Here—Offers City Inside Track to E.L. Club," *WG&B*, 5 January 1944, 6; "Eastern League Meeting Called for February 6—League to Continue," *WG&B*, 28 January 1944, 10.

15. James P. Quigel Jr. and Louis E. Hunsinger Jr., *Gateway to the Majors: Williamsport and Minor League Baseball* (University Park, Pennsylvania: The Pennsylvania State University Press, 2001), 57–61.

16. "Mass Meeting of Baseball Fans Thursday—Rally Called to Rush Action on Baseball Plans," *WG&B*, 8 March 1944, 2; "Decision Made to Buy Eastern Loop Franchise—Williamsport Returns to Eastern League," *WG&B*, 10 March 1944, 1, 12. Richardson's marketing instincts proved correct. In a 1945 recap of the previous season the *WG&B* reported: "The ever-chattering Ohioan [Manager Kolp] and his trackmen, while failing by an eyelash to make the Governor's Cup set, salvaged the accolade as the best road attraction in the circuit." See "Lightning Latins Apt to Surprise E.L. Foes Again," *WG&B*, 2 May 1945, 4.

17. "Local Group, John Cambria Complete Negotiations—Agreement is Reached for 3-Year Period," *WG&B*, 7 April 1944, 4; Bealle, 163.

18. "Ray Kolp Selected As Manager of Local Ball Club," *WG&B*, 18 April 1944, 6; "Grays Slated to Undergo First Test on Friday," *WG&B*, 27 April 1944, 6; Quigel and Hunsinger, 115.

19. Journalists of the era commented on the Cubans' tough adjustment to cold weather and night baseball in America. Ossie Bluege, the Senators' farm director in the early 1950s, offered this prescription to the organization's minor league managers : "Keep the Cubans bundled and pray for warm weather." See Small, 28; Al Decker Oral History Interview, interview conducted by the author and Louis E. Hunsinger Jr., 27 January 1992, Williamsport Baseball Oral History Collection, audiotape cassette recording in the possession of the author (hereafter cited as Al Decker Oral History Interview).

20. See Louis Pickelner "A Little Extra — Answer to Riddle," *WG&B*, 13 September 1945, 6.

21. The younger Cuban baseball players tended to stick together as a group, on and off the field. For a first-hand account of the socialization process for Cuban baseball players, see Preston Gomez's recollections in Goldstein, 189–191; James P. Quigel, Sr., conversation with the author, 12 August 1992 (hereafter cited as James P. Quigel Sr., Reminiscence). There is no paper documentation regarding the exact location of the housing quarters for the Cubans who played in Williamsport. Several interviewees for our Williamsport Baseball Oral History Project recalled that the Haleeka area — at one time a motel and camp grounds— was the site where the Cubans were housed for the season. None could recall the Cubans securing apartments or boarding room within the city limits.

22. John Cambria appointed a trusted associate, Ted Laviano, to serve as business manager for the Williamsport Grays. Originally hired to handle the Cambrias' legal affairs, Laviano managed their minor league baseball interests. Fluent in Spanish, he served as the team interpreter. Laviano's younger brother, Julie, was signed as a reserve catcher for the Grays in 1944 and also assisted the Cubans with their English. See "Teddy Laviano, Business Manager Of the Williamsport Grays, Has A Very Interesting Life, *Williamsport Sun* (hereafter cited as *WS*), 18 August 1944, 15.

23. Al Decker Oral History Interview.

24. James P. Quigel Sr., Reminiscence.

25. Dorothy Parson Oral History Interview, interview conducted by the author and Louis E. Hunsinger, Jr., 21 February 1992, Williamsport Baseball Oral History Collection, audiotape cassette recording in the possession of the author.

26. *Ibid.*

27. Louis Pickelner, Sports Editor for the *Williamsport Gazette and Bulletin*, credited *Scranton Tribune* writer Chick Feldman with dubbing the Cuban contingent by these monikers. By today's standards, such terms can be perceived as not being politically correct. Pickelner wrote that "Feldman has taken a definite liking to Kolp's 'Laughing Latins' and 'Rumba Rascals,' as he calls 'em ." See "A Little Something Extra," *WG&B*, 13 May 1944, 2.

28. Decker Oral History Interview.

29. *Ibid.*

30. "Speed Zardon Hurt As Grays Win 2nd from Luckless Sens," *WG&B*, 20 May 1944, 7; "Grays Run Wild," *WS*, 13 June 1944, 9. "Joe Zardon, Leading Base Stealer of the Grays One of the Fastest Men in Baseball—Beat Case 5 Times," *WG&B*, 20 July 1944, 9; "Kolp's Twin Win Specialists Make it 9 For Season—Zardon in Great Comeback," *WG&B*, 3 July 1944, 4.

31. "Grays, Laurels Share Bill," *WG&B*, 22 May 1944, 2; "A Little Something Extra," *WG&B*, 23 May 1944, 6.

32. "Zardón Ejected After Near Fight in Second," *WG&B*, 5 June 1944, 2. Zardón was fined $25 by EL president Tommy Richardson. Sports columnist Louis Pickelner believed that Zardón's action had " … its inception Saturday night when the [Wilkes-Barre] Barons, who have accumulated considerable notoriety as bench jockeys, picked on Joe with a duster." See "Extra Bases," *WG&B*, 5 June 1944, 2; Zardón was also ejected from a game against the Hartford Laurels for tossing his bat twenty-five feet after a disputed third-strike call by the umpire. See "Zardon Ejected in Sixth for Tossing Bat After Fanning," *WS*, 22 June 1944, 17.

33. "Parra Wins Own Game as Grays Even Triplet Series—Zardon Severely Injured,"

WG&B, 31 August 1944, 6; "Grays Lose Fourth Place on Final Day by Dropping Double," *WS*, 11 September 1944, 9.

34. "A Little Something Extra," *WG&B*, 13 September 1944, 4.

35. The local press reported that Gallardo returned to Cuba to tend to his wife and a sick child. There was some conjecture on the part of club officials that Gallardo may have left Williamsport one step ahead of the U.S. Selective Service and the draft. See "Second Sacker Decides to Jump Club — Team Loses Double Header," *WS*, 4 August 1944, 15. Pickelner wrote, "Gallardo, the most valuable bric-a-brac on John Cambria's roster, left a hole in the infield that could not be plugged." See "A Little Something Extra," *WG&B*, 13 September 1944, 4.

36. Francisco "Sojito" Gallardo played for Almendares, Cienfuegos, and Habana in the Cuban Professional League from 1947 to 1952, and five seasons with the Havana Cubans of the Class B Florida International League. He was named Rookie of the Year in the Cuban professional league in 1947–1948. See Jorge S. Figueredo, *Who's Who in Cuban Baseball, 1878–1961* (Jefferson, North Carolina: McFarland & Company, 2003), 151 (hereafter cited as Figueredo, *Who's Who*).

37. Parra was best noted for his Cuban Amateur League career and membership on Cuba's Amateur World Series teams in 1942 and 1943. See González Echevarría, 230, 247, 249; Parra pitched in the Cuban professional league for Almendares (1944–45); Marianao (1945–46); and Oriente (1946–47); and two seasons for the Havan Cubans of the Florida International League. In 1947, he won 11 and lost 4 for the Havana Cubans. See Figueredo, *Who's Who*, 245; "Parra Choice for First — Southpaw Breezes into Grays Camp in Fine Condition," *WG&B*, 21 April 1945,4; "Cuban Cuties of the Grays' Mound Staff, *WG&B*, 26 May 1945, 2.

38. "Grays Catching Department Rates As Good as Any Team in the League — One Reason Locals Are in Third Place,"*WS*, 21 July 1944, 15; "A Little Something Extra," *WG&B*, 13 September, 1944, 4; Rogelio Valdés played four seasons with Marianao and Oriente in the Cuban Professional League, but only compiled a career batting average of .163. He had one career at bat for Washington in 1944 before being farmed out to Chattanooga. See Figueredo, *Who's Who*, 202–03.

39. *WG&B* Sports Editor Louis Pickelner singled out Scranton Miners' manager, Heine Manush as an *agent provocateur*. Pickelner wrote: "Manush's mean and profane remarks resulted in several altercations between the two clubs." See "A Little Something Extra," *WG&B*, 12 October 1944, 4.

40. "Roger Valdes and Tony Napoles, '44 Players Check In," *WG&B*, 16 April 1945, 4.

41. Manuel "Chino" Hidalgo impressed Manager Kolp and the Williamsport sports press corps with "the lightning manner which he got rid of the ball." See "Extra Bases," *WG&B*, 17April 1945, 4; Hidalgo's Chinese heritage is mentioned in González Echevarría, 117, 230.

42. In order to play in 1945, Gallardo had to have his eligibility restored by the National Association's president, Judge William Bramham, after he jumped the Grays to return to Cuba in 1944. See "Extra Bases, *WG&B*, 19 April 1945, 8; "Lightning Latins Apt to Surprise E.L. Foes Again," *WG&B*, 2 May 1945, 4. Goicochea did not arrive in Williamsport until late May, but he would figure prominently in Williamsport's rivalry with the hated Utica Blue Sox. See "Idle Grays Tie for Lead with Help of Binghamton," *WG&B*, 22 May 1945, 4; Fernando "Trompoloco" Rodríguez enjoyed a lengthy pitching career in the Cuban professional league, pitching for both Almendares and Habana between 1947 and 1961. He also reached the majors, appearing in eight games with the Chicago Cubs (1958) and the Philadelphia Phillies (1959). In May of 1946, Rodríguez pitched a no-hitter as a member of the minor league Havana Cubans. See Figueredo, *Who's Who*, 252.

43 Hidalgo was a career .300 hitter with the Class B Havana Cubans (eight seasons) of the Florida International League, and twice captured the league's Most Valuable Player Award (1946 and 1947). See Jorge S. Figueredo, *Cuban Baseball: A Statistical History, 1878–1961* (Jefferson, North Carolina: McFarland & Company, 2003), 290–95(hereafter cited as Figueredo, *Statistical History*); Figueredo, *Who's Who*, 162–63; González Echevarría,53–55, 314–315.

44. Figueredo, *Who's Who*, 122; Figueredo, *Statistical History*, 271,289; González Echevarría, 270, 294.

45. "Rain Ends Most Dismal Year In Grays' History," *WG &B*, 10 September 1945, 4.

46. "Grays Play Usual Game — Lose Double to Scranton Team," *WS*, 9 August 1945, 16.

47. Even before July, the Grays had been involved in several scraps with Eastern League teams and umpires leading to riotous fan behavior. See "Utes Spoil Welteroth Debut in Stormy 6–3 Tussle," *WG&B*, 1 June 1945, 10; "Riot Squad Called to Escort Arbiter From Playing Field," *WS* 1 June 1945, 9 ; "Extra Bases," *WG&B*, 2 June 1945, 4.

48. Described as a "tobacco farmer" by the Eastern League press, Tyson targeted the Cubans because of their racial pedigree. His running feud with Cubans heated up as the season progressed, especially after Cuban pitchers began to throw inside to intimidate Tyson. See "A Little Extra-Harmful Tactics," *WG&B*, 20 July 1945, 12.

49. "Near Riot As Utes Cop Twin Bill From Slipping Billtown," *WS*, 9 July 1945, 11; "Three Others Punished for Part in Riot," *WG&B*, 10 July 1945, 6; "Three More Players Fined but Nothing Is Done to Umpires," *WS*, 10 July 1945, 9. In addition to "Turkey" Tyson, Eastern League president Tommy Richardson fined Williamsport pitchers Leonardo Goicochea and Felipe Jiménez, and Utica catcher Joe Antolick.

50. "Tyson Suspended — Fined $50 for Inciting Riot," *WG&B*, 9 July 1945, 4.

51. "Fodder For the Fans," *The Grit*, 15 July 1945, Sports Section, 8.

52. "Dugout Scrap Proves Costly to Grays," *WG&B*, 12 July 1945, 6; "Internal Friction Threatening to Tear Local Club Asunder, *WS* 12 July 1945, 12.

53. "Three Players Are Banished As Grays Drop Double Bill," *WS*, 17 July 1945, 9. Richardson came down hard on Tyson after the second brawl with the Cubans by levying a fifteen-day suspension in addition to the standard $50 fine. See "Richardson Suspends Turk Tyson Again for Gray-Baiting Tactics," *WG&B*, 18 July 1945, 4; "Grays Unable to Shake Blue Sox Jinx — Richardson Suspends Tyson For Actions Last Monday Evening," *WS*, 18 July 1945, 11.

54. "A Little Extra," *WG&B*, 2 August 1945, 6.

55. "Rain Ends Most Dismal Year In Grays' History," *WG&B*, 10 September 1945, 4; "Chino Hidalgo Named on Eastern's All-Star Team," *WG&B*, 15 November 1945, 10.

56. "Cambria to Stick to Agreement — Reports of Franchise Transfer are Spiked, *WG&B* 19 September 1945, 4; "Grays Tie up with Buffalo," 8 December 1945, 4; "Grays Going South to Train," *The Grit*, 9 December 1945, Sports Section, 1. Beginning in 1946, many of the former Williamsport Cuban players under contract to the Senators were assigned to play for the Havana Cubans of the Class B Florida International League. The team, co-owned by Clark Griffith, Joe Cambria, and Cuban sports entrepreneur Roberto Maduro, dominated league play and captured consecutive championships from 1947 to 1950. See González Echevarría, 295–97.

57. "Fodder for the Fans," *The Grit*, 5 August 1945, Sports Section, 8.

The Chinese Wall and Murakami, Too: The Baseball Establishment and Post–World War II Perceptions of the Asian Other

Ron Briley

On March 8, 1958, *The Sporting News* printed a rather astounding full-page cover cartoon portraying a gigantic Chinese figure dressed as a "coolie." Featuring a round face, slanted eyes, buck teeth, and long moustache, the Chinese gentleman looms over a baseball fence labeled 250 feet and is offering peanuts to a pitcher from the Dodgers, who is already crowded by two outfielders standing atop the pitcher's mound. For the uninitiated, the cartoon was actually a reference to the Brooklyn Dodgers moving to Los Angeles following the 1957 season. While the stadium at Chavez Ravine was being constructed, the Dodgers were to play their home games at the Los Angeles Coliseum, which had to be readied for baseball. A major problem with the project was that the left field fence was an incredibly short 251 feet from home plate. This potential cheap home run was, then, referred to as a "Chinese homer," and the short left field porch was termed the "Chinese wall."[1]

The cartoon, drawn by Willard Mullin of the New York *World Telegram & Sun*, makes use of dialect to further its racial representation and supposed humor. The Chinese figure is labeled as One Flung Wong, reminding readers that one poorly thrown pitch could result in a cheap home run. He has a bag of peanuts in his hand and is saying to the Dodgers players, "Likee Peanut. Tomorrow Bling [sic] Litchi Nut!" The cartoon also includes the following caption:

> Chop! Chop! When we lived in L.A., Chinatown was down around Alameda & Aliso Streets.... But, then, that was a quarter of a century

ago.... It was moved once (WW II) out to the N. Figueroa area.... But
it ain't there no more! It is now in left field at the Colesium.[2]

Cultural historian Iris Chang argues that the Chinese represented an
ancient civilization coming into contact with a newly developing country.
However, the racist caricature employed by Mullin is indicative of what
scholar Robert G. Lee describes as the effort by American popular culture to
portray Asians and their ancient civilizations in "yellowface." Lee asserts,
"Yellowface marks the Oriental as indelibly alien. Constructed as a race of
aliens, Orientals represent a present danger of pollution. An analysis of the
Oriental as a racial category must begin with the concept of the alien as a pol-
luting body."[3]

In *The Sporting News* front page cartoon of March 5, 1958, the Chinese
"coolie" is portrayed as a threat to the purity of America's national sport. The
Oriental in this case will pollute the American sense of fair play and achievement represented by the traditions of baseball. Nonetheless, *The Sporting
News*, under the editorship of J. G. Taylor Spink, insisted that there was no
racial prejudice involved with the concept of the "Chinese wall" and cheap
home run. In fact, the paper reported so much reader interest in the term
that another Mullin cartoon was published, as well as a piece on the origins
of the "Chinese wall" concept.

In his cartoon appearing May 7, 1958, in *The Sporting News*, Mullin
depicts another towering Chinese figure who is ostensibly the Chinese
philosopher Confucius. But in his rather sinister appearance and hands with
long finger nails reaching out to clutch handfuls of baseballs, Mullin's Confucius figure recalls the diabolical Chinese villain and stereotypes perpetu-
ated by author Sax Rohmer's Fu Manchu and his cinematic incarnation Boris
Karloff.[4] In this Mullin drawing, Confucius presides over the "great wailing
wall," while rendering a proverb in dialect, "One pop fly make one home
lun — one line dlive tliple [sic] make one long single." Again, the Chinese
theme is used to demonstrate the corruption of American sport and competition.

The accompanying caption also plays upon the fear of Chinese hordes
overrunning the world and threatening the quality of American life. Mullin
writes, "The most famous Ripley 'Believe It or Not,' wherein it is stated, 'If
all the Chinese in the world were to march four abreast, they would never
pass a given point,' is being proved at One Flung Wong, O'Malley's little joss
house in Los Angeles." Mullin was referring to Walter O'Malley, principal
owner and president of the Dodgers, whom the cartoonist characterized as
so wealthy that he really should be represented by a Mandarin rather than a
Chinese "coolie" or fisherman. Yet, Mullin appeared sensitive enough to recognize that some might find the "Chinese wall" terminology offensive and

sought to disassociate himself from the concept's origins. *The Sporting News* evidently failed to understand such discomfort and ran a headline proclaiming, "Artist Mullin Ducks Credit for Originating 'Chinaman.'"[5]

Mullin observed that when he arrived in New York as a young reporter in the mid-1930s, the phrase was already in common usage to describe the short left and right field foul lines at the Polo Grounds where the New York Giants played their home games. Accordingly, *The Sporting News* reproduced some of Mullin's earlier cartoons, including one from 1947 depicting Giants manager Mel Ott introducing rookie hitter Clint Hartung to the short left field porch as a looming Chinese figure smokes a long-stemmed pipe; this Chinese gentleman is more sedate than malevolent, thus conjuring up images of the Chinese as opium addicts. Ott tells the rookie that there are some "fellows" at the Polo Grounds that he should get to know — "One Flung Wong and One Home Lun [sic]."[6]

Once again, *The Sporting News* expressed no reservations about reprinting these cartoons, and editor Spink, in response to what he described as reader curiosity, not disapproval, penned a piece on the derivation of the "Chinese home run." Relying upon the accounts of veteran sportswriters, Spink concluded that usage of the phrase could be traced back to the 1920s and writer Thomas A. (Tad) Dorgan, who developed a dislike for the Giants manager John McGraw. To antagonize McGraw, Dorgan would belittle Giants victories by asserting that they were the result of cheap or "Chinese home runs" hit in the Polo Grounds. Dorgan, who worked for the New York *Journal*, was from San Francisco and perhaps carried with him the prejudice of many Anglos in California that the Chinese were a threat to white labor and social mobility. The association of the Chinese with cheap "coolie" labor resonated despite the corrective efforts of Ronald Takaki and other scholars. Takaki wrote,

> Contrary to the popular stereotype and myth, these Chinese migrants were not "coolies" — unfree laborers who had been kidnapped or pressed into service by coercion and shipped to a foreign country. Actually, they had come to America voluntarily as free laborers: some of them paid their own way, and probably most of them borrowed the necessary funding through the credit-ticket system.[7]

While contemporary scholars would certainly perceive Dorgan as perpetuating racial stereotypes, Spink of *The Sporting News* was quick to defend Dorgan and the "Chinese home run" from charges of racism. Observing that Dorgan had adopted two sons of Chinese ancestry, Spink quotes Joseph M. Sheehan of *The New York Times* as insisting, "In fairness to Dorgan, a benign and "gentle" satirist, it should be stressed that in introducing the 'Chinese homer' phrase, he had no thought of disparaging the Chinese people."[8]

The Sporting News continued to perpetuate the representation of the

Chinese as alien Orientals by featuring a piece on a letter written to the Los Angeles *Times* by Travis McGregor of Beverly Hills, California, who described himself as an old-time San Francisco sportswriter. According to McGregor, Dorgan had drawn his inspiration for the "Chinese homer" from a Chinese youth with a Stanford degree who yearned to be a sports reporter. Around 1912, he would hang out at ballparks in San Francisco and Oakland, entertaining the sportswriters by announcing the games in dialect and referring to "Chinese homers," while batters striking out were "Mandarins waving fans." However, none of the Anglo writers could pronounce the young man's name, so he was simply called Mike Murphy. Apparently unaware that his comments could be considered condescending, McGregor concluded his letter by noting, "For two or three seasons Mike was a riot — an Oriental Fred Allen, and Tad Dorgan drew a number of cartoons featuring Mike's comments."[9]

The Sporting News apparently perceived the McGregor letter as indicative of curiosity rather than offensive representation of the Chinese as the alien outsider. Of course, the newspaper was simply following a well-established tradition of treating the Chinese in a patronizing fashion. For example, in 1912, *Baseball Magazine* published a piece commenting upon Sun Yat-sen's modernizing revolution and reporting increasing interest by the Chinese in American baseball. Singing the praises of baseball's civilizing mission, the editorial asserted,

> The twentieth century seems destined to rank as an era of surprises in every feature of human endeavor, and its most striking feature up to this date has been the moral, mental and political regeneration of the nation which numbers as its citizens one-fourth of the entire population of the world.[10]

Baseball Magazine evidently found little of value in China's ancient civilization and hoped that baseball would bring Western values to the land of Confucius and tame the "yellow peril." Similar expectations were expressed by American diplomats and baseball executives regarding Imperial Japan. Baseball's civilizing mission in Japan, however, was aborted with the attack on Pearl Harbor.[11] Meanwhile, in American culture, especially Hollywood cinema, the Chinese were replaced by the Japanese as representative of the alien hordes who were a threat to American values and traditions. During the late 1930s and early 1940s, the Chinese were increasingly depicted, in films such as *The Good Earth* (1937) and *Thirty Seconds Over Tokyo* (1944), as America's loyal and humble ally.[12]

Nevertheless, Mao Zedong's communist revolution in China and the Korean War once again encouraged the representation of the Chinese in American popular culture as a clear and present danger to the United States and its quality of life. Thus, *The Sporting News* characterization of the Chinese as exotic and different, or un-American, should be placed within the historical context of American foreign policy concerns over the alleged expansionist plans of the People's Republic of China. Americans were told that an invasion of Formosa (Taiwan) might initiate World War III, and Chinese designs on the islands of Matsu and Quemoy became a major issue in the Presidential election of 1960.[13]

The representation of the Asian as an alien threat was only one trope used to stereotype Asian Americans. For example, during the Cold War years of the 1950s, Asians were often described as the model minority who could assimilate into the American mainstream, thus providing a countervailing argument to the African- American civil rights movement's challenge to the postwar consensus. And the reaction of baseball fans, management, and writers to Major League Baseball's first Asian player, Masanori Murakami from Japan, who appeared in the major leagues in 1964, only six years after *The Sporting News* pieces on the "Chinese home run," fits well into the apparently more positive model minority image.

Lee, however, observes that one should be careful regarding the artificial designation of positive and negative stereotypes. He opines, "The Yellowface coolie and model minority, despite their apparent contradiction, not only coexist but, in fact, can become mutually reinforcing at critical junctures because neither is created by the actual lives of Asians in America." Lee insists that the very success of the model minority may become perceived as a "camouflage for subversion," such as Asian capital threatening American economic interests. Thus, the model minority may be quickly replaced by the image of "the gook" in American popular culture.[14] While "the gook" is a rather extreme analogy for the experience of Murakami in the Untied States, the story of Murakami's saga from model minority to disenchanted athlete within two years raises questions about his initial favorable reception. The problems with Murakami's brief major league career blocked further Japanese integration of the major leagues for another thirty years.

Murakami was born May 6, 1944, in Otsuki, Japan. The six-foot, 180 pound, left-handed pitcher was an outstanding high school athlete, who was signed by the Nankai Hawks following his graduation. As a nineteen-year-old, he appeared in three games for the Hawks in 1963.[15]

Through the efforts of Tsunco "Cappy" Harada, who served as a scout for both the Nankai Hawks and San Francisco Giants, the promising young left-hander and two other Japanese youngsters, Hiroshi Takahashi and Tatsuchiko Tanaka, were sent to gain a year of seasoning in the United States in the Giant organization. Commenting upon the transaction, Jack Schwarz, administrative secretary of the Giant farm system, asserted, "It's a great benefit to Japanese baseball because they'll get a year of development in our farm system. And if one of them should be a Willie Mays or Mickey Mantle, we'll certainly put him right on our roster." Following spring training, Takahashi and Tanaka were assigned to the Giant affiliate in the Idaho rookie league, while Murakami was placed with the Class A Fresno franchise of the California League.[16]

Although he was welcomed by the Japanese community in Fresno, Murakami struggled with the English language. According to Fresno manager Bill Werle, "Naturally Murakami has picked up some English from his teammates. But wouldn't you know it, they're all four letter words." Werle also used the model minority concept to describe his pitcher, stating, "He's a model athlete, both on and off the field — and the team likes him." However, the manager expressed some frustration regarding his efforts to communicate with his young pitcher.[17]

On the other hand, Murakami did not appear to require a great deal of guidance from Werle. In his first appearance with Fresno on April 4, 1964, Murakami pitched five hitless innings of relief and was the winning pitcher in a 5–4 victory over Santa Barbara. Enjoying considerable success out of the bullpen, Murakami was assigned his first start as a part of a Fresno Japanese Day promotion. Playing before a crowd of 1,593 fans, Murakami, joined by former teammates Takahashi and Tanaka who were give special permission to play one game for Fresno, struck out thirteen batters while pitching the Fresno Giants to a 3–2 victory over Reno. Employing themes of assimilation associated with the model minority, the evening was presided over by Fresno Mayor Wallace Henderson and the city's chamber of commerce. The Japanese athletes were presented with gifts by the local branch of the Bank of Tokyo and Marie Nakai, Fresno Nisei beauty queen.[18]

Despite the fact that Murakami evidently had some interest and talent in performing as a starting pitcher, the Fresno Giants continued to use Murakami in relief. He responded with an outstanding season, leading his club to the California League championship, while earning league rookie honors with a record of eleven wins and seven losses to go along with eleven saves, 159 strikeouts as opposed to 34 walks, and a superlative 1.78 earned run average. The Giants then shocked many in baseball by summoning the twenty-year-old pitcher to the major leagues on September 1, 1964. Murakami flew immediately to New York City, where the Giants were playing the Mets, amid the media flurry over the first Japanese player to be placed on a major league roster. Before the evening contest, there was confusion when Giants vice president Chub Feeney attempted to stage the signing of Murakami to a contract as a media event. The pitcher balked at signing the document, but after a club house meeting between Feeney, manager Alvin Dark, an interpreter, and Murakami, a contract was agreed upon. Feeney explained to reporters that it was all a misunderstanding and that Murakami wanted to pitch for the Giants. The club executive concluded, "He had signed a minor league agreement in Fresno and thought he had already signed a Giants contract."[19] Nevertheless, this little misunderstanding, as Feeney termed it, was a foreshadowing of contract difficulties between the Giants and Murakami.

In the bottom of the eighth inning with the Giants trailing 4 to 0, Dark called Murakami into the game. Ironically, Dark, who weeks earlier had raised the ire of his players by complaining about the number of African-American and Latino athletes on the team, was given the distinction of placing the first Japanese-born major leaguer into the lineup.[20] Aware of the historical circumstances, the New York crowd of over 40,000 fans rose to its feet and gave Murakami an enthusiastic greeting. The young pitcher appeared unruffled by the hoopla. The first batter he faced was Charlie Smith, who struck out on four pitches. After giving up a single to Chris Cannizaro, Murakami fanned Ed Kranepool and retired shortstop Roy McMillan on a ground ball. The Giants rallied to score one run in the ninth, but the story of September 1, 1964 was not the defeat of the Giants who were now seven and one-half games out in the pennant race, but rather Murakami's impressive debut.

During his tenure in Fresno, Murakami played in a community with a supportive Japanese-American community, but the national press coverage of his major league premiere documented that representation of even a model minority Asian citizen could contain elements of the "Oriental" as an alien other in American culture. Bob Stevens of the San Francisco *Chronicle* described Murakami as "a handsome young man with a cherubic face and a glistening look about him, studied English for six years, but he has trouble understanding and communicating." While patronizing, Stevens's portrayal of Murakami did not employ the racial vocabulary of the caustic Dick Young, who would grow increasingly reactionary in dealing with societal and baseball change in the 1960s. Young entitled his piece for the New York *Daily News*, "Giants Spring Oriental Lefty, But Honorable Mets Go, 4–1." The reporter praised the Japanese pitcher's control and fastball, but Young concluded his piece by observing that "new breed" Mets fans were not really so bad. After all, they did not unfurl a banner proclaiming, "Remember Pearl Harbor." In raising the specter of World War II, Young broached a subject which most writers tended to avoid with Japan emerging as America's major Asian ally in blocking the assumed expansionist plans of communist China.[21]

Young's old fashioned stereotypical language was missing from a more balanced account by George Vecsey, who noted the irony of Dark being the man to bring in the first Japanese pitcher. Vecsey also concluded that while Murakami struggled with the English language, he was "smart enough to demand explanation when contracts were pushed in front of him." Nevertheless, Vecsey could not refrain from referring to Murakami's fast ball as the Orient Express. Likewise, Red Smith was complimentary of Murakami, and the veteran columnist stated that he was not surprised that a nation with so much passion for baseball would produce a major league player. However, Smith could not resist a little cultural commentary, observing that Murakami was not "big enough for a Suma wrestler," so he had no alternative than to play baseball.[22]

Stereotypes aside, Smith was certainly on target regarding Japanese enthusiasm for baseball, and Murakami's debut was the subject of considerable media attention by the Japanese press. Murakami's parents reported that they were deluged by neighbors and messages of congratulations. The proud parents attributed their son's baseball success to his stubborn character. Despite plans for their son to become a doctor, Murakami preferred baseball, and his family reluctantly agreed to his participation in the sport. Murakami's father, a postal worker, told reporters, "Now we're beginning to understand and like the game and we only hope our son continues playing baseball and does not forget what we once told him — 'If you want to be a ballplayer, you will have to be the best in Japan.'"[23] In the hoopla over Murakami's performance in the United States, his father's comments about playing in Japan gained scant attention at the time.

Meanwhile, Murakami was warmly embraced by San Francisco and its Japanese-American community. San Francisco Major John F. Shelley sent a welcoming telegram to the pitcher, asserting, "We are proud of Japan's gift to San Francisco." When the Giants returned from their road trip, over 100 members of the Murakami fan club were present at the airport. Public acceptance of the Japanese pitcher was made easier with his outstanding September performance for the Giants. He notched one victory and one save with a 1.80 earned run average. In fifteen innings of work, Murakami struck out fifteen batters while walking one. In a profile for *The Sporting News*, Jack McDonald emphasized the Americanization of the Giants' pitching discovery. McDonald observed that his teammates liked the Japanese youth, nicknaming him "Mashie." According to McDonald, Murakami found American ice cream to be "O, so good," and when he encountered difficulty reading a menu, the pitcher simply ordered "ham and eggs." A quote from Giants starting pitcher Bob Hendley firmly placed Murakami within the model minority construct. Speaking of his Japanese teammate, Hendley remarked, "He has three big objectives. He wants to stay here and learn the American way of playing baseball. He wants to learn to speak fluent English. And he wants to make a lot of money over here."[24]

Despite reports that his family expected Murakami to return home following his September stint with the Giants, Horace Stoneham insisted that his latest acquisition spend the winter pitching in the Arizona Instructional League. Murakami adhered to the wishes of the Giants management, continuing his fine pitching and adjustment to American culture during his sojourn in Arizona. Murakami hurled 43 innings in Arizona, striking out 30 and walking only two, with the league's lowest earned run average of 1.05.[25]

Following his achievements in Arizona, Murakami traveled to Japan, and the Giants expected him to report for spring training in February 1965. Upon his arrival in Japan, reports began to surface that his father expected Murakami to remain home and that the Nankai Hawks were recalling their young player. According to published reports, the Hawks insisted that Murakami was still their property, asserting that the $10,000 fee paid by the Giants to the Japanese franchise was simply for the pitcher's services during the 1964 season. The Giants disputed the claims made by the Japanese club, arguing Murakami had signed a 1965 contract to pitch with San Francisco. Replying to allegations by the ownership of the Nankai Hawks that the Giants had engaged in deception and forgery in signing Murakami, Giant vice president Feeney retorted,

> We deceived no one and know nothing of any forged papers. We're ready to go to court to prove it. We have Murakami's signed contract, a $10,000 cancelled check from the Hawks for Murakami's option and a release signed by Murakami himself. You'd think Murakami was Christy Mathewson come back to life instead of a relief pitcher who worked only 15 innings for us last season.[26]

As Lee suggests in his study of Orientalism, the representation and language of the model minority could rapidly move in a negative direction if perceived as a threat to American interests.

In the San Francisco *Chronicle*, Stevens used unnamed sources to report that Murakami was under tremendous pressure to remain in Japan. Stevens indicated that Murakami preferred to play with the Giants, but his parents, Japanese baseball fans, and the Nankai Hawks were prevailing upon the young man to stay in his native land. Furthermore, while San Francisco was offering the pitcher a contract for approximately $10,000, the Hawks were allegedly prepared to pay him in the neighborhood of $30,000. Stevens, however, maintained that Murakami's long-term earning potential was greater in the United States.[27]

Apparently bending to the pressures described by Stevens, Murakami penned a letter to Giants owner Stoneham stating that he would not be returning to the San Francisco team. Murakami explained,

> I am the only son in our family and I feel that my place is here in Japan with my family. Upon returning here, I have been treated very well. I did not realize until my return how much I missed Japan and its ways, and the thought of returning to the United States makes me homesick. I have come to the realization that I will not be happy in the United States and therefore feel that I must tell you that I am not returning. I am also thinking of getting married and this has also been a consideration in this decision.[28]

In making his case based on personal issues, Murakami was appealing to a hardship or homesickness clause in his contract.

The Giants, however, viewed Murakami's reluctance as motivated by the financial interests of the Nankai Hawks. After failing to reach an understanding with the Japanese club, San Francisco appealed the Murakami case to Major League Baseball commissioner Ford Frick. After meeting with former major league pitcher Joe Stanka, representing the Hawks and Murakami, Frick issued a decree on the Murakami matter. In a terse statement, Frick declared, "I have all the documents on this case, and it shows that the Giants purchased Murakami. The Giants sent $10,000 to the Japanese for Murakami. The check has been cashed — and endorsed by their people." Frick also revealed that he had dispatched a telegram to Japanese baseball commissioner Yushi Uchimura, threatening to sever all relations between Major League Baseball and Japan, including trips by American teams, until the Murakami matter was resolved in favor the San Francisco Giants. Frick declared, "I have sent out a bulletin to every one of our clubs that there will be no further relations with Japanese baseball until this thing is settled to my satisfaction. I have heard nothing from the Japanese Commissioner." Ko Ihara, secretary general to Uchimura, found Frick's comments to be abrasive and abrupt, especially since the American knew that his Japanese counterpart was ill with a bladder inflammation.[29]

Frick's threat of economic sanctions against the Japanese enjoyed the support of *The Sporting News*. In an editorial, the paper described the Japanese as ungrateful for the historical role played by the Giants in promoting baseball in Japan. The newspaper concluded,

> Murakami may be homesick. His team may need him. But the Giants think they can use him, too, and they have followed legal procedures. Commissioner Frick has had to lay down the law, approving the purchase by the Giants. The Japanese must recognize this as official.[30]

In the eyes of Major League Baseball and its quasi-official newspaper organ, the model minority Japanese needed to be taught a lesson. The arrogant American position espoused by Frick amounted to the internationalization of baseball management's notorious reserve clause. If Murakami did not play with San Francisco, he would not participate anywhere. And if the Japanese did not agree, there would be economic reprisals. Evidently, the diplomatic failures of the 1930s were lost upon Frick and the baseball establishment, who demonstrated that perceptions of the model minority and ally could be quickly altered if there was an economic challenge to American hegemony.

Fortunately, Uchimura recovered from his illness and proposed a compromise to settle the Murakami issue. He suggested that Murakami return to America and play for the Giants in 1965. After the 1965 season, Murakami would then have the right to render a decision on his future. He would be free to remain in the United States, or if he decided to return to Japan and play for the Hawks, he would be placed on the voluntarily retired list by San Francisco, who would retain their rights to Murakami if he should choose to come back to the United States at some later date. Until the issue was resolved, Uchimura ruled that Murakami could practice with the Hawks, but he would not participate in game action.[31]

The initial response by the Giants was that Uchimura's compromise, which had the support of Murakami's parents, was completely unacceptable. So the Giants opened the 1965 season without Murakami, but the team's slow start made it apparent that the Giants were lacking left-handed pitching. And the American position began to soften. *The Sporting News* questioned its earlier bellicose gunboat diplomacy, observing,

"It is somewhat difficult to determine what can be achieved if pitcher Murakami just doesn't want to pitch in the United States any more. Short of sending a platoon of Marines after him, there doesn't seem to be any way to get him to return if he doesn't want to." Fearing that the Murakami affair might endanger relations with America's Far Eastern ally in the Cold War, *The Sporting News* urged that the Japanese compromise be accepted. Meanwhile, the Giants, desperate for pitching help, announced that Murakami would be free to decide his fate after the 1965 season. Giants vice president Feeney proclaimed that their dispute was not with Murakami, but rather with the Nankai ownership. Murakami was welcomed back into the fold, and Feeney asserted, "We're hoping he'll stay with us."[32]

As for Murakami, he insisted that he was ready to pitch for the Giants, and on May 4, 1965, he was met by an enthusiastic crowd at the San Francisco airport. However, he refused to answer questions as to where he might play in 1966. While Murakami was eager to pitch, he had missed spring training and almost a month of the season. He was effective, but not as overpowering as he had been in September 1964. Murakami also expressed an interest in serving as a starting pitcher. Pulling out all the stops to keep their prospect, Murakami's wish was granted when the Giants arranged a Masanori Murakami Day at Candlestick Park, complete with the presentation of a new Datsun convertible. However, the Phillies knocked Murakami from the mound during the third inning, although the Giants rallied to win the contest.[33]

Reflecting the hope that Murakami would remain in the United States, press coverage of the Japanese pitcher was generally favorable although often patronizing. This positive tone, however, was marred by a Missouri letter writer who threatened to kill Giants manager Herman Franks (who had replaced Alvin Dark) if he continued using Murakami. The writer based his threat on the fact that the Japanese pitcher should not be in the country because his relatives might have killed Americans during World War II.[34] The Asian as alien or "gook" was apparent in this letter, but the dominant representation in the press was that of assimilation or the model minority.

Prescott Sullivan of the San Francisco *Examiner* was pleased to see Murakami argue with an umpire, demonstrating that the Japanese pitcher was adapting to the less traditional American lifestyle. Sullivan concluded, "Japanese teen-agers are swinging with the Beatles and abandoning their manners to back-talk their elders, including their folks. And with these changes, the day of the Hon. Umpire has come to an end." Perhaps this new tone of defiance would make it easier for Murakami to defy his parents and stay in the United States. In the San Francisco *Chronicle*, Stevens also reported on the growing Americanization of Murakami. After describing Murakami's growing appreciation for the beauty of American women, Stevens observed that the pitcher spoke "with humor, with depth of thought, and from behind a smile that makes you want to grab the nearest phone and fly to Japan and see if all these people are as happy as 'Mashi.'"[35]

The Americanization of Murakami also included another successful season on the mound. During his 1965 campaign with the Giants, Murakami appeared in 45 games, with a 4–1 won-loss record and a 3.75 earned run average. He pitched 74 innings, giving up only 57 hits, striking out 85 batters and walking only 22. The Giants finished two games behind the Dodgers in the chase for the National League pennant, and many observers wondered whether the Giants might have caught the Dodgers with Murakami's services for the entire season. Therefore, the Giants were eager to sign the Japanese pitcher to a 1966 agreement. Teammates added their voice to that of management in a united front to keep Murakami within the Giant community. Even San Francisco Mayor John Shelley got into the act, informing Murakami, "Your great performance thrilled all of us Giants fans and even though we didn't win, this season was a memorable one for us. You may be sure that we have the highest hopes for next year."[36]

But the hopes of Shelley and Giants fans everywhere were crushed when Murakami informed San Francisco management that in 1966 he would return to Japan and pitch with the Nankai Hawks. The response by the Giants to this decision was conciliatory and respectful, keeping the door open for future seasons. After all, at this point Murakami was only twenty-one years of age. Thus, Murakami continued to represent the model minority who might be assimilated into the American mainstream. Giants owner Stoneham wrote to the pitcher, asserting, "You were a very fine pitcher for the Giants, and I am sure that you found it a very interesting experience. Your personality and ability was reflected in the high regard in which you were held by your teammates, the fans in San Francisco and all the members of the Giants' organization." Hoping to keep alive the possibility of Murakami again wearing a San Francisco uniform, vice president Feeney penned a note to Murakami's father, explaining,

> We were extremely happy to have as fine a boy as your son as a member of our team. He is both a fine pitcher and a very fine person. He is extremely well-liked by his teammates, our management and the many baseball fans of San Francisco. He has reflected great credit on his family and his country while in the United States. We sincerely hope that he will pitch again for the Giants in the future and assure you that every care will be taken of him if he does.[37]

Feeney's letter reflects the general consensus that family obligations were the crucial factor in Murakami's return to Japan. Considerable speculation also centered upon whether he would earn more money pitching for Nankai or San Francisco in 1966, but most observers believed that his long-range financial prospects were brighter in the United States. However, this line of reasoning failed to factor in the corporate ties of Japanese baseball, which tended to include more long-term security arrangements.[38]

While Murakami continued to communicate with San Francisco management and former teammates, including Hal Lanier, he did not rejoin the Giants. He pitched in the Japanese leagues from 1966 through 1982 with the Nankai Hawks, Honshin Tigers, and Nippon Ham Fighters. While he enjoyed a solid career, Murakami failed to fulfill the promise demonstrated during his brief stint in the United States. In his seventeen-year Japanese career, he won 103 games while losing 82 with a career earned average of 3.64. Some observers believe that Murakami had trouble readjusting to Japanese baseball after his flirtation with Major League Baseball in the United States. And, indeed, Murakami always expressed regret that his American baseball career was so brief. In fact, after his retirement from Japanese baseball, Murakami attended spring training with the Giants in 1983, but he failed to make the ball club. Murakami went back to Japan, where he pursued a career in coaching and broadcasting.[39]

Sportswriter Gordon Sukamoto believed that Murakami would be a Japanese Jackie Robinson, breaking down major league barriers for Japanese players.[40] However, when San Francisco honored Murakami on the thirtieth anniversary of his Giants debut (the event was staged 1995 due to the strike-shortened season of 1994), he was still, at the time, the only Japanese-born player to have played in the American major leagues. It is interesting to remember that many journalists had once employed the cultural construct of race, referring to Murakami as the first "of his race" in the major leagues, as if race were a biological fact, indicating the persuasive hold of cultural perceptions regarding the Asian as alien.[41] By the 1990s, however, such language had generally disappeared from the nation's sports pages.

The financial bickering between the Nankai Hawks and San Francisco

Giants, along with the persistence of cultural stereotyping, held back the integration of Asian players until the Los Angeles Dodgers signed Nomo Hedeo in 1996, opening up Japan to the economic penetration of American corporate baseball interests. In the modern era, characterized by such baseball stars as the Japanese Kazuhiro Sasaki and Ichiro Suzuki of the Seattle Mariners and Korean Chan Ho Park of the Texas Rangers, in addition to aggressive marketing tailored to the Asian-American and international communities of the Pacific Rim, it is sometimes difficult to acknowledge that in the late 1950s and early 1960s the baseball establishment racially profiled the Asian as the other. Yet doubts about the ability of Hideki Matsui, the New York Yankees' Japanese import, to hit for power indicate that cultural stereotypes are hardly limited to the past.[42]

Nevertheless, the change from the representation of the "Chinese wall" in the late 1950s to the chants of Ichiro in Seattle in the early twenty-first century is evidence of a considerable leap for cultural understanding in the United States. But it is well worth recalling that the "Chinese wall" cartoons and the odyssey of Murakami were only a short forty years ago. As we move in the direction of a corporate global economy, which may threaten the indigenous baseball leagues of Japan and Korea, it is well worth remembering how the Asian other has been represented, and continues to be portrayed, in American popular and sporting culture, recalling how quickly the representation of the "model minority" may degenerate into a threatening alien presence.

Notes

1. For the shift of the Dodgers from Brooklyn to Los Angeles see Neil J. Sullivan, *The Dodgers Move West* (New York: Oxford University Press, 1987).

2. For the Mullin cartoon see *The Sporting News*, 5 March 1958, 1; and accompanying article by Roscoe McGowan, "Easier Target for Dodgers' One-Two Punch?" 1–2.

3. Iris Chang, *The Chinese in America: A Narrative History* (New York: Viking, 2003); and Robert G. Lee, *Orientals: Asian Americans in Popular Culture* (Philadelphia: Temple University Press, 1999), 2.

4. For Fu Manchu see Tina Chen, "Dissecting the 'Devil Doctor': Stereotype and Sensationalism in Sax Rohmer's Fu Manchu," in Josephine Lee, Imogene L. Lim, and Yuko Matsukawa, *Recollecting Early Asian America: Essays in Cultural History* (Philadelphia: Temple University Press, 2002), 218–237.

5. For the Mullin Confucius cartoon see *The Sporting News*, 7 May 1958; and accompanying article, "Artist Mullin Ducks Credit for Originating 'Chinaman,'" 3.

6. The New York cartoons from Mullin are reproduced in *The Sporting News*, 7 May 1958, 4.

7. Ronald Takaki, *A Different Mirror: A History of Multicultural America* (Boston: Little, Brown and Company, 1993), 193. For the Chinese in California see Sucheng Chan, *This Bitter-Sweet Soil: The Chinese in California Agriculture, 1860–1910* (Berkeley: University of California Press, 1986).

8. J. G. Taylor Spink, "Expression to Anger McGraw," *The Sporting News*, 7 May 1958, 3.

9. "Traces 'Chinese HR' to Oriental 'Murphy,'" *The Sporting News*, 28 May 1958, 14.

10. "A New Feature of the Yellow Peril: Baseball As a Factor in the Progress of Civilization," *Baseball Magazine* (April 1912), 80.

11. For studies on the role of baseball in Japan see Richard Crepeau, "Pearl Harbor: A Failure of Baseball?," *Journal of Popular Culture*, 15 (Spring 1982), 67–74; Donald Roden, "Baseball and the Quest for National Dignity in Meiji Japan," *American Historical Review*, 85 (June 1980), 511–534; and Robert Whitney, *The Chrysanthemum and the Bat: Baseball Samurai Style* (New York: Dodd, 1977).

12. For Hollywood and representation of Asia see Dorothy B. Jones, *The Portrayal of China and India on the American Screen, 1896–1955* (Cambridge: MIT Press, 1955); Gina Marchetti, *Romance and the 'Yellow Peril': Race, Sex, and Discursive Strategies in Hollywood Fiction* (Berkeley: University of California Press, 1993); and Eugene Franklin Wong, *On Visual Media Racism: Asians in the American Motion Pictures* (New York: Arno Press, 1978).

13. For U.S. relations with Mao's China see Foster Rhea Dulles, *American Policy Toward Communist China, 1949–1969* (New York: Thomas Y. Crowell, 1972).

14. Lee, *Orientals*, 12–13 and 10–11.

15. For an overview of Murakami's career see Larry Whiteside, "Murakami Hardly a Trailblazer," Boston *Globe*, 2 November 1992; and Jack Gilbert, "Masanori Murakami's Historic Return," n.d., Masanori Murakami File, Baseball Hall of Fame Museum and Library (BHFML), Cooperstown, New York.

16. Bob Stevens, "Giants Tap Fresh Talent Pool, Sign Three Japanese for Farm," San Francisco *Chronicle*, 7 March 1964; and Tom Meehan, "Fresno Giants Will Keep Southpaw Japanese Pitcher Murakami, Sends Two to Twin Falls," Fresno *Bee*, 21 April 1964, Murakami File, BHFML.

17. Dan Hruby, "Fresno Giants Masanori Murakami Handicapped by English Language," Fresno *Bee*, 18 August 1964, Murakami File, BHFML.

18. "Murakami Turns in Great Performance in American Debut," Fresno *Bee*, 25 April 1964; and Tom Meehan "1,593 Fans Watch Murakami Win First Game as Starter," Fresno *Bee*, 22 May 1964, Murakami File, BHFML.

19. Dick Young, "Ne'er the Twain," New York *Daily News*, 2 September 1964, 78, Murakami File, BHFML.

20. For coverage of Dark's racial comments see *The Sporting News*, 22 August 1964; Charles Einstein, *Willie's Time: A Memoir* (New York: J. B. Lippincott, 1979); and Alvin Dark, *When in Doubt Fire the Manager: My Life in Baseball* (New York: E. P. Dutton, 1980).

21. Bob Stevens, "Masanori's 1st Day in the Big Leagues," San Francisco *Chronicle*, 2 September 1964, 49; and Dick Young, "Giants Spring Oriental Lefty, but Honorable Mets Go, 4–1," New York *Daily News*, 2 September 1964, 78, Murakami File, BHFML.

22. George Vecsey, "Newest Giant Pitcher Gets Quick Orientation," *The New York Times*, 2 September, 1964; and Red Smith, "Murakami," Binghamton *Press*, 3 September 1964, 23, Murakami File, BHFML.

23. "Masanori Made Folks Proud," San Francisco *Chronicle*, 5 September 1964, 38, Murakami File, BHFML.

24. John F. Shelley, "Message of Congratulations," 5 September 1964; and Jack McDonald, "Ice Cream, Ham and Eggs High on Murakami's 'Oh So Good' List," *The Sporting News*, 3 October 1964, Murakami File, BHFML.

25. Jack McDonald, "'No Tug-of-War Over Murakami,' Say Giants—'He's Our Property,'" *The Sporting News*, 12 December 1964, 13, Murakami File, BHFML.

26. Jack McDonald, "Giants Furious—Deny Charge of Forgery in Murakami Case," *The Sporting News*, 6 March 1965, Murakami File, BHFML.

27. Bob Stevens, "Will Masanori Play for S. F. Giants or Nankai Hawks?," San Francisco *Chronicle*, 7 January 1965, Murakami File, BHFML.

28. Masanori Murakami to Horace Stoneham, 8 February 1965, Murakami File, BHFML.

29. "Japanese Given Warning," and "Murakami Belongs to San Francisco," San Francisco *Chronicle*, n. d., Murakami File, BHFML.

30. "International Incident Over Hurler," *The Sporting News*, 20 February 1965, Murakami File, BHFML.

31. Bob Stevens, "Murakami's Return Ok'd—for '65," San Francisco *Chronicle*, 17 March 1965, Murakami File, BHFML.

32. "Why Ignite International Incident?" *The Sporting News*, 13 March 1965; and Bob Stevens, "Giants Make Move to Get Murakami," 27 April 1965, 45, Murakami File, BHFML.

33. Glen Dickey, "Yes, Fans, There Is a Murakami," San Francisco *Chronicle*, 5 May 1965; and "Giants Move to Within 2 _ Games of LA," San Francisco *Chronicle*, 17 August 1965, Murakami File, BHFML.

34. Bob Stevens, "Anti-Japanese Man Threatens Giants Pilot Herman Franks," San Francisco *Chronicle*, 18 June 1965, Murakami File, BHFML.

35. Prescott Sullivan, "Masanori Murakami Does Unexplained Thing Other Night — Argues with Honorable Umpire," San Francisco *Examiner*, 19 June 1965; and Bob Stevens, "Americanization of Masanori Murakami Coming Along Nicely," San Francisco *Chronicle*, 29 June 1965, Murakami File, BHFML.

36. John Shelley to Masanori Murakami, 5 October 1965, Murakami File, BHFML.

37. Horace Stoneham to Masanori Murakami, 18 December 1965; and Charles Feeney to Kiyoshi Murakami, 6 December 1965, Murakami File, BHFML.

38. James K. McGee, "More Work but Less Money," San Francisco *Examiner*, 26 February 1966; and Leslie Nakashima, "Mashi's Tough Decision," 18 August 1965, Murakami File, BHFML.

39. For Murakami's later career see Bill Francis, "First Japanese-Born MLB Player Pays Visit to HOF," The Freeman's *Journal*, 15 January 1998; Art Spadner, "'Mashi Takes Hike to U.S.," *The Sporting News*, 28 February 1983, 10; and Rita Ferrandino, "Hall in Japan for Opener," Cooperstown *Crier*, 6 April 2000, Murakami File, BHFML.

40. Gordon Sukamoto, "Jackie Robinson Did It for Negroes and Murakami May Do It for Japanese," 21 September 1964, Murakami File, BHFML.

41. For examples of the cultural construction of race in coverage of Murakami see Jack McDonald, "Ice Cream, Ham and Eggs High on Murakami's 'Oh So Good' List," *The Sporting News*, 3 October 1964, Murakami File, BHFML.

42. Tom Verducci, "Waiting for Godzilla," *Sports Illustrated*, 27 January 2003, 69–70.

Part IV

BASEBALL MEDIA: LITERATURE, JOURNALISM, AND AUDIOVISUAL REPRODUCTION

Imagining the Action: Audiovisual Baseball Game Reproductions in Richmond, Virginia, 1895–1935

Eric Dewberry

Before the advent of radio and television, fans across the nation received play-by-play coverage of games through audiovisual reproductions via mechanical and electronic display boards. Spectators did not have to wait for the daily newspaper the following day to receive information about a game. Instead, enthusiasts experienced instant re-creation of the game through a running account provided by telegraph reports. These audiovisual display boards provided early coverage of the World Series. For nearly the first three decades of the twentieth century, thousands of fans from coast-to-coast gathered annually at theaters, armories, saloons, fairs, dancehalls, and outside of newspaper offices to "watch" the Fall Classic. Surprisingly, historians have failed to critically analyze the relationship between audiovisual reproduction, baseball, and the American culture.[1] Employing a case study approach, this study examines audiovisual reproductions of baseball games in Richmond, Virginia, from 1895–1935, within a social and cultural framework.

The first attempts at providing up-to-the-minute sports coverage took place in the 1870s and 1880s; saloon and billiards hall owners kept their customers informed of boxing, track, and baseball results by way of decoded telegraph messages provided directly from the event.[2] During this time, baseball was maturing into a popular form of commercial entertainment. Several factors, however, threatened the game's potential growth. Inadequate transportation posed one impediment to fans frequenting ballparks. As a result, an untapped audience emerged, demanding live audio and visual baseball game reproductions away from the ballpark. Entertainment entrepreneurs seized the opportunity, utilizing various mechanical and electri-

141

cal devices that depicted the action of the game directly from the field of play.

One of the earliest documented attempts at audiovisual reproduction of a baseball game occurred in 1894 at Baltimore's Ford Opera House during the Temple Cup Playoffs, forerunner to the World Series.[3] Known as "Compton's Electrical System," the device consisted of a ten-by-ten foot vertical display board of a baseball diamond. An outline of the field marked the center of the scoreboard, and electric bulbs designated bases and positions, player line-ups, and game situations, including balls, strikes, outs, bunts, home runs, sacrifices, double plays, and errors. A telegrapher, receiving play-by-play coverage directly from the game, would flash the respective bulbs for the player batting, nature of the play, and location of the action. The telegrapher also scribbled the results down on paper for an announcer, equipped with a megaphone, to broadcast it to the crowd.[4]

On April 22, 1895, Samuel R. Crowder, an electrician for Richmond's Western Union Telegraph branch, introduced to the city a similar, yet more elaborate mechanical play-by-play device that graphically simulated the away games of the city's beloved minor-league Bluebirds. Known as the "Little Men," the instrument was housed at the city's "legitimate" theater, the Mozart's Academy of Music.[5] The apparatus, consisting of a five-by-seven footboard outlined with a baseball diamond, was set on an incline so that the audience could see the field. Tiny wooden figures standing seven inches high represented the players. Capable of moving their arms and legs, the "little automatons" were arranged so that they could slide back and forth from base to base, or from one position on the field to another. To further re-create the game, miniature wooden balls attached to wires were raised and lowered underneath each manikin, mimicking the progress of the baseball. Operators hid stealthily beneath the board and controlled the movements of the players by twisting and squeezing numerous triggers and levers. R. L. Gill, lead operator under the board, invited a reporter from the Richmond *Times* to witness the complex operation. The reporter explained:

> When the "ticker" announced a player up, one of Mr. Gill's assistants puts the diminutive player on the field, and by working the trigger the audience sees the little fellow walk towards the plate, pick up his bat, and square himself to "swipe" anything that comes his way. Then the telegraph says "Ball one," and Mr. Gill informs his assistants of this fact, at the same time causing the little pitcher to deliver the ball, while "Sammy" announces the fact to the audience. And so it goes throughout the game, every play being made just at the instant it takes place on the real diamond, miles away.[6]

"Sammy," dressed as an umpire, colorfully commentated on the action to the audience. Two large blackboards, standing adjacent to the diamond, completed the invention: one board displayed the names and lineups of the two teams, and the other recorded runs, hits, and errors.

One hundred and fifty enthusiastic fans witnessed the opening day of "Little Men." What spectators watched, however, was hardly an accurate depiction of a baseball game. Crowder had hastily rushed the debut of his invention to cover the Bluebird's first away series in Lynchburg. His technicians had yet to master the difficulty of maneuvering the figures, and the board itself was incomplete. Only nine figures were ready on opening day, thus representing only one team. On one occasion during the series, a player lost his head while "gliding" after a pop fly. Another player "made a bold dash for first base, backwards."[7]

Despite the clumsy and imperfect transmission of the contest, Crowder's invention generated excitement. By the end of May, attendance at the presentations ran as high as 800 people a game. Local newspapers reviewed almost every performance of the "Little Men." The sheer novelty of the "Little Men" contributed to the popularity of the entertainment. The *Times* reported that "the playing off bases and rushing together of the players, popping their little heads like walnuts, is quite amusing, and the manner in which they imitate sliding ... never failed to raise a laugh."[8] The invention's realism impressed others. One female fan enjoyed the lifelike manner in which the "Little Men" interacted with the crowd. After seeing a performance, she was quoted as saying, "Aren't they just the dearest, cutest little fellows you ever saw, and so polite; why they bow as sweetly as 'real live men' when applauded."[9]

In June of 1895, inspired by the enormous popularity of the "Little Men" in Richmond, Crowder ventured north to market his invention. Leaving behind assistants to continue operating the board at the Academy until his return, Crowder traveled to the cities of Baltimore, Philadelphia, Pittsburgh, New York City, Boston, and Atlantic City.[10] Northern reaction to the "Little Men" was overwhelmingly positive. A Baltimore *Sun* reporter was captivated at how the "figures move their arms, legs, and bodies."[11] The "Little Men" proved successful in these cities, as well as others, and sold abundantly throughout the country.[12]

In Richmond, the "Little Men" remained extremely popular. Games recreated in the posh Academy of Music offered an alternative environment to the ballpark. The theater offered a virtuous and hospitable atmosphere compared to the ofttimes rowdy behavior associated with the Bluebirds' West End Park. Although spectators at West End Park were largely white middle-class men, possessed of enough disposable income to afford a ticket and spare time to enjoy an afternoon ball game, blue-collar fans also attended.[13] Generally, middle-class fans sat in the more expensive awning-covered grandstand located behind home plate, while working-class fans opted for the cheaper bleacher seating, stretching down the first and third base lines. With beer sold underneath the bleachers, the blue-collar fans had a well-earned reputation for rowdiness; they enjoyed spitting, kicking, drinking, smoking, excessive yelling, and even throwing objects at the umpire.[14] Undoubtedly, such saloon-like behavior in the stands, and sometimes equally disreputable behavior exhibited by the players on the field, dissuaded some fans from attending the games, especially women.[15]

Unlike the ballpark, however, the strictest order was always observed at the Academy. Crowder provided a respectable environment for the audiences of the "Little Men." He encouraged families to attend the games, and many times admitted women into the Academy free of charge.[16] A *Times* reporter proclaimed that the "Little Men" audience was saved the "kicking against the umpire, the yell of 'Here's your cigars, cigarettes, peanuts, and chewing gum.' The leather lung boy, the clouds of cigar smoke, and other nuisances that must be born at the base-ball park."[17] In contrast, Academy games attracted well-dressed, respectable citizenry, including the mayor and other public officials.[18] The climate within the Academy appealed to women. Local newspapers reported that ofttimes more "ladies" were present than men at the presentations.[19] The atmosphere was even suitable for children. During one game, 150 orphans, sponsored by the Masonic Lodge, enjoyed peanuts and lemonade as they watched the "Little Men" play.[20] In addition to avoiding rowdy behavior, fans also avoided harsh weather elements inherent with the ballpark. Spectators were so caught up in "imagining" the game that, as the *Times* reported, they often forgot they were "deprived of the discomforts of the sunshine, heat, and occasional shower."[21] The inviting conditions provided at the Academy attracted spectators who otherwise would not frequent baseball games. In an era when women and children were increasingly touted as consumers in society, Crowder reaped profits by maintaining a reputable environment.

Blacks were allowed to attend the Academy, but were relegated to segregated seating and forced to use a separate side entrance, accessed from the alleyway, when entering and exiting the building. African-American baseball fans faced equivalent discrimination at West End Park. The ensuing embarrassment blacks faced when confronted with such inequalities at the theater or ballpark prompted many to remain at home rather than attend a show or ballgame. Moreover, the seats available to blacks in the Academy occupied the last two rows of the balcony, and the chance of actually seeing the miniature seven-inch tall manikins from atop the structure was improbable.

The orderly conduct expected at the Academy did not put a damper on the crowd's spirit. Fans enjoyed themselves immensely while rooting for the "Little Men." Commenting on audience behavior, the Richmond *Dispatch* reported, "The crowd was wild, calling to the players just as if they were at

West End Park. The rooters did duty when rooting was needed and applauded every play."[22] Fans who went to West End Park to watch the Bluebird's home games ofttimes frequented the "Little Men" games. Two "old-time rooters, the 'Umbrella Man' and 'Old Man Scissors,'" regularly led the audience in cheering with the "beat of their bugles."[23] Women even joined in the revelry by enthusiastically "waving their handkerchiefs" and applauding for good plays.[24] Nevertheless, when rooting became too raucous, Crowder seized control of the situation. He guaranteed women that men would not cheer directly into their ears or otherwise annoy them, thus encouraging their attendance.[25] Maintaining a spirited, yet disciplined environment proved beneficial to the "Little Men's" success.

Added to the suitable setting and entertainment value at the "Little Men" presentations, play-by-play commentary offered an easy opportunity for people to learn the game. Coinciding with the action reproduced on the board, Crowder provided a complete description of each play in a clear and concise manner between pitches and innings. He became somewhat of a local celebrity and the prototype of modern sportscasters, entertaining the audience with comic asides and commentary.

The "Little Men" broadcasts appealed to women and small girls who had not previously known the rules of baseball. The "ladies were completely captivated over the new game," reported the *Times*. "They keep the score, applaud, and take, if it be possible, more interest in the game than the men."[26] Eleven-year-old Laura M'Cabe witnessed a "Little Men" re-creation, admitting that initially she "could not understand it as much as the boys could." She learned enough of the game, however, to provide a detailed overview of the action in a letter to the *Dispatch*. She remembered numerous catcher/pitcher changes during the contest and a game winning hit by a Bluebird player.[27] Callie Ryland, a special female correspondent for the *Times* who knew nothing about baseball, "often wondered how so many intellectual men, as well as others, could go every afternoon to see the 'Little Men' play." Given an exclusive opportunity to report on the "Little Men," Ryland admitted she learned a great deal about baseball from the "Little Men." Witnessed a dramatic, game winning home run by a Bluebird player, Ryland confessed that the game was so competitive that she found herself highly entertained.[28]

For the remainder of the 1895 season, the "Little Men" continued to attract large audiences, as the Bluebirds convincingly advanced through their schedule to win the Virginia League pennant.[29] So profitable was the first season, that for the upcoming 1896 season, Crowder leased a "larger and cooler" building on the corner of Twelfth and Main Streets to house the "Little Men." Since almost all theaters in the South closed in the summer due to the excessive heat, Crowder advertised that electric fans cooled the "Little Men's" new home. In addition to the electric fans, Crowder constructed a larger steel board, scheduled every Bluebird's away game, and promised to broadcast all the performances personally.[30] Fans enjoyed the new accommodations, and, coupled with the continuing enthusiasm over the Bluebirds on-field success, the "Little Men" remained popular throughout the 1896 season. The Bluebirds brought home their second straight pennant at season's end; however, the Virginia League collapsed after only two years in existence due to poor ticket sales in other cities.[31] In 1897, the Bluebirds entered the Atlantic League, and, for unknown reasons, Crowder transferred the "Little Men" back to the Academy.[32] This was the last season for the "Little Men." Perhaps, after two years, the novelty of the invention waned. In addition, since the Atlantic League consisted primarily of Northeastern teams, civic rivalry — so existent in the close-knit Virginia League — declined, and interest in road coverage of the Bluebirds declined.[33] In 1898, attendance at Atlantic League games plummeted, and, midway through the 1899 season, the League disbanded.[34]

After the turn of the century, mechanical and electronic baseball reproduction display boards popped up in cities nationwide. The popularity of display boards coincided with soaring interest in the game, stimulated by the creation of the World Series. The press was also instrumental in the growth of the baseball reproduction display boards. In the first two decades of the twentieth century, newspaper companies increased their baseball coverage immensely. Stanley Walker, editor of the *New York Herald Tribune*, believed that the paper's sports audience was probably larger than their general clientele.[35] As the World Series grew in popularity, newspaper companies, already equipped with telegraphy and a large fan readership, graphically simulated the games on display boards.

During the cross-town World Series between the Cubs and the White Sox in 1906, Chicago hosted the first audiovisual scoreboard re-creations of the Series. The *Chicago Tribune*, taking advantage of the overwhelming demand for tickets to sold-out games, rented several theaters and armories in the city, furnishing each with crude "twenty-by-twenty foot wooden boards" with "windows representing each base on the diamond." To reproduce the action, *Tribune* employees placed numbered cards, symbolizing each player in the corresponding windows depending upon the results from the field.[36]

Richmond did not receive audiovisual re-creations of the World Series until October 14, 1911, when the Richmond *Times-Dispatch* gave the city its first live reproduction of a baseball game since the "Little Men." Fifteen hundred people jammed Main Street between Ninth and Tenth Streets to watch Philadelphia battle the New York Giants in the World Series.[37] Reproduction of the game was cast on a primitive electronic scoreboard similar to the "Compton" device. Hanging from a second story window of the *Times-Dispatch* office, the board was equipped with electric lights that displayed the player at bat, the bases occupied, strikes, balls, and outs.[38] The scoreboard, displayed outdoors on the public streets, was available for all to view for free. The *Times-Dispatch* utilized the scoreboard as a public relations gimmick, not as a direct profit-making event. The paper sarcastically advised that a fan could save his "Christmas money" by watching the scoreboard rather than exhausting funds traveling miles away to see games in person like a "less frugal brother."[39] Heeding the advice, tens of thousands of fans, by week's end, had viewed the scoreboard.

Inspired by the overall popularity of the *Times-Dispatch* display board, numerous Richmond entrepreneurs and business owners offered a variety of outlets for audiovisual reproduction of the World Series. The first venture hailed from the *Times-Dispatch*'s cross-town competitor, the Richmond *News Leader*. On October 2, 1912, the *News Leader* introduced an electric scoreboard at the Virginia State Fair, located on the city's north side. The scoreboard's construction was nearly identical to the *Times-Dispatch* board; yet, it was not free like the *Times-Dispatch* scoreboard as State Fair visitors were charged an admission price.[40] The *News Leader* scoreboard was positioned in front of a 5,000-seat grandstand, intended to seat patrons at a variety of entertainments, most notably horse racing and vaudeville acts. Confusingly, these different amusements transpired simultaneously. Nevertheless, the board proved to be the center of attention. The *News Leader* reporting that the grandstand filled with spectators each day, sarcastically offered their apologies to the "race horse men ... for drawing everybody's interest from the horses to the electric World Series scoreboard."[41] The guarantee of a large audience at the State Fair made the scoreboard a success.

Other venues for audiovisual re-creation of the World Series in Richmond were not as popular. In 1912 and 1913, moving picture footage, fifteen to twenty minutes in length, of the World Series was presented to Richmonders at the Colonial Theater, a vaudeville house owned by Jake Wells, former player-manager of the Bluebirds. The coverage was not successful because the pictures were shown nearly a month after the Series had ended. With few film distribution centers and a limited number of World Series reels for rent, exhibitors were forced to wait weeks to obtain the special "feature" length coverage of the games.[42]

Another unsuccessful audiovisual World Series reproduction endeavor was introduced to Richmonders on October 25, 1913, when George Coleman of Washington D.C. presented his "Coleman Baseball Players" at Belvidere Hall, a saloon and billiard hall that catered to working-class men.[43] Coleman re-created the World Series on his board nearly two weeks after the Series ended through transcribed game logs. The "Coleman Players" resembled the "Little Men." The "Players" were tiny semi-transparent figures, representing the players. Flashing lights behind the figures illuminated the action, while grooves cut throughout the board allowed the "Players" to move around the diamond. Mechanically, a light bulb, simulating a baseball, moved across the board through a set of grooves, replicating the action of the ball in flight, an enhancement absent from the other display boards. The "Coleman Players" performed in the evening. This offered working-class men and those who could not take time off from work during the afternoon a chance to "see" a World Series game. In addition, within the bar, patrons could indulge rowdy behavior — drinking, smoking, and hollering — associated with the ballpark. Savoring this male-bachelor subculture, though, was not enough to sustain the "Coleman Players" in Richmond; this was their first and last performance in the city. As with moving picture footage, delayed coverage hurt the "Coleman Players."

In 1915, the Academy of Music, coincidentally now owned by Jake Wells, offered live play-by-play coverage for twenty-five cent admission on its "Electraboard." Its construction was virtually identical to the newspaper's electronic scoreboards. Although spectators had indoor and spacious seating, this was the only year the Electraboard was displayed in the Academy. The opportunity to see newspaper scoreboards for free proved a deterrent to Wells' venture.

Throughout the 1910s, the *Times-Dispatch* and *News Leader* scoreboards attracted tens of thousands of fans annually. Fans enjoyed the instantaneous results, economic accessibility, and the appeal of rooting side-by-side with thousands of fans. The sea of people crowded around these boards was a spectacle in itself; spectators could converse and share the game's emotional highs and lows with others. When games are played in front of an audience, the audience itself becomes a source of excitement.[44]

The social-makeup of fans differed greatly at the respective newspaper-sponsored display boards. The *Times-Dispatch* office was located in Richmond's business district on Main Street. Many businessmen made up the daytime crowd at the board, stopping to see the scoreboard on their way to and from work, meetings, or lunch breaks. Some would even watch the board directly from work. The *Times-Dispatch* reported that during the 1913 World Series "ten floors of bristling faces" occupied the west façade of the American National Bank Building. Lawyers, realtors, and insurance men drew up their chairs to the windows and watched the electric record like occupants of $30 reserved seats at the Polo Grounds.[45]

The *Times-Dispatch* scoreboard was free, and the newspaper reported that the fans on the ground included "white and black, old and young, and beggars and brokers."[46] Astonishingly, unlike the separate seating in ballparks and theaters, segregation did not exist on the public streets during the scoreboard reproductions. African Americans rooted side-by-side with whites. Annual photographs of the crowds at the *Times-Dispatch* scoreboard reveal many black faces intermingled with those of whites. The newspaper reported that the positive spirit of the baseball game "overshadowed the caste and color" of the crowd.[47] For black and white fans alike, the experience was surreal.

Women, however, rarely attended the *Times-Dispatch* re-creations. Photographs of the crowd indicate that few women were present. The location of the *Times-Dispatch* office within Richmond's business district discouraged their turnout given the separate sphere ideology that dominated the era.[48] Women were more likely to be found thronging the retail district located along Broad Street, a few blocks away. Many men deemed it improper to have their wives join them as part of the scoreboard crowd, and middle-class women felt uncomfortable viewing the board by themselves. Instead, they waited elsewhere. The *Times-Dispatch* reported that the women "without getting weary" stood by for their husbands in nearby Capitol Square, a more reputable location.[49] Contrasted to the indoor reproductions, the corporate climate connected to the *Times-Dispatch* scoreboard did not appeal to middle-class women.

The audience present at the *News Leader* scoreboard differed from that congregated at the *Times-Dispatch* device. Unlike the predominately male, business-class crowd found on Main Street, patrons at the State Fair display board represented a wider cross-section of Virginia society. Providing an assortment of entertainment and exhibits, the Fair attracted men and women, rural and urban people, black and white, and the young and old.[50] Examination of photographs of the State Fair grandstands, located in front of the scoreboard, shows women intermixed with men. These photographs, however, reveal no African Americans within the crowd. Apparently, as at the ballpark, segregated seating prevailed at the State Fair grandstand.[51]

Attendance at baseball games soared in the 1920s, as leisure time increased for many. During the "golden age" of sport, baseball magnates and newspaper companies collaborated to increase the popularity of sport. They sold baseball as a nationalizing force, and the game took on mythic proportions. Intellectual Morris Raphael Cohen contended, "Baseball emerged as America's secular national religion." The press and baseball magnates manufactured sports heroes like never before.[52] The public's identification with Babe Ruth and other compensatory heroes helped Americans cope with the rigors of daily life in a fast-paced, changing world.[53] For many fans across the nation, the closest they could come to "watching" their heroes play was through audiovisual reproductions of the World Series.

During the 1920s, as more and more spectators flooded city blocks in Richmond to watch the World Series, both the *News Leader* and *Times-Dispatch* made changes in their coverage. In 1923, the *News Leader* moved their coverage of the World Series from the State Fair to their new office, located downtown. Christening their new home, the company introduced a new, graphically enhanced, electromagnetic scoreboard to cover the World Series. Erected atop a wooden platform outside of their office, an aluminum sphere, representing a baseball, moved along a series of wires, while white squares flashed individually, mimicking the base runner's every move.[54] A bell rang when denoting a base hit, and a *News Leader* employee served as announcer, narrating each play through a loudspeaker system.

In 1924, the *Times-Dispatch* introduced a new graphically illuminated electronic scoreboard named the "Playograph." Individual flashing lights simulated the progress of the ball and base runners on the scoreboard. Unlike the *News Leader* board, the "Playograph" did not need the aid of play-by-play broadcasting from an announcer. Game situations, including singles, doubles, triples, wild pitches, and balks, were flashed at the bottom of the board. In addition, both the *Times-Dispatch* and *News Leader* scoreboards listed the names of the players.[55]

With these enhanced graphical capabilities, fans could follow play-by-play illustration more easily. The *News Leader* boasted that their scoreboard "left little to the imagination," claiming that "everything but the personality of the player was supplied," and the audience, asserted the paper, had "imagination sufficient for that."[56] The new scoreboards were more informative, and, like the "Little Men," they served as a teaching tool for spectators who did not understand the game. As the "Playograph" labeled numerous game situations at the bottom of the board, fans, without the aid of play-by-play broadcasting, could easily follow the game. A spectator of the *Times-Dispatch* scoreboard claimed that he enjoyed not hearing an announcer broadcast the game: "Though I'm not exactly an expert at the sport. I can follow each play with ease on the board."[57]

The crowds present at the display boards during the World Series constituted the largest single day public amusement event in Richmond. In 1924 and 1925, both newspaper scoreboards averaged from 10,000–14,000 spectators, as the Senators, from Washington, the major league city closest to Richmond, played in the World Series. Like other forms of commercial entertainment in the early twentieth century, including motion picture theaters and amusement parks, the scoreboards came under scrutiny from cultural guardians. Controversy arose when fans demanded operation of World Series scoreboards on Sunday, thus challenging existing blue laws, restricting Richmonders from engaging in any business or amusement activities on the Sabbath. Sunday blue laws in Richmond dated back to the colonial era, and in the 1890s city officials banned the playing of baseball on the Sabbath.[58] In respect to the law, both the *News Leader* and *Times-Dispatch* refused to cover World Series games played on Sundays. C. C. Stockton, a baseball fan from Richmond, believed that the Sunday laws were "ancient and archaic," and that showing Sunday games "would benefit all classes concerned in this great American sport."[59]

Supporters of the blue laws praised the newspaper companies for not showing World Series games on Sunday. O. A. Hawkins, a member of Battery Park Christian Church, thanked the newspapers on behalf of "10,000 men in Bible classes on Sundays and thousands of women and children in Sunday-schools." Members of the baseball fraternity, however, proposed change. Since World Series games were played in the afternoon, one enthusiast suggested that people could attend church in the morning, watch the scoreboard in the afternoon, and return to church in the evening. The fan asked, "What chance does a man that works in a shop ... have to see a game except on Sunday?" He challenged all "baseball fans to wake up and demand the operation of the scoreboard on Sunday."[60]

In 1926, the *News Leader*, reversing their approach to the city's blue laws, chose to operate their scoreboard on a Sunday to reproduce a World Series game. The newspaper could not use the public streets, so they cut a deal with Jake Wells, now owner of the local minor-league baseball stadium, Tate Field, to erect it there. The venture was a huge success. Sixteen thousand fans crowded into the stadium to "watch" the St. Louis Cardinals play the New York Yankees. Placed behind second base, the scoreboard faced home plate, allowing spectators to enjoy the comfort of the grandstands. Nonetheless, some fans were forced to take seats in the far bleachers where they could hear, but not see, the playing of the game.[61] The next day, a *News Leader* editorial asserted, "We do not know if Mayor Bright was in the crowd, or how many of the council were there. If the Mayor and the city-lawmakers did go ..., they must have pondered the demand for recreation [on Sunday] disclosed by the tremendous turnout."[62]

In addition to the newspaper scoreboards, the rise of radio in the 1920s offered a new medium by which Richmond could receive World Series coverage. Broadcasting baseball games seemed natural for radio. In 1922, several radio stations first broadcast live play-by-play coverage of the World Series to an estimated five million listeners nationwide.[63] The number of listeners would grow throughout the decade.

Surprisingly, radio's coverage of the World Series did not immediately hurt the popularity of the newspaper scoreboards. A limited number of sets and shoddy reception circumscribed early radio. In the late 1920s, attendance at the *News Leader* and *Times-Dispatch* scoreboards averaged 4,000–5,000 spectators per game at each venue.[64] Yet, the *News Leader* and WRVA, Richmond's local radio station, collaborated on World Series coverage, as the newspaper allowed the station to broadcast directly from their office via telegraph.[65] It was estimated that the dual coverage served upward of "50,000 Richmonders" throughout the World Series.[66]

Radio would ultimately be the downfall for the World Series reproduction display boards, as its coverage possessed certain advantages over the newspaper scoreboards. In time, with a twist of the dial, any listener from anywhere in Richmond, or America for that matter, had access to a variety of programming that stretched from coast-to-coast.[67] In 1928, WRVA affiliated with national broadcasting company, NBC, increasing its listening potential by 300 to 400 percent. WRVA installed a new, and more powerful, 5,000 kilowatt antenna.[68] In addition, radio set ownership increased. In 1922, it was estimated that 400,000 sets existed; by 1930, the number had jumped to approximately thirteen million.[69] Throughout the decade, World Series broadcasting matured as well. Inspired by the pioneering Graham McNamee, sportscasters increasingly incorporated colorful description and commentary into game coverage, providing details about how the game felt and looked. Some of the early World Series broadcasts were covered live from the seats in the grandstands rather than in separate press booths.[70] Such broadcasting conveyed the intimacy of rooting beside thousands of cheering fans, transmitting sounds of the game such as the crack of the bat hitting a ball or the smack the ball makes as a pitch hits the catcher's mitt.[71] Improvements in World Series broadcasts, augmented by colorful realism, snap, and sound, simulated the sensory experience of being at the game. Fans, at home or elsewhere, could savor having the World Series come to them. Indeed, radio coverage offered almost everything the graphically enhanced scoreboards did and then some. By the late 1920s, "talkies" brought new sights and sound to motion picture newsreel coverage. As a result, thousands of scoreboards were retired across America, including, in 1934, those of the *Times-Dispatch* and *News Leader*.[72]

It can be argued that the graphically illuminated re-creations radically altered the nation's cultural identity. Richmonders and others across America gathered in front of these display boards to watch the World Series in an "imagined community of interest," encouraging spectators to share similar symbols, heroes, stories, and ideas that revolved around baseball and American culture. These display boards were one of the many forces building a national mass culture. Similar to nationally marketed periodicals, consumer goods, and entertainment products, the display boards opened up new possibilities for expressions of community and collective identity in disparate locales.[73] The new baseball fans had their counterparts in new groups of shoppers, movie patrons, diners, and travelers.

The reproduction display boards were instrumental in encouraging the development of the sport. Abetting baseball's transformation into commercial entertainment, the audiovisual reproductions brought coverage to fans who otherwise could not have seen Major League Baseball. New recruits included workers, women, and blacks. Reproductions, from diverse backgrounds, offered fans accessibility to baseball, providing alternative environments to watch the sport, at prices more affordable than at the ballpark. In addition, the reproductions also served as a teaching tool for the game with easy to follow play-by-play action.

For Major League Baseball, the scoreboards infiltrated geographical boundaries. In Richmond's case, and for much of the South, the Washington franchise was the closest major league team. For fans in the far West, the nearest teams were in Chicago and St. Louis. For these distant spectators, the audiovisual reproductions of the World Series approximated the experience of actually "seeing" their favorite heroes and teams play.

The audiovisual display boards were also influential for future modes of baseball coverage. The experience of receiving instantaneous results, the spectacle of large crowds, and the demand to broaden one's imagination to visualize the action on the field re-created the sensation of attending a game. Robert Harper, sports reporter for the *Times-Dispatch* during the 1920s, perhaps best explains the sensory experience of viewing audiovisual reproduced baseball games on a display board. He wrote:

> The climax of a baseball season, reported play by play on a scoreboard, affords a thrill.... There is something gripping in watching a game via the scoreboard route. To keep one's eyes glued on the little electric bulbs, ears attuned to catch the faintest ringing of the bell denoting a base hit, and giving vent to one's emotions, just as if the athletes in person were dancing about the scoreboard, keeps one in a state of suspense, which gives a greater thrill to some people than being on the scene of the conflict.[74]

The "thrill" of imagining the action through audiovisual coverage of baseball served as a precursor to radio, television, and Internet broadcasting. The sensory experience that reproductions provided fans influenced the attempt of future media to capture the look and feel of being at the game.

Notes

1. Norman L. Macht, "Watching the World Series," *American History Illustrated* 26 (September–October 1991): 49–51. For brief mentioning, see Harold Seymour, *Baseball: The Early Years* (New York: Oxford University Press, 1960), 79; Jules Tygiel, *Past Time: Baseball As History* (Oxford: Oxford University Press, 2000), 65–68; Benjamin Rader, *Baseball: A History of America's Game* (Urbana, IL: University of Illinois Press, 1992), 160–161; and Stacy L. Lorenz, "'A Lively Interest on the Prairies': Western Canada, the Mass Media, and a 'World of Sport,' 1870–1939," *Journal of Sports History* 27 (2): 195–227.

2. Richard D. Mandell, *Sport: A Cultural History* (New York: Columbia University Press, 1984), 184–185; and Steven J. Smethers and Lee Joliffe, "The Role of Telegraphy in the Development of Radio Broadcasting." Paper presented at the AEJMC Annual Meeting (Boston, MA, 7–11August 1991), passim.

3. Macht, 49–50; and *The Sun* (Baltimore) 14 October 1894. For a description on this

and other audiovisual scoreboards, see "Mechanical Baseball Bulletin Boards," *Scientific American* (October 11, 1913), 285.

4. Macht, 50–51; and *United States Patent and Trade Organization*, #543,851, available from <http://www.uspto.gov.>

5. For more information on social class and theater, see: Richard Butsch, *The Making of American Audiences: From Stage to Television, 1750–1990* (Cambridge, Cambridge University Press, 2000).

6. *Richmond Times*, 25 August 1895. Hereafter cited *RT. Sporting News*, 23 March 1895, 2.

7. *RT*, 23 April 1895.

8. Ibid.

9. *RT*, 7 May 1895.

10. *RT*, 6 June 1895.

11. *The Sun* (Baltimore), 20 June 1895.

12. *The News Leader* Richmond), 25 February 1938. Hereafter cited *NL*.

13. Steven A. Riess, *Touching Base: Professional Baseball and American Culture in the Progressive Era* (Westport, CT: Greenwood Press, 1980), 26–30.

14. David Nasaw, *Going Out: The Rise and Fall of Public Amusement* (New York: Basic Books, 1993), 100–102.

15. Seymour, 328–329.

16. *RT*, 5 May 1895.

17. *RT*, 23 April 1895.

18. *RT*, 30 May 1895.

19. *RT*, 10 May 1895.

20. *Richmond Dispatch*, 24 May 1896. Hereafter cited *RD*.

21. *RT*, 7 May 1895.

22. *RD*, 13 August 1895.

23. *RT*, 9 May 1895.

24. *RT*, 27 August 1895.

25. *RT*, 9 May 1895.

26. *RT*, 10 May 1895.

27. *RD*, 26 May 1896.

28. *RT*, 30 May 1895.

29. *RD*, 29 August 1895.

30. *RT*, 19 April 1896.

31. *RD*, 10 July, 23 August 1896.

32. W. Harrison Daniel and Scott P. Mayer, *Baseball and Richmond: A History of the Professional Game*, (Jefferson, NC: McFarland and Company, Inc., 2002), 37.

33. Riess, 13–14.

34. Eric Dewberry, "Jake Wells, Entertainment Entrepreneur of the South: A Study of His Career in Richmond, Virginia, 1894–1927," MA Thesis (Richmond: Virginia Commonwealth University, 2003), 38.

35. Wayne M. Towers, "Gee Whiz!' and 'Aw Nuts!': Radio and Newspaper Coverage of Baseball in the 1920s." Paper presented at the Annual Meeting of the Association for Education in Journalism (Sixty-second, Houston, TX, August 5–8, 1979), 3.

36. Macht, 50.

37. *Times-Dispatch* (Richmond), 15 October 1911. Hereafter cited *RTD*.

38. *RTD*, 14 October 1911.

39. *RTD*, 18 October 1911.

40. Michael A. Trotti, "When Coney Island Arrived in Richmond: Leisure in the Capital at the Turn of the Twentieth Century," *Virginia Cavalcade* 51 (Autumn 2002): 168–179.

41. *NL*, 2 & 9 October 1912.

42. See Benjamin B. Hampton, *A History of the Movies* (New York: Arno Press & The New York Times, 1970), 116; and Kathryn H. Fuller, *At the Picture Show: Small-Town Audiences and the Creation of Movie Fan Culture* (Washington, DC: Smithsonian Institution Press, 1996), 47–48.

43. YWCA Papers "Know Your City Survey, 1911," Virginia Commonwealth University

Special Collections, Richmond, Virginia, Box 35, folder 11. Richmond City Directory, Hill Directory Company, 1913, 1134.

44. Benjamin G. Rader, *In Its Own Image: How Television Has Transformed Sports* (New York: The Free Press, 1984), 10.

45. *RTD*, 8 October 1913.

46. Ibid.

47. Ibid.

48. Kathy Peiss, *Cheap Amusements: Working Women and Leisure in Turn-of-the-Century New York* (Philadelphia: Temple University Press, 1986), 4–6.

49. *RTD*, 9 October 1912.

50. For a discussion on fairs in the South, see Ted Owenby, *Subduing Satan: Religion, Recreation, and Manhood in the Rural South, 1865–1920* (Chapel Hill: University of North Carolina Press, 1990).

51. For specific information on blacks and the Virginia State Fair, see Trotti, 168–179.

52. Morris Raphael Cohen, "Baseball," *Dial*, 47 (26 July 1919): 57–58. Cited in Riess, 39.

53. Rader, *In Its Own*, 14–16.

54. *NL*, 11 October 1923.

55. *RTD*, 2 October 1924.

56. *NL*, 11 October 1923.

57. *RTD*, 15 October 1923.

58. Samuel C. Shepherd Jr., *Avenues of Faith: Shaping the Urban Religious Culture of Richmond, Virginia, 1900–1929* (Tuscaloosa: University of Alabama Press, 2001), 93–96; and Dewberry, 92–97.

59. *NL*, 15 October 1925.

60. *NL*, 6 October 1927.

61. *NL*, 11 October 1926.

62. Ibid.

63. Towers, 1 and 5.

64. Averages come from author's calculations of newspapers annual estimated headcount. In 1924 and 1925, the newspaper scoreboards reached attendance figures upwards of 10,000 spectators a day because the Washington Senators were in the World Series. For example, see *RNL*, 8, 9 October 1925; and *RTD*, 8, 9 October 1925.

65. *NL*, 2 October 1926; Macht, 5; and Smethers and Joliffe, 17–19.

66. *NL*, 8 October 1925.

67. *NL*, 11 October 1926.

68. Papers of Calvin T. Lucy III, Virginia Commonwealth University Special Collections, Box 5, Misc. folder, Coverage Map, 1935.

69. Melvin Defleur, *Theories of Mass Communication*, Second Edition (New York: David McKay Company, Inc., 1970), 66.

70. Later, broadcasters would remain in local studios and reproduce the games from telegraph messages. They used taped recordings of audience cheering, and baseball sounds as heard from the grandstands to further recreate their broadcast. Broadcasters even mimicked sounds of the game manually. For example, they hit pieces of wood together to simulate a bat hitting a ball.

71. Susan J. Douglas, *Listening In: Radio and the American Imagination, from Amos 'n' Andy and Edward R. Murrow to Wolfman Jack and Howard Stern* (New York: Times Book, 1999), 204–205.

72. *RNL*, 6 October 1934.

73. Lorenz, 195–227.

74. *RTD*, 10 October 1923.

Joe McCarthy and the Fourth Estate: A Window onto Baseball and Media Relations in the Mid-Twentieth Century

Alan H. Levy

The role of the press in the history of baseball (and of sports more generally) has clearly been a most significant facet in the development of the game's popularity. Since the beginning of professional baseball in the nineteenth century, the media has played a vital role. Professional baseball would likely have never succeeded without the presence of an active press. Public interest in each of America's professional baseball cities first grew in significant measure due to press coverage. In some respects, the counterpoint was also true — newspaper sales grew with the coverage given to baseball and other sports. Editor/publisher Joseph Pulitzer was among the first newspapermen to recognize the need to provide the reading public with more extensive coverage in areas of interest beyond the "straight news." First in St. Louis, and subsequently in New York, Pulitzer pioneered the establishment of separate sections in his papers, especially in his deftly expanded Sunday editions. Among the most important and popular of these "papers within papers" were the sports pages.[1] Polls in various decades of the twentieth-century have steadily shown that significant numbers of Americans turn first to the sports section when they open a newspaper. With such expansions and specializations, and the copying of Pulitzer's structure by other editors who saw that his system sold copies, teams of reporters emerged who devoted their professional energies exclusively to the world of sports.

Just like some reporters who camped out at city hall and covered just the city government, early twentieth-century baseball scribes increasingly lived within and for the national pastime. The ways they covered teams and people associated with baseball and other sports took on an unprecedented intensity. The tonality in the coverage shifted markedly over time and place. The shifts in the reporters' ways were part of the overall evolution of the public's perception of the appropriate role of journalists in society. Chroniclers of facts, snoops, muckrakers, analysts, psychologists, cheerleaders, nay-sayers, optimists, cynics, proud parents, stern parents, lap dogs, guard dogs, attack dogs, gossipers, prosecutors, defense attorneys, dispassionate judges—the list of journalistic styles is long, and each label has had its day in regard to evolving public perceptions of the media's legitimacy as well as its inappropriateness. The forces involved in the changing attitudes about the media in baseball (and in society more generally) mirror some of the key political, economic, and social trends in the past century of American history as well as some key developments within the history of baseball.

Much has been written about the ways that reporters covered stars in such a sports heyday as the 1920s in contrast to the media's ways in more recent decades. While not wrong, it is somewhat too neat and simple to say that the media has simply changed from a group that looked the other way in regard to personal faults and foibles of stars into one which incessantly "digs up the dirt." That sea change has certainly been a major overall trend in both sports and politics. While such a change from cheerleader to muckraker is certainly in evidence, a more careful look at the history of the media in sports and politics shows much more texture and subtlety beyond a straight line of ascent (or descent) from optimist to cynic. In the early twentieth century, baseball already presented media figures of varying media cast, from the villainous Ty Cobb to the saintly Christy Mathewson. Babe Ruth, exciting and charismatic as he was, proved, of course, the perfect figure for the media as it emerged in both size and social significance after the First World War. Both he and the media were New York-based, and that importance cannot be overstated. His endearing nature, furthermore, was perfect for the generally positive spin that journalists knew best to put upon their stories, for that was clearly what sold copies among 1920s Americans who looked for roaring good times coupled with tinges of innocence and nostalgia.[2] In the 1920s, had a personality like Ty Cobb been based in New York, the press would not have known what to do with him. Ruth's talent and contrasting warmth worked wonders, and he towered over all other baseball and indeed over all other sports figures between World War I and the Depression. As much of the public saw a speak-easy frequenter as someone doing nothing wrong, it would have been bad salesmanship, as well as personally hypocritical, for most newspapermen to take any moral high ground with Babe Ruth.

Ruth's decline came with the Depression, and the search for new sports/media idols then occurred amidst very different social circumstances.

This was the very time when Joe McCarthy emerged as the New York Yankees' manager. A significant symbol of the contrast between the new and old eras was indeed the Ruth/McCarthy conflict. Their uncomfortable relationship, which began the day McCarthy became the Yankees' manager in 1931, was in itself a story for the press and readers of the day. The story was symbolic of even more, however. Ruth had epitomized the devil-may-care days of the Roaring Twenties. What writers like Frederick Lewis Allen had sentimentalized about the 1920s amidst the economy's collapse made memories of Babe Ruth's prime years seem all the more romantic.[3] In the 1930s, some yearned for such non-conformity and swagger to reappear. This yearning found form in the national pastime in such figures as Dizzy Dean and his teammates on the St. Louis Cardinals' Gas House Gang who gave American sports fans tidbits of such romantic innocence and care-free nostalgia. But, without any doubt, the triumphant team of the decade of the 1930s was the New York Yankees, and they were no Gas House Gang. They traveled in suits and ties and disdained virtually all cults of personality. The early Yankees "dynasty" of the 1920s had been but one of several that gained the utmost respect of baseball fans. The Yankees of the mid-1930s and early 1940s were the team that truly eclipsed all the perceived "dynasties" which had preceded them. No one had ever won four straight pennants, or seven in eight years, or four straight World Series, or seven in twelve years. Furthermore, no one had ever achieved such victories in such an utterly crushing manner. The Yankees' seven Series titles from 1932 to 1943 yielded a won/loss record of 28 and 5. Their pennants were each won by very wide margins (the narrowest in 1942 was by nine games). By 1938, one Cleveland newspaper was printing only the standings of the second to eighth place teams in the American League. Amidst this total domination of the game, when one newspaperman asked Yankee catcher Bill Dickey "what makes the Yankees go?" he glanced at the reporter, calmly pointed his figure, and stated "that man." He was pointing to Manager Joe McCarthy.

McCarthy's presence as a force in baseball was well established by the mid-1930s. Because he held a place of such undeniable greatness, McCarthy was always under the microscope of the media. He had been so ever since the beginning of his major league managerial career in 1926. Always in the spotlight, but the very opposite of Babe Ruth, McCarthy could not have been a less media-oriented character if he had tried to be. Indeed, many scribes felt McCarthy did make a fetish of media inaccessibility. Dan Daniel of the *New York World Telegram* wrote: "you reach what seems to be a thick plate of glass through which you can see McCarthy, but beyond which he will not let you advance." All others encountered the same, and many did not reflect upon the encounters so nicely or dispassionately. Some reporters frankly hated him. Others who respected him certainly recognized his reclusive nature. In his day only a few gentlemen of the press were openly willing to concede his greatness.[4]

The nature of the evolution of McCarthy's relations with the press provides a vantage onto the changing nature of the media's role in the game of baseball from the Babe Ruth era into the post-World War II boom years. McCarthy arrived in Major League Baseball during Babe Ruth's heyday. His first big break as a manager had come at the end of the 1925 season. Previously, he had been managing for Louisville in the American Association. There he was highly successful, and the press in Louisville gave him nothing but raves. More significantly, so did the sports writers of rival American Association cities. As one Kansas City writer extolled, "Joe McCarthy's club is not beaten until the last man is out." Among Louisville sports fans, as one Kentucky writer later reflected, "everyone knew he was destined for the big show."[5]

It was McCarthy's reputation at Louisville and throughout the American Association that caught the notice of the Chicago Cubs owner, Philip K. Wrigley, and his club president, William Veeck, Sr. The Cubs had been mired in hard times since the war, and Wrigley hired McCarthy to whip the team back into a unit of which Wrigley, Veeck, and Chicago could once again be proud. He did not disappoint. In 1926, the Cubs surprised the National League, contending for first place throughout much of the summer, finishing fourth, and winning the open respect of everyone in the league, including veteran rival skippers like Wilbert Robinson and John McGraw. From the outset, the Chicago press was also full of praise for McCarthy. They all noted their frustrations over his laconic manner. Sometimes, indeed, if a reporter actually secured some substantive information from McCarthy, a paper would headline an article with a sardonic quip like: "Extra, McCarthy Talks About the Team!" But while McCarthy's taciturn ways were regularly noted, the general tone was always respectful. The basic reason for this was the undeniable fact that McCarthy had turned the Cubs back into contenders. He had made some gutsy moves to do this, especially when he got rid of pitcher Grover Cleveland Alexander in June, 1926. Chicago fans loved "Alex," but when McCarthy got rid of him, Wrigley and Veeck supported the move, and the press echoed their confident enthusiasm. Even though Alexander put in two more good seasons with the rival St. Louis Cardinals and beat the Cubs in some key games, the Chicago press never chided McCarthy about his decision. In regard to McCarthy's "in charge" regimen, it was Harry Niely of the *Chicago Evening American* who in 1926 gave McCarthy the nickname that stuck with him the rest of his life — "Marse Joe." The racism implicit in the nickname cannot be denied, but sensitivities of that era were not what they have become. The name was raised with both humor and respect, and was received by the fans, as well as by McCarthy, in that very way. McCarthy never minded that press moniker. There would be another he would utterly detest, however.[6]

The culmination (and denouement) of McCarthy's Chicago press relations came in 1929 when the Cubs won the pennant but lost what was for them a horrible World Series to the Philadelphia A's. Two famous things happened there. One involved Connie Mack's decision to start the undistinguished Howard Ehmke in Game One, ahead of his two 20-game winners, George Earnshaw and Lefty Grove. Ehmke's slow, sloppy, underhand curve balls baffled McCarthy's great right-handed hitters. He struck out 13, and the Cubs were embarrassed. Over the next days, the press's reflections on the game emphasized the point that Mr. Mack had put one over on everyone, hence that Manager Joe McCarthy had met his match and then some. During the Series, the Ehmke victory looked as though it would fade in significance, as toward the end of Game Four it looked like the Cubs were about to even up the Series. Down two games to one, but up 8–0 going into the seventh inning of Game Four, the Cubs felt they were back on par and looked forward to winning two of the next three games. Then in the bottom of the seventh inning, "an 'inning' which will live in infamy …" for Cub fans, the A's scored 10 runs. World War I had given rise to the term "shell shock," and reporters and fans freely used it as they witnessed McCarthy's Cubs going harmlessly in the next two innings and then appearing to let a close one slip away the next day to hand the Series to the A's. Some said that Mr. Wrigley never really recovered from the events. Others in Chicago also reflected grimly, pointing out a few weeks later that while the rest of the country may have gone into a deep Depression at the end of October, 1929, Chicago was already there. Joe McCarthy hardly felt good about it. Reporters did criticize him for not moving more quickly to the bullpen during the A's 10-run rally. For years, McCarthy paled at any reminders of the Series, and he could not bring himself to cash his loser's share World Series check for a full eight months.[7]

In 1930, reporters found themselves even less cordially waved off whenever they asked McCarthy anything either about the 1929 Series or about the upcoming season. Still, the Chicago press did not hound him unduly, especially since the following season McCarthy again had the Cubs in the thick of the pennant fight. (They actually hounded centerfielder Hack Wilson more, as he had lost two fly balls in the sun during the A's fateful Game Four rally.) While the press respect for McCarthy was still generally high, it was Mr. Wrigley, and consequently Bill Veeck, who harbored grudges. The press did not so much take sides in the disputes as they duly reported both statements from Wrigley and the fact that McCarthy steadily offered no comment. It was indeed remarkable that McCarthy's Cubs stayed in the pennant race as they did in 1930. Not only was second baseman Rogers Hornsby out for most of the season with a broken ankle, but as the season wore on there were less than confident expressions coming from the front office. The pennant eluded the Cubs that September, and as it did, McCarthy was released 10 days before the season was over. The Chicago press tone was largely neutral in the shifts. If anything, they tilted toward McCarthy, noting conspicuously, for example, how Wrigley and his new field boss, Rogers Hornsby, encountered a loud chorus of boos from the Cubs' faithful when Hornsby first stepped onto the field and shook hands with Wrigley on the afternoon of his managerial debut. Chicago reporters also gave generous coverage to the going-away party that other prominent Chicagoans gave McCarthy before he left the city. So the positive relations between McCarthy and Chicago press held even in the tumultuous weeks of September 1930.[8]

The Cubs of that era had certainly given reporters grist for muckraking. At first there had been Grover Alexander's escapades. Hack Wilson was also a notorious drinker and fighter. Meanwhile Rogers Hornsby was always stirring up controversies. Many reporters could have thus peppered McCarthy with countless questions and expressed umbrage at his non-responsiveness, but the general tenor of Chicago's and baseball's journalistic protocols at that time did not embrace the idea of slinging mud, especially with one so successful and obviously competent as Joe McCarthy. It was also a member of the Chicago press corps, Warren Brown, who helped McCarthy secure his next managerial post — with the Yankees. It was Brown who served as the messenger for Col. Jacob Ruppert and Ed Barrow to find out if McCarthy was interested in signing with New York. Brown was one of McCarthy's favorite reporters in Chicago, and the fact that Brown never made public his role in the New York dealings for fifteen years underscored to McCarthy the legitimacy of his friendship with Brown as well as his distaste for what he saw as the rest of the press's contrasting untrustworthiness.[9]

While McCarthy had had an enthusiastic press in Louisville and largely the same in Chicago, New York proved a more complex matter. In the first place, the media there was so much more sizable and diverse. Secondly, while the Yankees had not then won a pennant in several years, the situation there was hardly the "rock bottom" affair he inherited in Chicago. In this context, the memory of the late Miller Huggins made invidious comparisons an inevitable hurdle for anyone who would take over the team. Gratitude would not be easily earned. It had certainly hurt Huggins immediate successor, Bob Shawkey. Beyond the point that many players and reporters had established senses of excellence from the Huggins era, Joe McCarthy was also inheriting a phenomenon — Babe Ruth. Much has been written about the tension between the two, and there is no question about the fact of its existence. Two points are key here. One is that in the first two years of McCarthy's Yankees reign, Babe Ruth was still very much an active player. Ruth himself saw it this way. Retirement was not yet fully on his mind, so McCarthy sitting in the chair of field manager was something he could begrudgingly accept, for the time being, with the childish fantasy that when the time came all would fall into place as he imagined it should. McCarthy made allowances for Ruth traveling with his entourage and hosting parties and taking his meals in his room, things no one else on the team were allowed to do. Reporters generally took note of the latitude given Ruth, as well as of the fact that McCarthy would not discuss anything about the situation with anyone. Much like McCarthy (as well as Col. Ruppert and Ed Barrow), reporters were content to let the situation play itself out.

By 1933, and fully in 1934, matters turned especially bad. Ruth was then clearly past his peak. He increasingly resented McCarthy's leadership, and chafed at many of McCarthy's decisions to "spell" him towards the end of many games. The press' coverage required little digging. They did note that thousands of fans headed for the exits whenever McCarthy replaced Ruth. For "inside dope," they did not need to go much farther than to approach Ruth and let him blow off steam, and this he certainly did. Meanwhile, McCarthy had impressed most of the New York reporters since his first spring with the team in regard to his leadership and baseball knowledge, "McCarthy'll do," being the simple summary of one. With the championship of 1932, this sense was confirmed, and with Ruth's carping and moaning, McCarthy's naturally laconic tendencies struck many as the better, contrastingly mature approach to the situation. There were some rumors that McCarthy was easing out some of the players who seemed to be in Ruth's "camp." Shortstop Lyn Lary seemed a conspicuous example here. McCarthy cut him, but few could quarrel with the quality of McCarthy's preference, Frankie Crosetti. Ruth regularly growled at any reporter who expressed anything positive about McCarthy's field management. However they may have felt, reporters clearly gathered that McCarthy had impressed Col. Ruppert and Ed Barrow, and, of course, that was the clincher. Thus when Ruth presented Ruppert and Barrow with the demand that they release McCarthy and make him their manager, he got nothing but an offer to manage the Newark farm club and then a sale to the Boston Braves.[10]

McCarthy had won the Ruth War. Additionally, he had fully gained the respect of the Yankee players, especially the player leadership that had succeeded Ruth in such men as Lou Gehrig and Bill Dickey. At that point, the New York media could do little but marvel at the results, and the successive championships from 1936 to 1939 could yield little but awe (as well as resentment). There was little criticism of the team in those years. Apropos of the popular movie of the day, one tongue-in-cheek criticism involved a characterization of McCarthy looking like one of the Seven Dwarfs in the Walt Disney movie *Snow White*. The criticism here was that McCarthy's uniform was too baggy. It was a matter indeed raised in the sardonic context of "Aha! Here at last: something to criticize about McCarthy and the Yankees." Otherwise the press had noted the apparent arrogance of the Yankees under McCarthy and did so with a vintage New York sniggering jest. When Ruth was still with the team, McCarthy's new regimen of coats and ties on the road and no card playing in the clubhouse met with some consternation. After 1935, his inflexible ways drew only respect, and the quiet arrogance of it all was a perfect tonality for late 1930s New Yorkers. In late 1938, for example, reporters chuckled as they noted the team had bought McCarthy a Christmas present — a silver platter with all the players' signatures engraved around a heading proclaiming "World Champions, 1938." The punch line of the December story was that the players had bought and inscribed the platter in August, and McCarthy knew it. New Yorkers further relished the story of a reporter asking a Yankees rookie "Are you married?" and the young man nervously responding: "I don't know, sir. You'd better ask Mr. McCarthy." Reporters wrote of, and fans grinned at, how McCarthy had the Yankees uniforms and caps cut ever so slightly larger to make the squad loom ever more intimidating to the opposition. The whines that came from opposition city reporters were of no consequence. Meanwhile, stories of awe were all about the Yankees in the late 1930s. Reporters clearly grasped that, with such a perspective of invincibility regularly reinforced, the baseball public gained a great sense of security and satisfaction, something for which the era clearly called. Critics elsewhere around the American League scoffed that rooting for McCarthy and the Yankees was "like rooting for U.S. Steel." But the point was that in the wake of all the traumas of the Great Depression, it hardly seemed like a bad thing to root for, or bank on, U.S. Steel or the New York Yankees. The raucous St. Louis Gas House Gang may have inspired some romantics in the Depression era, but it was McCarthy's Gray-Flannel Suit Yankees that inspired the deepest awe.[11] Other societies' Depression-driven Romanticism for bygone times of alleged happiness and glory had wrought political disaster; McCarthy's Yankees, even to Yankees haters, were national pastime symbols of a "Can't Happen Here" America that faced a terribly harsh reality squarely in the face and triumphed. Some press and fans may have found the American League boring, but boredom can be a welcome emotion in the wake of severe depression. Few late-1930s media people cared or dared to challenge such a sensibility.

The decline of Lou Gehrig in 1939 was, of course, the major bump in the Yankees' road to unprecedented dynastic status in these years. The way McCarthy and the Yankees handled the tragedy only added to their mystique. Throughout the ordeal, McCarthy and the Yankees rallied around their captain, inspiring nothing but respect from the media and the fans. In addition to holding a memorable ceremony for Gehrig that summer on July 4th, McCarthy kept Gehrig on the team throughout the season. Reporters had grown increasingly aware of McCarthy's shrewd psychological sense. Gehrig himself had made note of it in his famous July address, referring to McCarthy as "that smart student of psychology." McCarthy's keeping Gehrig on the bench certainly showed psychological savvy as well as humanitarianism, and reporters acknowledged it. Gehrig's presence snuffed out many mental slumps on the Yankees, and it unnerved more than a few opponents when he limped out to home plate before every game with the lineup card. Again the sense of the press and the public here was 100% positive, as the supposedly merciless McCarthy Yankees could now be seen not merely as damnably great players but as genuinely great men who shouldered their own worst troubles and triumphed not just in spite of but because of the commitment. The sweep of Cincinnati that fall in the World Series, and the churlish little fact that most of the team departed from the train trip home at 125th Street rather than taking the time to go downtown, was also taken with a nodding smile. This team and its leader had proven they were of such greatness that they could legitimately win another Series and do it all in stride. (Only a few fans were waiting to greet the team downtown anyway.) Gehrig's day was special; a World Series win was but another October day at the U.S. Steel office, and at the end of the day there was simply the matter of there being less traffic at 125th Street than around Grand Central Station.[12] The Yankees had triumphed in the Depression era. Now on top, there was no place for 1920s-style ballyhoo. Some reporters may have wanted more juice, but McCarthy was not going to give it to them. His only product was hard, stainless steel baseball. It was hard to find nay sayers here, even among the hard-bitten New York press.

In 1940, when the Yankees at last lost a pennant, and by the narrowest of margins, no one blamed McCarthy. When the team had fallen to last place that May, reporters noted admiringly how McCarthy showed no urge to lash out at anyone but calmly counseled the team that they behaved like champions in good times, that he knew they would do so in these leaner times, and that he knew that if they maintained their poise they would assuredly come back. McCarthy did not even flinch when one reporter, Jimmy Powers from the *New York Daily News*, in what may still be considered the most offensive article in the history of sports journalism, offered speculation that August that the 1940 Yankees' poor play was due to their possibly having somehow caught Lou Gehrig's germs and were thus all suffering from the early stages of his sclerosis. Other Yankees wanted to prove to Powers (on his face) that they indeed had not lost much muscle, but McCarthy knew it best to let Powers' idiocy do him in without any extra jabs and uppercuts. Newspapermen recognized McCarthy's sagacity here too, and Powers did later print a note of apology. On the last day of the 1940 season, the Yankees lost and finished the campaign in third place, two games out. Trying to induce some emotion, for once, a reporter earnestly asked McCarthy what the team's third-place share of World Series money would be. McCarthy looked at him with a steady, three-second glare (that felt like an hour) and then deadpanned: "I dunno, I haven't looked it up." He then turned and finished clipping his toenails in front of everyone. No one asked such a question again, and when McCarthy's team won the next three pennants, 1940 seemed all the more aberrational.[13]

McCarthy was in his heyday, and the media could and would do little but applaud. What was there to criticize? His taciturn ways continued, but the reporters simply accepted it with few expressing any entitlement-driven frustration. Across the river in Brooklyn, the young manager Leo Durocher may have always been better, more entertaining copy, but Manager McCarthy had assumed virtually mythic dimensions. "An all-seeing, silent Buddha figure," as one reporter rhapsodized, who apparently saw all, which for the most part he did. About the only leader of any institution in New York who could match Joe McCarthy for respect at this time was Arturo Toscanini of the NBC Symphony, and when he did not want to talk to a reporter no one dared take it as a slight there either. One heard everything, one saw everything, and no one doubted each was the absolute master of his craft.[14]

What changed everything for McCarthy was, of course, the same thing that changed everything for baseball and for the nation at that time — the War. As many players went into the service, President Roosevelt still called for professional baseball to continue, and so it did, although many minor leagues closed. McCarthy continued to win pennants through 1943, and he nearly won in 1944 despite having a complete sham of a team. Such skillful managing could have provided a basis for many in the media to extend their praise for McCarthy's ability to manage lesser players, as he had in Louisville and Chicago. Some such praise was there, but it was minimal. The war had simply altered everyone's perspective. It was not so much that McCarthy's personal prestige took a dive, but the fact that the game of baseball had diminished. It was no longer so meaningful a metaphor for the nation with respect to leadership and accomplishment. Now the people no longer looked for metaphors of greatness; they were looking in earnest for the real thing. Like everything and everyone else in baseball, McCarthy became a sideshow. He never complained about any perceived loss of status, about losing any players to the service, or about any travel or training restrictions or other Spartan conditions under which he and the rest of baseball had to labor. The war simply knocked out the symbolic value of what he had been doing his entire career. Literally and figuratively, he was now on the back pages of the news. As long as the President said that a little baseball was good for the nation, he would continue to do his job of serving that need as best he could uncomplainingly.

It was in the context of this diminished status that the press hit McCarthy with a new nickname that stuck with him for the rest of his life, one that he did not like one bit. In the winter, before the opening of the 1944 training camps, Chicago Manager Jimmie Dykes wisecracked that with all the players in the military, Joe McCarthy was going to have more trouble, adding "He won't be able to sit back and push buttons anymore." Dykes' little swipe caught on in a way that even he never anticipated. Dykes later confessed, indeed, that he had no idea that his little comment would have such impact as it had. Ever the wise guy, however, he still hastened to add: "the statement was not without some merit." For so many people in baseball, the notion of a push-button manager somehow reified what they had wanted to believe for so many years — that anyone could win with the kind of teams that McCarthy had seemingly had placed in his lap. While playing baseball at the level of Joe DiMaggio indeed looks easy to the untutored, the fact that virtually all fans have themselves played the game at one time or another mitigates any "that's easy" sense from being taken too seriously. The sense of ease at managing teams like the Yankees of the late 1930s never had nearly such a strong reality-dimension correcting the fancies of most fans, as few of them had ever coached or managed, let alone at a serious level.

Reporters asked McCarthy for reactions to Dykes' comment, and he bristled. "Yes," he snapped, "I spend all my summers in Atlantic City and only come back for the World Series." After years of non-reactions and of terse retorts like "let me worry about that," reporters now relished the fact that they could get a reaction, and an emotionally-charged one no less, out of the great McCarthy. The game's diminished status in the war years added a sense that no mere baseball man had the right to be haughty anyway. McCarthy would not, could not but show his displeasure, so the media naturally kept the spotlight on the issue. Cheerleading, respect, awe — these press tones were long gone. At a baseball writers' dinner in late February of 1944, organizers felt it might be fun to have McCarthy sit in front of the room during the after-dinner speeches and push a button before each speaker came to the podium. It showed just how much the little statement had penetrated the sports world. When asked to take part, McCarthy again showed not a hint of amusement and did not cooperate. Some writers criticized his recalcitrance.

One of McCarthy's many talents as a manager was to pinpoint opponents' weaknesses and exploit them. Were another manager's vulnerability so exposed, he would never have quashed any bench jockeying. Now he was simply going to have to take it. He shouldered on, just as he had when he first came to the Cubs and endured the constant barbs about having had no major league experience. With regard to the "push-button" label, winning the 1944 pennant would have been a nice bit of revenge for him, and he certainly came close, but it would not come to pass. As the next season approached, with the War's pressures greater than ever, the "push button" taunts continued unabated, as did questions from reporters. A few scribes sought to address the unfairness of the "push button" label, but few took heed. The War had leveled many of the relative strengths and weaknesses of most of the teams, and it had temporarily removed the awe in which professional baseball had been held. Approaching the age of 60 and having bought a retirement home outside Buffalo, McCarthy had clearly been considering stepping down. But he wanted to go out with a last hurrah. With the felt disrespect and with the sacrifices of the War seasons, he wanted one more win when things were back to normal. Here he would learn that the muses of baseball, like those of Las Vegas, are not always kind to those who want to keep playing just until they get one more big win.[15]

By the time the War ended another war had already begun for McCarthy. After Col. Ruppert died in 1939, Ed Barrow continued to run the team, but the actual ownership of the Yankees fell into abeyance until 1944 when it was bought by Dan Topping and Del Webb. At first, their ownership was accompanied by one Larry MacPhail, the team's new president and business manager. As has been well chronicled, Mr. MacPhail and McCarthy did not get on well. With the accession of MacPhail, fans and reporters fell into two camps as the new Yankee era commenced. One hoped that MacPhail would jazz up the Yankees; the other feared that MacPhail would jazz up the Yankees. A vaudeville and Broadway show lover, McCarthy was no fan of jazz, literally or metaphorically, and he did not like "Loud Larry" one bit, nor did he like many of the changes and personnel he brought. Back in 1942, while McCarthy was filling out his lineup card before a game, reporter Arthur "Red" Patterson of the *New York Herald Tribune* was seated nearby. McCarthy was placing no surprise entries on the card, nevertheless he drew away from Patterson, snapping nastily at him for "sticking his nose where it does not belong." The story then was of no great consequence, but in 1945 MacPhail made Red Patterson the Yankees new traveling secretary and head publicity man. Patterson then began dutifully pumping McCarthy for news for the club's publicity office. Newspapers noted the growing tension over these and other matters. McCarthy was galled further to distraction, and further to drink.[16]

Joe McCarthy had always been a drinker, but then so had virtually every reporter who had followed him in the minors, as well as in Chicago and New York. On several occasions beginning in 1940, McCarthy had taken a few days off due to illness. Several reporters had made references to McCarthy "riding the White Horse," a reference to his preferred brand of Scotch. Each time McCarthy was "ill," there were no references to any problem with alcohol, however. The common term was that "his gall bladder was troubling him again." (He never had a gall bladder operation.) In the 1930s and 1940s, attitudes toward drinking, including chronic drinking and alcoholism, were certainly different than they have become. In the true clinical sense of the term, McCarthy was probably not an alcoholic, in that he did not appear to have any kind of physiological allergy or addiction. There were no known alcohol incidents in Buffalo, either in the off-season or during his retirement years. But while in Major League Baseball, especially as he got older, the pressures of management and the spotlight definitely wore on him. Thus whatever the verdict on the medical issue of alcoholism, Joe McCarthy did have a drinking problem while a manager. A couple of glasses of scotch in the evening was typical for him, and many times this got out of hand, especially in his later years.

One feature of McCarthy's game management was that he rarely came out of the dugout. Early in his managerial years, in Louisville, most of the time in Chicago, and occasionally in his first Yankees years, McCarthy coached third base, but by 1932 he was exclusively a bench manager. Lou Gehrig, or a coach, always turned in the lineup card to the umpire before the game, and McCarthy rarely argued with umpires. When he did it could be a real corker, but he was ejected from a game a total of but six times in his entire career. Thus if there was drinking affecting his actual game work, few, including the press corps, were able to see it the way they later could with such managers as Billy Martin. Significantly, McCarthy's game ejections, few as they were, came more frequently in his late career when the glasses of Scotch were sometimes more than he could handle. While there were a few "gall bladder" troubles for McCarthy before 1945, the first year with Larry MacPhail brought on the first big one. It was in July that season that McCarthy took his first extended leave — three weeks— because of pressures and drinking. Here the press was generally charitable, and when he returned to the team amidst the tumultuous pennant fight of that August and September he was peppered with few questions about his health. Subsequent popular and media sensibilities would have yielded much more invasive probings.[17]

In 1946, McCarthy's last year with the Yankees, the drinking and the distaste for MacPhail proved too much. With all his star players again on hand, he had obviously come back for what he hoped would be a final championship. The Yankees played well, but the Boston Red Sox were simply better. They quickly jumped out to a huge lead, and it was clear that they were not going to be headed. Drinking and a few tough losses in Cleveland in May put McCarthy in a terrible state. In earshot of reporters and teammates, he chewed out pitcher Joe Page on a plane to Detroit. (Before then, he had always done anything like that in private quarters.) The Red Sox happened to be leaving the Detroit airport when the Yankees arrived there. Uncharacteristically, an inebriated McCarthy took the opportunity to taunt Red Sox owner Tom Yawkey. Then, with less publicity, he abused a limo driver, as well as a couple of assistants, on route from the Detroit airport to his hotel. The next morning he left the team, flew home to Buffalo, and soon resigned from the Yankees. The chief press reaction did not mention alcohol. Scribes noted that McCarthy was not well, and they reflected the sense of the players— that McCarthy was spiraling ever more out of character, that it was unfortunate that he left as he did, but that it was obviously the best thing. Dan Daniel of the *World Telegram* eulogized that "he should have walked out of the Stadium with music playing and banners flying." Few others raved so, but the respect was there.[18]

Had McCarthy's career ended in the unceremonious way that it did in 1946, the issue of his relations with the press would have merited some note, the main point being that he steadily gave reporters very, very little, but that he was able to get away with it, in large measure because his incredible success before the War had to be admired, a gray tone that very much fit the sensibilities of a people and a city struggling their way out of the Depression. But, of course, McCarthy did not end his career in New York. After the close of the '47 season, McCarthy signed with Tom Yawkey and Joe Cronin to manage the Boston Red Sox.

The attraction of the job of managing the Red Sox lay in their obvious potential to become a truly outstanding team. What also lay ahead was the famed Boston press who many predicted would be ready to engage in rhetorical duels with the acerbic McCarthy. Apropos of McCarthy's anticipated arrival in Boston, New York writer Milton Gross warned, "When a Boston writer sits down, he puts on his spurs before opening his typewriter case." Scarcely a month after his appointment as Red Sox manager, McCarthy did fire Boston's popular trainer, Win Green.[19] Among the Boston press, Win Green's departure caused some ripples right off the bat. Green was an icon, and with his departure, the press' knives were out even more. Gross claimed, "The ink-stained wretches of the Hub [Boston] may not have invented the second guess, but they have certainly refined it to an incisive art." The city had not won a World Series since 1918. The press thus felt both the utmost of entitlement in being critical and absolutely no reason for deference. The Boston press was mean during Babe Ruth's Yankees heyday. Perhaps the Red Sox long decline from champion to doormat after Ruth's sale marked a heightened sense of entitlement in the media's coarse demeanor. In any case, by the time McCarthy arrived as manager it was a deeply ingrained habit. As likeable a manager as there ever was in baseball, McCarthy's predecessor Joe Cronin had been anything but immune from the Boston press' barbs. Already full of self-importance, the Boston press now had Joe McCarthy to add to the subjects to be put under their microscopes.[20]

The Boston press' extraordinary sense of entitlement was greater than that of any other major league city. Already present among the press and fans (never among the players) was the sense of the team being "cursed" as a result of the selling of Babe Ruth to the Yankees in 1919. The narrow loss of the 1946 World Series deepened it. The fully perceived sense of "the curse" would not emerge for another two years, however. At the outset of the 1948 season, Boston fans, players, and writers were of the belief that their hour had at long last come around. Until Tom Yawkey bought the team in 1932, the Boston press often gave more coverage to the Braves. Then Mr. Yawkey began to spend lavishly, and the Red Sox built up a potent team. A belief in Boston was that the talent Yawkey had assembled by the late 1930s would have been enough for several pennant contenders but for the War. The 1946 season proved Boston's superiority, and the loss that October to St. Louis was just a bad break; 1947 was an off year. Then before the 1948 season came several key trades and the hiring of McCarthy. Now was the time for Boston. The Yankees had had their day in the late 1930s. Now the true "Yanks" were going to step forth and displace New York as the game's premier team. For the Boston media, these lofty expectations underscored to them their self-entitled role of watchdog. The city expected championships, and anything that would appear to be detracting from that was going to be more than fair game for a reporter.

Pressure on newspapers' circulation figures from the new medium of television added to the sense of urgency among Boston reporters to do all they could to get a good story, hence rake the muck, since that was something TV could not do so effectively. A few papers had closed, notably the *Boston Transcript*. So reporters had every reason to believe that if they did not work hard for juicy stories, circulation could be affected and they could find themselves in dire straits. Along with these pressures, young, aggressive sports reporters also entered the Boston arena from many New England locales from Connecticut to Maine. Amidst this new atmosphere, Mr. Yawkey no longer picked up press expenses as he had before the war. Perhaps most importantly, the open bar Yawkey had previously maintained for the press at Fenway was no more. It was a different world. In 1946, one Red Sox official, Larry Woodall, told every rookie, as he had apparently done before, "Don't talk to the Boston writers; they can't be trusted." When opposite sides in a struggle each feel a sense of moral righteousness, it is difficult if not impossible for the conflict to do anything but grow more and more intense. Considering the city's Irish heritage, reporters and fans could also regard a rebuff from a member of Yawkey's Red Sox as a sports version of the old barrier: "No Irish Need Apply." Ted Williams was already infamous for stiffing the press. It was into this atmosphere of perceived wounding, self-righteousness, name-calling, and high expectations that Joe McCarthy stepped when he became the Red Sox manager.

Early into his tenure with Boston, McCarthy began to answer lots of reporters' questions with the refrains that New York reporters had endured season after season: If they got any detail, it would be mere reminiscences about the Yankees or the Cubs, and to direct questions about the Sox there was one basic response: "let me worry about that." The fight was on.[21] Merely by the end of spring training, much of the Boston press corps was bristling with resentment at McCarthy. The term "Cold War" was just coming into vogue in American foreign affairs, and its use resonated among Bostonians trying to describe McCarthy's relations with the press. By the end of spring training, "Cold War" was exactly what people called the state of affairs between McCarthy and the Boston media. As the 1948 season unfolded, McCarthy's recurring "let me worry about that," caused yet more irritation among Boston's scribes. Their egos were bruised, *and* the Red Sox were not living up to expectations. By late May, the team was mired in seventh place, and the press was chortling. At the nadir of this May slump, McCarthy had an apparently bad bout with the bottle. Reports speculated that he was going to resign and that Joe Cronin went down to Washington D.C. and sat up with him in his hotel room, persuading him not to quit. Press frustrations grew here over the fact that neither McCarthy nor Cronin would let anyone know the details of what went on in Washington.[22] As the team began to win steadily in June, McCarthy made a key personnel move, placing Billy Goodman at first base. One reporter with the *Boston Herald* had previously written that this move was in the works. McCarthy was irked that anyone had known about this, and mocked the press about the fact that at least no one surmised that he was going to place Goodman in the leadoff position in the lineup. McCarthy was concerned most with the idea of minimizing the pressure which Goodman would feel in taking over first base. But to the press, it was another example of McCarthy's irritatingly secretive proclivities.[23]

Over the summer of 1948, the Red Sox were the hottest team in baseball. In two months, they jumped from seventh place to first. This certainly muted much of the anger with McCarthy, but even here some hard-bitten scribes could not but seek out points of criticism. In September, Al Hirshberg of the *Boston Post* unashamedly wrote in praise of the real reason for the Red Sox magnificent turn-around — Joe Cronin. If the *Post* received any letters of criticism against Hirshberg and in defense of McCarthy, they did not publish them.[24] Of course, the outcome of the 1948 season underscored the prejudices of anyone, press or fan, who wanted to be negative about McCarthy. In September, Cleveland overtook Boston (and New York). Boston beat the Yankees twice over the season's final weekend, and when Cleveland lost their last game to Detroit, the Indians and the Red Sox finished the season dead even, prompting the only one-game pennant playoff in the history of the American League. Cleveland won the game, and their victory prompted as much second-guessing as almost any game in the history of baseball. McCarthy was at the center of the hubbub because of his choice of starting pitcher. People had been expecting him to start Mel Parnell, or possibly Jack Kramer, but McCarthy gave the ball to an older, and frankly mediocre, journeyman, Denny Galehouse. Galehouse's record to that point in the season was 8–7. That afternoon, Cleveland hit Galehouse freely and took the pennant. The next day, the *Boston Post* had nothing about the game on the front page; their sports section began on page twenty-one where they noted that Indians were to open the Series against the Braves that afternoon. Barebones coverage of the Sox loss to Cleveland did not come until page thirty-eight, after the hunting and fishing section.[25]

Boston was disconsolate, and as fans could apparently not put the loss behind them, reporters focused endlessly on the game and especially on McCarthy's choice to start Galehouse. Dozens of contradictory stories emerged, and McCarthy, of course, gave the press no resolution. All he said was a shrugging, "These things happen. We played Cleveland even all year; they just got the odd game.... I've been whipped before, and I can take it. I just feel sorry for the boys." Later, dismissively shooing all the gossip about the Galehouse matter, he sniffed, "No matter what you do, you get second guessed." McCarthy lived to the age of ninety, and a year before he died he said he had never stopped getting letters asking him about his decision to start Denny Galehouse.[26]

The Boston media and fans had all winter to stew over the horrible loss. Knowing the public appetite for further speculation about the game, the following March at spring training, the press peppered the Red Sox with questions about it. Because they gathered much contradictory information, some naturally turned to McCarthy who again gave them nothing. Despite this continued barrier, some felt the Boston press felt a trifle guilty about their relations with McCarthy in 1948, so at the outset of 1949 a few sensed a little warming.[27] But when the Red Sox again started the season poorly, reporters felt an even higher sense of entitlement in "going after" McCarthy and the rest of the faltering team. By June the Red Sox were below .500 and had been as low as seventh place. At that point in the spring, former British Prime Minister Winston Churchill was speaking at the Massachusetts Institute of Technology. Borrowing from Churchillian prose, one reporter rhapsodized about another apparent Red Sox collapse. Cheekily noting that thirteen members of the highly paid Red Sox owned Cadillacs that year, he intoned: "Never have so many been paid so much for doing so little."[28] Again, reporters were sharpening their razors.

As in 1948, in the summer of 1949 the Red Sox again ignited and tore through the league. From July 4 to September 30, their record was 61 and 20. Boston fans were ecstatic. Still, with all the bad blood of the previous two seasons, some elements of the press continued to pound away at McCarthy as well as at some of the Red Sox players, especially Ted Williams. When talking to reporters, one of Joe McCarthy's "deflection" devices continued to involve reminiscing about past teams and players with the Cubs and the Yankees. Reporters naturally knew what he was doing, but they had no choice but to go along. (Additionally, they garnered an occasional tidbit that could spice up a story, if not then but at another time.) Boston scribes did not mind the stories about the Cubs. Any McCarthy reminiscences about the Yankees days of old, however, fueled steady (and absurd) suspicions that he harbored divided loyalties, and in 1949 the AL race was strictly between New York and Boston. In regard the 1948 playoff loss to Cleveland, some reported that in the final two regular season games of the season, against the Yankees, McCarthy had kept Denny Galehouse warming in the bullpen for much of both games, hence he was starting a tired pitcher against Cleveland. The argument here was not so conspiratorial as to say that McCarthy intentionally fatigued Galehouse before starting him against the Indians. It went, rather, that McCarthy held such an excessive fear of the Yankees that he used up his staff that weekend. Other items also fueled rumors. Until the Red Sox traded for Al Zarilla in May of 1949, right field had been the weak spot in their lineup, and McCarthy reportedly made invidious comparisons between his various mediocre right fielders and his old Yankee reliable Tommy Henrich. Several times, McCarthy referred to pitcher Mickey McDermott as "Gomez." Most glaringly, reporters fixated on the respect McCarthy held for Joe DiMaggio. In 1948, Boston pitcher Tex Hughson drilled DiMaggio in the ribs with a fastball. DiMaggio then angrily flipped his bat toward the dugout and trotted down to first. As DiMaggio stood at first base, McCarthy was reported to have admiringly predicted "watch him; he won't rub it." Thereafter, Hughson always maintained that McCarthy never gave him a fair chance, and many reporters were primed to receive such views.[29] Later in 1948, in a key game with the Yankees, McCarthy chose to leave a struggling pitcher, Rex Caldwell, in a tight spot. Joe DiMaggio slammed a game winning grand slam home run off him, and whispers flew about the press that McCarthy wanted to give his former star the opportunity for such a dramatic moment.[30]

At the end of the 1948 season, the Yankees lost two games to the Red Sox. DiMaggio had been playing with flu symptoms, and when he withdrew himself toward the end of the last game, the fans at Fenway gave him a gracious cheer. Similarly, in June 1949, when DiMaggio dramatically returned to the Yankee lineup after months of suffering from a bone spur injury and hit six home runs in three days, some Boston fans cheered DiMaggio *and* booed Ted Williams. No one accused the Red Sox fans of harboring divided loyalties (although perhaps a death wish). Nevertheless, at the outset of the June 1949 Yankee series when DiMaggio returned to the lineup, McCarthy cautioned some who speculated that DiMaggio may not be able to run well. "Just watch him," McCarthy warned. Even though a plane circled over Fenway with a banner which read "The Great DiMaggio," some reporters fastened onto McCarthy's warning as further proof of his divided loyalties. In the final weekend of the 1949 season, when the Red Sox lost two in New York to lose the pennant, the Yankees held a ceremony honoring DiMaggio. In his "thank you" address, DiMaggio went out of his way to praise his former manager, and McCarthy came out to shake DiMaggio's hand. A few Boston writers scowled. "The old skipper," snarled one, "could not seem to shake his conviction that the Yankees were somehow tougher than his boys. McCarthy's fear did his ball club no good."[31] There were no fears in McCarthy, nor on the Red Sox. They were aplenty among Boston reporters, however, and in a time in which Americans were inclined to see key matters of world politics in fearful terms of "5th Column" conspiracies, the "We lost China" outlook of 1949 had its counterpart in the way many New Englanders accounted for the outcome of the American League pennant race. To Red Sox fans, the Yankees did not win the pennant, "we lost it." The major contrast between the paranoia in national politics and Boston baseball was that in Boston "Joe McCarthy" was on the receiving end of the suspicions.

The final game of the 1949 season — with New York — was another heart breaking loss for Boston. The winner of the game took the pennant. In the game, McCarthy made a tough decision. In the top of the eighth inning, he was down 1–0. With one out, he chose to pinch-hit for pitcher Ellis Kinder. Kinder had been undefeated since June 9, and he appeared unhittable that afternoon. But McCarthy chose to pinch hit for him. The pinch-hitter, Tom Wright, drew a walk, but, uncharacteristically, Dom DiMaggio then grounded sharply into a double play to end the inning. From there a tired relief staff could not hold the Yankees in the bottom of the eighth. New York scored four more runs, and a Red Sox rally in the top of the ninth netted but three. (Kinder had said that if the Sox scored three runs, he would win the game.) On the train back to Boston, Kinder downed his usual quantity of beer and began to complain: "Goddammit," he yelled, "if that old man McCarthy had let me stay in, we would'a won it all." Various reporters, and countless fans, quoted this widely and began second-guessing McCarthy's decision to pinch-hit for Kinder. The controversy rivaled the "Denny Galehouse" matter of 1948. Indeed, in 1973, when the American League instituted the designated hitter rule, Harold Kaese of the *Boston Globe* tersely wrote: "the new rule is 24 years too late for Joe McCarthy." Few Red Sox fans needed any clarification. Trying to criticize McCarthy, Al Hirshberg of the *Boston Post* argued that Kinder was a very good hitter. That season, however, Kinder had but twelve hits, batting a mere .130.[32] As with the other Joe McCarthy, when people believe in conspiracies, facts do not always matter terribly much.

After the Sox lost the pennant to the Yankees, McCarthy went over to the Yankee locker room to congratulate Manager Casey Stengel and the team.

Again, the Boston press corps scowled. With two pennants in a row lost on the last day of the season, it was easy for Boston fans and reporters to fixate on any one point that could have "made the difference." Notions of McCarthy's divided loyalties fit the mood. For fans in a city with the hubris to regard itself as "the Hub" and which simultaneously carries a Puritan legacy, believing that one must strive for perfection while knowing one will likely fail, and for fans of a city whose other chief ethnicity maintains what James Joyce dubbed "the Irish romance of failure," the denouements of the 1948 and 1949 seasons were bitterly perfect fulfillments. While the lean years of the 1920s and 1930s and the loss in the 1946 Series had already started the talk, the notion of a team "cursed" received full confirmation for Boston in the McCarthy years. Given the *Scarlet Letter*-ending to the team's two cursed seasons, the press could thus readily see itself ever more as a Roger Chillingworth. After 1948-1949, many scribes relished this role ever more.

While some reporters had sensed an effort at warmer media relations when training camp commenced in 1949, no one detected any such efforts in 1950. The knives were out, and there was not even a pretense of good manners. The players generally did not like it. Ted Williams was certainly disgusted. "I think without question," he later wrote,

> that Boston had the worst bunch of writers who ever came down the pike in baseball. I think any professional sport has to have color written about the teams, but can you do all that without being unfair, without picking on somebody, without making a damned mountain out of a molehill, without putting somebody on the spot?[33]

Amidst the pressures, McCarthy continued his laconic ways. Reporters asked him as many questions about the end of the 1949 season, and he was as reticent then as he had been the previous spring about Denny Galehouse. "McCarthy would never talk about the decisions he made," moaned one reporter. "You couldn't get McCarthy to say anything. Nothing. You'd look in [his office] and he'd be smoking a cigar and you'd say 'Hi, Joe' and that was it. He wouldn't tell you a f_____ word. Nothing." With McCarthy, echoed another, "I sat one day in the Red Sox clubhouse with some fifteen other scribes for fourteen minutes on my watch, and nobody said a thing but 'How've you been?' and 'Lend me a match.' Mr. McCarthy sat facing us like a House Un-American Activities witness standing on his constitutional rights. ... [One would] have thought the whole scene had been painted." Young Casey Stengel was the opposite of McCarthy here. He would talk incessantly, often nonsensically, but the reporters loved it. Even if they never got a straight answer to their original questions, they could always come away with a quotation and a story. As the public seemed to like the stories, everyone was happy. Stengel could thus make himself the issue. McCarthy could never do that. To him, baseball was always the issue, and when he provided the press with nothing, that became the issue. In this new, nervously affluent, cold-war climate, the public often sought reassurance. Aided by the presence of the more superficial venue of television, the media catered to this need by providing what Daniel Boorstin called "pseudo-events." The contrasting press relations of Stengel and McCarthy illustrates Boorstin's point. Casey Stengel's often weird words usually shed no light on the actual games at hand, but they were great copy, and, ever increasingly, great copy was the game.[34]

The tensions between McCarthy and the press reached even greater heights as the 1950 season began. If McCarthy had any thoughts about what had happened to the Red Sox in 1948 and 1949, he likely believed that the slow starts of each April and May were to blame. He and the players were determined not to let that happen again. Boston did start fast—for the first six innings of the first game. Opening against the Yankees, the Sox were up 9–0 and ended up losing 15–10 in what Joe DiMaggio called "the strangest game of baseball I have seen, played in, or heard of." The next morning, one paper ruefully quipped: "Short Season, Wasn't It?" Reporters, of course, descended on the Red Sox with a bevy of "What happened's?" Tired of the incessant pressure and the sniping, perhaps remembering Game Four of the 1929 World Series, McCarthy banned the press for a full half hour after each game. The team unanimously concurred.[35]

Naturally, the half-hour ban irked the hell out of the Boston press corps. Again drawing upon Churchill and popular political references, they referred to the ban as "The Iron Curtain." Several times after games Ted Williams opened the door to them only for the purpose of immaturely yelling, "Not yet, you chowder heads, not yet!" By the time they came in, some players had already left, and the emotional reactions for which they hoped were muted. As for McCarthy, it was more of the same. Interviewing him, whined one scribe, "is like removing the teeth of a bucking bronco with an oyster fork. The man is so cautious he does not dare say 'Good Morning' for fear the weather will change."[36]

McCarthy's reticent nature had been the source of general good humor and respect in Chicago and New York. By 1950, there was little humor and only biting sarcasm left in Boston. Later that April, on McCarthy's 63rd birthday, reporters sent him a telegram that said: "Do not read this telegram until 30 minutes after you have opened it." McCarthy chuckled, but he did not change the club's press rule. As the opening of the 1950 season again went poorly, tensions remained high. Attempting to demonstrate that the anger with McCarthy was not a *sui generis* press concern, papers began to print letters from fans. Most were highly critical of McCarthy. In a fit of Fourth Estate egomania, some writers also began to speculate that it was impossible for the half-hour press ban to have been genuinely supported by the majority of players. They argued that it must have been the work of Williams, McCarthy, and a few others of similar sensibility, "but it is inconceivable," confidently asserted one, "that it could have been voted unanimously." On May 2, the team answered that point. They took another vote and kept the ban. The vote was 23 to 3, with 3 newcomers abstaining. That spring, with all the Cold War tensions in the world, the young evangelist Billy Graham held a mass prayer meeting at noon on Boston Common. Over 40,000 people gathered on the Common, and Rev. Graham called for prayers for world peace and for national repentance and spiritual humility. Some said many of the Bostonians assembled that hour were praying along those very same lines—for the Red Sox.[37]

Joe McCarthy, snarled the ever-critical Al Hirsberg of the *Boston Post*, has become "a sour, disillusioned man who looked upon the world with a jaundiced eye of a violinist about to change a tire." He indeed seemed a tired man, and his drinking continued. Some said only Ted Williams would sit near McCarthy on the bench, as no one else could stand his breath. While drinking had been a problem at times in New York, it was usually overlooked just like that of many others. On several occasions, McCarthy had had some bouts with the bottle in Boston. At the point in May of 1948, when Joe Cronin apparently talked him out of resigning, he had also rescued McCarthy from a stupor. In August of 1948, there was an incident in a game in St. Louis, when outfielder Sam Mele injured his ankle sliding into third. As the team and the trainer gathered around Mele, McCarthy was seen wandering up the first base line, with the fans along the railing taunting him, fully aware of his condition. None of the Boston dailies mentioned the incidents and their obvious connections to alcohol. They continued to look the other way with regard to drinking, a testament far more to attitudes toward alcohol in that era than to any softness of feeling toward Joe McCarthy in Boston.[38]

In 1950, Ellis Kinder's drinking was getting the better of him too, and with his demise, the Red Sox pitching never fully recovered. The 1950 team had a few good spurts in April and June, including a two-game splurge of offense against St. Louis in which they scored 20 and 29 runs, still the major league team marks for one-and two-game run production. But the Red Sox' play was inconsistent, and the league leaders (New York and Detroit) appeared insurmountably ahead. In June, drinking more, McCarthy was reported "ill" with influenza and pleurisy. On a game day in Chicago on June 20, he did not leave his hotel room. The next day he flew home to Buffalo, officially retiring on June 24, 1950. The papers were full of rumors, but focusing mostly on whether the retirement was genuine. When the finality of McCarthy's decision became clear, the press finally withdrew. The *Boston Herald* graciously noted, albeit ungrammatically: "Nothing but vultures are indelicate enough to rattle their wattles before a potential casualty becomes a *corpus delicti*."[39]

The Red Sox once again gathered force that summer. By September 20, under new Manager Steve O'Neill, they had pulled to within a half game of the league leading Yankees. Then they fell back, finally eliminated with a loss to Washington (whose starter that day was Gene Bearden).[40] O'Neill could not win a championship. With the aging of the stars of the late 1940s, the 1950s teams faded from contention. Years later came such close calls as those of 1967, 1974, 1975, 1978, 1986, 1990, and 2003. It took a while, but the fans and press of Boston concluded that if there was a curse, it was at least a lot bigger than Joe McCarthy.

McCarthy lived out a happy life in retirement on his "Yankee Farm" outside Buffalo. Reporters there all found him open for lots of chats. He lived to just four months shy of his 91st birthday. A local reporter, Ralph Hubbell, was with him when he died.

Several years after McCarthy's passing, Joe DiMaggio strode into the lobby of Buffalo's Hyatt Regency Hotel for an afternoon event. Naturally, all eyes turned upon him. While some fans approached for autographs and conversation, most of the reporters gathered for the event knew better than to try to approach Joe DiMaggio for any reflections or information. DiMaggio had long made it clear to all that he was not to be bothered. Some said that a disdain for the press was one of several deep bonds of friendship between DiMaggio and McCarthy. A young Buffalo reporter dared approach DiMaggio that afternoon, however. Instantly, Joe DiMaggio snapped: "Are you a reporter?" When the young writer acknowledged he was, DiMaggio waved him off and began walking away, sniffing: "I don't want to talk." But the young reporter pressed lightly and asked DiMaggio if he would just answer a few questions about Joe McCarthy. The reporter recalled: "DiMaggio took a few more steps, then suddenly stopped. 'Wait a minute,' DiMaggio asked, 'are you from Buffalo?'" When the reporter nodded yes, DiMaggio's entire countenance and tone changed. "'Joe was from Buffalo,' he recalled with a smile, 'go ahead and ask your questions.'" The young man got his interview right on the spot, and the rest of the press gathered in the lobby were absolutely flabbergasted at the sight of this young upstart somehow getting the great DiMaggio to talk to him.[41] Joe DiMaggio and Fourth Estate may have hated each other; Joe McCarthy and the Fourth Estate may have hated each other. But the affection and respect that bonded DiMaggio and McCarthy to one another and from the press was something that, even after McCarthy died, could apparently break through the press walls of Joe DiMaggio and let him be human once in a while. We can blame the press for some of the bad blood here. The magnificent on-field qualities of men like McCarthy and DiMaggio make it easy to sympathize with them, in regard to the media pressures they endured. In McCarthy's case, unlike DiMaggio, he made little or no fetish about the pressure from the media. He just had a career-long habit of calmly stiffing them. That was his nature. The press may have changed from cheerleading, to respectful deference, to criticism, to nagging, but McCarthy never changed, and he managed himself into the Hall of Fame always true to his nature. Even though he and Joe DiMaggio may not have drawn the greatest joy from the point, we also have the press to thank for much of the wonderful details of their deeds, as well as for the broader story of the relationship of press and sports figures, one which McCarthy's and DiMaggio's careers illustrate, and one which continues to be an evolving, ever-more important element of modern social history.

Notes

1. George Juergens, *Joseph Pulitzer and the New York World* (Princeton: Princeton University Press, 1966), pp. 93–174; James Wyman Barrett, *Joseph Pulitzer and His World* (New York: The Vanguard Press, 1941), pp. 55–83.

2. Warren Susman, *Culture as History: The Transformation of American Society in the Twentieth Century*. (New York: Pantheon Books, [1973] 1984), pp. 105–121.

3. Frederick Lewis Allen, *Only Yesterday: An Informal History of the Twenties*. (New York and London, Harper & brothers, 1931), *passim*.

4. *New York World-Telegram*, May 25, 1946, p. 12.

5. *Kansas City Journal*, July 17, 1923; Harry J. Rothberger, Jr., "Joe McCarthy's Ten Years as a Louisville Colonel," from *A Celebration of Louisville Baseball in the Major and Minor Leagues*. (Cleveland: The Society for American Baseball Research, 1997), p. 7; *New York Evening Post*, April 6, 1933, p. 11.

6. *Chicago Daily News*, March 3, p. 21; *Chicago Herald and Examiner*, March 1, 1926, p. 13, March 10, p. 13, March 16, p. 13, March 17, p. 15, March 31, 1926, p. 13, April 1, p. 21, April 5, p. 15, April 12, p. 17, June 16, p. 11, June 18, p. 14; *Chicago Tribune*, February 12, p. 19, March 4, p. 17, March 16, p. 21, June 16, 1926, p. 21, June 27, section 2, p. 2.

7. *Chicago Daily News*, October 8, 1929, p. 1, October 9, p. 1, October 11, pp. 1, 18, October 12, p. 1; October 14, p. 1, Oct 15, p. 29; *Chicago Herald and Examiner*, Oct. 9, p. 15, Oct. 10, p. 17, Oct. 12, p. 17, Oct. 13, section 3, p. 1, Oct. 14, p. 17, Oct. 15, p. 17, Oct. 18, p. 17; *Chicago Tribune*, Oct. 9, p. 24, Oct. 10, p. 23, Oct. 13, section 2, p. 1, Oct. 15, p. 31, Dec. 5, p. 28; *The Sporting News*, November 10, 1954, p. 15; *Philadelphia Evening Public Ledger*, Oct. 13, 1932, p. 22; *Baseball Digest*, April 1948, pp. 7–8; Edwin Pope, *Baseball's Greatest Managers*. (Garden City, N.Y.: Doubleday and Co., 1960), p. 142; Joe McCarthy, "How Pennants Are Really Won," *Liberty Magazine*, September 30, 1933, p. 4; Warren Brown, *The Chicago Cubs*. (Carbondale: Southern Illinois Press [1946] 2001), p. 117; Donald Honig, *The Man in the Dugout, Fifteen Big League Managers Speak Their Minds* (Chicago: Follett Publishing Co., 1977), pp. 82, 281; Harvey Frommer, *Baseball's Greatest Managers*. (New York: Franklin Watts, 1985), p. 192; Ed Burns, "The Chicago Cubs," *Sport Magazine*, September, 1950, p. 82; Joe McCarthy Clippings File, Baseball Hall of Fame, Cooperstown: Cancelled check, National City Bank, New York, June 7, 1930.

8. *Chicago Herald and Examiner*, September 22, 1930, pp. 1, 19–21, Sept. 23, p. 19, Sept. 26, p. 19; *Chicago Tribune*, Sept. 22, p. 21, Sept. 26, p. 33.

9. Warren Brown, *The Chicago Cubs*. (Carbondale: Southern Illinois Press [1946] 2001), pp. 118–20; Tom Meany, *The Yankee Story*. (New York: E.P. Dutton and Co., Inc., 1960), p. 104–05; Ed Hurley, *Managing to Win*. (New York: Pellicino, Inc., 1976), pp. 42–44; Will Wedge, *New York Sun*, April 4, 1932, p. 34; Edward Grant Barrow, *My Fifty Years in Baseball*. (New York: Coward-McCann, Inc., 1951), p. 165; Barrow, "The Greatest Manager," *Collier's*, June 24, 1950, p. 28; Frank Graham, *Lou Gehrig: A Quiet Hero*. (New York: G.P. Putnam's Sons, 1942), p. 139.

10. *New York Times*, March 4, 1931, p. 24, March 10, p. 28; *Philadelphia Record*, February 23, 1931, p. 17; *New York Daily News*, March 1, 1931, pp. 74, 77, March 4, p. 50; *New York Sun*, March 16, p. 37; *New York World Telegram*, July 31, 1931, p. 9; *Philadelphia Public Ledger*, July 4, 1931, p. 14; Harvey Frommer, *Baseball's Greatest Managers*. (New York: Franklin Watts, 1985), p. 158; Jim Enright, *Baseball's Greatest Teams: The Chicago Cubs*. (New York: Collier Books, 1975), p. 100; Edwin Pope, *Baseball's Greatest Managers*. (New York: Doubleday and Co., Inc., 1960), p. 144; Robert Creamer, *Babe: The Legend Comes to Life*. (New York: Simon and Schuster, 1974), p. 352; Dan Shaughnessy, *The Curse of the Bambino*. (New York: Penguin Books, [1990] 1991), p. 77; Marshall Smelser, *The Life That Ruth Built: A Biography*. (Lincoln: University of Nebraska Press, 1993), pp. 427, 432; Joe DiMaggio, *Lucky to Be a Yankee*. (New York: Grosset and Dunlap, 1951), p. 18; Ed Linn, *The Great Rivalry: The Yankees and the Red Sox, 1901–1990*. (New York: Ticknor and Fields, 1991), pp. 180, 184.

11. *New York Daily News*, September 2, 1939, p. 28, Sept. 17, p. 84, Sept. 26, p. 27; Anthony Violanti, *Miracle in Buffalo: How the Dream of Baseball Revived a City* (New York: St. Martin's Press, 1991), pp. 63–64; David Quentin Voigt, *American Baseball*, vol. II. (University Park, Pa.: Penn State University Press, 1983), pp. 197–98; Richard Lally, *Bombers: An Oral History of the New York Yankees*. (New York: Three Rivers Press, Crown Publishers, 2002), p. 179; Leonard Koppett, *The Man in the Dugout: Baseball's Top Managers and How They Got That Way*. (Philadelphia: Temple University Press, 2000), p. 98; Richard Ben Cramer, *Joe DiMaggio: A Hero's Life*. (New York: Simon and Schuster, 2000), pp. 137–38; Tommy Henrich, *Five O'Clock Lightening: Ruth, Gehrig, DiMaggio, Mantle, and the Glory Years of the New York Yankees*. (New York: Birch Lane Press, 1992), p. 62.

12. *Buffalo Evening News*, October 11, 1939, pp. 37, 39; Gordon Cobbledick, "Break Up the Yankees!" *Collier's*, February 25, 1939, p. 19; Joe DiMaggio, *Lucky to Be a Yankee*. (New York: Grosset and Dunlap, 1947), p. 130; Tommy Henrich, *Five O'Clock Lightening*, pp. 20–21.

13. *New York Daily News*, July 13, 1940, p. 67, July 16, p. 57, July 21, p. 64, August 2, p. 38, Aug. 5, p. 35, Aug. 6, p. 40, Aug. 18, p. 70, Sept. 28, p. 28, Sept. 29, p. 85, Sept. 30, p. 42; *New York Times*, Aug. 20, p. 25, Aug. 21, p. 25, June 3, 1941, p. 26; *New York World-Telegram*, October 10, p. 34; *New York Sun*, January 13, 1942, p. 24; Tommy Henrich, *Five O'Clock Lightening*, pp. 83, 87, 112;

14. Joe Williams, "Busher Joe McCarthy," *Saturday Evening Post*, April 15, 1939, p. 12.

15. *New York Daily News*, May 16, 1944, p. 32; *New York Times*, November 10, 1943, p. 32; June 25, 1950, section 5, p. 2; *New York World Telegram*, March 28, 1944, p. 20, April 13, p. 17, Arthur Daley, "McCarthy Could Manage," *Baseball Digest*, vol. 9, no. 9, Sept. 1950, p. 62; Associated Press Biographical Sketch, No. 3002, November 15, 1942; Edwin Pope, *Baseball's Greatest Managers*, pp. 134–35; Donald Honig, *The Man in the Dugout*, pp. 288–89; Harvey Frommer, *Baseball's Greatest Managers*, p. 156; Richard Goldstein, *Spartan Seasons: How Baseball Survived the Second World War*. (New York: MacMillan Publishing, Inc., 1980), p. 157; Donald Honig, *Baseball Between the Lines: Baseball in the Forties as Told by the Men Who Played It*. (Lincoln: University of Nebraska Press, 1976), p. 374.

16. *New York Daily News*, April 14, 1945, p. 43; Milton Gross, *Yankee Doodles* (Boston: House of Kent Publishing Co., 1948), pp. 58, 164, 234.

17. *New York Daily News*, June 13, 1945, p. 53, June 22, p. 38, July 1, p. 56, July 2, p. 36, July 3, p. 25, July 22, p. 80, July 24, 1945, p. 41, July 25, p. 49; *New York Times*, July 23, p. 22; *Buffalo Evening News*, July 24, p. 18, July 25, p. 30, August 8, p. 30, August 16, p. 19; *Buffalo Courier-Express*, July 22, p. 18; *New York Journal-American*, July 24, p. 19.

18. *New York Sun*, May 22, 1946, p. 35, May 23, p. 33; *New York World Telegram*, May 25, p. 12, May 27, p. 25.

19. *The Sporting News*, October 8, 1947, p. 3; Harry Frommer, *Baseball's Greatest Managers*, p. 192; Milton Gross, *Yankee Doodles*, p. 144; Harry J. Rothberger, Jr., "Joe McCarthy's Ten Years as a Louisville Colonel," p. 7.

20. Milton Gross, *Yankee Doodles*, pp. 59, 62; Al Hirshberg, *What's the Matter with the Red Sox*. (New York: Dodd, Mead and Co., 1973), p. 18.

21. Al Hirshberg, *What's the Matter with the Red Sox*, pp. 8, 18, 123, 130, 133; *The Sporting News*, April 14, 1948, p. 6.

22. *Boston Herald*, May 27, 1948, p. 26, May 28, p. 1, May 29, p. 8, May 31, p. 36; *Boston Globe*, May 30, p. 1, *Boston Post*, May 28, pp. 1, 22, May 29, p. 8, May 30, p. 9, May 31, p. 38,

June 1, p. 20, June 2, p. 16, June 3, p. 18; Peter C. Bjarkman, ed., *Encyclopedia of Major League Baseball — American League.* (New York: Carroll and Graf Publishers, 1993), p. 28.

    23. *Boston Post,* June 7, 1948, p. 1, June 25, pp. 1, 19- 20; Ed Linn, *The Great Rivalry,* pp. 184–5; Tom Meany, *The Boston Red Sox.* (New York: A.S. Barnes and Co., 1956), p. 159.

    24. *Boston Post,* September 9, 1948, p. 19.

    25. Ibid., October 5, 1948, p. 38.

    26. *Boston Post,* October 5, 1948, pp. 38, May 20, 1949, p. 31; Donald Honig, *The Man in the Dugout,* p. 93; Bill James, *The Bill James Guide to Baseball Managers from 1870 to Today.* (New York: Scribner's, 1997), p. 118; Harry Frommer, *Baseball's Greatest Managers.* (New York: Franklin Watts, 1985), p. 161; Hank Nuwer, *Strategies of the Great Baseball Managers.* (New York: Franklin Watts, 1988), p. 81; Dan Shaughnessy, *The Curse of the Bambino,* pp. 80–83; Ed Linn, *The Great Rivalry,* pp. 196–98.

    27. *Boston Globe,* February 28, 1950, p. 16, March 1, p. 26; *Boston Post,* March 24, p. 35.

    28. *Boston Post,* May 17, 1949, p. 18, May 31, p. 16, June 6, pp. 1, 18, June 11, p. 8; Al Hirshberg, *What's Wrong with the Red Sox,* p. 104.

    29. Al Hirshberg, *What's Wrong With the Red Sox,* pp. 70–71.

    30. *Boston Post,* September 11, 1948, pp. 1, 8; Joseph Durso, *Joe DiMaggio: The Last American Knight.* (Boston: Little, Brown, and Co., 1995), p. 173; Ed Linn, *The Great Rivalry,* pp. 185–7.

    31. *Boston Post,* June 30, 1949 p. 15, July 1, p. 16, October 2, pp. 38–9; *Boston Herald,* Oct. 2, p. 51; Donald Honig, *Baseball Between the Lines,* p. 89; Peter Goldenbock, *Fenway: An Unexpurgated History of the Red Sox.* (New York: G.P. Putnam's Sons, 1992), p. 180; Ed Linn, *Hitter: The Life and Turmoils of Ted Williams.* (New York: Harcourt Brace and Co., 1993), p. 311; Dan Shaughnessy, *The Curse of the Bambino,* p. 84–5; Joe DiMaggio, *Lucky to Be a Yankee,* p. 27; Richard Ben Cramer, *Joe DiMaggio: The Hero's Life.* (New York: Simon and Schuster, 2000), pp. 266–68. (In his apparent desire to demonize Joe DiMaggio, Cramer appeared logically compelled to criticize McCarthy, as the two had been cast as a perfect compliment to one another — always mindful and seemingly without joys. (Cramer, p. 93) McCarthy and DiMaggio each had joys, and McCarthy had no divided loyalties when managing in Boston.) Al Hirshberg, *What's Wrong with the Red Sox,* p. 91; Ed Hurley, *Managing to Win.* (New York: A.J. Pollicino, Inc., 1976), p. 89.

    32. *Boston Post,* October 3, 1949, p. 18, *Boston Herald,* Oct. 3, p. 1, *Boston Globe,* Oct. 3, p. 8; Al Hirshberg, *What's Wrong with the Red Sox,* pp. 100–02; Bill Madden, *Pride of October: What it Was to be Young and a Yankee.* (New York: Warner Books, 2003), p. 116.

    33. Quoted in Dan Shaughnessy, *The Curse of the Bambino* (New York: Penguin Books, [1990] 1991), p. 61.

    34. *Boston Herald,* June 23, 1950, p. 18; Shaughnessy, *The Curse of the Bambino,* pp. 76–7; Daniel Boorstin, *The Image: A Guide to Pseudo-Events in America.* (New York: Harper and Row, 1961), *passim.*

    35. *Boston Post,* April 14, 1950, p. 29, April 18, p. 1, April 19, pp. 36–37; *Boston Globe,* April 14, p. 24, April 17, p. 20; *Look Magazine,* July 4, 1950, p. 71; *Newsweek,* April 17, 1950, p. 62.

    36. *Boston Globe,* April 16, 1950, p. 46, April 19, p. 28; *Boston Post,* April 22, p. 7; Edwin Pope, *Baseball's Greatest Managers.* (Garden City, NY: Doubleday and Co., Inc., 1960), p. 134; Harry Frommer, *Baseball's Greatest Managers,* p. 162.

    37. *Boston Post,* April 23, 1950, pp. 1, 37- 38, April 24, pp. 1, 19; *Boston Globe,* April 24, pp. 1, 8, April 25, p. 17.

    38. Ed Linn, *Hitter: The Life and Turmoils of Ted Williams.* (New York: Harcourt Brace and Co., 1993), p. 311.

    39. *Boston Globe,* June 24, pp. 1, 6; *Boston Herald,* June 23, p. 18, June 25, p. 11; *The Sporting News,* December 18, 1957, p. 18; Pope, *Baseball's Greatest Managers,* p. 135; Peter Goldenbock, *Fenway,* p. 186.

    40. *Boston Post,* June 26, 1950, p. 18; *Boston Globe,* September 19, 1950, p. 1, Sept. 20, p. 14, Sept. 21, p. 23, Sept. 24, p. 1, Sept. 25, p. 1, Sept. 28, p. 12.

    41. Anthony Violanti, *Miracle in Buffalo: How the Dream of Baseball Revived a City.* (New York: St. Martin's Press, 1991), pp. 62–3.

Playing Catch Inverted: August Wilson's *Fences* and Other Departures from Baseball's Cultural Stereotypes

Edward J. Rielly

Baseball is perhaps, of all sports, the richest in cultural traditions. Its traditions are steeped in myth, hallowed with long practice, and rooted in the most fundamental values associated with the human condition. It is no coincidence that baseball has long been described in religious terms (e.g., the ballpark as a cathedral), or that students and fans of the game have viewed the game in metaphoric terms. At the same time, baseball is perceived as a powerful bonding agent between father and son, their eternal connection created in a game of catch in the backyard.

Baseball as religion has been presented in film and fiction and dissected in scholarly tomes. The speech by Annie Savoy (played by Susan Sarandon) in the film *Bull Durham* about the "church of baseball" has received wide currency. The speech concludes with her affirmation: "The only church that truly feeds the soul day in day out is the church of baseball."[1] In the novel *Shoeless Joe*, Ray Kinsella, preparing for a nocturnal visit to the Minnesota stadium with J. D. Salinger and Moonlight Graham, opines, "A ballpark at night is more like a church than a church."[2] Later in the book, Eddie Scissons, who falsely passes himself off as the oldest living Chicago Cub, leads Ray, Ray's family, and Ray's ghostly baseball guests in a litany, not on the church of baseball but, more fundamentally, on the word of baseball:

"The word is baseball," we barely whisper.
"Say it out loud," exhorts Eddie.
"The word is baseball," we say louder, but still self-consciously...
"The word is what?"
"Baseball ..."[3]

And the litany continues, evoking unmistakable echoes of the opening of John's gospel: "In the beginning was the Word, and the Word was with God, and the Word was God."[4]

The implied identification of baseball with the divine might seem excessive, if not blasphemous, to most people, and writers usually try to walk the frail line between religion and religion-like. Recent books about the religious dimensions of baseball try, not always successfully, to avoid crossing it.

Andrew Cooper begins his *Playing in the Zone: Exploring the Spiritual Dimensions of Sports* by quoting former Giants catcher Wes Westrum: "Baseball is like church. Many attend, but few understand."[5] For Cooper, sport, "in its ability to provoke wonder, to elicit deep feeling, to grace our lives with glimpses of timeless beauty and freedom ... is, though not religion, something religious."[6] That dividing line sways badly at this point, hanging together by a frayed string or two: "Like drama, music, and poetry, the beginnings of sport go back to the religious rites of the ancient world.... [T]hrough most of human history, before modern times, sport has maintained some explicit connection with its sacred origins."[7] Cooper applies the term "secret life" to this hidden religious character of sport, defining the term as "religion as it emerges from the depths of the self."[8]

While Cooper attempts an inclusive discussion of sport in general as religious (or something like religious), true believers realize that the authentic religion of sport is baseball. James Penrice takes an explicitly didactic approach in *Crossing Home: The Spiritual Lessons of Baseball*. He tries to make his position clear in the first sentence of the book: "Baseball is a lot like religion"— not actually religion itself.[9] Far less inclusive than Cooper, Penrice acknowledges his personal Catholicism as a framework for discussion. He accepts the superficiality of many common comparisons of baseball to religion, e.g., stadiums as temples,[10] but then steps very close to the line between is and like:

> But just as in religion, the true spirituality of baseball lies deep beneath the surface of ritual. I invite you to explore with me beyond this surface, to probe the essence of Christian values which saturate the game and the institution of baseball. If you love God and love the game, come with me.[11]

Penrice then offers twenty-three meditations on ways in which baseball can enhance one's Christian faith. Chapter titles include: "The Parable of the Free Agent," "Let the Children Come, and Do Not Hinder Them," "Wherever Two or More Are Gathered." To avoid mistaking the point, Penrice makes generous use of capitalization throughout: "The Umpire," "The Owner," "Biggest Fan" (all referring to God, although other baseball theologians might prefer the devil for "The Owner"); "The Opponent" (the devil in this exegesis); "The Game" (the Christian's life); "Home" (heaven). As a sort of epigraph, the author offers a tortured parallel on the word "cross," likening crossing home plate to the role of the Christian cross in bringing people home to God.[12]

Even the greatest of authors, though, can merge baseball with religion. F. Scott Fitzgerald, in *The Great Gatsby*, has Nick Carraway describing a conversation with Gatsby about an underworld figure, Meyer Wolfsheim:

> "Meyer Wolfsheim? No, he's a gambler." Gatsby hesitated, then added coolly: "He's the man who fixed the World's Series back in 1919."
> "Fixed the World's Series?" I repeated.
> The idea staggered me. I remembered of course that the World's Series had been fixed in 1919 but if I had thought of it at all I would have thought of it as a thing that merely *happened*, the end of some inevitable chain. It never occurred to me that one man could start to play with the faith of fifty million people — with the single-mindedness of a burglar blowing a safe.[13]

Fitzgerald's reference supplies the title for a collection of essays edited by Christopher H. Evans and William R. Herzog II — *The Faith of Fifty Million: Baseball, Religion, and American Culture*, an examination of baseball within the context of Protestant Christianity and democratic ideals. In the essay "Baseball As Civil Religion: The Genesis of an American Creation Story," Evans writes that "civil religion describes how Americans throughout the nation's history have created a collective national identity through bestowing sacred meaning on a variety of secular symbols, rituals, and institutions."[14] For Evans, "At the center of baseball's symbolic power there resides a unique language of civil religion, proclaiming that the game can redeem America and serve as a light to all nations."[15] Baseball thus became America's national pastime because it represents the nation's soul.[16]

Similar estimations of baseball's utility in inculcating America's moral and democratic principles have been formalized by countless individuals, including early player, manager, club president, and sporting-goods tycoon Albert Spalding. In *Base Ball: America's National Game*, first published in 1911, Spalding combines moral certainty with a flair for alliteration:

> I claim that Base Ball owes its prestige as our National Game to the fact that as no other form of sport it is the exponent of American Courage, Confidence, Combativeness; American Dash, Discipline, Determination; American Energy, Eagerness, Enthusiasm; American Pluck, Persistency, Performance; American Spirit, Sagacity, Success; American Vim, Vigor, Virility.[17]

General Douglas MacArthur, commander of the occupying force in Japan after World War II and a former baseball player at West Texas Military Academy and West Point, viewed the game from a similar vantage point. MacArthur encouraged the rebirth of baseball in Japan as a means of grafting American democracy onto Japanese traditions. The general so enjoyed the sport that he occasionally would pause on his drives between his residence at the American Embassy in Tokyo and headquarters to watch sandlot games.[18]

Evans also discusses baseball in relation to "liberal-Protestant, Progressive-Era reformers."[19] Contending that "turn-of-the-century liberal Protestantism believed baseball embodied the virtues of Christian recreation," Evans examines the very public role of pitcher Christy Mathewson as a "Christian Gentleman." Evans asserts that "baseball embodied what many liberals saw as the chief cornerstone of the kingdom of God in America — a faith in Christian democracy."[20]

As it is a small step from religion to myth, or vice versa, so it is a small step from the religion of baseball to baseball's position in the great myths that help to define the human condition, especially humankind's eternal dreams and aspirations. Without entirely abandoning the notion of baseball as somehow religious, A. Bartlett Giamatti, former Yale president, commissioner of baseball, and the most illustrious explicator of the game's mythos, endeared himself to owner and fan alike in an increasingly money-driven world (and sport) by romanticizing and ennobling what otherwise might be categorized as just another big business.

Giamatti proposes in *Take Time for Paradise: Americans and Their Games* that organized sport "mimics the ritual quality of religious observances even when sport is no longer, if it ever was, connected to a formal religious act of worship."[21] However, he finds that sport differs from religion by not including the typical religious consequences, such as "religion's moral strictures or political power or endless promises."[22] What is particularly important about sport, for Giamatti, is that "play aspires to the condition of paradise," a condition in the Western world typically envisioned "as a garden, sometimes on a mountaintop, often on an island, but always as removed, an enclosed, green place."[23] He reflects, "It is a dream of ourselves as better than we are, back to what we were."[24] According to Giamatti, "Between days of work, sports or games only repeat and repeat our effort to go back, back to a freedom we cannot recall, save as a moment of play in some garden now lost."[25]

Baseball, for Giamatti, reenacts that drive to return. Baseball is thus "the story of going home after having left home,"[26] home being, rather than a place, "a state of mind where self-definition starts."[27] Baseball is "a narrative, an epic of exile and return"; it also is a "Romance Epic of homecoming America sings to itself."[28] Baseball "sends its players out in order to return again, allowing all the freedom to accomplish great things in a dangerous world. So baseball restates a version of America's promise every time it is played."[29] And that promise begins, Giamatti reminds the reader, in childhood. Much of what we love about baseball, that "most strenuously nostalgic of all our sports,"[30] is that it recalls to mind our earliest sense of self, memories not just of a game but of "a time when all that would be better was before us, as a hope, and the hope was fastened to a game."[31]

For many writers about baseball, as well as fans of the game, that sense of nostalgia is the dominant tone. Roger Kahn was a young newspaperman covering the Brooklyn Dodgers in the early 1950s, that time of life, as he writes of himself in *The Boys of Summer*, "when one is through with boyhood, but has not yet discovered how to be a man."[32] Almost twenty years later, in the autumn of those players' lives, he set about discovering how the passage of time had treated his Brooklyn heroes—Jackie Robinson, Pee Wee Reese, Duke Snider, Billy Cox, and the rest.

Another nostalgic trip occurs in Maury Allen's book about Joe DiMaggio. The title comes from a Paul Simon song and reflects the sense of a modern era without genuine heroes: *Where Have You Gone, Joe DiMaggio?*[33]

Baseball nostalgia frequently evokes childhood memories of the sort that the poet Donald Hall uses in the title for a collection of essays: *Fathers Playing Catch with Sons: Essays on Sport [Mostly Baseball]*. In fact, for Hall, "baseball is fathers and sons playing catch,"[34] and he chronicles the long, continuous progression of baseball in terms of that father-son relationship:

> my father and my son, and my mother's father when the married men played the single men in Wilmot, New Hampshire, and my father's father's father who hit a ball with a stick while he was camped outside Vicksburg in June of 1863, and maybe my son's son's son for baseball is continuous, like nothing else among American things, an endless game of repeated summers, joining the long generations of all the fathers and all the sons.[35]

Baseball is about fathers and sons pursuing a dream to return home, and in the midst of that pursuit bonding in an unending chain of fathers and sons. All of this is either overtly religious or something akin to the religious experience — and if not religiously religious, at least a matter of civil religion. It is about America: sound moral and democratic principles rooted in family, served with apple pie and wrapped in the stars and stripes. But is this all of the story? Some people, including the playwright August Wilson, say no.

August Wilson, one of America's greatest playwrights, chronicles the history of African Americans within this nation's social and political movements, and he does so through one play for each decade of the twentieth century. The play for the 1950s is *Fences*, first produced in 1985 and winner of the 1987 Pulitzer Prize for Drama.[36]

Set in 1957, ten years after Jackie Robinson integrated Major League Baseball, *Fences* is about many things, including baseball, integration, the death of dreams, and family relationships. And integration, lost dreams, and family relationships revolve around baseball in the play. Throughout the drama, the grand and noble concepts of the game are sharply inverted, even down to the baseball metaphors that define life.

The main character in *Fences* is fifty-three-year-old Troy Maxson, a former Negro League star who came along too early to have a chance to play in the major leagues and now makes a living by collecting garbage. His son, Cory, is a star high school athlete who has an opportunity to receive a scholarship to play college football.

The play takes place in the front yard of the Maxson home, framed by a partial fence that Rose, Troy's wife, is trying to get him to complete and a ball hanging from a tree. From time to time, Troy takes some swings with his bat at the ball. In fact, as Sandra D. Shannon has written, Troy is "constantly at bat" throughout the play.[37]

The fence recalls both the fences Troy was adept at hitting baseballs over and the unfinished status of his own life while also symbolizing, as Troy's friend, Bono, explains, Rose's attempt to keep her family together.[38] *Fences* is a powerful exposition of the impact of racial discrimination, with African Americans' exclusion from Organized Baseball the root cause for much of the action in the play. Consequently, as Kim Pereira has written, the fence also acts as "a symbol of separation."[39]

In the standard mythos of baseball, the game binds father and son forever, but here sport is what drives them apart. Frustrated by his own unfulfilled dreams as a baseball player and certain that whites have stacked the deck against African Americans, Troy commands his son to get a useful trade like car repairing and forget sports. There is no defining of baseball here in terms of a father and son playing catch. Baseball is just another manifestation of racial injustice. It is not about going home; it is about being driven from home, as Cory finally runs away, not returning until the day of his father's funeral. The last scene in which both father and son are present dramatically inverts Hall's defining image of a father and son playing ball together. Cory, outraged by his father's marital infidelity and failures as a father, claims that Troy has tried to make both Cory and Rose afraid of him. The verbal exchange increases in intensity, and Troy orders Cory out of the yard. Cory backs away until he comes up against the tree from which the ball hangs and against which the bat is leaning. He grabs the bat and threatens Troy: "I ain't going nowhere! Come on ... put me out! I ain't scared of you."[40] Cory twice swings the bat, not at a pitched ball from a loving father, but against the father himself. Both times he misses, at which point Troy wrestles the bat away from Cory and orders him to leave. When Cory says that he will be back for his things, Troy angrily says, "They'll be on the other side of that fence."[41]

The social and political philosophy that Troy recognizes is not baseball as civil religion but the game as one more white trick perpetrated on blacks.

In his misguided way, Troy loves his son, although he cannot even admit to Cory that he likes him, and tries to save his son from what he believes will be a great betrayal. As he explains to Rose, "I got sense enough not to let my boy get hurt over playing no sports."[42] Unwittingly, Troy, who cannot accept that times have changed, deprives his son of his great opportunity to achieve both academic and athletic success, at the same time driving him away from home.

So bitter is Troy that he mocks the accomplishments of the early black stars of Major League Baseball. "I done seen a hundred niggers play baseball better than Jackie Robinson," Troy says.[43] After Cory mentions that Hank Aaron had recently hit two home runs, Troy answers: "Hank Aaron ain't nobody. That's what you supposed to do…. Hell, I can hit forty-three home runs now!'[44]

Like so many commentators on the game, Troy employs life-and-death metaphors drawn from baseball, but with a striking inversion of normative usage. He employs, for example, baseball metaphors to justify his marital infidelity, the tenor of such metaphors far removed from Giamatti's desire to return to one's origins, to one's unlimited promises. Troy remarks that he was born with two strikes on him and had to guard the plate, "always looking for the curve-ball on the inside corner."[45] But, Troy says, he fooled "them" (an undifferentiated them) by bunting, that is, by finding Rose and Cory and "a halfway decent job."[46] Troy fooled them and found himself standing safe on first base, "looking for one of them boys to knock me in. To get me home."[47] He recalls, "Then when I saw that gal … she firmed up my backbone. And I got to thinking that if I tried … I just might be able to steal second. Do you understand after eighteen years I wanted to steal second."[48]

Rose, hurt and bewildered by Troy's actions, which include not only an extramarital affair but also fathering a child by the other woman, responds, "We're not talking about baseball! We're talking about you going off to lay in bed with another woman … and then bring it home to me. That's what we're talking about. We ain't talking about no baseball."[49] Rose's comments add another layer of irony to the now popular myth of baseball being about returning home.

Throughout the play, Troy bats the ball hanging from the tree, but he never plays ball with Cory. In fact, his primary partner in baseball is death, as Troy explicates his mortal struggle in metaphorical terms of a batter facing a pitcher. "Death ain't nothing," he says early in the play, "but a fastball on the outside corner." Troy continues, "And you know what I'll do to that! Lookee here, Bono … am I lying? You get one of them fastballs, about waist high, over the outside corner of the plate where you can get the meat of the bat on it … and good god! You can kiss it goodbye."[50] Ultimately, Troy misses that nice, fat pitch, suffering an apparent heart attack during his accustomed batting practice. As Rose explains to the returned Cory:

He still got that piece of rag tied to that tree. He was out here swinging that bat. I was just ready to go back in the house. He swung that
bat and then he just fell over. Seem like he swung it and stood there
with this grin on his face ... and then he just fell over.[51]

Troy uses a similar batting metaphor to chastise Cory. At the end of Act
One, Cory and Troy engage in a verbal exchange over Troy's telling the high
school football coach that Cory "can't play football no more" and that the
college recruiter should forget about Cory.[52] Cory accuses Troy, who never
had a chance, of being afraid that his son may surpass him, leading Troy to
warn Cory: "I'm gonna tell you what your mistake was. See ... you swung at
the ball and didn't hit it. That's strike one. See, you in the batter's box now.
You swung and you missed. That's strike one. Don't you strike out."[53]

The next inverted time at bat occurs the following morning. Cory leaves
the house at the moment when Troy had grabbed Rose by the arm during an
angry exchange about Troy's affair and fathering a child. Cory grabs his father
and throws him down. Rose holds onto Troy, who stops just before hitting
Cory back. But Troy warns Cory that he has strike two on him and had better not strike out.[54]

Strike three occurs eight months later in the previously mentioned scene
when Cory swings a bat at his father. Troy does not have to remind Cory that
the swing constitutes strike three. His command that Cory leave demonstrates that, for him, Cory has struck out. As soon as Cory exits, though,
Troy grabs his bat, crouches as if waiting for a pitch, and resumes his con-
frontation with death, daring death to try to strike him out.[55] It is the last
time that the audience sees Troy. The next scene, the final one in the play, is
set in 1965 on the day of Troy's funeral, Troy finally having missed the "fastball on the outside corner" of the plate.[56]

Fences is one of the most powerful and artistically successful departures
from baseball stereotypes, but it has much company. Baseball is about dreams,
as Giamatti argues, but the commissioner and purveyor of baseball myth
does not admit that they often are failed dreams. That certainly is the case
in *Shoeless Joe*, W. P. Kinsella's classic baseball novel.

In the end, baseball reunites father and son in Kinsella's novel (and in
the film version, *Field of Dreams*). But it must play this role only because in
"real life" it was the source of Ray's father's great disappointments, with his
failed baseball career (never rising above Class B teams), and the fate of his
baseball hero, Shoeless Joe Jackson, banished from baseball for life for helping to throw the 1919 World Series.[57] The film version adds the theme of baseball as a source of division between father and son, with Ray at seventeen
leaving home after insulting both his father and Shoeless Joe with the statement, "I could never respect a man whose hero was a criminal."[58]

Francis Phelan, protagonist in William Kennedy's *Ironweed*, ironically never has the opportunity to play catch with one of his sons because he drops the infant, accidentally killing him, perhaps the ultimate fielding error in baseball literature. This from a former great defensive third baseman with the Washington Senators, a "damn fieldin' machine," as Phelan remembers himself.[59] The mortal error reduces Phelan to a life as a hobo. Finally, he returns, although only temporarily, to his family after an absence of some twenty years. Phelan retrieves an old ball and glove from an attic trunk, giving these reminders of his earlier life to his grandson and surviving son. Phelan's final baseball epiphany, however, is not familial, but is with other transients in a squatters' camp against raiders attempting to eliminate the hobos. The raiders' attack, with bats, is another inversion of baseball. Francis Phelan survives the attack and catches a freight train out of town.

Heroes are part of the grandeur of baseball. Joe DiMaggio and Ted Williams are two obvious examples. DiMaggio, the subject of the aforementioned Paul Simon song and Maury Allen book, was revered by fan and teammate alike for his talent, grace, and dignity. Always impeccably dressed, he was ever conscious of his image and that of the Yankees. The son of immigrants, DiMaggio, courageously battling illness and injury, attained greatness. Impressed, Ernest Hemingway, the ultimate macho writer, depicted DiMaggio as the hero of his fisherman protagonist in *The Old Man and the Sea*.[60] Finally, when age and injury caught up with him, Joltin' Joe retired, unwilling to play out the string as a mediocre player. Until his death in 1999, DiMaggio was routinely referred to and introduced (by his demand) as the greatest living ballplayer.

After his death, though, the DiMaggio reputation lost some of its heroic luster, due to Richard Ben Cramer's revisionist *Joe DiMaggio: The Hero's Life*. Cramer presents a DiMaggio defined by loneliness, hunger for money, and failed family relationships. Cramer's controversial book concludes with a portrait of DiMaggio as a sick old man controlled by his lawyer, confidant, and business manager, Morris Engelberg. Engelberg, according to Cramer, pushed DiMaggio to sign memorabilia and controlled who would have access to the Yankee Clipper, even attempting, during Joe's final illness, to deny access to his brother Dominic. Cramer claims that Engelberg orchestrated DiMaggio's death, ordering the removal of the life-support respirator.[61]

As rival player and legend, Ted Williams was often compared to DiMaggio. If DiMaggio was the greatest living player, Williams was the greatest living hitter, possibly the greatest hitter of all time. Like DiMaggio, Williams was a heroic figure, larger than life and notable for his exploits on and off the field. A pilot in World War II and the Korean conflict, Williams flew dangerous combat missions. Williams also gave generously of his time to the Jimmy Fund, aiding children battling cancer.[62] Although Williams was often surly to sportswriters and fans, few denied his greatness.[63]

The multiple dimensions of Williams' heroics were dramatized at the Fenway Park tribute to the deceased slugger on July 22, 2002. The event was divided into nine parts, labeled "nine innings to honor number nine."[64] Presenters at the Williams' memorial included: teammates Dom DiMaggio, Jerry Coleman, and Johnny Pesky; Carl Yastrzemski, who succeeded Williams in left field; former astronaut and Senator John Glenn, Williams' squadron leader in Korea; filmmaker Ken Burns; ex-pitcher Earl Wilson, one of the first blacks to play for the Red Sox; and former Boston infielder and current chair of the Jimmy Fund, Mike Andrews.[65]

Unfortunately, shortly after Williams' death on July 5, 2002, a macabre form of immortality beckoned. Although family is an essential part of the baseball myth, the dysfunction of the Williams family had provided press fodder for decades. Ted himself had lamented to longtime teammate and friend Dom DiMaggio "that he had made something of a mess of his life."[66] This was apparent in Williams' failed marriages and the distance that often separated him from his children.

Following Williams' death, the public learned that his last years bore similarities to DiMaggio's. John Henry Williams, Ted's son, financially and psychologically manipulated his father. Purporting to be following his father's wishes, a claim strongly denied by Dom DiMaggio and Williams' oldest child, Bobby-Jo Ferrell, John Henry announced plans to have Williams' body frozen. Cryonics, considered a crackpot science by most scientists, aims at freezing the dead body until the subject can be brought back or cloned. Bizarre descriptions of what this would entail quickly surfaced: Ted Williams suspended upside down in an aluminum pod of nitrogen vapor at -320 degrees at the Alcor Life Extension Foundation in Scottsdale, Arizona, his blood and brain fluid replaced with a preservative solution, or perhaps only his head preserved. John Henry apparently discussed cloning his father, leading to conjecture that he might be planning to sell Ted's DNA.[67]

A bitter fight ensued, with another daughter, Claudia Williams, siding with John Henry against Bobby-Jo. Ultimately, John Henry triumphed, apparently keeping Ted Williams' remains in cold storage. Only the credulous could believe cloned Splendid Splinters will someday thump home runs out of Fenway Park. Sadly, posterity is deprived of a lingering image of the great slugger playing catch with son John Henry in some backyard paradise; instead, Williams, apparently decapitated, grotesquely spends eternity in bitterly cold nitrogen.

Despite the wonderful cinematic evocation of the All-American Girls Professional Baseball League, mothers and daughters complicate baseball mythology. In reality, many girls and women embraced baseball within a familial context. In *Wait till Next Year: A Memoir*, Doris Kearns Goodwin lovingly describes keeping box scores of Brooklyn Dodgers games for her father.[68] Grounded in his daughter's love of baseball, Ralph Schoenstein's *Diamonds for Lori and Me* described his thrill upon hearing Lori belt out "Take Me Out to the Ball Game" at Shea Stadium.[69] In Don J. Snyder's novel *Veterans Park*, Bobbi Ann Mullens regularly takes her dreams and her daughter Zoey to the ballpark.[70]

Psychologist Sherry Moss, a diehard Red Sox fan, describes her joy at attending games at Fenway with her father and her struggles to transform her two sons into Red Sox adherents. She recalls the moment when her boys finally began (or perhaps pretended) to come around:

> Recently, I confronted my sons. What about the home team, I asked. They looked at me, I thought, almost sympathetically. Jacob asked me to help him find a book on Ted Williams, and Ben asked about going to Fenway (OK, to see the A's). But this time I thought I saw a glimmer of recognition in their eyes. My father and me at Fenway. My sons and me at Fenway. Hopes that carry memories, like a ball aloft in the wind ... flying forever toward the left-field wall.[71]

Then, there is a certain grandmother with whom this writer has shared his dugout for thirty-plus years. She works diligently on her grandson's swing (nice and level, no uppercutting); this same woman bribed her son with dimes to get him to stand up at the plate and take a good cut at the fastball rather than fall away from it.

These selected departures from the stereotypes do not destroy, may not even seriously weaken, the cultural myths that accompany baseball. However, they do demonstrate that the normative baseball narrative is more complex than many envision it. Baseball is a cultural narrative, but one with a variety of plots, some of them contradictory, a few shameful, some very welcome indeed. Heroes are important, but they are not gods; like other humans, they possess a variety of imperfections. The ideal is just that, which is to say, not fully achieved. While myth certainly includes some truth, it is only a partial truth. This recognition should not make baseball less satisfying, but it may reduce the prevalence of disappointment. After all, is it not nicer to long for a return to a home where the backyard was the setting for a good four-way game of catch, where mother and daughter, along with father and son, shared in that innocent moment of happiness?

Notes

1. *Bull Durham*, dir. Ron Shelton, perf. Kevin Costner, Susan Sarandon, and Tim Robbins, Orion Pictures, 1988.
2. W. P. Kinsella, *Shoeless Joe* (1982; New York: Ballantine Books, 1996), 160.
3. Ibid., 227–228.
4. John 1.1 (King James Version).

5. Andrew Cooper, *Playing in the Zone: Exploring the Spiritual Dimensions of Sports* (Boston: Shambhala, 1998), 1.

6. Ibid., 1.

7. Ibid., 1–2.

8. Ibid., 2.

9. James Penrice, *Crossing Home: The Spiritual Lessons of Baseball* (New York: Alba House, 1993), 1.

10. Ibid., 1–3.

11. Ibid., 3.

12. Ibid., ix.

13. F. Scott Fitzgerald, *The Great Gatsby* (1925; New York: Collier Books, 1992), 78.

14. Christopher H. Evans, "Baseball as Civil Religion: The Genesis of an American Creation Story," in *The Faith of Fifty Million: Baseball, Religion, and American Culture*, ed. Christopher H. Evans and William R. Herzog II (Louisville: Westminster John Knox Press, 2002), 14.

15. Ibid., 15.

16. Ibid., 27.

17. Albert G. Spalding, *Base Ball: America's National Game* (1911; San Francisco: Halo Books, 1991), 2.

18. For a discussion of MacArthur's relationship to baseball, see Edward J. Rielly, "Baseball Haiku: Basho, the Babe, and the Great Japanese-American Trade," in *The Cooperstown Symposium on Baseball and American Culture, 2001*, ed. William M. Simons (Jefferson, NC: McFarland, 2002), 250–251.

19. Christopher H. Evans, "The Kingdom of Baseball in America: The Chronicle of an American Theology," *The Faith of Fifty Million: Baseball, Religion, and American Culture*, 37.

20. Evans, "The Kingdom of Baseball in America," 39–40.

21. A. Bartlett Giamatti, *Take Time for Paradise: Americans and Their Games* (New York: Summit Books, 1989), 33.

22. Ibid., 37.

23. Ibid., 42.

24. Ibid., 43.

25. Ibid., 44.

26. Ibid., 90.

27. Ibid., 91.

28. Ibid., 95.

29. Ibid., 103–104.

30. Ibid., 67.

31. Ibid., 82.

32. Roger Kahn, *The Boys of Summer* (1971; New York: New American Library, 1973), xi.

33. Maury Allen, *Where Have You Gone, Joe DiMaggio?* (1975; New York: New American Library, 1976). The Paul Simon song is "Mrs. Robinson" recorded by Simon and Art Garfunkel on their album *The Graduate*, released by Columbia Records in 1968.

34. Donald Hall, *Fathers Playing Catch with Sons: Essays on Sport [Mostly Baseball]* (San Francisco: North Point Press, 1985), 30.

35. Ibid., 46.

36. August Wilson, *Fences* (New York: Penguin, 1986). *Fences* rain for 526 performances on Broadway in the 46th Street Theatre, earning a Tony for James Earl Jones as Troy Maxson. For these and other details of the play's performance, see Yvonne Shafer, *August Wilson: A Research and Production Sourcebook* (Westport, CT: Greenwood, 1998), 123–124.

37. Sandra D. Shannon, *The Dramatic Vision of August Wilson* (Washington, DC: Howard University Press, 1995), 110.

38. Wilson, *Fences*, 61.

39. Kim Pereira, *August Wilson and the African-American Odyssey* (Urbana, IL: University of Illinois Press, 1995), 50.

40. Wilson, *Fences*, 88.

41. Ibid., 89.

42. Ibid., 39.

43. Ibid., 10.

44. Ibid., 34.

45. Ibid., 69.

46. Ibid., 69–70.

47. Ibid., 70.

48. Ibid., 70.

49. Ibid., 70.

50. Ibid., 10. Peter Wolfe discusses the relative ease with which this type of pitch can be hit in his *August Wilson*, Twayne's United States Authors Series, ed. Frank Day (New York: Twayne, 1999), 72.

51. Wilson, *Fences*, 95–96.

52. Ibid., 57.

53. Ibid., 58.

54. Ibid., 72.

55. Ibid., 89.

56. Ibid., 10.

57. Kinsella, *Shoeless* Joe, 6–8.

58. For the film version, see *Field of Dreams*, dir. Phil Alden Robinson, perf. Kevin Costner, Amy Madigan, James Earl Jones, Ray Liotta, and Burt Lancaster. Universal, 1989.

59. William Kennedy, *Ironweed* (1983; New York: Penguin, 1984), 50.

60. See Ernest Hemingway, *The Old Man and the Sea* (New York: Charles Scribner's Sons, 1952).

61. Richard Ben Cramer, *Joe DiMaggio: The Hero's Life* (New York: Simon and Schuster, 2000). Engelberg answers Cramer's accusations in his and Marv Schneider's *DiMaggio: Setting the Record Straight* (Osceola, WI: MBI, 2003).

62. The Jimmy Fund raises money for the Dana-Farber Cancer Institute in Boston.

63. According to Bill Koenig in "A Splendid Life," *USA Today Baseball Weekly*, 11–16 July 2002, 3–6, Mel Webb, a Boston sportswriter, left Williams entirely off his Most Valuable Player ballot in 1947, causing Williams to lose out by one point to DiMaggio as American League MVP.

64. For a published agenda of the event, see "Ted Williams: A Celebration of an American Hero," *Boston Sunday Globe*, 21 July 2002, C5.

65. A succinct biography of Coleman occurs in *Baseball: The Biographical Encyclopedia*, ed. David Pietrusza, Matthew Silverman, and Michael Gershman (New York: Total Sports Illustrated, 2000), 221–222.

66. David Halberstam, *The Teammates: A Portrait of a Friendship* (New York: Hyperion, 2003), 22.

67. See, for example, Dave Kindred, "A Cryonic Shame," *The Sporting News*, 29 July 2002, 64; Larry Tye, "With Loss of Independence, Sadness," *Boston Sunday Globe*, 7 July 2002, A10; and Raja Mishra and Scott Bernard Nelson, "Feud Follows Williams Death," *Boston Sunday Globe*, 7 July 2002, A1, A10-A11.

68. Doris Kearns Goodwin, *Wait till Next Year: A Memoir* (New York: Simon and Schuster, 1997).

69. Ralph Schoenstein, *Diamonds for Lori and Me: A Father, A Daughter, and Baseball* (New York: Beech Tree Books, 1988).

70. Don J. Snyder, *Veterans Park* (New York: Franklin Watts, 1987).

71. Sherry Moss, "How About a Cheer for the Home Team?" *Boston Sunday Globe*, 8 April 1990, Sports section, 52.

Part V

THE BUSINESS OF BASEBALL

Yankees Profits and Promise: The Purchase of Babe Ruth and the Building of Yankee Stadium

Kenneth Winter and Michael J. Haupert

The New York Yankees are the juggernaut of Major League Baseball both on and off the field. With four appearances and three titles in the past five World Series, they are annually regarded as the favorites to take the title. With an estimated net worth hovering near one billion dollars and the highest payroll in the league, they are titans off the field as well. However, the Yankees were not always so successful on the field or in the profit column. It wasn't until the 1920s that the team consistently turned a profit or began to win. The Yankees ascended to the top of the baseball world behind a solid business plan implemented by the savvy owners of the team — owners who took over in 1915 and built a model franchise that continues to dominate the game into the twenty-first century.

In this paper, we review those early years of the Yankees by using the original accounting records to analyze the financial performance of the team from 1915–1929. This time period covers the sale of a struggling franchise to the beginning of the Great Depression — the building years of the Yankees dynasty. This time period allows us to focus on the impact two major investments had for the team: the purchase of Babe Ruth and the construction of Yankee Stadium.

It will come as no surprise to any baseball fan that the purchase of Babe Ruth was a wise move on the part of the Yankees. However, for the first time we can now learn exactly how good a move that purchase was. In addition, we take a close look at the construction of Yankee Stadium and the creative ways in which the Yankees exploited their new home for enormous financial profit. By focusing on two events, we will show how the Yankees owners, Colonels Jacob Ruppert and T. L. Huston, created a model for profitable operation of a baseball franchise that has been copied by owners for the past three-quarters of a century.

Historical Background[1]

The New York Yankees, the most storied franchise in Major League Baseball history, had an inauspicious beginning. The team was moved from Baltimore in 1903 as the American League, a recent challenger to the established National League, sought to establish a foothold in New York. The team was sold to two local owners, William Devery and Frank Farrell, who were able to accomplish something that Ban Johnson, President of the American League, had been attempting to do for two years: secure enough land in Manhattan to construct a ballpark. The rival leagues went beyond mere refusal to cooperate: they resorted to out and out war. Andrew Freedman, owner of the National League New York franchise, was a Tammany Hall insider, and he used his political connections to keep the American League at bay by preventing them from securing the necessary land to construct a stadium in which to house a team.[2]

However, when Tammany power lapsed, the new powers were aligned with Farrell and Devery. Johnson took advantage of this connection when he sought out the pair to purchase the Baltimore team and transfer it to Manhattan. Their first order of business was to build a ballpark.

The stadium was constructed at a cost of $300,000 on acreage on Washington Heights overlooking the New Jersey palisades. The AL franchise eventually took on the nickname Hilltoppers, in reference to the location of their stadium. Hilltop Park, like its contemporaries, was a wooden structure. A wooden fence surrounded the field with a double-decked grandstand between first and third base. Seating 16,000, it was an average capacity ballpark. Ballparks of this era were relatively small, cheap to build, and not typically exploited as revenue-generating investments in and of themselves.

The Yankees left Hilltop Park in 1913 and became tenants of the Giants at the Polo Grounds. Their rent for the first two years was $55,000 per year. For that amount they used the park for 72 home games, bore no maintenance or game-day expenses, and received a nominal amount of concession revenue from the Giants. This relationship lasted through the 1922 season although the rent increased as the Yankees became more successful.

Devery and Farrell sold the franchise after the 1914 season for a reported $460,000. The new owners of the Yankees were a pair of well-heeled local businessmen — Colonel Tillinghast L'Hommedieu Huston and Colonel Jacob Ruppert. Equally as important as their wealth was their business acumen. Ruppert had been raised in the brewery business, and Huston was a successful engineer. Both men had an interest in baseball, and an interest in making money as well.

At the time of sale, the franchise, by this time known as the Yankees, was virtually bankrupt. Newspapers reported that the Yankees had only earned a profit once in the previous decade. Primary information from the ledgers from 1913 and 1914 suggests that the profits were not quite as bad as the papers implied, but the balance sheet was awful. The ledgers show that the Yankees earned a profit of almost $22,000 in 1913 but had a loss of almost $96,000 in 1914. The Yankees' surplus, what we now call retained earnings, was negative $83,273 just before the sale. The negative balance in surplus means that dividends (there were none in 1913 or 1914) and losses are greater than profits. Yankees attendance varied widely from 211,000 to 500,000 (see Table 1 at the end of this chapter) under Devery and Farrell, so it seems likely that they earned a profit more than once in 10 years. However, the Yankees clearly were not profitable overall and would have been unable to pay their bills in 1915.

The balance sheet for the Yankees prior to the sale is a true disaster. The ledger data allows for the construction of an approximate balance sheet at the time of sale (Table 2). The Yankees' circumstances prior to the sale were dire. They had almost no liquid resources ($5,000 including cash and receivables) and over $300,000 in debt. Of particular importance is the $17,000 in accrued interest. Accrued interest means that the interest is owed but not yet paid and the Yankees had no way of paying it without raising capital.

The lack of financial success under Devery and Farrell was no accident. The team contended for a pennant in two of its first three years, but thereafter never came closer than 21 games out. The last three years were particularly dismal as the Yankees averaged 41 games behind.

The before and after ledgers show the terms of the deal between the colonels and Devery and Farrell. The colonels got the Yankees franchise and the Yankees' debts were paid off. Devery and Farrell got to keep Muscoota Realty and got some cash. Muscoota seems to be unrelated to the Yankees although the term does refer to the north of Manhattan. Using the reported purchase price of $460,000, Devery and Farrell received $160,000 for the franchise and rid themselves of all its debts.

Knowledge of the dismal conditions of the Yankees brings up two obvious conjectures. First, why would the colonels not let the Yankees go bankrupt and pick them up more cheaply? Second, why did these astute businessmen seem to negotiate so poorly? The answer to the first question is the American League. The American League had worked diligently to get a franchise in New York. They were unlikely to let it go bankrupt and, of course, if the American League took over the Yankees then the colonels might be left out of the bidding.

It seems like poor negotiation to pay $460,000 for a bankrupt franchise that had rarely earned a profit. The Yankees franchise was unprofitable but valuable because of the operating leverage. Yankees attendance had the potential for substantial increases. Attendance would cause revenues to increase faster than expenses. It is also a reasonable conjecture that the price is over-stated, as most reported (but unverifiable) figures about baseball finances are. The data from the ledger suggests how this could be done. The colonels say, "We paid the owners $150,000 and settled debts of over twice that." The enterprising scribe does the arithmetic and comes up with $460,000. The only problem with the computation is the assumption that the colonels paid 100 cents on the dollar to settle the debts. With the creditors holding off bankruptcy pending the sale, it seems unlikely that the creditors received anywhere near 100 cents on the dollar. Thus, the reported price of $460,000 must be taken as an upper bound.

The first declared intention of the new owners was to build a new sta-dium, which they promised in the near future. In fact, it took nearly a decade to fulfill this promise. To be fair, World War I should shoulder part of the blame for the delay. The result, however, was the grandest stadium in the game at the time (some would argue that it still is) — one that would set a new trend in stadium construction and prove to be a source of profit in its own right.

Ruppert and Huston made money with the Yankees by spending money wisely. Player purchases were modest in the lean years (1915–1919) but accel-erated in the twenties. Their two most famous investments were the purchase of Babe Ruth from the Boston Red Sox and the construction of Yankee Sta-dium. The former transaction was completed in January of 1920 for a total of $100,000. The latter was completed in the early spring of 1923 for a total cost of $2.3 million.

Ruppert and Huston did the right things to turn the Yankees into a profitable enterprise. They hired skilled management who could make good decisions regarding personnel. This resulted in a winning team on the field. They also put an entertaining product on the field, featuring the one and only George Herman "Babe" Ruth.

The colonels saw that the management team had the resources to com-pete. No dividends were paid to the owners during the entire period consid-ered here, 1915–1929. During the lean years (1915–1918) the owners lent money to the team so it had the necessary resources to grow. The lending relationship was additional evidence of the business atmosphere. Ruppert lent money to the Yankees, and they paid it back plus 6% interest per annum. The owners did not take any salary until July 15, 1919, when the team was profitable. Owners' salaries were another good business decision because the Sixteenth Amendment, legalizing income taxes, and World War I tax rates made it a good decision to transfer money to the owners by a payment that was tax deductible to the Yankees.

The Yankees had been playing in the shadow of the Giants since their arrival in town. Now that men with sufficient funds owned the team, the Yankees made the necessary moves toward profitability. They began by improving the playing talent, resulting in a more competitive team, which in turn generated greater fan interest and paid attendance. After Ruppert and Huston bought the team, the Yankees improved in the standings from sixth place in 1914 to consecutive third place finishes in 1919 and 1920, followed by three straight trips to the World Series. Table 3 summarizes the Yankees' success.

During the winter of 1919–1920, the Yankees purchased the contract of Babe Ruth from the Boston Red Sox. The purchase of Ruth, one of the best young players in baseball at the time, made sense from a talent perspective, and would turn out to make even more sense from an entertainment perspective. Babe Ruth became the greatest draw in the league, and was a primary catalyst for the Yankees to finally build their own ballpark. The stadium, which was built to showcase the talents of Ruth as a home run hitter, was also built to capitalize on his popularity.

Yankees Profits

The returns to ownership in first few years were unstable, ranging from a loss of $73,000 in 1915, the first year under the new owners, to a profit of just under $107,000 in 1919. By way of comparison with other financial assets (Table 5), however, the relative performance of the team in those years was a reflection of the American economy. While returns on the team were negative in three of the first five years, so were returns on the Dow Jones Industrial Average (DJIA). The DJIA lost ground in 1917 and 1918, the same years the Yankees lost money. Since these were years of world war, it is understandable that the nation was distracted from watching men play ball. The manpower needs of the military were such that the Yankees' schedule was shortened to 123 games in 1918. After 1918, the Yankees would not show a negative return for an individual year again.

Through the first five years of their ownership, Huston and Ruppert lost a total of $30,000. This was more than made up for in 1920, when the team turned a profit of more than $370,000. They lost money in three of the first four years they owned the team, but beginning in 1919 they turned a profit for 13 consecutive years— no mean feat considering the country was plunged in to the Great Depression in 1929. What is impressive is not that the Yankees made money, but how much money they made.

The return to capital figures calculated in Table 5 is based on an investment of $460,000, the price of the team. The rate of return is calculated by dividing the profit for the year by the original investment. For purposes of comparison, we have included in the chart some standard financial figures – the rate of return earned in the stock market, as represented by the Dow Jones

Industrial Average (DJIA), and the annual interest rate paid on high quality bonds (AAA rated) and the higher return to be earned on slightly riskier bonds (BAA rated).

When compared to the rather conservative bond market, the Yankees were a stunning investment success. They out-earned the AAA bond market by a factor of between three and 20 each year during the comparison period. In six years, the Yankees earned more than ten times what bonds returned. When compared to the BAA bonds, the comparison still looks impressive. The Yankees were no less than twice as profitable as the bonds in any year, ranging up to fifteen times as profitable in 1926.

During a decade of impressive growth in the stock market, the Yankees were out-earning the market by leaps and bounds. In only two years during the period 1919–1929 could the colonels have earned more money in the stock market than with the Yankees, and then just barely. In five of the years the Yankees earned about twice as much as the market, and twice they out-gained the market by a factor of 40 or more. It should be noted that in four of the years from 1919–1929 the DJIA lost money, something the Yankees never did during this period.

The Yankees fared well relative to the rest of the league as well. Six times during the decade of the 1920s they led the league in profits, and in each year but 1925 they exceeded the league average – by a margin of at least two, and as high as five. The year 1925 was aberrant for the Yankees because it was the only annum during the period that their earnings were merely very good — an impressive 16.9% return to capital. Every other year the Yankee returns were gaudy, ranging from 34% to 107% on profits of $106,000 to $666,000 (Table 5).

The Ruth Purchase

The most famous and financially successful move the Yankees made was the purchase of Babe Ruth. Ruth contributed to a Yankee powerhouse that appeared in six World Series in the decade following his arrival in town.

Ruth cost the Yankees $100,000 in January of 1920. Baseball lore has always claimed that the Boston Red Sox, owned by Broadway magnate Harry Frazee, sold Ruth because Frazee was strapped for cash after the dismal failure of one of his shows. The legend further adds that the sale price of Ruth was only part of the purchase agreement. In addition, the Yankees allegedly loaned Frazee in excess of $300,000 to shore up his theaters or pay the former owners of the Red Sox. No evidence exists in the Yankees account books that such a loan took place. The $100,000 purchase price (erroneously reported as $125,000 in many contemporary newspapers) is well documented.

It took the form of $25,000 in cash plus three $25,000 promissory notes due on November 1 of 1920, 1921, and 1922. The interest rate was 6%. One interesting discovery in the accounting records is that the Red Sox paid part of Babe Ruth's salary in 1921.

The matter of the loan is harder to analyze without any evidence. While it is possible the loan took place, depending on its terms, it may have had no relation to the Ruth purchase. The decision to loan money to Harry Frazee was a separate financial decision. The only way in which it would have an impact on the value of the Ruth purchase was if the terms of the loan were better than the market rate. In other words, if a condition of the sale of Ruth to the Yankees was that Jacob Ruppert loan Harry Frazee $300,000 at zero interest over a period of 10 years, then the true cost of Ruth increases by the amount of interest that Ruppert would have collected on the $300,000.

There are a couple of problems with this scenario, however. First, it is apparent from examining the Yankees account books that the loan, if it was ever made, was not made by the Yankees. It could only have been made by Ruppert or Huston privately. Since Ruppert was the primary negotiator in the Ruth deal, it stands to reason that if any loan was made, it would have been from Ruppert.

If the loan was made by Ruppert, then it seems unlikely that he would have made it at below market rates. The deal to secure Ruth provided revenues to the Yankees, of which Ruppert was only a 50% owner. In addition, it seems even less likely that he would make such a financial arrangement given the strained relationship that existed at the time between Ruppert and Huston. The rift between the two men would eventually grow to the point where Ruppert bought out Huston in 1923, becoming sole owner of the franchise for the remainder of his life.

If a loan was made from Ruppert to Frazee as a condition of the Ruth sale, but the loan was at the market rate of interest, then it had no bearing on the value of the Ruth deal. The decision by Ruppert to loan Frazee money would have been made on the same basis that Ruppert would make any other decision regarding his personal finances: what would earn him the best return given his current financial situation?

Until such time as evidence regarding the details of the alleged loan surfaces, we cannot make a complete analysis. However, it seems reasonable to assume that the cost to the Yankees of Babe Ruth was the purchase price of $100,000 and no more. Our analysis of the return to the Yankees on the purchase of Ruth will proceed along these lines.

The purchase of Ruth in 1920 immediately paid off for the Yankees. Yankees home attendance nearly doubled from 619,000 in 1919 to almost 1.3 million in 1920. As a result, home receipts more than doubled each of the next three years. The team appeared in the World Series in 1921, 1922 and 1923, earning an additional $150,000 in revenues, and the Yankees share of road receipts more than doubled in each of the next three seasons. Figure 1 indicates that while attendance did increase around the league during the period from 1915 to 1929, the Yankees were an outstanding outlier. Their attendance exploded in 1920, the first season Ruth played for the team. From 1920 through Ruth's final season with the Yankees in 1934, the Yankees failed to lead the league in attendance only twice. The first instance was 1925 when Ruth played in only 98 games due to injuries and suspensions. This was the fewest number of games he would play in as a Yankee. In 1934, the Yankees also failed to lead the league in attendance during Ruth's final season in New York. After leading the league in attendance during 13 of 15 years during the Ruth era, the Yankees led the league only three times in the next six years.

Of course, not all increases in revenue can be attributed to the popularity of Ruth or his admittedly tremendous impact on the quality of the team's play. As a result, these calculated returns are certainly upwardly biased. Even then, the return is not as far-fetched as it may seem. The Yankees roster was not substantially different, except for Ruth, from 1919 to 1920. The team finished in third place in both seasons, but did increase their win total and was more competitive, finishing a mere three games out of first place, an improvement from 7.5 games the previous season. The combination of a marquee gate attraction and improved team, both in the person of Babe Ruth, was a significant factor in the improved fortunes of the Yankees.

Was $100,000 an unusual amount of money to spend for one player? Certainly it was an outstanding sum, but it was not as breathtaking as it may at first seem. First of all, the purchase and sale of ballplayers was much more frequent in those days than it is today. Second, it was a very common way for an owner to make ends meet when finances got tough. On more than one occasion Connie Mack settled his bills by dismantling a World Series championship team by peddling his players for cash. After paying his bills, he then used the remaining cash to acquire young talent and develop it into a winner. Mack was not the only owner to follow this path to success. In fact, the Red Sox were on the buying side of this very formula when they won the World Series in 1918. So when the Red Sox sold Ruth, the sale itself was not unusual. Even selling a future Hall of Fame player was not unusual. What made this sale unique was the enormous impact that Ruth had on the Yankees, both on the field and at the box office.

By way of comparison, consider another young lefthander who was sold to New York by Boston in 1919. He led New York to pennants and World Series victories. The lefty was Art Nehf, the teams were the Braves and the Giants, and the price was $55,000. Nehf led the National League in complete games with 28 (the Braves only played 124 games) in 1918. Art won 17 games in 1919 splitting his time between the Braves and the Giants. He averaged twenty wins for the next three seasons as the Giants won two pennants and two World Series. Art Nehf was a good investment at $55,000. While Ruth cost nearly twice as much, he was an everyday player coming off a record-setting home run season. The price may have been a stretch at the time, but it was not preposterous.

In analyzing a financial return for Babe Ruth, we must consider the investment, the change in revenue resulting from the investment, and the additional costs. The investment, of course, was the purchase of Ruth for $100,000. The return on that investment is calculated as the additional revenue Ruth generated less the additional costs to the Yankees due to Ruth. We measure the additional costs simply as salary. The additional revenues are a bit trickier to capture. We focus only on Ruth's impact on the gate revenue as his revenue contribution. This shows up in two ways: the superstar effect, that is some people come out to the park just to see Ruth, and his impact on the quality of the team, and the subsequent increase in demand for Yankee tickets that a higher quality team generates.[3] We ignore the additional concession revenue that Ruth generated for the Yankees when Yankee Stadium opened.

For our purposes, we do not need to differentiate between these two sources of increased demand for Yankee tickets, only the change in demand. We do this simply by looking at home and road gate receipts and comparing them to 1919, the year before the Yankees purchased Ruth. While Ruth was a major box office draw, it is unrealistic to think that he was the sole cause of all increased gate and road revenues, though he was likely a major source of it.

We follow the recent literature in assigning to Ruth the cause of half of the increase in gate revenue. By assuming that Ruth is personally responsible (in either of the two above-mentioned ways) for half of the increase in gate receipts, we are able to calculate revenue increases. Recent works on the "superstar effect" for NBA players such as Michael Jordan, Larry Bird, and Shaquille O'Neal has shown that these players are responsible for 50% of the increase in gate revenue both at home and on the road.[4] These studies are conducted using changes in game-by-game attendance depending on the presence of the selected superstar. The same type of study is not possible with Babe Ruth because of the lack of individual game attendance figures during this period of baseball history. However, annual home and road attendance figures are available. Using the annual attendance figures and the 50% figure realized by the basketball superstars, we calculate the impact of Ruth on gate receipts both at home and on the road, comparing 1919 with the years 1920–22 and 1927–29 (see Table 6). These years are chosen because of availability of data. We do not have detailed home and road receipt data for the years 1923–26.

A quick glance at the table will reveal that the financial return earned by the Yankees on the purchase of Babe Ruth was nothing less than spectacular. Keep in mind that this is a conservative estimate of the financial impact of Ruth on the Yankees. We have not attempted at this stage to estimate the on-field performance of the team without Ruth. To the extent that replacing Ruth with an average right fielder would have made the Yankees a weaker club (certainly a credible assumption) that would not have won as many games, this would have had a negative impact on attendance and hence profits. Also not included in this calculation is the additional revenue the Yankees earned from their appearances in six World Series in the 1920s or the additional revenue from concessions after Yankee Stadium opened in 1923.

In an era when an annual return of 30% on the stock market drove investors to giddy heights, the Yankees were returning more than ten times that amount on their investment in Ruth in three of the six years cited. The leanest Ruth year was 1929, when the team earned a paltry 196% return on Ruth.

Perhaps no better anecdotal evidence for the importance of Babe Ruth to the Yankees can be provided than the 1925 season, one of the worst in Ruth's career. Due to injury and suspension, Ruth played in only 98 games that year — the fewest of his Yankees career. He batted only .290, fifty points below his career average, and hit only 25 of his trademark home runs, the lowest production since before he became a mostly fulltime player in 1919, and a figure he would not see again until 1934, his final year in a Yankees uniform.

The impact of his absence from the lineup was felt by the Yankees on the field and in the pocketbook. On the field, the Yankees collapsed from an 89 win season and second place finish in 1924 to seventh place and 69 wins in 1925. It was the only year that the Yankees had a losing record in Ruth's tenure with the team. At the box office, the absence of Ruth and the poor performance of the team was just as evident. The Yankees attendance fell 33% to under 700,000, the first time they failed to draw over a million fans since the arrival of Ruth and the only time except his final season with the team they would not lead the league in attendance. Overall revenue for the team in 1925 was off 25% from the year before, dropping the Yankees below the league average in profits for the only time during the decade.

Yankee Stadium

A complement to owning a Major League Baseball team in the 1920s, as it is now, is owning (or in the contemporary case, leasing) a stadium, which not only serves a purpose as a necessary component in the production of a ballgame, but can also serve as a source of additional income on the 280-odd days on which the team does not play in it.

In an attempt to gauge the returns earned purely from extracurricular rental of Yankee Stadium, we have calculated a return to capital on the stadium, using only those sources of revenue that are solely due to the stadium. These funds included rental of the stadium for professional and college football, boxing matches, and Negro League baseball games. Of course, the stadium also contributes to increased revenue for the team during the season. A modern stadium is an attraction in and of itself. At the time of its construction, Yankee Stadium was the largest and most modern stadium in professional baseball, and certainly contributed to the increased crowds at Yankee games. For the purposes of our analysis here, however, we are interested only in calculating a minimum return on the stadium. For that reason, we ignore all baseball income, and focus solely on the income earned from non-baseball sources. Specifically we ignore the $100,000 that the Yankees had paid to rent the Polo Grounds and the $86,000 increase in park privileges or concession revenue.

The calculated returns on the stadium investment are downward biased on two margins. First, the revenues are understated, as they include only the extracurricular revenues mentioned above. Second, all stadium costs, apart from game day expenses, are attributed to the stadium profit calculation.

The accounting records reveal a hitherto unknown profit on Yankee Stadium. In 1926 the Yankees sold part of the land to Stanley Murray at a profit of $121,082. The problem for our analysis is whether to reduce the investment in Yankee Stadium by the cost of the real estate ($125,575) or the price it was sold ($250,000). There was also a small amount of selling expenses to lead to the final profit. We chose to reduce the investment by the cost because a larger denominator would lead to a lower return. For the same reason, we used the gross investment (cost) rather than the net investment (cost — accumulated depreciation).

The return on the stadium investment (see Table 8) was modest for the four years for which data exist, with positive returns ranging from just under 4% to almost 8%. While these are modest returns when compared to the team as a whole or the investment in Babe Ruth, they do compare favorably with the bond market. In addition, keep in mind that these are returns based only on non-baseball use of the stadium. In other words, these are minimum estimates of the returns the Yankees would have earned on the stadium had they built it but never played baseball in it.

Another way to view the importance of Yankee Stadium as a revenue source is to look at the impact it had on the team's revenue distribution (see Table 7). During the first decade of ownership, Ruppert and Huston took in two-thirds to three-quarters of all their revenue at the gate in Yankee Stadium. After the construction of Yankee Stadium, gate receipts declined to half of total revenues as the importance of rental income from the stadium increased.

What is not included in any of these calculations on the profitability of the stadium is the opportunity cost of renting the Polo Grounds. From 1913 to 1922, the Yankees were tenants of the Giants at the Polo Grounds. Not only did they not have any non-baseball income earning ability as tenants, but they were paying annual rent of $55,000 beginning in 1913 and increasing to $100,000 per year in 1921 and 1922. If we consider the savings of the rent the Yankees were paying in 1922, the annual return to the stadium would nearly double.

Of course, the impact of the stadium on baseball earnings must also be considered. While this is a goal of our future research, it is not possible at this time due to the lack of individual game attendance figures. This is an important fact to keep in mind when considering the enormous profitability of the stadium for the Yankees, and the fact that contemporary stadiums are profitable for teams almost exclusively due to their impact on baseball revenues through the increased attendance caused by the novelty of the stadium and the added revenues from luxury seating and advertising. Little income is currently generated by teams leasing their stadiums for non-baseball events.

Conclusion

The Yankees started life like many new businesses: undercapitalized and poorly managed by owners who were not astute businessmen. The vast majority of new businesses fail for the above-stated reasons, and the Yankees were proving to be no exception until new owners stepped in to save the insolvent franchise. Colonels Ruppert and Huston proved to be savvy businessmen who recognized how to make a dollar on a baseball game: offer a quality product in an inviting atmosphere. The quality product was a winning team built around one of the greatest gate attractions of the twentieth century, and the inviting atmosphere was the grandest stadium in the game. That same formula has been employed by team owners ever since — the only improvement to the original Yankees method is the ability of current owners to get somebody else to put up the capital for the stadium.

While this lesson is certainly worthwhile for current team owners, it is also a revelation concerning the role of business in Major League Baseball in the early part of the twentieth century. Contrary to the wistful reminiscences of some sportswriters and baseball enthusiasts, the good old days of Major League Baseball, when everyone was involved for the love of the game and not the money, never existed. The game has always been about the money — there is just a greater focus on it now than there was a century ago. Baseball was, is, and will continue to be a business. It attracts a lot of press and passion, but the bottom line is profit — and the Yankees have excelled at this for three-quarters of a century using the Ruppert model.

Table 1

DEVERY AND FARRELL'S YANKEES

Year	Wins	Loses	Win %	GB	Attendance
1914	70	84	45.5	30.0	359,477
1913	57	94	37.7	38.0	357,551
1912	50	102	32.9	55.0	242,194
1911	76	76	50.0	25.5	302,444
1910	88	63	58.3	14.5	355,857
1909	74	77	49.0	23.5	501,700
1908	51	103	33.1	39.5	305,500
1907	70	78	47.3	21.0	350,020
1906	90	61	59.6	3.0	434,700
1905	71	78	47.7	21.5	309,100
1904	92	59	60.9	1.5	438,919
1903	72	62	53.7	17.0	211,808
Average	72	78	48.0	24.2	347,439

Source for individual years: http://newyork.yankees.mlb.com/NASApp/mlb/nyy/history/year_by_year_results.jsp

Table 2

YANKEES BALANCE SHEET
PRIOR TO THE 1915 SALE

Assets		Liabilities and Stockholders' Equity		
Cash	471	Accrued Interest	17,053	
Receivables	4,535	Bills Payable	85,000	
Muscoota Realty	65,060	Loan Payable	50,000	
Franchise	457,268	Cert of Indebtedness	150,000	
Missing asset*	446	Total Liabilities		302,053
		Stockholders' Equity		
		Capital	300,000	
		Surplus	(83,273)	216,727
Total	518,780	Total		518,780

* Analysis of the ledger accounts has not revealed the missing asset yet.

Table 3

RUPPERT'S YANKEES 1915–1929

Year	Wins	Losses	Win %	GB	Attendance
1929	88	66	.571	18.0	960,148
1928	101	53	.656	-	1,072,132
1927	110	44	.714	-	1,164,015
1926	91	63	.591	-	1,027,675
1925	69	85	.448	28.5	697,267
1924	89	63	.586	2.0	1,053,533
1923	98	54	.645	-	1,007,066
1922	94	60	.610	-	1,026,134
1921	98	55	.641	-	1,230,696
1920	95	59	.617	3.0	1,289,422
1919	80	59	.576	7.5	619,164
1918	60	63	.488	13.5	282,047
1917	71	82	.464	28.5	330,294
1916	80	74	.519	11.0	469,211
1915	69	83	.454	32.5	256,035
Average	86	64	.572	16	832,323

Source for individual years: ory/year_by_year_results.jsp

Table 4

YANKEES PROFITS 1915–1929

Year	Profit on Team	and Depreciation	Team Profit before Taxes
1915	(73,362)	(73,362)	(73,362)
1916	40,995	40,995	40,995
1917	(58,036)	(57,847)	(58,036)
1918	(46,651)	(46,481)	(46,651)
1919	106,971	106,971	106,971
1920	374,079	666,353	666,353
1921	176,502	340,517	339,984
1922	270,875	316,029	315,420
1923	494,071	595,972	532,139
1924	351,695	441,640	363,279
1925	77,624	156,250	77,165
1926	393,272	624,226	544,124
1927	567,664	682,484	601,351
1928	297,060	422,057	333,326
1929	229,919	355,791	259,195

Profits are based on nominal accounting data.

Lack of taxes in 1916 and 1919 probably results from the ability to carry losses forward to reduce taxable income in a future year.

Table 5

ANNUAL RETURN TO SELECTED FINANCIAL ASSETS 1915–1929

Year	Dow Jones Industrial Average (DJIA)	Annual Growth Rate of DJIA	Moody's Seasoned AAA Corporate Bond Yield	Moody's Seasoned BAA Corporate Bond Yield	Return to Capital New York Yankees	Return to Capital Yankee Stadium*
1915	55.44				-15.95%	
1916	98.81	78.23%			8.91%	
1917	96.4	-2.44%			-12.62%	
1918	74.85	-22.35%			-10.14%	
1919	82.45	10.15%	5.35%	7.12%	23.25%	
1920	108.85	32.02%	5.75%	7.78%	81.32%	
1921	72.67	-33.24%	6.14%	8.50%	38.37%	
1922	78.9	8.57%	5.34%	7.70%	58.89%	
1923	98.06	24.28%	5.04%	6.98%	107.41%	
1924	96.54	-1.55%	5.09%	7.24%	76.46%	
1925	119.46	23.74%	4.95%	6.44%	16.87%	
1926	158.75	32.89%	4.82%	6.09%	85.49%	
1927	155.16	-2.26%	4.66%	5.61%	78.66%	7.78%
1928	203.55	31.19%	4.46%	5.35%	34.13%	3.97%
1929	297.7	46.25%	4.62%	5.63%	42.50%	3.91%

* Yankee Stadium was constructed in 1923, but detailed stadium receipts and expenses are not available until 1927

Table 6

RETURN ON INVESTMENT IN RUTH
ASSUMING 50% IMPACT ON GATE RECEIPTS

Year	Ruth Salary	Change in home receipts from 1919	Change in road receipts from 1919	Return on Ruth purchase
1920	$17,570	$526,532	$180,691	336%
1921	$39,638	$526,962	$139,490	363%
1922	$54,103	$384,558	$160,583	231%
1927	$76,190	$448,334	$192,858	304%
1928	$70,000	$394,467	$167,805	268%
1929	$70,000	$332,632	$198,673	196%

Table 7

RELATIVE REVENUES AND EXPENSES 1915–1929

Year	Team Salary as percentage of Expenses	Team Salary as percentage of Revenues	Home Gate Receipts as Percentage of Total Revenue
1915	35.62%	59.71%	63.37%
1916	38.11%	39.70%	71.90%
1917	34.59%	49.21%	65.72%
1918	26.32%	37.06%	74.94%
1919	28.46%	25.21%	76.88%
1920	22.23%	10.67%	72.16%
1921	14.55%	11.74%	66.29%
1922	26.88%	20.92%	65.82%
1927	32.33%	18.07%	44.75%
1928	19.60%	22.41%	45.99%
1929	40.17%	27.21%	49.41%

Table 8

PROFITABILITY OF YANKEE STADIUM 1927–1930

	1927	1928	1929	1930
College Football	$ 108,543	$ 140,612	$ 101,750	$ 87,841
Boxing	$ 124,451	$ 52,142	$ 45,345	$ 60,568
Professional Football	$ 7,063	$ 7,648		
Colored Baseball	$ 2,500		$ 52	$ 3,989
Total Non-baseball Receipts	$ 242,581	$ 200,403	$ 147,147	$ 152,399
Stadium Net Profit	$ 191,989	$ 111,672	$ 110,343	$ 120,399
Stadium cost	2,466,411	2,813,573	2,818,846	2,836,745
Return to Stadium Investment before baseball	7.78%	3.97%	3.91%	4.24%

Source: Celler Monopoly Hearings

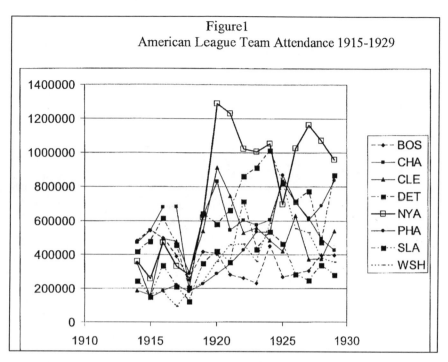

Figure1
American League Team Attendance 1915-1929

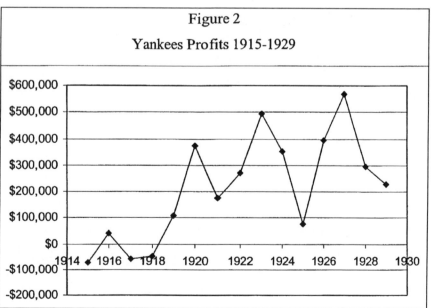

Figure 2
Yankees Profits 1915-1929

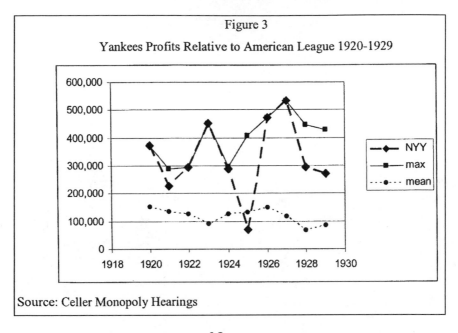

Figure 3

Yankees Profits Relative to American League 1920-1929

Source: Celler Monopoly Hearings

Notes

1. This section borrows substantially from Michael Haupert and Kenneth Winter, "Play Ball: Estimating the Profitability of the New York Yankees, 1915–1937," *Essays in Economic and Business History* XXI (2003), 89–102.

2. For a full discussion of the politics surrounding the New York stadium situation, see Neil J. Sullivan, *The Diamond in the Bronx: Yankee Stadium and the Politics of New York* (New York: Oxford University Press, 2001).

3. See Glenn Knowles, Keith Sherony and Michael Haupert, "The Demand for Major League Baseball: A Test of the Uncertainty of Outcome Hypothesis," *American Economist* 36:3 (Fall1992), 72–80.

4. Jerry Hausman and Gregory Leonard, "Superstars in the National Baseball Association: Economic Value and Policy," *Journal of Labor Economics* 15:4 October 1997), 586–624.

Evolution of the Sunday Doubleheader and Its Role in Elevating the Popularity of Baseball

Charlie Bevis

The Sunday doubleheader was a staple of Major League Baseball (MLB) during the middle third of the twentieth century. During that era, teams often played two Sunday games, and fans were admitted for the price of a single contest. Examination of the Sunday doubleheader's evolution illuminates baseball history and American culture. Widely embraced due to the financial despair of the 1930s, the Sunday doubleheader played a significant role in reshaping MLB during the Great Depression and in the decades that followed.

Baseball historiography neglects the role of the Sunday doubleheader in reviving the popularity of the national pastime. Instead, commentators cite night baseball, radio, minor-league farm systems, and the media. As a corrective, it is necessary to explore the antecedents of both Sunday baseball and the doubleheader.

Sunday Baseball

In the late nineteenth and early twentieth centuries, laws in many states continued to prohibit most labor as well as numerous other activities on Sundays. Sabbath laws, originating in the seventeenth century, reflected the religious influence of the Puritans. Subsequently, these "blue laws" were justified by reference to the state's interest in regulating the health and welfare of its citizens through a weekly "day of rest."

Convoluted legal rationales often justified the "coincidence" that Sunday, the religious day of rest, was also designated as the state-mandated day of rest. The text that follows, from the 1898 ruling of the Ohio Supreme Court in *State v. Powell*, illustrates this phenomenon:

> Though the day adopted for the observance of rest may coincide with the religious persuasion of a large part of the people, but not with all, this is not regarded as infringing on the rights of the latter, since no religious observance of any kind is enjoined. Those who desire can devote the day to religious observances. Others may do as they see fit, so [long as] they do not engage in such secular pursuits as, in accordance with the policy of the law, are prohibited.[1]

Sunday baseball was once a divisive issue. America struggled with changing Sunday from a day of rest to a day of leisure to, ultimately, a day of recreation. In areas of the Northeast, once dominated by Puritanism, as well as in Ohio, settled by transplanted New Englanders, old-stock Anglo-Protestants, motivated by a combination of nativism, a commitment to social control, and tradition, supported Sabbatarian restrictions. The typical workweek for the laboring class encompassed six days, with Sunday for respite. "Sunday stood in opposition to relentless work for the majority of nineteenth-century Americans," Alexis McCrossen wrote in *Holy Day, Holiday: The American Sunday.* "The six working days blended into one unit — the workweek — in contrast to Sunday, the day of rest."[2]

In an era in which the East confined MLB exclusively to the daytime, Monday through Saturday, spectators consisted of those with the job flexibility to attend an afternoon contest. Not only did the comfortable classes possess the time and money to attend games, they, believed baseball magnates, helped legitimize baseball as a respectable recreation. Thus, baseball owners appealed to middle-class patrons to fill ballpark seats. Industrial workers found it difficult to attend MLB games:

> The result of an onerous work load was that it was difficult for craftsmen and almost impossible for unskilled personnel to attend a ball game unless they worked unusual hours like a baker, took time off from work, were unemployed, had a rare holiday, or lived in a city that permitted Sunday baseball.[3]

In addition to state laws, the National League, as a matter of policy, prohibited Sunday games prior to 1892. Then, in 1892, St. Louis and Louisville joined the National League. The St. Louis and Louisville franchises were formerly part of the now defunct American Association, a major league that had allowed Sunday games since its inception in 1881.[4]

In those Midwestern cities with MLB games on Sundays, working people flocked to the ballpark, making Sunday the best attendance day of the week. Teams subject to Sabbatarian prohibitions often went to great lengths to play Sunday games on the road, as even a visitor's share of a Sunday gate was often larger than receipts from a poorly attended weekday home gate. Sunday baseball slowly gained acceptance, moving from the Midwest to the East. Conflict over Sunday activities raged for decades in courts and state legislatures. As late as 1910, only Detroit, Chicago, Cincinnati, and St. Louis had legalized MLB games on Sunday. It took nearly twenty-five years for Sunday baseball to gain legal sanction in the remaining host cities: Cleveland (1911), Washington (1918), New York (1919), Boston (1929), Philadelphia (1934), and Pittsburgh (1934).[5]

The Doubleheader

Due to the popularity and profitability of Sunday baseball in its own right, owners were understandably loath to play doubleheaders on Sunday. Although Decoration Day, the Fourth of July, and Labor Day often called for two games, these holiday affairs had separate admissions for morning and afternoon games; thus, they were not considered true doubleheaders. The doubleheader is "a set of two games played in succession on the same day between the same two teams and to which spectators are admitted for the price of a single game." The first doubleheaders, desperation moves by owners suffering financial difficulties, were disdained by most baseball magnates.[6]

On Monday September 25, 1882, the National League's first "two-for-one" doubleheader was played in Worcester, Massachusetts. Expelled from the league several days earlier to make room for a Philadelphia franchise and with but one more week of major league affiliation, the Worcester club had little incentive to adhere to league protocol concerning the rescheduling of its September 22 rainout with Providence. The Worcester club, plagued by poor attendance, utilized the two-for-one approach to attract spectators.[7]

Prior to 1925, doubleheaders were most often employed to make up postponed games. The concept pioneered in Worcester in 1882 gained general acceptance within a few years. MLB developed a taxonomy of protocols involving doubleheaders:

- Level 1—Make up a postponed game.
- Level 2—Enhance attendance by rescheduling a weekday game that would otherwise generate limited spectatorship.
- Level 3—Optimize attendance on the team's best attendance day of the week during non-peak periods of the baseball season.
- Level 4—Employ the Level 3 approach during peak periods of the season.

Before World War II, the business of baseball operated under the assumption that profit equaled gate receipts minus the combined expenses of player salaries, ballpark costs, and travel to road games. Gate receipts thus drove the owner's bottom line. Such reasoning was not hospitable to doubleheaders.

Despite the financial benefits of a Level 2, 3, or 4 doubleheader, owners, prior to 1925, rarely designated a single-admission doubleheader on the initial season schedule. There are at least four reasons for the owners' aversion to scheduling doubleheaders:

The first reason was physical considerations. The results of the second game could be unduly influenced by the stamina, rather than the skill, of participants. In addition, not all starting players, notably catchers, would appear in both games of a doubleheader.

Moral considerations were a second reason. The sanctity of the game could be compromised if the games were more about attendance than the championship. In 1926, *The Sporting News* editorialized, "There is not a sound argument for a double-header, except to swell the gate receipts of a ball club, and when men arrange baseball games to swell receipts and not to play them for a championship, they hippodrome the sport." Overflow crowds on the outfield in small ballparks changed the game due to "ground rules" for balls hit into the assemblage. Furthermore, second games were often curtailed before nine innings were played, due to darkness, delimiting the opportunity for a comeback victory.[8]

The third reason was perception. Not considering themselves in the entertainment business, MLB owners were reluctant to adopt promotional techniques, especially ones like the doubleheader associated with low-brow venues like the minor leagues, professional basketball, or the Negro Leagues. The short-lived Federal League (1914–1915) had made extensive use of the doubleheader, further adding to its disdain amongst National and American League owners.

Inevitably, financial considerations were another reason for the aversion. Generally parsimonious, owners did not like to give away anything. The second game of a doubleheader, essentially a "free" game for the spectators, was viewed by the owners as lost revenue. This "preserve the gate" mentality reflected the belief that middle-class spectators would avoid weekday games if a Sunday two-for-one doubleheader was available.

Sunday Doubleheaders

Nonetheless, during the 1880s American Association franchises in St. Louis, Louisville, and Brooklyn intermittently hosted Sunday doubleheaders. Then, in the 1890s, Sunday baseball was institutionalized in Chicago, Cincinnati, and St. Louis. During the first three decades of the twentieth century, Sunday doubleheaders were occasionally deployed in the non-peak stages of the baseball season as well as under the following circumstances:

- dates preceding a holiday or a long road trip;
- games against inferior competition; and
- dates deep in the hot summer when shoreline amusements beckoned.

Typically, a Level 2 doubleheader would be slated for a Saturday, with a single game on Sunday, to optimize attendance on both days. In 1929, for example, the Washington Senators played a doubleheader at Griffith Stadium with the Philadelphia Athletics on Saturday, May 18, and then the two teams played a single game on Sunday, May 19. It was not until the Great Depression of the 1930s, however, that the Sunday doubleheader, in a Level 4 fashion, truly began to change baseball.

St. Louis provided the precursor to the Level 4 Sunday doubleheader. By 1925, Sunday baseball in St. Louis had notched more than forty seasons, making it commonplace, in contrast to New York where it was in its fifth year. Augmenting Sunday baseball, St. Louis owner Sam Breadon brought it to Level 4. Of Breadon's strategy, *The Sporting News* commented, "Sam Breadon has been the target for considerable raillery, because of his Sunday doubleheaders, but he knows his St. Louis and he knows its workers do not take afternoons off during the week for amusement." In 1930, Breadon organized Sunday doubleheaders during peak periods, and St. Louis gained notoriety as the birthplace of the Sunday doubleheader. Other teams emulated Breadon's Level 4 usage.[9]

During the early 1930s, America suffered through its worst economic depression. Attendance at major league ballparks plummeted by 40 percent, from a 1930 peak of ten million to six million for the 1933 season. Yet, Sunday doubleheaders, often of the Level 4 genre, accelerated in frequency during the Great Depression. Within a five-season period from 1929 through 1933, as shown in the table below, Sunday doubleheaders increased three-fold, from 27 to 109. As a percent of total games played in a season, contests that were part of Sunday doubleheaders rose from 4.4 percent to 17.8 percent.[10]

Year	No. of Sunday Doubleheaders	Percent of Games in Total Season
1929	27	4.4%
1930	48	7.8%
1931	69	11.1%
1932	67	10.9%
1933	109	17.8%

The substantial increase in Sunday doubleheaders during the 1929–1933 period increasing the popularity of baseball in three ways:

First, it rescued the game. Since fewer people could afford to attend baseball games in the early 1930s due to hard times, doubleheaders on Sunday helped to attract spectators on the day that people who did continue to hold jobs could get to the ballpark.

Second, it expanded urban attendance opportunities. Compared to a solitary game, the two-for-one Sunday doubleheader attracted more urbanites to the ballpark, enlarging attendance opportunities for the city dweller.

Third, it broadened interest in rural areas. Radio broadcasts of Sunday doubleheaders expanded MLB games beyond the city into rural areas; on Sundays rural workers could listen to broadcasts. Radio familiarity encouraged people to travel long distances to attend Sunday games. In the 1930s, the St. Louis Cardinals often had star pitcher Dizzy Dean start one game of a Sunday doubleheader to attract spectators from outlying areas: "Farmers came from Arkansas, Illinois, western Tennessee, and Kentucky — even northern Mississippi and western Indiana."[11]

Without the 1929–1933 expansion of Sunday doubleheaders, the attendance decline would have been far worse for MLB owners. Despite the Depression, crowds flocked to Sunday doubleheaders in 1933. Newspapers highlighted attendance at Sunday doubleheaders, as evidenced by these *New York Times* headlines from a Monday edition in August:

- "60,000 See Indians Divide Twin Bill"
- "Braves, Reds Split As 40,000 Look On"
- "50,000 See Giants Lose, Then Tie"[12]

Sunday doubleheaders contributed mightily to gate receipts. Cincinnati owner Powell Crosley asserted, "In Cincinnati during 1934, 70 percent of the Reds' gross home attendance for the year was recorded on only fifteen playing days, these including opening day, Sundays and holidays."[13] Yet, amazingly, despite their popularity with ballpark spectators and radio listeners, Sunday doubleheaders in the 1930s were almost never pre-scheduled before the season: they were scheduled on an ad hoc basis during the campaign.

Both leagues would release initial season schedules sans a trace of a Sunday doubleheader. After opening day, owners would adjust their schedules by moving up a Monday game or a late-season weekday game, making it the second game of a Sunday doubleheader. Also, following the inevitable weather-related postponements of games in the spring months, the leagues would announce adjusted schedules; many of these rainouts became the second games of Sunday doubleheaders.[14]

"If Sunday doubleheaders are to become a regular thing, they should be so incorporated in the schedules," asserted *The Sporting News* in 1933. "We know nothing more meaningless than the present schedules, with games charted for as late as September being moved up at the whim of a club owner to create a Sunday doubleheader in May."[15] *The Sporting News* further noted,

> Fear is voiced in some quarters that baseball is going to become a weekend sport, instead of a daily affair. Its possibility does counsel serious consideration of the probable effects of the arbitrary shifting around of week-day games to make possible double-headers on Sunday. There is such a thing as carrying the practice so far that the fans through habit will expect double bills as a regular diet.

There was also the insidious question "whether approximately the same number of fans wouldn't be attracted by single games on Sunday."[16]

Moreover, several owners despised the Sunday doubleheader, then referred to as a "synthetic doubleheader" because Level 2, 3, and 4 Sunday doubleheaders were, unlike a Level 1 contest, man-made rather than naturally formed (due to weather postponements). Nonetheless, the times demanded innovation. Many minor league teams, attempting to remain financially viable, had been scheduling Sunday doubleheaders and playing night games since 1930. But MLB was more resistant to change. "We are not going in for any hippodrome stuff," said Clark Griffith, owner of the Washington club, in regard to a 1933 proposal by Chicago Cubs owner William L. Veeck for interleague play during the hot summer interval from July 5 to mid-August. "The American League is a big league, asserted Griffith. "Our business has held up at least as well as any other. We're going on just the way we are."[17]

After a dismal 1933 season on the financial front, MLB owners voted to curtail Sunday doubleheaders, not permitting them before June 15. At the owner meetings, magnates failed to respond creatively to fan receptivity to Sunday doubleheaders during the 1933 season. Instead, the owners voted to use a uniform baseball in both leagues. "I think the decision to adopt a uniform ball is one of the most constructive moves in baseball history. From now on every major league player will hit and throw the same ball. Finer comparisons can be drawn from batting averages of both leagues," asserted National League president John Heydler.[18] Compared to the Sunday doubleheader, the uniform ball was a fairly minor matter. Yet, rather than directly addressing economic issues through the Sunday doubleheader, moguls facilely viewed the uniform ball as a panacea.

In December 1934, however, National League owners did approve the installation of artificial lights to inaugurate night games in 1935. Lest there be too drastic a change, however, no franchise was to exceed seven night games for the season. Nonetheless, night baseball helped salvage MLB since it exponentially opened up more opportunities for spectatorship.

Sunday doubleheaders facilitated the emergence of night baseball. The Sunday doubleheader absorbed the brunt of owner opposition to innovation in the early 1930s, softening up management to other changes later in the decade. Furthermore, the Sunday doubleheader prompted the scheduling of night games, as owners (and players) preferred not to play an afternoon game on the day following a night game. Without the synthetic doubleheader, the addition of seven night games to a team's schedule would have necessitated an open day, thus expanding the season schedule by a week: such a contingency would have delayed the adoption of night baseball for several more years.

Indeed, it was night baseball that finally put the Sunday doubleheader on the preliminary season schedule. In 1939, with three teams playing night games, the National League scheduled twelve Sunday doubleheaders specifically related to night games in Cincinnati, Brooklyn, and Philadelphia. Commenting on the proliferation of Sunday doubleheaders on the National League schedule, *The Sporting News* observed, "As a result of the open dates which usually follow night games, an unusually large number of Sunday doubleheaders have been scheduled, to enable teams to provide for the engagements which otherwise would follow the nocturnal battles."[19]

Over the next two years, more teams in both leagues adopted night baseball, leading MLB to prominently feature the Sunday doubleheader in their 1941 schedules: sixteen for the American League and twenty-five for the Nationals. "Taking official cognizance of the growing practice of some clubs in arranging Sunday double-headers after the season starts, the American League schedule sets a precedent this year by definitely charting 16 Sabbath twin-bills in advance," reported *The Sporting News*.[20]

Advance scheduling had meaning for fans. "There has been entirely too much subterfuge in postponing regularly-carded contests during the week to create synthetic twin-bills," opined *The Sporting News:*

> As a result, carefully-prepared schedules became mere scraps of paper before the season had gone far, and the fans were lost in a maze of altered dates, which made it impossible for them to tell when games would be played. The American League schedule, announced this week, restores permanency to the dates, and fans once more can depend upon the annual chart issued in the spring.[21]

Proliferation of the Sunday doubleheader happened at an opportune time. The United States' entry into World War II, following the attack on Pearl Harbor on December 7, 1941, transformed baseball. President Franklin D. Roosevelt's "green-light letter" enabled MLB to continue during the war years, and the Sunday doubleheader was important to that continuance. In wartime, the frequency of Sunday doubleheaders skyrocketed, exceeding the 1933 peak. On the home front, the Sunday doubleheader accommodated both civilian workers and those servicemen stationed stateside. During World War II, Sunday doubleheaders encompassed more than one-quarter of the entire playing schedule per annum. In 1944, Sunday doubleheaders accounted for nearly 28 percent of games played, as the table below illustates.[22]

Year	No. of Sunday Doubleheaders	Percent of Games in Total Season
1942	155	25.3%
1943	166	26.8%
1944	172	27.7%
1945	156	25.4%

Nonetheless, MLB attendance declined during the war years, dropping from nine million in 1941 to seven million in 1943. With restrictions on pleasure travel, the Sunday doubleheader prevented an even more precipitous decline in spectatorship during World War II.[23]

In the postwar era, the Sunday doubleheader survived, although the factors that formerly drove its popularity lost relevance. New conditions were less hospitable to the Sunday doubleheader, including:

- *The "weekend."* In the aftermath of World War II, the normative workweek declined from six days to five, giving most working people two consecutive days off, creating a new social institution — the weekend. Suddenly, attending a ball game on Saturday afternoon was a pleasure many more people could and did enjoy.
- *Television.* TV undermined ballpark attendance. People increasingly watched baseball on the new electronic medium, avoiding the travel and expense associated with live attendance.
- *Night baseball.* A novelty before the war, night games greatly proliferated during the postwar era. By 1948, all MLB parks, save the Cubs' Wrigley Field, possessed night lights. Dominating Monday through Friday scheduling, night baseball eliminated most poorly attended day games during the workweek: hence, fewer games were candidates for addition to a Sunday date. A Friday night game could outdraw a Sunday game, something unthinkable in the 1930s. Management incentive for providing a second "free" game on Sunday eroded. Sunday baseball lost its special niche. Working people now had more opportunity to attend games on other days (more typically nights) of the week.

  Commercialism, consumerism, and mass leisure transformed the American Sunday. "During the 1950s and 1960s commercialism and materialism intensified their pressure on all aspects of American life, including Sunday," social scientist Alexis McCrossen observed in

Holy Day, Holiday: The American Sunday. "Blue laws were amended to provide more time for commercial activity."[24]

The growth of highways, suburbs, television, and discretionary purchasing power increased during the postwar years, providing baseball with additional competition. In the postwar years, baseball moguls, employing the Level 4 strategy of the "free" second game, continued to schedule Sunday doubleheaders. Although Sunday doubleheaders remained a MLB staple well into the 1960s, several factors contributed to their decline:

- *New cities.* Franchise relocations in the 1950s to Milwaukee, Baltimore, Kansas City, Los Angeles, and San Francisco, as well as franchise expansion in the 1960s, had consequences for the Sunday doubleheader. The novelty of MLB in these new locations was enough of an attraction to draw crowds on Sunday without a doubleheader.
- *TV revenue.* Gate receipts declined in importance as television revenue increased.[25] Night games began to draw higher viewer ratings than weekend games, adding pressure to drop Sunday doubleheaders. Furthermore, since television executives were generally not interested in televising the second game of a doubleheader, baseball owners lost potential TV revenue on such a contest.
- *Longer game times.* As average game time grew from two hours to three, fewer spectators were willing to sit through both games of a doubleheader. Whereas a doubleheader could be completed in four to five hours in the 1930s, it was not unusual in the 1970s for a doubleheader to take up six to seven hours of a Sunday.
- *New stadiums.* Aging edifices like Shibe Park, Forbes Field, and Sportsman's Park were replaced in the 1960s and 1970s by more modern facilities. Baseball management believed that these new facilities would draw fans on Sundays sans doubleheaders.
- *Football.* By the late 1950s, Sundays in September were increasingly dominated by pro football. Baseball pennant races lost ground to the gridiron.

Sunday crowds, by the 1960s, whether for a doubleheader or a single game, diminished as changing attitudes and the erosion of legal prohibitions encouraged other commercial options. Now working people could shop as well as indulge in amusements on Sunday.

By the mid-1970s, the Sunday doubleheader had disappeared from the schedules of a number of successful, big market clubs, including the Boston Red Sox and Los Angeles Dodgers. Other franchises gradually abandoned the Sunday doubleheader. In 1984, only seven teams had a Sunday doubleheader on their playing schedule, and with the exception of the Giants, it was just one Sunday doubleheader (the Giants scheduled two). By 1986, the Sunday doubleheader was virtually extinct in the major leagues.

Summary

The Sunday doubleheader merits more study. It contributed to the survival of MLB during the Great Depression and World War II. Moreover, it augmented attendance opportunities for working people. The Sunday doubleheader also contributed to the rise of night baseball. Beyond the foul line, the rise and decline of the Sunday doubleheader reflected the larger American culture.

Notes

1. *State v. Powell*, 58 Ohio St. 324, 50 N.E. 900 (1898).

2. Witold Rybczynski, *Waiting for the Weekend* (New York: Viking Penguin, 1991), 132; and Alexis McCrossen, *Holy Day, Holiday: The American Sunday* (Ithaca, NY: Cornell University Press, 2000), 8.

3. Steven Riess, *Touching Base: Professional Baseball and American Culture in the Progressive Era* (Westport, CT: Greenwood Press, 1980), 31.

4. Charlie Bevis, *Sunday Baseball: The Major Leagues' Struggle to Play Baseball on the Lord's Day, 1876–1934* (Jefferson, NC: McFarland & Company, 2003), 271–273.

5. Ibid.

6. Paul Dickson, *The New Dickson Baseball Dictionary* (New York: Harcourt Brace, 1999), 163.

7. *Complete Baseball Record Book*, 2003 edition (St. Louis: Sporting News Books, 2003), 130.

8. "The Double-Header," *The Sporting News*, 12 August 1926, 4.

9. "Letting in More Light," *The Sporting News*, 25 January 1940, 4; and "B.R. Disowns Sunday 2-for-1," *The Sporting News*, 1 July 1943, 1.

10. Robert Tiemann, "Major League Attendance," *Total Baseball*, seventh edition (Kingston, NY: Total Sports Publishing, 2001), 76; Underlying data to construct table obtained online from the Retrosheet database of major-league game results are available at <www.retrosheet.org> (9 April 2003); 11; and Robert Hood, *The Gashouse Gang* (New York: William Morrow, 1976), 88–89.

11. All three headlines from *The New York Times*, 28 August 1933, 16.

12. John Drebinger, "Night Baseball on Limited Scale Adopted Unanimously by National League," *New York Times*, 13 December 1934, 31.

13. For examples of adjusted schedules, see "Lists 15 Double-Headers," *New York Times*, 17 May 1931, sec. 10, 6; and "Double Bills Listed," *New York Times*, 17 July 1936, 10.

14. "Synthetic Double-Headers," *The Sporting News*, 25 May 1933, 4.

15. Ibid.

16. "Griffith Opposes Inter-League Plan," *The New York Times*, 24 August 1933, 21.

17. "Big Leagues Vote for Uniform Ball," *The New York Times*, 15 December 1933, 31.

18. "Arcs Give N.L. More Sunday Twin Bills," *The Sporting News*, 9 February 1939, 2.

19. "16 Sabbath 'Twins' Scheduled by A.L.," *The Sporting News*, 30 January 1941, 2; and "25 Sunday Bargains on N.L. Date Chart," *The Sporting News*, 6 February 1941, 2.

20. "At Last a Permanent Schedule," *The Sporting News*, 30 January 1941, 4.

21. Underlying data to construct table obtained online from the Retrosheet database of major league game results are available at <www.retrosheet.org> (9 April 2003).

22. Tiemann, 76.

23. McCrossen, 105–106.

24. Foster Rhea Dulles, *A History of Recreation* (New York: Appleton-Century-Crofts, 1965), 351–352.

The Kansas City Royals' Baseball Academy: Expanding the Science and Pedagogy of Baseball

Richard J. Puerzer

"The Book," the mythical set of traditional methods governing the management of baseball, both on and off the field, has defined the game for most of its history. Innovation regarding training, strategy, statistical analysis, and general knowledge of baseball has come in fits and starts. Within this context, the Kansas City Royals' Baseball Academy constituted an important revisionist venture in the development and training of players. The Baseball Academy attempted to create baseball success through the application of science, technology, and improved pedagogy.

The Kansas City Royals' Baseball Academy, established in 1970, was the brainchild of Royals' owner Ewing Kauffman. Kauffman, a self-made multimillionaire and founder of the giant Marion Labs, attempted to bring his entrepreneurial spirit to baseball ownership through the establishment of the Baseball Academy. The goal of the Academy was the development of its students/players. Academy students deviated from the traditional baseball population, and the methods employed at the Academy were anything but by "the Book."

The Establishment of the Kansas City Royals

The Kansas City Royals entered the American League in 1969 as an expansion team. Prior to 1969, Kansas City had been home to many major and minor league teams, including the Packers of the Federal League, the Blues of the American Association, the Monarchs of the Negro Leagues, and the Athletics of the American League. Following the 1967 season, the Athletics, owned by the contentious Charlie O. Finley, departed for Oakland,

California. Ewing Kauffman was then awarded the new Kansas City franchise In contrast to Finley, Kauffman immediately established a positive relationship with the denizens of Kansas City, pledging that the team would not move from the city during his lifetime.[1] Kauffman also promised that he would provide the financial support necessary to field a winning baseball team.

True to his word, Kauffman recruited experienced and knowledgeable baseball personnel to run the club. He hired Cedric Tallis as executive vice president and general manager. Tallis, a veteran baseball executive, had spent the previous seven years with the California Angels. Recognizing the need to immediately plan for the expansion draft and develop a minor league system, Tallis named Charlie Metro director of personnel. A consummate baseball man, Metro, between 1937 and 1953, played on diverse levels of Organized Baseball, from the lower classifications of the minors to the major leagues. Metro had also managed in both the majors and minors from 1947 to 1966. Immediately prior to joining the Royals, Metro scouted for the Cincinnati Reds. Previously associated in the minor leagues, Metro and Tallis shared a mutual respect. Metro viewed Tallis as one of the game's preeminent judges of baseball talent.[2] Tallis subsequently designated Lou Gorman, formerly director of minor league operations for the Baltimore Orioles, the Royals' director of player development. Tallis, Metro, and Gorman would play prominent roles in the formation and decline of the Baseball Academy.

The Management Approach of Ewing Kauffman

Kauffman was intrigued with the opportunity to apply to baseball the management principles he had successfully utilized in the pharmaceutical industry. He had earned a reputation as an innovative and compassionate leader. Entering the pharmaceutical industry with an investment of $5,000 in 1950, Kauffman sold his controlling interest in Marion Laboratories in 1989, with the company reporting annual sales exceeding one billion dollars. Three dictums shaped Kauffman's business philosophy: treat others as you want to be treated, share life's rewards with those who make them possible, and give back to society.[3] In keeping with this philosophy, Kauffman pursued a multitude of philanthropic ventures, including funding the mass teaching of cardiopulmonary resuscitation and the creation of a program to encourage entrepreneurship in the United States. Kauffman's management vision facilitated rapid and enduring success for the Kansas City Royals.

Shortly after acquiring the team, Kauffman announced that he was including profit sharing in the benefit package for Royals' non-player personnel.[4] Kauffman's goal in instituting profit sharing was two-fold: to attract excellent employees and to motivate those employees to work toward the success of the franchise. Kauffman also did not shy away from spending money in order to hire talented coaches and managers in the farm system, recognizing that these men were necessary to develop neophyte players. Under Kauffman's mandate, the Royals' farm system employed more minor-league coaches than other organizations, providing prospects with a singular level of personalized training.[5] Kauffman also worked to establish an open relationship with his players, offering them counsel regarding personal finances.[6] Denying altruism, Kauffman stressed that improvement in the performance of his players would benefit team revenues.

Kauffman's entrepreneurial approach was most evident in the genesis of the Baseball Academy. After reflecting on the traditional methods of player development, Kauffman was disheartened by the extremely slow process of acquiring, developing, and promoting players to the major league level.[7] Likewise, he was disenchanted with the baseball establishment's resistance to change. The conservative traditions of baseball differed from the business environment that Kauffman knew, where without innovation and improvement, companies failed. Kauffman was chagrined that baseball was resistant to innovative ideas. So, employing his entrepreneurial acumen, Kauffman sponsored the creation of the Kansas City Royals' Baseball Academy.

Previous Efforts Similar to the Academy

Although the Royals' Baseball Academy was without question an innovative undertaking, it was certainly not the first attempt to improve the training of players. Although nothing came of it, John Heydler, president of the National League in the 1920s, suggested that Major League Baseball should sponsor a "baseball school."[8] Branch Rickey introduced several innovations for the training of players during his long career in baseball management. Rickey utilized such teaching tools as sliding pits, batting tees, batting cages, and pitching machines to teach the fundamentals of baseball play.[9]

In 1938, the Chicago Cubs hired Coleman R. Griffith, then known as the father of sport psychology in America, as a consultant to the team. During his two-year tenure with the Cubs, Griffith pursued many new methods in an attempt to build a scientific training program. With the Cubs, as with the Royals under Kauffman, it was an innovative and business-minded owner, Philip K. Wrigley, who sought to improve his team through untraditional means. While working with the Cubs, Griffith used such techniques as filming players, recommending improved training regimes, the documentation of player progress through charts and diagrams, and changes in batting and pitching practice in order to make the practice sessions more closely resemble game conditions. Griffith suffered through acrimonious relationships with the two Cub managers he worked with, Charlie Grimm and Gabby Hartnett; they undermined much of Griffith's work. Despite producing some 400 pages of reports, including documentation on the use of methods and measures later employed at the Baseball Academy, Griffith's work for the Cubs was essentially for naught.[10]

The St. Louis Browns employed another psychologist, David F. Tracy, in 1950. Tracy took an entirely psychological approach to improving player performance, working with players through relaxation techniques, autosuggestion, and hypnosis during spring training. Although Tracy was apparently well received by both the Browns' players and management, he did not have a significant impact on team performance.[11]

Other efforts to improve player skills outside of the regular spring to fall cycle of baseball development and play appeared. During the early 1950s, Casey Stengel, then manager of the New York Yankees, utilized a post-season camp in an effort to expedite the development of players. Mickey Mantle, Gil McDougald, and future Baseball Academy director Syd Thrift took part in the camp.[12] The camp was effective in refining the talents of many players, and fostering their transition to the major leagues. However, unlike the target group of the Royals' Baseball Academy, all of the players taking part in Stengel's initiative were already professional ballplayers.

The "Research Program for Baseball," a project underwritten by Philadelphia Phillies owner Bob Carpenter and carried out by professors from the University of Delaware and scientists from DuPont between 1963 and 1972, also merits note.[13] Through this research, the study of hitting encompassed the measurement of bat velocity, bat acceleration, and total force. Another project concerned the impact of player vision on hitting, pitching, and fielding. Although Carpenter's initiative advanced the science of the game, it was generally scoffed at by the baseball establishment, including scouts who were perhaps not eager to allow science to replace their expert opinion.

The Creation of the Kansas City Royals' Baseball Academy

Kauffman believed that the four traditional ways of acquiring players—the free agent draft, the minor league draft, trades with other teams, and purchases from other teams—would not allow the Royals to quickly develop a winning team.[14] Kauffman therefore sought a nontraditional method for gaining good players. This search gave birth to the Baseball Academy, a school which would teach how best to play baseball. The Baseball Academy sought to create players from nontraditional personnel. Kauffman's asserted that an athlete did not necessarily have to play baseball for many years in order to become a major leaguer.

This notion of turning a good athlete into a good baseball player may have been influenced by the performance of Royals Lou Pinella, American League Rookie of the Year in 1969. In high school, Pinella was primarily renowned for his basketball talent, even eschewing baseball for a year.[15] Kauffman believed that the Academy could fashion major league prospects from individuals with limited baseball backgrounds but possessed of a high degree of athleticism.

In order to ascertain the physical and mental abilities necessary to excel at baseball, Kauffman hired Dr. Raymond Reilly, a research psychologist with previous experience at NASA and the Office of Naval Research.[16] Approximately 150 players, mainly from within the Royals organization, were tested in order to help establish the requisite abilities to be a professional baseball player. The vision, psychomotor responses, and psychological makeup of the players were tested.[17] The four determining attributes for prospective players were excellent running speed, exceptional eyesight, fast reflexes, and superb body balance. Likewise, Reilly believed that potential players should have specific personality traits, including the need for success and achievement. He also determined that players should be of above average intelligence with a good memory for facts and figures.[18] These requirements were summarized in advertising tryouts for the Academy:

> the only requisites for consideration: an applicant must (a) have completed his high school eligibility, (b) be less than 20, (c) be able to run 60 yards in 6.9 seconds in baseball shoes (the average of major leaguers is somewhat above 7.0), and (d) be neither enrolled in a four-year college nor have been drafted by a major league team.[19]

The Academy's scouts sought good athletes who had never concentrated on baseball in the past. Kauffman was correct in assuming that these athletes existed, for among the applicants in the first year were a New Mexico high school state wrestling champion, a Missouri high school sprint champion, a collegiate pole vaulter, an excellent bowler and weight lifter, and a former high school quarterback who had set his school's record in the javelin throw.[20]

The construction of the Academy began in early 1970 with Lou Pinella, representing the Royals, turning the first shovel of dirt.[21] The Academy was located in Sarasota, Florida, enabling the team created at the Academy to play in the Florida Instructional League, and for the Royals organization to use the facilities year round.[22] The 121-acre campus featured five baseball diamonds, four of which were to be used for training and instruction and one with a grandstand and lights for full-scale games. All five of the fields were built to the precise dimensions of the future Royals stadium that was to be opened in Kansas City before the 1972 season.[23] The campus also featured a fifty-room dormitory for players, offices, lecture halls, laboratories, tennis courts, and a swimming pool. The cost of construction was reported to be $1,500,000, with an additional $500,000 to be spent on establishing the Academy in its first year.[24]

Syd Thrift, who had originally been hired as the Royals' supervisor of scouting for the eastern United States, was named director of the Academy. Thrift had formerly pitched in the New York Yankee minor league system and scouted for the Pittsburgh Pirates. Thrift hired Steve Korcheck to be the Academy's coordinator of instruction; Korcheck's background included four seasons as a backup catcher for the Washington Senators during the 1950s and a stint as varsity baseball coach at George Washington University. Carlton "Buzzy" Keller, the former baseball coach at Texas Lutheran, was also hired, eventually managing the Academy team in the Gulf Coast League. In addition, several other ex-major league players were employed as instructors at the Academy, including former Detroit Tigers first baseman and Cincinnati Reds manager Johnny Neun, former Washington Senators player and manager Jim Lemon, former Boston Red Sox pitcher Chuck Stobbs, former Senators pitcher Bill Fischer, former Royals manager and Yankees/Cleveland Indians second baseman Joe Gordon, and former Yankees right-fielder Tommy Henrich.

Several part-time or full-time members of the Academy staff were hired despite having no baseball experience. George Bourette, who was a high school football coach in Missouri for twenty-six years, worked with the players on losing or gaining weight while increasing strength through exercise.[25] Mickey Cobb, athletic trainer at the Academy, later served as trainer for the organization's major league team. Bill Easton, the track coach at the University of Kansas, and Wes Santee, an ex-Olympian formerly known as America's greatest miler, were hired to work with the players on their base running.[26] The aforementioned Dr. Ray Reilly was actively involved in the physiological and psychological testing of players. Two ophthalmologists, Bill Harrison and Bill Lee, were involved in the testing and improvement of vision.[27] In retrospect, this cadre of professionals constituted the first concerted effort to measure, evaluate, and improve both baseball players and the way that baseball is played.

The Science and Pedagogy Used at the Academy

Players were selected for the Academy based on their performance at tryout camps held throughout the United States. It was envisioned that 50 players would be selected from the several thousand who would take part in the tryouts. The first of these camps was held in Kansas City from June 4–6,

1970.[28] In the first year, 128 tryout camps were held for 7,682 candidates. From these candidates, forty-three athletes hailing from twenty-three different states were selected for the initial class.[29] Orestes Minoso Arrietta, stepson of former Negro Leaguer and Chicago White Sox outfielder Minnie Minoso, was the only player of notoriety in this first group. Although Arrietta would never reach the majors, three future big leaguers were in the first class: Bruce Miller, a light-hitting infielder who would appear in 196 games for the San Francisco Giants between 1973 and 1976; Ron Washington, another infielder who played for five different teams including a six-year stint with the Minnesota Twins; and Frank White, the star pupil of the Academy who would go on to an outstanding career with the Royals. Another member of the first year class was Hal Baird. Although Baird did not reach the majors, he went on to a distinguished tenure as head baseball coach at Auburn University, where he would tutor Bo Jackson, Frank Thomas, Tim Hudson, Gregg Olson, and other future baseball luminaries.[30]

Players were to train and study baseball at the Academy for a minimum of ten months. Academy players were paid a modest monthly salary, beginning at $100 to $200 a month in the first year and increasing to $500 a month in the second year. Likewise, they received free room, three diet-planned meals a day, uniforms, health and life insurance, and a round-trip plane ticket home for the Christmas holidays. In keeping with Kauffman's belief that an educated individual made a good baseball player and that all of the players should have education to fall back on should their baseball career not work out, it was required that each player attend classes three mornings a week at nearby Manatee Junior College.[31]

On the mornings that players did not attend junior college classes, they received classroom instruction on baseball at the Academy. Every afternoon they played baseball. First-year players played approximately 150 games, first in exhibitions against collegiate and professional teams and then later in Gulf Coast League competition.

Much of the Academy's program differed significantly from standard practices of the time. For example, in the average minor league camp a hitter might spend but a few minutes in the cage for batting practice. At the Academy, players were given 30 minutes a day for batting practice, against both live pitching and a pitching machine.[32] Another unique training method involved the use of pitching machines for fielding practice. As the pitching machine could create a uniform velocity and bounce, it was used to test the reaction and dexterity of infielders. Likewise, it could repetitively drill infielders for work on their lateral range and footwork. These drills were supplemented with machines that could produce non-uniform ground balls, similar to those caused by a bat hitting a ball.[33]

Foot speed, especially on the basepaths, was a priority at the Academy.

Several approaches were utilized to improve base running. Wes Santee set up a running and conditioning program for the improvement of running form. Base-stealing ability was improved through the development of the timed, measured lead. By timing an opposing pitcher's delivery and his pick-off throw, it was determined that an average runner could take a twelve-foot lead off of first base, with faster runners taking slightly bigger leads. Likewise, a lead of twenty-seven feet could usually be taken safely from second base. With this knowledge, players were instructed precisely how far they could venture off base. This knowledge improved performance and instilled confidence in the players. The now ubiquitous approach of using stopwatches on the ball field was then quite novel. As the time required for a catcher to receive a pitch and get a throw to second base was recorded, base runners could determine the likelihood of a steal based on specific battery combinations. Prospects were also trained in the proper use of the delayed steal and the double steal.[34] Academy teams invariably led the league in steals. These base-stealing and base-running techniques would have a great impact on the running game in the major leagues during the 1970s and 1980s. The Royals' proficiency on the base paths also influenced players in other organizations. Tom Treblehorn, for example, familiarized himself with the Academy approach to base stealing, passing his knowledge on to Rickey Henderson while managing Henderson in the minor leagues.[35]

Doctors Reilly, Harrison, and Lee worked with players on improving their mental approach to the game. One technique that they employed called for players to "center their concentration," on one aspect of instruction until it became second nature, enabling them to focus much more clearly on the task at hand.[36] Another technique for the improvement of performance was "visualization," the ability to readily obtain mental pictures and use these visual images for the enrichment of performance. It was believed that visualization would reduce stress, thereby improving timing and balance.[37] George Brett was one of the first major league players to utilize visualization, claiming that it helped him to concentrate and break bad patterns of performance.[38]

Several other innovative physical training methods were utilized at the Academy. Under the direction of trainer Mickey Cobb, the Royals organization was the first to employ a mandatory stretching program. Also, they were the first team to utilize exercises performed in a swimming pool as a part of rehabilitation programs for a multitude of injuries. Cobb and strength/conditioning coach George Bourette developed innovative resistance training methods that used rubber bands and rubber chains. Methods for the use of resistance tools improved strength and provided increased protection against injuries.[39] Academy instruction also stressed the negative consequences of drug and alcohol abuse.[40] (It is ironic that this topic was addressed at such a relatively early time by a team that a decade later would be plagued by drug problems.[41])

The result of all of these innovative training methods was not a "eureka moment" for any of the players or personnel at the Academy. Instead, the success of the teams and players came as a result of the screening of players, traditional and innovative training methods, and months of practice and games. The Academy work did indeed culminate in the transformation of capable athletes into gifted baseball players.

The Academy Experiences of Frank White

Frank White, a member of the Academy's initial class, was the program's first graduate to reach the major leagues. Regarded as one of the finest defensive second basemen in the game's history, he earned eight Gold Gloves. Named to five American League All-Star teams, White played second base for the Royals for eighteen seasons.

Frank White grew up in Kansas City, living but ten blocks from old Municipal Stadium, and attended Lincoln High School, located right across the street from the stadium. He did not play varsity baseball because there was no team at his high school. However, he did participate in Ban Johnson and Casey Stengel leagues.[42] According to White, he was not scouted because in the late 1960s scouts, who were predominantly white, avoided inner city areas.[43] White was reluctant to go to the Academy tryout, but was encouraged by his wife and given the day off from his job at a local sheet metal company. His performance at the tryout earned him a place in the Academy's initial class. Reflecting on the idea behind the Academy, White believed that it was "the wisdom of Mr. Kauffman to bring instructors to the players," which made the Academy a successful venture. For Frank White, it created a life in baseball.

Nonetheless, White does not romanticize his time at the Academy, recalling it as akin to boot camp, with 6 a.m. wake up calls, classes, near constant practice sessions, and curfew. As none of the players had cars, they would all ride into town each Wednesday night on the team bus for their limited leisure time. White remembers Academy time revolving around baseball. Although he recollects feeling as something of "a guinea pig in a grand baseball experiment," White also remembers the many innovations that were explored, strategies that stayed with him throughout his baseball career. According to White, the strong point of the Academy was the teaching of fundamentals; he also believes that the concentrated Academy approach turned him into a major league baseball player in a few short years. White recalls the Academy as "a great, great experience." In many ways, White embodied Kauffman's idea of the Academy: an excellent and intelligent athlete can be molded and transformed into a quick, resourceful, exceptional baseball player.

White was promoted to the Royals in June 1973, just three years after joining the Academy. He recalls learning that Royals manager Jack McKeon encountered resistance to the promotion. Some within the organization did not want to see White succeed because they wanted to prove to Kauffman that there was no merit in the Academy idea. Nonetheless, White became one of the primary components of a championship team, and influenced the play of second basemen on artificial turf. In evaluating White's career, statistical guru Bill James describes it as interchangeable with that of Bill Mazeroski, who was elected to the Baseball Hall of Fame in 2001 primarily on the strength of his defensive prowess.[44]

The Performance of Academy Teams

The first Academy team began play in the Gulf Coast League during the 1971 season against rookie clubs of the Pittsburgh Pirates, St. Louis Cardinals, Cleveland Indians, Chicago White Sox, Cincinnati Reds, and Minnesota Twins. Skeptics wondered if the team would be able to compete against baseball talent discovered in the traditional manner. Yet the Academy team ran away with the Gulf Coast League championship.[45]

The Academy team finished first with a record of 40–13, for a .755 winning percentage, while leading the league in both team batting average (.257) and ERA (2.07).[46] This team stole 103 bases, 48 more than the next closest team, while being caught stealing only 16 times. Clearly the team coalesced in the months of training prior to league play. This success brought many, including Kauffman and Thrift, to extrapolate the success of players into the future and wonder as to their potential on the major league level.[47] Fifteen members of the first-year class were promoted into the upper levels of the Royals organization.[48]

Despite the great success of that first season, the role of the Academy began to be downgraded, signaling the opposition of traditionalists to the Academy idea. The reassignment of Syd Thrift from director of the Academy to his former position of eastern scouting supervisor provides evidence of this process. Furthermore, Lou Gorman, already director of the scouting staff and minor league operations, would also assume the duty of directing the Academy. Moreover, the second Academy class was limited to 20 players, with the restriction that only 17 to 19 year-old players could attend. (Players already in the Royals farm system could be assigned to the Academy for two months time after their regular season ended.)[49]

In 1972, the performance of the second class of the Academy remained excellent, as reflected in a record of 41–22, a winning percentage of .651, and finishing in a tie atop the Gulf Coast League. The team again led the league in batting average (.257) and stole an astounding 161 bases. They also pitched well, posting a team ERA of 2.81, good for second in the league. Rodney Scott, who would later enjoy a substantial major league career, was perhaps the most outstanding player on this team.

The third class of the Academy would fare well neither on the field nor in the collective mind of the Royals' front office. On the field, the 1973 Academy team finished with a record of 27–28. The team hit but .224 and posted a 3.87 ERA, both marks near the bottom of the league. One bright spot: the contingent still led the circuit in stolen bases with 96, exceeding the next closest team by 21 steals, but the Academy was closed before the next season.

The Closing and Legacy of the Academy

In early 1973, three years after the opening of the Academy, Ewing Kauffman was asked to reflect on its performance. At this juncture, the Academy had cost Kauffman $1,500,000 for construction and $700,000 per year in operating expenses, a rather large investment for that time. Although several Academy graduates had moved into the Royals farm system, the Academy had yet to create a major league player, let alone a superstar. The Academy was also having trouble finding qualified students, as evinced by the decline in the size of its class from 43 in 1971, to 26 in 1972, to but 14 in 1973. Moreover, almost all of the students had considerable baseball background, contradicting the theory that a great many gifted athletes with little baseball experience would have the desire to attend the Academy. A believer in the training and instruction at the Academy, Kauffman still saw promise in the institution, stating that it would remain active for at least another five years.[50] However, a little over a year later, in May 1974, the Academy was closed.

It was with a heavy heart that Kauffman closed the Academy. He was quick to point out the Academy did get results, as Frank White was now with the big league Royals, but Kauffman acknowledged that for the costs involved there should have been a bigger impact.[51] With a downsized staff, accelerated instructional camps used the site for several months of the year. And, in 1979, the Royals abandoned the complex, donating it to the YMCA.[52]

At the time, it was generally reported that the Academy was closed primarily for financial reasons. In retrospect, however, it is easy to see that the Academy received little support from much of the Royals front office, notably general manager Cedric Tallis and player development director Lou Gorman. Rather than being seen as an integral part of the Royals player development system, it was seen as competition, utilizing resources, especially financial, which could have been used in traditional player development programs. Syd Thrift, a believer in the Academy, resigned out of frustration in 1972, disappointed that only Kauffman shared his belief in the program.[53] Conversely, Charlie Metro faults Thrift, claiming that Thrift ignored most of the advice Metro had to offer on the recognition of talent and the training of players.[54] Metro termed the Academy "something of a disaster," full of "crazy instruction." Metro's views were indicative of the contentiousness surrounding the Academy due to the traditionalism of the career baseball men running the Royals at the time.[55] Despite acquiescing to his baseball people and closing the Academy, Kauffman remained frustrated by the inertia he found in baseball concerning innovation. He later stated that he believed that the Royals would have been better off retaining the Academy.[56]

Eventually, fourteen graduates of the Academy were called up to the major leagues. The most successful of the group were: the aforementioned Frank White; U. L. Washington, who played in the major leagues for ten years, primarily at shortstop with the Royals; Rodney Scott, a second baseman who played seven years in the majors, enjoying his best years with the Montreal Expos; and Ron Washington, who played twelve years in the majors, mainly with the Minnesota Twins, and subsequently served as a coach for many years. Given that fourteen Academy alumni reached the majors leagues, its existence was not without significance.

The Academy left a lingering legacy. As a player and instructor, Frank White found that "the Academy experience made an indelible impression on his approach to the game."[57] Steve Boros reflects that "a day doesn't go by where I don't use the things I learned at the Academy."[58] Likewise, Syd Thrift called the Academy "the most stimulating baseball experience I have ever been a part of."[59]

Conclusions

The Kansas City Royals' Baseball Academy was a genuinely innovative endeavor that challenged the hidebound methods of the baseball establishment. The science employed at the Academy, the use of technology such as radar guns, video technology, strength and conditioning equipment, and stopwatches soon became ubiquitous among all major league teams. Likewise, many of the Academy's training methods became commonplace throughout Organized Baseball. However, as was found at the Academy, it is very hard to transform an athlete sans significant diamond experience into a baseball player. A baseball adage holds that the hardest thing to do in all of sports is to hit a baseball; the experience of Academy alumni provides some validation to that observation. The Academy graduates who reached the major leagues were, without exception, no more than fair hitters.

An interesting comparison can be made between the innovative efforts of the Royals in operating the Academy and the methods utilized in recent years by Oakland A's general manager Billy Beane.[60] Both organizations have pursued the same end, the identification of unrecognized and therefore economically viable baseball talent. However, the Royals and A's identified this talent from markedly different vantage points.

The players who tried out for the Academy were essentially unwanted by other organizations. Academy selection criteria derived from generic athletic measures, such as foot speed. Conversely, although Oakland looked for underappreciated talent, the A's sought athletes with significant prior experience in baseball. Eschewing generic athletic ability, the A's instead looked for evidence of superior baseball skills in specific areas, such the ability of a batter to get on base, as measured by on-base percentage, and a pitcher's control, as exhibited through strikeout-to-walk ratio. The A's often forego scouting players, relying instead on evaluations based on widely available performance statistics. The passage of time will allow historians of the future to more fully compare the A's approach to that of the Royals.

The Royals' Baseball Academy was innovative, representing the cutting edge in the science and pedagogy of baseball. This program enabled several players who probably would not have played professional baseball to reach the major leagues, and the Academy advanced the scientific approach to physical and mental training. Yet this innovative approach led to the downfall of the Academy by creating fear in the minds of baseball traditionalists who, as Bill James sarcastically stated, "didn't want to be associated with any commie pinko radical ideas."[61] Nonetheless, Ewing Kauffman's vision that the Baseball Academy would bring science and an innovative business approach to the game had an important, albeit insufficiently acknowledged, impact on modern baseball.

Notes

1. Sid Bordman, *Expansion to Excellence: An Intimate Portrait of the Kansas City Royals* (Kansas City, MO, no date), 8.
2. Charlie Metro with Tom Altherr, *Safe by a Mile* (Lincoln, NB: University of Nebraska Press, 2002), 226.
3. Anne Morgan, *Prescription for Success: The Life and Values of Ewing Marion Kauffman* (Kansas City, MO: Andrews and McMeel, 1995), 2–3.
4. Ibid., 249. It should be noted that Major League players had their own retirement package offered through the players' union.
5. Joe McGuff, "Royals to Place a Coach With Every Farm Team," *The Sporting News*, 21 February 1970, n.p.
6. Joe McGuff, "Royals Offer Players $$$ Counsel," *The Sporting News*, 11 July 1970, n.p.

7. Morgan, *Prescription for Success*, 251.

8. Bill James, *The New Bill James Historical Baseball Abstract* (New York: The Free Press, 2001), 504.

9. Murray Polner, *Branch Rickey: A Biography* (New York: Atheneum, 1982), 134.

10. For an in depth description of Griffith's work with the Cubs, see: Christopher Green, "Psychology Strikes Out: Coleman Griffith and the Chicago Cubs," *History of Psychology* 6, no. 3 (2003): 267–283.

11. For a description of Tracy's work with the Browns and its impact on baseball, see: Alan Kornspan and Mary MacCracken, "The Use of Psychology in Professional Baseball," *Nine: A Journal of Baseball History and Culture* 11, no. 2 (2003): 36–43.

12. Brad Wilson, "College Courses Part of Royal Academy Program," 13 June 1970, with incomplete citation from Kansas City Royals File, National Baseball Hall of Fame.

13. Kevin Kerrane, *Dollar Sign on the Muscle: The World of Baseball Scouting* (Lincoln, NB: University of Nebraska Press, 1999 reprint of the 1984 edition), 153–156.

14. Morgan, *Prescription for* Success, 252.

15. Lou Pinella and Maury Allen, *Sweet Lou* (New York: G.P. Putnam's Sons, 1986), 34–42.

16. Morgan, *Preription for Success*, 253.

17. Syd Thrift and Barry Shapiro, *The Game According to Syd: The Theories and Teachings of Baseball's Leading Innovator* (New York: Simon and Schuster, 1990), 27.

18. Morgan, *Prescription for Success*, 253–254.

19. "SUAB Branch of Baseball: KC Academy," June 16, 1972, with incomplete citation from Kansas City Royals File, National Baseball Hall of Fame.

20. Thrift and Shapiro, *The Game According to Syd*, 27.

21. Joe McGuff, "Work Starting on Royals' Academy," *The Sporting News*, 7 February 1970, n.p.

22. The exact location of the academy was 6700 Clark Road in Sarasota, Florida on State Highway 72, six miles east of its junction with U.S. 41.

23. Thrift and Shapiro, *The Game According to Syd*, 29.

24. Joe McGuff, "Royals Will Build Florida Academy; Cost Is $3 Million," *The Sporting News*, 27 September 1969, n.p.

25. Spike Claussen, "K.C. Baseball Academy Dedication on March 21," *The Sporting News*, 27 February 1971, n.p.

26. Thrift and Shapiro, *The Game According to Syd*, 29.

27. Jerome Holtzman, "Kauffman Never Ignores a Bright Idea," 1 April 1972, with incomplete citation from Kansas City Royals File, National Baseball Hall of Fame.

28. Brad Wilson, "College Courses Part of Royal Academy Program," 13 June 1970, with incomplete citation from Kansas City Royals File, National Baseball Hall of Fame.

29. Spike Claassen, "K.C. Baseball Academy Dedication on March 21," *The Sporting News*, 27 February 1971, n.p.

30. Information on the coaching career of Hal Baird at Auburn can be found at *www.auburn.edu/athletics/base/baird.html*.

31. Harold Claassen, "15 Selected for Royals' Academy," *The Sporting News*, 25 July 1970, n.p.

32. George McClelland, "Royals' Academy Makes It a Whole New Ballgame," *The Virginian-Pilot*, 27 August 1972, E2.

33. Thrift and Shapiro, *The Game According to Syd*, 125–126.

34. Ibid, 102–110.

35. Ibid, 34.

36. Holtzman, "Kauffman Never Ignores," n.p.

37. "Royals Sharpen Wits for Hits," *The New York Times*, 21 January 1973, with incomplete citation from Kansas City Royals File, National Baseball Hall of Fame.

38. Thrift and Shapiro, *The Game According to Syd*, 147–148.

39. Ibid, 31–32. Also see Joe McGuff, "Royals Adopting Mod Look in Training Camp Techniques," *The Sporting News*, 24 March 1973, 44.

40. Thrift and Shapiro, *The Game According to Syd*, 32.

41. Morgan, *Prescription for Success*, 278.

42. Joe Posnanski, "Extra Innings: Frank White is Back in the Games, Hoping to Lead a Royals Rally, *The Kansas City Star*, 21 September 1997, n.p.

43. Frank White, phone interview by Richard J. Puerzer, 4 February 2003.

44. James, *The New Bill James*, 504.

45. C.C. Johnson Spink, "We Believe...," *The Sporting News*, 11 September 1971, n.p.

46. All statistics related to the performance of the Academy teams in the Gulf Coast League were found in the *1972, 1973, and 1974 Official Baseball Guides* (St. Louis, MO: The Sporting News).

47. Joe McGuff, "Fast-Moving Royals Junk Timetable," *The Sporting News*, 25 September 1971, n.p.

48. "Royals Promote Grads," 13 May 1972, with incomplete citation from Kansas City Royals File, National Baseball Hall of Fame.

49. Joe McGuff, "Royals Extending Academy Plan to Farmhands," *The Sporting News*, 5 August 1972, n.p.

50. Joe McGuff, "Kaycee Academy Grooms Rejects, But Cost Is High," *The Sporting News*, 21 April 1973, 17.

51. Sid Bordman, "Royals Close Their Academy," 18 May 1974, with incomplete citation from Kansas City Royals File, National Baseball Hall of Fame.

52. "Owner of Royals Donates Baseball Complex to 'Y'," 23 December 1979, with incomplete citation from Kansas City Royals File, National Baseball Hall of Fame.

53. Thrift and Sapiro, *The Game According to Syd*, 33.

54. Charlie Metro, phone interview with Richard J. Puerzer, 19 June 2003.

55. Metro with Altherr, *Safe by a Mile*, 331.

56. Morgan, *Prescription for Success*, 260.

57. White interview.

58. Thrift and Sapiro, *The Game According to Syd*, 34.

59. Ibid, 25.

60. Michael Lewis, *Moneyball*, (New York: W.W. Norton & Co., 2003), passim.

61. James, *The New Bill James*, 504.

The Cost of Competitiveness in Major League Baseball

Herbert F. Lewis, Thomas R. Sexton, and Kathleen A. Lock

The dramatic growth of free agency in Major League Baseball (MLB) since 1975 has caused great concern about the ability of some teams, particularly those in smaller markets, to compete. To test the validity of that concern, this study examines: (1) the minimum total player salary required to be competitive in each nonstrike year since 1985; (2) the trends in the minimum total player salary required to be competitive; (3) the number of teams that were noncompetitive either due to low total player salary or for other reasons; and (4) the relationship between competitiveness and market size. These questions generate answers that challenge conventional wisdoms.

MLB teams, like other sports franchises but unlike other business enterprises, depend on stiff competition for economic survival. To be sure, winning increases fan interest, brings more people to the ballpark, improves television ratings, and bolsters sales of team-related merchandise, all of which add to franchise prosperity. However, baseball is entertainment; tight division races, unpredictable playoff series, and the periodic emergence of new champions enhance the entertainment value of the sport, ensuring its fan base and its future.

Baseball entered the era of free agency on December 23, 1975, and player salaries have since grown to controversial levels. In 1975, the average player salary was $44,676; in 2002, it was $2,384,779, an average annual growth rate of nearly 16 percent per year for twenty-seven years.[1] Few industries could absorb such a cost increase while growing by 25 percent, as MLB did in expanding from twenty-four to thirty teams. Some teams, notably those located in larger markets and those possessing greater financial resources, found it easier than other franchises to sign free agents to high-salary, multiyear contracts, thereby cornering the market on the most talented players and threatening the competitive balance on the field.

Major League Baseball expressed its concern in July 2000 when the Commissioner's Blue Ribbon Panel on Baseball Economics (2000) reported on the revenue disparities in MLB. The Panel found disparities affecting competition and growing worse while the limited revenue sharing and payroll taxes approved in the 1996 labor agreement with the players were having little effect. Moreover, the Panel concluded that the cost of trying to be competitive was raising ticket and concession prices, jeopardizing MLB's position as the affordable family spectator sport. The Panel's recommendations included greater revenue sharing and a competitive balance tax, both of which are part of the 2002 labor agreement with the players. The Panel also recommended franchise relocation. Following the 2001 season, MLB went further, attempting to contract two teams. Nonetheless, the attempt failed, and the 2002 labor agreement guarantees no contraction through 2006.

Methodology

The Blue Ribbon Panel defined *competitive balance* as the state in which "every well-run club has a regularly recurring reasonable hope of reaching postseason play."[2] To define "well-run," turn to the theory of productive efficiency in the management science and economics literature. This study deems a team *well run* if its relative efficiency score is 100% when measured using Data Envelopment Analysis (DEA).[3] Analysts have applied DEA in a broad array of settings over the past twenty-five years. Using this definition, a team is well run if no other team has won as many games in a given season while spending less on total player salaries (TPS). The DEA results are used to determine the number of games each team would have won, given its TPS, had it been well run. This number is the team's *efficient games won* (EGW).

For each season, the probability that a team would qualify for the playoffs if every team in its league were equally talented is computed. This means that each team in a given division would have the same likelihood of qualifying for postseason play. Thus, the phrase "reasonable hope of reaching postseason play" is interpreted to mean that a team must have at least this probability of making the playoffs.

Next, logistic regression[4] is employed to model the relationship between the number of games won and the probability of making the playoffs. This study employs the logistic regression model to compute MGW, defined as the minimum number of games a team must have won to achieve the minimum probability of making the playoffs for its league and year. A team is defined as *competitive* in a given year if its EGW equals or exceeds its MGW. In other words, a team is competitive if it would have won enough games to have a reasonable hope of reaching postseason play had it used all of its player salary money efficiently.

Then, the minimum TPS needed to be competitive in each year is determined. This is the *competitive salary* for that year. To do this, teams are clustered into two groups: those below a selected TPS and those above this value. A standard clustering index, the Gini index[5], is employed to identify the TPS that places primarily noncompetitive teams in the lower cluster and primarily competitive teams in the upper cluster. The competitive salary for that year is the lowest TPS of any team in the upper cluster.

The trends in competitive salary are examined relative to the trends in minimum, maximum, and mean TPS, identifying noncompetitive teams in each year due to low TPS (and other reasons). Next, this study evaluates the relationship between noncompetitiveness and the size of the market in which the team plays.

Analysis of Competitiveness in MLB

The analysis begins by computing the efficiency of every MLB team during the study period, defined as the nonstrike years between 1985 and 2002. The study views a MLB team as a two-stage production operation.[6] See Figure 1. In Stage 1, the team's front office uses resources (TPS) to acquire talent (offensive and defensive production). In Stage 2, the talent produces games won (GW) on the field.

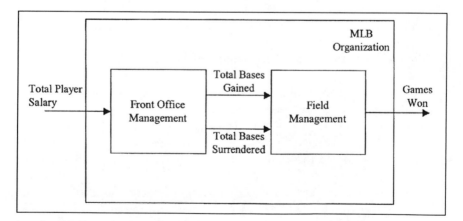

Figure 1: This study models a Major League Baseball organization as a two-stage production process. In the first stage, front office management spends money on player salaries and produces offensive and defensive performance, measured by Total Bases Gained and Total Bases Surrendered, respectively. In the second stage, field management converts these intermediate products into games won.

The offensive talent of a team is measured by its total bases gained (TBG) and its defensive talent by its total bases surrendered (TBS). MLB uses a statistic called *total bases* to measure offensive performance. Specifically, MLB's definition of total bases for a team in a single year is[7]

$$TB = S + 2D + 3T + 4HR$$

where S = the number of singles, D = the number of doubles, T = the number of triples, and HR = the number of home runs hit by the team. This definition is extended by adding W = the number of walks received by the team and E = the number of fielding errors committed by the opposing team. Thus,[8]

$$TBG = TB + W + E$$

TBS is defined identically except that the summands refer to the number of such hits and walks surrendered by the team, and the number of fielding errors committed by the team, in the given year.

This formulation is appealing because of the symmetric nature of TBG and TBS. If TBG is accepted as a natural Stage 2 input capturing the team's offensive contribution to the production of GW, then it follows logically that TBS is a natural Stage 2 input for the defensive contribution. Given the pure symmetry of the game, it is reasonable and desirable to formulate the model with symmetric Stage 2 inputs.

The study applies the two-stage DEA methodology described in Sexton and Lewis[9] to compute the efficiency of every MLB team. The DEA results are used to determine the number of games each team would have won had they been efficient, i.e., the team's efficient games won. Thus,

$$EGW = \frac{GW}{Efficiency}$$

Next, a logistic regression model is constructed for a team's probability of qualifying for postseason play using data for the years 1903 through 2002.[10] The independent variable in the model is GW; the dependent variable is equal to one if the team qualified for postseason play in that year or equal to zero if it did not qualify:

$$Playoffs = \begin{matrix} 1, \textit{ if team qualified for post-season play} \\ 0, \textit{ if team did not qualify for post-season play} \end{matrix}$$

This model also includes indicator variables that identify the playoff qualification conditions that applied to the league and division in which the team played in that year. Specifically, since 1903, there have been eight such conditions. Therefore, the logistic regression computes a team's probability of qualifying for postseason play given its number of games won and the playoff qualification conditions that applied to the league and division in which the team played in that year.

For each of the eight playoff qualification conditions, the model computes the probability that a team would qualify for the playoffs if every team in its league were equally talented, meaning that each team in a given division would have the same likelihood of qualifying for postseason play. This represents the minimum probability of qualifying for postseason play that a team must achieve to be competitive under the given playoff qualification conditions. Then, the results of the logistic regression model are used to compute MGW, the minimum number of games a team must have won to be competitive under those conditions. Thus, a team is competitive if and only if it would have won at least MGW had it been efficient. In other words, a team is competitive if and only if

$$EGW \geq MGW$$

Finally, within each year, teams are sorted according to TPS from low to high and the Gini index identifies a TPS that partitions the teams into two sets, one of which consists primarily of competitive teams and one of which consists primarily of noncompetitive teams. The competitive salary in that year is the TPS of the lowest paid team in the primarily competitive set.

Data Sources

The U.S. Bureau of the Census (2000) and Statistics Canada (2001)[11] provide market size data. Player salary data is extracted from the *USA Today* web site.[12] The Baseball Archive Database and the Major League Baseball Official Web Site[13] provide games won, whether the team qualified for postseason play, total bases gained,[14] and total bases surrendered.[15]

Results

Figure 2 illustrates the relationship between EGW and GW for all teams in the study period as determined by the DEA. The teams that lie along the line defined by EGW = GW are organizationally efficient. All organizationally inefficient teams lie above this line. Different symbols indicate whether the team was competitive, noncompetitive due to low TPS, or noncompetitive due to other reasons.

Table 1 shows, for each playoff qualification condition, the probability that a team would qualify for the playoffs if every team in its league were equally talented. For example, with 10 teams in the league and no divisions or wild card, each team would have a probability of 1 in 10, or 0.100, of qualifying for postseason play. With 14 teams in the league, comprised of two 7-team divisions, with no wild card, each team would have a probability of 1 in 7, or 0.143, of qualifying for postseason play. As a final example, consider a team playing in a 4-team division within a 14-team league with a wild card. This team has a

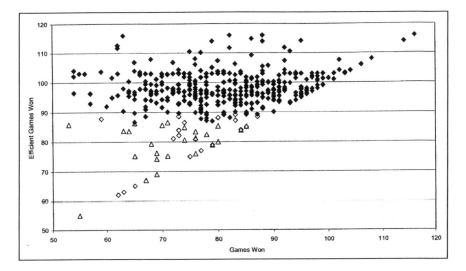

Figure 2: The relationship between EGW and GW for all teams in the study period as determined by the DEA. The teams that lie along the line defined by EGW = GW are organizationally efficient. All organizationally inefficient teams lie above this line. Solid diamonds indicate competitive teams, open triangles indicate teams that were noncompetitive due to low TPS, and open diamonds indicate teams that were noncompetitive due to other reasons.

probability of 1 in 4, or 0.250, of winning its division plus a probability of 1 in 11, or 0.091, of being the wild card team given that it is does not win its division. Thus, this team has a total probability of 0.341 of qualifying for postseason play. See Figure 3, which shows the logistic regression model for this condition. The model indicates that a team playing under such conditions must win at least 86.4 games to have a probability of qualifying for the playoffs equal to or greater than 0.341. Thus, under this playoff qualification condition, MGW = 86.4. Similar analyses lead to the MGW values shown in Table 1.

Number of Teams in League	Number of Teams in Division	Wild Card	Probability of Qualifying for Playoffs	MGW
10	—	No	0.100	92.8
8	—	No	0.125	88.9
14	7	No	0.143	89.5
12	6	No	0.167	88.2
16	6	Yes	0.244	87.5
16	5	Yes	0.277	88.5
14	5	Yes	0.291	85.9
14	4	Yes	0.341	86.4

Table 1: The table shows the proportion of teams in a league and division that qualify for the playoffs and the minimum number of games a team needs to win to have a probability of qualifying for the playoffs at least as large as this proportion (MGW).

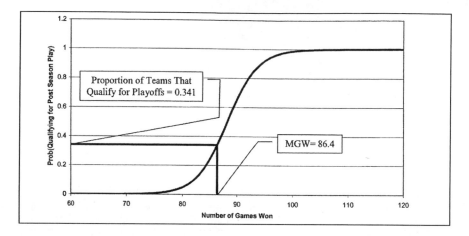

Figure 3: The logistic regression model represents the probability that a team in a 4-team division within a 14-team league qualifies for the playoffs. A team playing under such conditions must win at least 86.4 games to have a probability of qualifying for the playoffs equal to or greater than 34.1 percent.

Figure 4 shows the relationship between TPS and EGW for the 2000 season. Similar relationships hold in all other years in the study period. Three teams were noncompetitive in 2000, when the MGW was 85.9 in the American League East and Central, 86.4 in the American League West, 88.5 in the National League East and West, and 87.5 in the National League Central. They were the Minnesota Twins, the Florida Marlins, and the Houston Astros – their EGWs were 74.3, 79.0, and 81.1, respectively. The Gini index analysis indicates that the two teams with the lowest TPS (the Minnesota Twins and the Florida Marlins) were noncompetitive due to low TPS. The lowest TPS in the primarily competitive group is $23.13 million, belonging to the Kansas City Royals. Thus, the competitive salary in 2000 was $23.13 million.

It is not clear why the Houston Astros were noncompetitive in 2000 other than that it was not due to low TPS. However, 2000 was the Astros' first year in their new ballpark, one with dramatically different playing conditions than those found in the Astrodome. Note that the Astros were competitive in both 1999 and 2001.

Figure 5 and Table 2 show the competitive salary along with the team minima, mean, and maxima salaries for the non-strike years between 1985 and 2002. The competitive salary ranges from $6.19 million in 1985 to $38.67 million in 2002, an average annual growth rate of 10.7% per year. Interestingly, the team minimum, mean, and maximum salaries have risen at nearly the same average annual percentage rate, namely 11.2% for the minimum, 10.8% for the mean, and 12.1% for the maximum. This suggests that, since 1985, it has not become relatively more costly to be competitive in MLB.

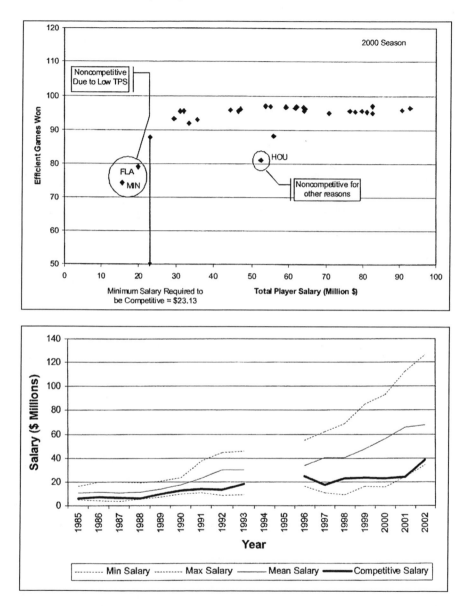

Top: Figure 4: The relationship between TPS and EGW in the year 2000. Three teams were noncompetitive, the Minnesota Twins, the Florida Marlins, and the Houston Astros. The Twins and the Marlins were noncompetitive due to low TPS. The minimum TPS to be competitive was $23.13 million, the TPS of the Kansas City Royals. *Bottom:* Figure 5: The heavy line shows the minimum TPS to be competitive along with the team minima, mean, and maxima for the non-strike years between 1985 and 2002.

Year	1985	1986	1987	1988	1989	1990	1991	1992	1993	1996	1997	1998	1999	2000	2001	2002
Minimum	5.10	4.26	3.56	5.41	7.19	9.50	10.72	8.46	8.83	16.26	10.77	9.16	16.18	15.65	24.13	34.38
Maximum	16.20	19.64	20.01	19.44	20.27	23.57	37.28	44.46	45.75	54.71	62.24	68.99	85.03	92.94	112.29	125.93
Mean	10.64	11.46	10.79	11.63	13.82	17.20	22.95	30.04	30.38	33.94	40.25	40.34	47.37	56.20	65.48	67.49
Median	10.81	10.93	11.56	12.33	14.05	17.65	23.01	30.15	33.01	32.12	41.85	40.60	46.76	57.49	64.00	61.11
Competitive	6.19	9.19	4.09	6.00	9.09	12.66	14.05	13.49	18.20	24.48	17.27	22.73	22.20	23.13	24.13	38.67

Table 2: The table shows the minimum, maximum, mean, and median total player salaries for the nonstrike years between 1985 and 2002. In addition, the table shows the minimum TPS to be competitive for each of the same years.

Moreover, the competitive salary has remained low relative to the mean TPS in each year. As Figure 6 shows, the ratio of the competitive salary in a given year to the minimum TPS in the same year has remained stable[16] around its mean of 1.5. Therefore, a rule of thumb is that a team's TPS must be at least 50% larger than the lowest TPS in a given year to be competitive.

In each year, there were between zero and four teams that were noncompetitive due to low TPS, as shown in Figure 7. In each year in the study period except for 2001, there existed teams that were noncompetitive due to low TPS and the number of such teams was relatively small. As Figure 7 also shows, there were between zero and eight teams that were noncompetitive for nonsalary reasons. These are teams whose total player salaries exceeded the minimum required to be competitive but whose EGW fell below MGW. The reason why these teams are noncompetitive is a matter for future research.

Figure 8 displays the years in which each team was noncompetitive either

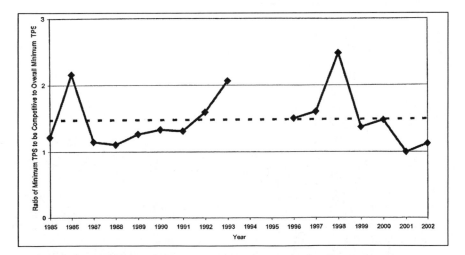

Figure 6: The ratio of the minimum TPS to be competitive to the overall minimum TPS has remained stable around a mean of approximately 1.5 between 1985 and 2002. The slope of the best-fit regression line, shown as dashed, is 0.0012, which represents the average annual change in the ratio during this period.

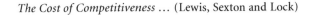

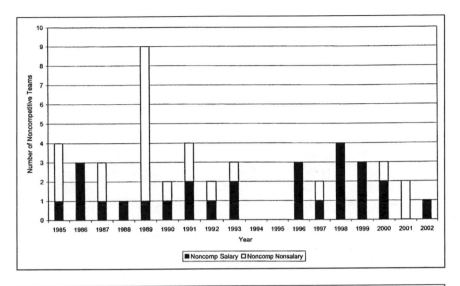

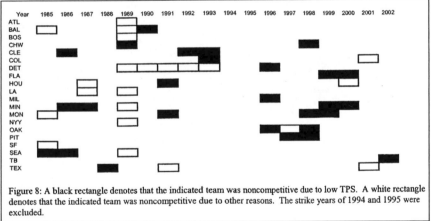

Figure 8: A black rectangle denotes that the indicated team was noncompetitive due to low TPS. A white rectangle denotes that the indicated team was noncompetitive due to other reasons. The strike years of 1994 and 1995 were excluded.

Top: Figure 7: The number of teams that were noncompetitive due to low TPS has remained stable between zero and four in every non-strike year between 1985 and 2002. In most years, there have been teams that were noncompetitive due to reasons other than low TPS. *Bottom:* Figure 8: A black rectangle denotes that the indicated team was noncompetitive due to low TPS. A white rectangle denotes that the indicated team was noncompetitive due to other reasons. The strike years of 1994 and 1995 were excluded.

for salary or non-salary reasons. Teams not shown in Figure 8 have been competitive in all years in the study. Note that no teams have been noncompetitive due to low TPS in more than four of the 18 years in the study period. The Seattle Mariners (1985–1986), the Cleveland Indians (1992–1993), the Pittsburgh Pirates (1997–1998), the Montreal Expos (1998–1999), the Minnesota Twins (1986–1987 and 1999–2000), and the Florida Marlins (1999–2000) were noncompetitive due to low TPS for two consecutive years. Thus, there is no evidence that being noncompetitive due to low TPS is a chronic condition.

Figure 9 shows the number of times each team was noncompetitive due to low TPS versus the team's market size, defined as the population of the team's metropolitan area according to the 2000 U.S. and 2001 Canadian censes. While the four teams in the two largest markets, two in New York and two in Los Angeles/Anaheim, were never noncompetitive due to low TPS, the Chicago White Sox, who play in the third largest market, were noncompetitive due to low TPS in two years (1989 and 1998). There is no evidence that the number of times that a team has been noncompetitive due to low TPS between 1985 and 2002 relates to the size of the market in which it plays. Seven of the eighteen teams that play in markets below five million people have not been noncompetitive due to low TPS. Only six such teams have been noncompetitive due to low TPS more than once in this period.

Figure 10 shows the relationship between efficient games won and market size for MLB teams during the study period. The regression line shown in Figure 10 has a slope of 2.262 games per 10 million people (P-value = 0.0019), suggesting that an efficient New York team, with market size approx-

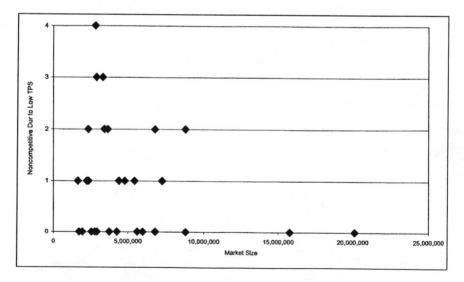

Figure 9: There is no evidence that the number of times that a team has been noncompetitive due to low TPS between 1985 and 2002 relates to the size of the market in which it plays. Seven of the eighteen teams that play in markets below five million people have not been noncompetitive due to low TPS in the nonstrike years between 1985 and 2002. Only six such teams have been noncompetitive due to low TPS more than once in this period.

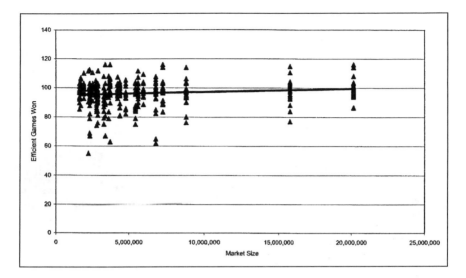

Figure 10: Efficient games won versus market size for MLB teams between 1985 and 2002 except for the strike years 1994–1995. The regression line shown in the figure has a slope of 2.262 games per 10 million people, suggesting that an efficient New York team, with market size approximately equal to 20.13 million, would win roughly four more games in season than would an efficient Milwaukee team, with market size equal to 1.65 million.

imately equal to 20.13 million, would win roughly four more games in a season than would an efficient Milwaukee team, with market size equal to 1.65 million.

Discussion and Conclusions

The first two questions concerned how much a team needed to spend on player salaries to be competitive in a given year. As demonstrated, this value has risen from $6.19 million in 1985 to $38.67 million in 2002, an average annual increase of 10.7%. Generally, the competitive salary has been about 50% more than the minimum TPS.

The third question dealt with the number of teams that are noncompetitive due to low total player salary in a given year. Analysis of the data found between 0 and 4 teams in this situation each year. Since 1985, 49 of the 442 teams (11.1%) have been noncompetitive, 27 (55.1% of the 49) due to low TPS, and 22 (44.9% of the 49) for other reasons.

The fourth question examined how non-competitiveness due to low total player salary relates to market size. Teams playing in New York and Los Angeles/Anaheim, MLB's largest markets, have not been noncompetitive due to low TPS since 1985. On the other hand, the Chicago White Sox, who play in MLB's third largest market, have been noncompetitive due to low TPS two times since 1985. Moreover, seven of the eighteen teams with market size below 5 million have not been noncompetitive due to low TPS since 1985. However, efficient large market teams will generally win more games than efficient small market teams, perhaps enough to decide a division or wild card race.

These conclusions challenge several common perceptions about competitiveness in MLB. First, the cost of competitiveness is less than many people suggest. Second, small-market teams can be competitive if they utilize their resources efficiently, although an efficient small market team can expect to win fewer games than an efficient large market team. Third, the number of noncompetitive teams has remained stable over the past two decades. Thus, the economic condition of baseball may be as dire as some think, and small market teams can compete effectively if they use their resources efficiently.

Notes

1. *USA Today.* <http://asp.usatoday.com/sports/baseball/salaries/default.aspx>.
2. Report of the Independent Members of the Commissioner's Blue Ribbon Panel on Baseball Economics, July 2000, 5.
3. DEA has become a widely used methodology for evaluating relative efficiency. It traces its mathematical development to: A. Charnes, W.W. Cooper, and E. Rhodes, "Measuring the Efficiency of Decision-Making Units," *European Journal of Operational Research* 2, no. 6 (1978): 429–444. Charnes, Cooper, and Rhodes built on the work of others, including: M.J. Farrell, "The Measurement of Productive Efficiency," *Journal of the Royal Statistical Society* Series A, III (1957): 253–290. DEA measures relative efficiency in situations in which there are multiple inputs and outputs, and there is no obvious objective way to aggregate either inputs or outputs into a meaningful index of productive efficiency. Several studies have applied DEA to baseball: H.F. Lewis and T.R. Sexton, "Network DEA: Efficiency Analysis of Organizations with Complex Internal Structure," *Computers and Operations Research*, forthcoming; H.F. Lewis and T.R. Sexton, "Data Envelopment Analysis with Reverse Inputs and Outputs," *Journal of Productive Analysis*, forthcoming; T.R. Sexton and H.F. Lewis, "Two-Stage Data Envelopment Analysis," *Journal of Productivity Analysis*, 19, nos. 2 and 3 (2003); T.R. Anderson and G.P. Sharp, "A New Measure of Baseball Batters Using DEA," *Annals of Operation Research*, 73 (1997): 131–155; M.J. Mazur in *Data Envelopment Analysis: Theory, Methodology, and Applications*, eds. A. Charnes, W.W. Cooper, A. Lewin, and L.M. Seiford (Dordrecht and Boston: Kluwer Academic Publishers, 1994), 369–391; and L.H. Howard and J.L. Miller, "Fair Pay for Fair Play: Estimating Pay Equity in Professional Baseball with Data Envelopment Analysis," *Academy of Management Journal* 36, no. 4 (1993):882–894: The technique appears widely in the management science literature. Web sites with extensive bibliographies of over 1000 articles that document the theoretical development of DEA and its broad range of application are provided by the following: T. Anderson, "DEA WWW Bibliography," < http://www.emp.pdx.edu/dea/deabib.html#Bibliography> ; and A. Emrouznejad, "DEA Bibliography," < http://www.csv.warwick.ac.uk/~bsr-llu/dea/deab/bib-a.htm>. A comprehensive bibliography of the DEA literature is provided in Gabriel Tavares, "A Bibliography of Data Envelopment Analysis (178–2001)," *Rutcor Research Report*, RRR 01–02, Rutgers University (2002).
4. Logistic regression is similar to the more familiar linear regression with one impor-

tant difference: the dependent variable in logistic regression is a binary variable that can only assume one of two possible values, namely zero and one. The logistic regression model produces a value between zero and one that we can interpret as the probability that the dependent variable equals one, given specific values for the independent variables, also known as predictor variables. For an excellent presentation of logistic regression analysis, see D.W. Hosmer and S. Lemeshow, *Applied Logistical Regression Analysis* (Hoboken, NJ: Wiley, 2000).

5. The Gini index uses a scale from zero to one to measure the extent to which members of a population are dissimilar from one another. Researchers have used the Gini index to measure income disparity: W. T. Wilson, *The Effect of Right-to-Work Laws on Economic Development* (Mackinac, MI: Mackinac Center for Public Policy, 2002); R.J. Harrison and D.H. Weinberg, "Racial and Ethnic Residential Segregation in 1990," Population Association of America Meeting (1992); and Pan American Health Organization, "Measuring Inequalities in Health: Gini Coefficient and Concentration Index," *Epidemiological Bulletin* 21, no. 4 (2001): 3–4. In addition, the Gini index provides a measure suitable for placing members of a population into two or more distinct clusters such that members within the same cluster are similar to one another and dissimilar from members of other clusters.

6. Sexton and Lewis, passim.

7. Major League Baseball Official Web Site, <http://mlb.com>.

8. Although not every error results in the batter reaching first base, each error results in at least one runner (and in many cases the batter) advancing at least one base. This study models errors as the approximate equivalent of singles and walks.

9. Sexton and Lewis, passim.

10. Except 1904 when there was no postseason and the strike years 1981, 1994, and 1995.

11. U.S Census Bureau 2000, <http://www.census.gov/>; and Statistics Canada (2001), <http://www12.statcan.ca/english/census01/release/index.cfm>.

12. USA Today.

13. Baseball Archive Database, Version 3.0, < http://www.baseball1.com/ >; and Major League Baseball Official Web Site.

14. This study was unable to find data on the number of opposition errors, which is required in the calculation of TBG. The study estimated this number for each team in each year by subtracting the team's own errors committed from the total committed in that team's league and dividing by one less than the number of teams in the league. This approximation ignores the minor effects of interleague play and the somewhat different schedules played by different teams, and assumes that teams are equally likely to commit errors against each team they play.

15. In addition, this study was unable to find data to support MLB's definition of TB in the calculation of TBS for years prior to 1999. The study estimated this quantity by identifying the relationship between total hits and total bases using regression analysis.

16. The least squares regression line has a slope that is very nearly zero (-0.0026 per year).

The Elements of
Major League Contraction

Paul D. Staudohar and Franklin Lowenthal

Under the current collective bargaining agreement in baseball, the parties agreed that no teams would be contracted during the life of the agreement, from 2003–2006. Thus, the earliest that elimination of a major league team could occur would be for the 2007 season. Despite this agreement, the issue of contraction remains important because it is apt to resurface in the future.

The major league owners voted on November 6, 2001, to contract two teams. That the vote was 28–2 indicated widespread support for the proposal. Not surprisingly, the vote caused a welter of controversy in the media, nearly all of it in opposition to contraction, and ultimately the owners decided to place the issue in abeyance.

This paper examines key economic, legal, and political aspects of contraction. It reviews the events leading to the provision in the collective bargaining agreement. Of particular interest is an analysis of whether it is economically feasible to contract. That is, whether remaining owners in the leagues would benefit sufficiently to warrant dropping teams. The leading candidates for contraction are examined in this regard. The analysis indicates that from a purely economic standpoint contraction makes sense because the remaining members of the cartel would be better off.

But there is also the legal and political overplay to consider. The players' union opposes contraction because it would eliminate jobs. Fans generally are opposed to the idea, especially in cities that might lose their teams. Were contraction to proceed it would generate vociferous reactions from opposing groups, perhaps leading to lengthy court battles and prohibitive legislation. There would also be a difficult problem of determining how players would be allocated among the remaining teams.

Background

Over the years, Major League Baseball (MLB) has had numerous franchise sales, relocations, and additions through expansions.[1] Four new franchises were added by MLB in the 1990s. Since 1901, however, when the American League was formed, there has not been a franchise abandonment.[2] In contrast, 14 NBA franchises were dissolved from 1946–1959; the NFL lost 38 franchises from 1920–1959; and the NHL shed 6 franchises from 1917–1979.[3]

Thus, for over a hundred years in baseball, and from 2–4 decades in other professional team sports, no franchises have been eliminated. Instead, the number of major league sports franchises has expanded significantly in recent years, perhaps by too much. Should MLB eliminate teams, it would not be surprising if other over-expanded sports leagues do likewise. This would end a long period of growth. Emphasis would shift from quantity to quality and to greater financial stability.

When MLB Commissioner Bud Selig announced the owners' vote, he did not specify the two teams, saying only that "the teams to be contracted have a long record of failing to generate enough revenues to operate a viable major-league franchise."[4] Because the owners who voted against contraction were Jeffrey Loria of the Montreal Expos and Carl Pohlad of the Minnesota Twins, speculation focused on their teams as the ones to be eliminated. As events unfolded, other teams were identified as candidates for elimination, apparently for subsequent years, with a likely total of four subtracted teams over a 2–3 year period.

Economic Rationale

As shown in Table 1, Montreal and Minnesota were the franchises with the lowest estimated values in 2001. Other low-ranked franchises that were considered candidates for elimination include the Tampa Bay Devil Rays, Kansas City Royals, and Florida Marlins. As indicated in the table, each of these teams lost money in 2001 and the amount of the losses was far in excess of the league average.

Table 1

FRANCHISES VALUES AND 2001 LOSSES

Team	Value Millions	Revenue Thousands	Expenses Thousands	Operating Loss Thousands
Tampa Bay	$150	$80,595	$103,438	$22,843

Team	Value Millions	Revenue Thousands	Expenses Thousands	Operating Loss Thousands
Kansas City	138	63,696	79,830	16,134
Florida.	128	60,547	88,288	27,741
Minnesota.	99	56.266	74,799	18,533
Montreal.	92	34,171	72,690	38,519
League Average	263	118,267	126,004	7,737

Sources: Estimated franchise values from *Forbes*, April 16, 2001, p. 148; other data from *Contra Costa* (California) *Times*, December 7, 2001, p. C2.

Whether to eliminate a franchise can be viewed as a capital budgeting decision based on models that include the time value of money. Using the net present method, it can be shown that contraction is a sound course of action for owners functioning as a league or single business entity.

The financial impact of contraction would be different for each of the owners of the remaining 28 teams; the exact impact on each is impossible to predict since it is unknown how revenue sharing would be revised among the surviving teams once contraction occurs. Since we cannot ascertain the future cash flows for each of these teams, it is impossible to use a capital budgeting model to formulate a decision for each of these teams. Instead we will consider the remaining 28 teams to constitute a single business entity, and we will analyze the contraction decision as a decision that is made by this business entity (e.g. we consider MLB to be a partnership with 28 partners buying out the other two partners). In this analysis, the revenue flow, the expenses, the attendance, and the competitive level of the franchise that is the candidate for contraction all are irrelevant to our analysis (they are relevant only to the owner of the team that is being contracted). The only cash flows that are relevant are:

1. the buyout price;
2. the revenue currently allocated to the contracted franchise under revenue sharing;
3. the portion of the revenue generated by MLB's TV contract that is received by the contracted franchise;
4. the luxury tax payment received by the contracted franchise;
5. the increased revenue from attendance when a team with low fan interest is replaced as the visiting team by one with a high (or at least higher) fan interest — this last item although potentially important is difficult to measure and will be omitted from our analysis.

The buyout price is unknown, although franchise values are estimated by sources such as *Forbes* magazine. This lack of information on the actual buyout price is not a serious problem in the application of our capital budgeting model. Instead, we determine a "breakeven" buyout price. Then if the actual negotiated buyout price is less than this calculated "breakeven" price, the owners should buy out the franchise at that price. But if the negotiated price exceeds the "breakeven" price, then it would be a poor managerial decision for the owners to contract that franchise at that price.

The luxury tax was last paid in the 1999 season, before being renewed for the 2003 season. We do not include the luxury tax in our analysis because of uncertainty over amounts to be paid in the future. The annual TV contract currently pays Major League Baseball $559 million per year. Under the current configuration of 30 teams, each team receives approximately $18,633,000 annually from the TV contract. This would amount to an annual cash inflow to the business entity MLB of $18,633,000 if a single franchise were contracted. This amount could increase or decrease with the next TV contract but we will simply assume that the amount is constant for the foreseeable future.

The revenue sharing figures, released by the Commissioner's office, for 2001 were as follows: Montreal—$28,517,000; Minnesota—$19,069,000; Tampa Bay—$12,384,000; Florida—$18,561,000; Kansas City—$15,997,000. These figures represent the annual cash inflow to MLB if the respective franchise were contracted. If we linearly order these numbers and if we agree to ignore all other non-financial implications of contraction, then the candidates for contraction should be ordered as follows: Montreal, Minnesota, Florida, Kansas City, and Tampa Bay.

Next, we must decide on the time duration of the cash flows above. One possibility is to view these cash flows as perpetuities, continuing forever. A second possibility is to view them as annuities, having a limited life; for the sake of definiteness we will consider two cases: 10-year duration and 20-year duration of these annual cash flows.

Finally, we must choose a minimum desired rate of return (also called cost of capital) for MLB as this is required as input to the net present value model; we shall choose before-tax rates of 8% and 10%. Our analysis can be simply modified to incorporate any other rate as input. The formulas that we will use can be found in any text on cost accounting. In the case of perpetuity, the present value of the cash inflows is simply ACF/I where ACF is the annual cash inflow and I is the minimum desired rate of return. If, on the other hand, we assume an N year annuity, the present value is ACF*(1-v^N)/I where v = 1/(1+I) is the present value of $1 received 1 year in the future at discount rate I and ^ indicates that the financial implications extend for some time period into the future.

Contraction of the Montreal Expos

In this case, the annual cash inflow before taxes to MLB (the partnership of the remaining teams) is $18,633,000 + $28,517,000 = $47,150,000. Using the formulas above we obtain as the breakeven buyout price under the various scenarios considered the following figures:

Buyout Price	Duration	Minimum Desired Rate of Return
$471,150,000	Perpetuity	10%
$589,375,000	Perpetuity	8%
$401,414,500	20 years	10%
$462,925,700	20 years	8%
$289,716,300	10 years	10%
$316,380,300	10 years	8%

These figures do not represent the buyout price that actually will be negotiated. Rather they represent, under the corresponding scenario, the maximum buyout price that MLB should be willing to pay to the owners of the Montreal Expos to contract that franchise. For example, if the minimum desired rate of return is 10% before taxes and the annual cash inflow of $47,150,000 from contracting the Expos is expected to last for only 10 years, then the maximum buyout price is $289,716,300. Anything below that would represent a positive net present value in which case a buyout is appropriate while anything above that would represent a negative net present value in which case a buyout is not appropriate.

We applied the same analytical model to the other four teams considered for contraction in 2001.[5] This analysis demonstrated that apart from questions of competitiveness and that the economic pains of baseball divided between big market and small market teams, contraction was attractive simply because from the point of view of capital budgeting it is an excellent long-term investment for the remaining owners. The net present value model unequivocally demonstrates just how attractive contraction is. The Montreal Expos in 2001 could probably have been bought out at a price in the area of $100 million dollars. This cash outflow is offset by a present value of future cash inflows that range in our table from $289 million to $589 million depending on the chosen set of assumptions. No wonder the owners were overwhelmingly in favor of contraction.

Legal Overplay

We have seen that from a purely economic standpoint it is quite logical to eliminate teams. All of the owners gain from this transaction and the league becomes a healthier financial entity. But there are other parties that do not view contraction as being in their interests. The most powerful of these groups are the players and fans. The players are represented by a union that can fight against contraction or seek to minimize its impact. Fans are represented by public officials who can undertake legal action to prevent contraction.

Montreal was in the least favorable position. The Expos averaged only 7,935 fans per game in 2001, well under the league average of 30,054.[6] There were no plans to build a new ballpark and the frustrated club was even unable to sell the local television rights to its games. Conveniently, the team's stadium lease expired on November 30, 2001. Owner Jeffrey Loria, sensing the hopeless future, decided to bail out by selling the Expos in 2002 for $120 million to Baseball Expos LP, a Delaware limited partnership owned by the other MLB teams. Loria then purchased the Florida Marlins for $158.5 million from John Henry, who led the group that bought the Boston Red Sox for $660 million.

Thus the Expos began the 2002 season in limbo, not knowing whether the franchise would be dissolved or relocated. The only previous time that a MLB team was owned by a league was briefly between the 1942 and 1943 seasons. The National League took over the Philadelphia Phillies from owner Gerald Nugent who fell behind on his rent at Shibe Park, and sold the team five weeks later to William Cox, who was later banned from the sport by Commissioner Kenesaw Mountain Landis for gambling on Phillies games.[7]

Unlike the Expos, the Twins had loyal fans who averaged 22,286 at games in 2001. Although their payroll was the lowest in baseball at $24 million, the Twins competed well on the field in 2001, winning 85 games. The Twins franchise has a history of success, with World Series championships in 1987 and 1991, and three members of the Hall of Fame. In 1997, Carl Pohlad offered to turn over 49 percent of his club to the state of Minnesota, provided the state would agree to build a new ballpark. The Minnesota legislature, however, would not approve the deal, and there is still considerable resistance to building a new stadium with public funds.

About a week after the owners' contraction vote, a bill was introduced in Congress by the two Minnesota Senators, the late Paul Wellstone and Mark Dayton, and Representative John Conyers from Michigan. Called the Fairness in Antitrust in National Sports Act (S.B.1704), the bill would allow lawsuits against MLB when teams fold or relocate. Suits could be brought by an "injured party" like a governmental entity or a baseball player. Lack of support caused the proposed law to be shelved.

MLB has an exemption from the antitrust law under a 1922 decision by the U.S. Supreme Court. This exemption was modified in 1998 by passage of the Curt Flood Act, named after a player who had unsuccessfully challenged the exemption. The modification is for purposes of labor relations and allows players to bring an antitrust suit on labor issues but only after their relationship with the union has been severed. Although Congress did modify the exemption, it was for the limited context of labor disputes. Otherwise, it remains intact.[8]

There have been several bills introduced in Congress over the years that would have modified MLB's antitrust exemption. Apart from the Flood Act, none of these actions have succeeded. Even during the 1994–95 baseball strike, Congress adopted a "hands off" position on intervening. While the 2001 bill failed to result in law, the legislative hearings were useful. Commissioner Selig was summoned to Washington and asked to explain the position of MLB on contraction. Selig said that only five teams made money and the other 25 owners lost about $500 million in 2001.[9] But he was unable to square these assertions with the facts that franchises were being sold at record prices and the owners were continuing to sign players to astronomical contracts. *Forbes* magazine later estimated that MLB had an operating profit of $75 million in 2001.[10]

The Twins' lease, stipulating that they play in the Metrodome through the 2002 season, was a deterrent to contraction in 2002. The Minnesota Sports Facilities Commission sued to compel the Twins to honor the lease, and a county district court issued an injunction against the Twins and MLB, requiring the team to play at the Metrodome in 2002. An appeal was filed with the Minnesota Court of Appeals and plans were made to expedite the matter before the Minnesota Supreme Court. However, because the earliest the case could be heard was December 27 and MLB had to establish its schedule for the coming season, the contraction issue was put on hold for the time being. In February 2002 the Minnesota Supreme Court refused to consider the appeal of the injunction, keeping it in effect and forcing the Twins to stay put for the season.

Another important legal development occurred in December 2001, when the attorney general for the state of Florida sought disclosure of documents from MLB and the two Florida teams concerning contraction. A U.S. District Court judge ruled that MLB's antitrust exemption freed it from having to provide the information, and this decision was affirmed by the U.S. Court of Appeals.[11] Unlike the situation in Minnesota, the preemptive action failed in Florida. There will doubtless be more legal skirmishes ahead if contraction plans are revitalized.

Owners vs. Players

Since 1972 there have been eight work stoppages in baseball. That the sport was unable to get through a labor negotiation without a strike or lock-out was irksome to fans. This is why there was some cheer in that early negotiations to replace the collective bargaining agreement, which expired on November 7, 2001, were going well. As a result of cooperation on passage of the Curt Flood Act, labor and management finally seemed to be getting along. The union's executive director, Donald Fehr, and MLB negotiators Paul Beeston and Rob Manfred had a much-improved relationship compared to the roughhouse tactics of the 1994–95 negotiations that led to the longest strike in the history of professional sports.

Unfortunately, Selig subsequently decided he no longer wanted to be friendly with the union. This was apparently the result of being convinced by Sandy Alderson of the Commissioner's office and some of the hard-line owners that good labor relations would not be productive, at least for the time being. Beeston was essentially forced to resign as MLB's president and chief operating officer by Selig and hawkish owners such as John Moores of San Diego, Drayton McLane of Houston, David Glass of Kansas City, and Carl Pohlad of Minnesota.[12] He was replaced by Bob DuPuy, Selig's longtime lawyer. Moreover, the vote to shrink the league dashed optimism for a clear path to a new labor contract. As Fehr put it, the vote was a "severe blow to such hopes."[13] It could be that the whole contraction issue was just an attempt by MLB to gain leverage at the bargaining table.

The day before the collective bargaining agreement expired, the union filed a grievance against contraction, arguing that it violated several provisions of the agreement, major league rules, and all existing player contracts. The grievance was scheduled to be heard by baseball arbitrator Shyam Das, but meanwhile the parties tried to work out a negotiated understanding. In effect, the owners wanted the union to acknowledge that MLB had the unilateral right to fold franchises. Then, contended the owners, they would be obligated to bargain over the effects of contraction, such as how to allocate players among other clubs. The owners preferred that a dispersal draft be held, where teams would draft players in the reverse order of their 2001 won-lost records, and no-trade clauses would not be honored. The union, on the other hand, wanted all players on dissolved teams to become free agents. When the bargaining on contraction procedures collapsed, the parties moved forward on the arbitration case.

Following 20 days of hearings on the union's contraction grievance, Arbitrator Das announced that his decision would be forthcoming on July 15, 2002. However, the deadline was extended to August 15 to allow the owners to give the union a tentative schedule for the 2003 season. But the arbitration decision was never rendered. The reason is that the parties reached agreement in negotiations to delay possible contraction, and the grievance before Arbitrator Das was withdrawn by the union.

Outcomes

While contraction was forestalled for the 2002 season and put off until at least 2007, will the idea be revived? We would predict that there is a good chance that contraction will occur in the future. As noted above, contraction makes sound financial sense under the conditions that prevailed before the imposition of the 2003–2006 collective bargaining agreement. As a result of that agreement, nearly a billion dollars is expected to flow from richer teams to poorer ones.[14] With this significant increase in revenue sharing, the economic rationale for contraction would appear to be more compelling than ever.

But the future is full of surprises. Some of the clubs that are currently plagued with low revenues may become revitalized. On the other hand, teams that presently seem healthy financially could turn out to be candidates for contraction later on. How this scenario plays out will depend on a number of variables that are not easy to predict, such as won-lost records, fan attendance, and local television deals. Will certain teams build new stadiums? What relocations might occur? Will new owners who are willing to open their pocketbooks come into the game?

A case in point is the Florida Marlins, who struck gold in 2003 when they won the World Series despite having the fifth-lowest payroll in the majors. A few weeks after this astounding triumph, the Marlins and Miami-Dade County tentatively approved plans to fund a new stadium. If this stadium is built, it would get the Marlins off the contraction hot seat.

More importantly, the Montreal franchise appears to be headed to Washington D.C. for the 2005 season. Although they were taken over by MLB, the Expos continued to languish. The team lost about $45 million in 2002.[15] Beginning in 2003, 22 "home games" were played in San Juan, Puerto Rico, but this did little to reverse the financial tide. With every other MLB owner responsible for 1/29th of the losses and with contraction no longer an alternative, pressure mounted to relocate the franchise.

The new Washington team will try to succeed in a city whose two previous teams, known as the Senators, were relocated. Perhaps the third try will be a charm. The team anticipates playing its first three years in Robert F. Kennedy Stadium before moving into a new ballpark.

It is less likely that the Minnesota Twins will be contracted or relocated. The state legislature has proposed a new stadium costing an estimated $330 million, with $120 million of private financing required.[16] Although a new ballpark may not materialize for several years, the Twins' outstanding record on the field in 2002–2004 has revitalized attendance as well as the future of the franchise in Minnesota.

That the new collective bargaining agreement will redistribute more money from high revenue to low revenue teams will help the weaker teams financially and perhaps improve competitive balance on the playing field. On the other hand, the overall economic health of baseball is declining. Quite simply, baseball is now perceived by many as a bad business. Several owners have had significant problems in their outside businesses, as declining stock prices have eroded personal fortunes. Many major league clubs are for sale, but there are few buyers willing to pay high prices because there is no guarantee of a reasonable economic return. The three MLB teams owned by media companies that were up for sale in 2003 all sustained heavy losses in the preceding year: about $10 million for Disney's Anaheim Angels, $25 million for AOL Time Warner's Atlanta Braves, and $40 million for News Corp.'s Los Angeles Dodgers.[17] It is unlikely that the national television revenues to MLB will increase much, if at all, when the current agreements expire in 2005 (ESPN) and 2006 (Fox). On the other hand, MLB attendance continues to be strong, setting an all-time record in 2004.

Prominent baseball writer Roger Angell calls contraction a "euphemism for corporate death."[18] Avoidance of this outcome may be possible through relocation of moribund franchises, as by Montreal relocating to Washington D.C. Historically, MLB has frowned on relocation, although occasionally franchises have moved from one city to another with generally positive results. The problem today compared with the past is that there are not only fewer buyers with deep pockets but fewer attractive sites available.

Unless there is antitrust action by Congress barring contraction, the owners are legally able to allow teams to go under. Of course, a team cannot be contracted unless the owner of the team is compensated. If a favorable buyout price can be arranged, MLB owners can reap a windfall if the team that they acquire can be later unloaded at a higher price for a city eager for a team. Should a team actually be contracted, i.e., if the franchise is dissolved, then the remaining owners who bought the former team would be required to bargain with the union over what happens to the players from the team that is dropped. Owners are not required by law to remain in business, particularly if they are losing money.

Supposing that contraction does occur in the future, what about the effects on the cities involved? There will be difficulties for fans, especially those who have faithfully supported their teams. Minnesota District Court Judge Harry Crump recognized the public stake when he said that "baseball crosses social barriers, creates community spirit and is much more than a private enterprise."[19] Also, affected cities will lose some of their "major league" status, for what that is worth.

The economic impact on the community, however, will be minimal. Sports franchises contribute marginally to the local economy. Player salaries are mostly spent elsewhere, and jobs that are lost are far less than one percent of those in the area.[20] The spending that occurred on games and related accommodations and dining will simply be spent on other things. The net economic activity lost in Montreal will be only about $15–25 million, a tiny portion of the total economic product of this city. Roger Noll and Andrew Zimbalist note, regarding the economic impact of a professional sports team, that "... metropolitan and central city development is not likely to be affected...."[21] Fans too will get over the loss of their teams, which will be replaced by minor league franchises. A city that cannot support its team does not deserve to have one. If another city or area is willing to provide an attractive ballpark and support the team at a significantly higher level, relocation makes sense. It is clearly a more desirable alternative than contraction.

Notes

1. See generally, Frank P. Jozsa, Jr. and John J. Guthrie, Jr., *Relocating Teams and Expanding Leagues in Professional Sports* (Westport, CT: Quorum Books, 1999).

2. James Quirk and Rodney D. Fort, *Pay Dirt: The Business of Professional Team Sports* (Princeton, NJ: Princeton University Press, 1992), 26–27. An exception to this point is the Federal League, which is considered to have been a major league. The Federal League folded after just two seasons of play (1914–15), resulting in the demise of franchises that were not absorbed into MLB.

3. *Ibid.*, 30, 33, and 37.

4. Quotation from *Wall Street Journal*, November 7, 2001, 11.

5. Details of this analysis are in Paul D. Staudohar and Franklin Lowenthal, "Baseball's Contraction Pains," *NINE: A Journal of Baseball History and Culture*, Vol. 11, No. 2, Spring 2003, 77–80.

6. Data from *Los Angeles Times*, November 8, 2001, B1.

7. "Owners OK Sale of Teams," Newswire, *Los Angeles Times*, February 11, 2002, B10.

8. For further discussion, see Paul D. Staudohar, editor, *Diamond Mines: Baseball and Labor* (Syracuse, NY: Syracuse University Press, 2000).

9. Ross Newhan, "Selig Gets Big Show of Support," *Los Angeles Times*, November 28, 2001, B1.

10. Kurt Badenhausen, Cecily Fluke, Leslie Kump, and Michael K. Ozanian, "Double Play," *Forbes*, Vol. 169, No. 9, April 15, 2002, 92–98.

11. Daniel C. Glazer, "The Baseball Exemption," *Wall Street Journal*, June 13, 2003, A6.

12. Ross Newhan, "Again, Game on Dangerous Path," *Los Angeles Times*, March 17, 2002, B7.

13. John Shea, "Baseball Votes to Cut Two Teams," *San Francisco Chronicle*, November 7, 2001, . C1.

14. Paul D. Staudohar, "Baseball Negotiations: A New Agreement," *Monthly Labor Review*, Vol. 125 No. 12, December 2002, 21.

15. Ross Newhan, "Problem of Expos Not Eliminated," *Los Angeles Times*, September 8, 2002, B9.

16. "Lawmakers OK Twins Deal," *San Francisco Chronicle*, May 19, 2002, B4.

17. Stefan Fatsis, "Sports Teams for Sale," *Wall Street Journal*, March 13, 2003, B1.

18. Roger Angell, "Kiss Kiss, Bang Bang," *New Yorker*, November 25, 2002, 53.

19. Quotation from Bill Shaikin, "State Lawyers Will Be Tough," *Los Angeles Times*, November 18, 2001, B7.

20. Mark S. Rosentraub, *Major League Losers: The Real Cost of Sports and Who's Paying For It* (New York: Basic Books, 1997), 176.

21. Roger G. Noll and Andrew Zimbalist, eds. *Sports, Jobs and Taxes: The Economic Impact of Sports Teams and Stadiums* (Washington, D.C.: Brookings Institution Press, 1997), 496.

Index